EXOCET
FALKLANDS

Other books by Ewen Southby-Tailyour

Military Histories and Biographies

Falkland Islands Shores
Reasons in Writing: A Commando's View of the Falklands War
Amphibious Assault Falklands: The Battle for San Carlos
Blondie: A Life of Lieutenant-Colonel HG Hasler DSO, OBE
The Next Moon. A Special Operations Executive Agent in France
HMS Fearless: *The Mighty Lion*
3 Commando Brigade, Helmand
Commando Assault, Helmand
Nothing Impossible. A Portrait of The Royal Marines 1664–2010 (ed.)

Fiction

Skeletons for Sadness

Reference

Jane's Amphibious Warfare Capabilities (ed.)
Jane's Special Forces Equipment Recognition Guide (ed.)
Jane's Amphibious and Special Forces (ed., bi-annual publication)

EXOCET FALKLANDS

The Untold Story of Special Forces Operations

Ewen Southby-Tailyour

Pen & Sword
MILITARY

First published in Great Britain in 2014 by
PEN & SWORD MILITARY
An imprint of
Pen & Sword Books Ltd
47 Church Street
Barnsley
South Yorkshire
S70 2AS

ISBN 978-1-78346-387-9

Typeset by Concept, Huddersfield, West Yorkshire, HD4 5JL.
Printed and bound in England by CPI Group (UK) Ltd, Croydon CR0 4YY.

Pen & Sword Books Ltd incorporates the imprints of Pen & Sword Archaeology,
Atlas, Aviation, Battleground, Discovery, Family History, History, Maritime,
Military, Naval, Politics, Railways, Select, Social History, Transport, True Crime,
and Claymore Press, Frontline Books, Leo Cooper, Praetorian Press,
Remember When, Seaforth Publishing and Wharncliffe.

For a complete list of Pen & Sword titles please contact
PEN & SWORD BOOKS LIMITED
47 Church Street, Barnsley, South Yorkshire, S70 2AS, England
E-mail: enquiries@pen-and-sword.co.uk
Website: www.pen-and-sword.co.uk

Contents

List of Plates

Capitán de Corbeta Roberto Curilovic with Teniente de Navio Julio Barraza.

Capitán de Corbeta Alejandro Francisco returning from the 'attack' on HMS *Invincible*.

ARA *Hipolito Bouchard*.

ARA *General Belgrano* at anchor in the Beagle Channel.

HMS *Onyx* arriving at HMS *Dolphin*, Portsmouth, from the South Atlantic.

The crew of XV200 with members of Wideawake's RAF ground staff in 1982.

47 Squadron's Special Forces Flight's crest.

Super Étendard 202 showing Two Squadron's crest and marking the sinking of HMS *Sheffield* and a 'strike' against HMS *Invincible*.

Victor Charlie landed 6 Troop on the flat, grassy headland in the middle distance, near to Estancia Cameron.

One of the two entrances to the command bunker at Rio Grande airbase.·

The command bunker at Rio Grande.

A cluttered corner of Rio Grande airbase.

BIM 3 on the Chile/Argentina border.

Series II A 'pink panther' Land Rover similar to that used by R Squadron, SAS, at Laarbruch and those planned to be used by B Squadron on Operation Mikado at Rio Grande.

HMS *Onyx* in dry dock in Portsmouth, showing the underwater damage before the torpedoes were removed.

One section of B Squadron, SAS, arriving in the South Atlantic on 14 June, with the tug *Irishman* in the background.

A land-launched Exocet on its launching trailer.

An unexpended, ground-launched Exocet lying in a ditch outside Stanley after the conflict.

Nine of the Super Étendard pilots with their aircraft at Espora naval airbase.

Victor Charlie's crew thirty years after the conflict.

Introduction

This is the story of the French AM 39 Exocet: an air-launched, sea-skimming, anti-ship missile deployed by Argentina against the British during the Falklands campaign in 1982. This missile was a clear danger to the Task Force aircraft carriers, the loss of just one of which would have seriously prejudiced the outcome. By its mere presence the Exocet affected much of the strategic and tactical thinking of the British commanders at sea and in the United Kingdom.

It is also a narrative of three British Special Forces operations designed to destroy those missiles on the Argentine mainland before they could be launched by the Super Étendard fighter-bombers that carried them. Operation Plum Duff was a reconnaissance and, if the opportunity arose, a direct action operation by eight men of 6 Troop, B Squadron, 22 Special Air Service Regiment against the Argentine Navy's Rio Grande air base in Tierra del Fuego. It was aborted three days after it began. Why it was aborted has been the subject of much imprecise speculation.

Operation Mikado, also against Rio Grande, depended on the intelligence obtained during Operation Plum Duff. It would have been conducted by two Hercules C-130 aircraft of the Royal Air Force's 47 Squadron's Special Forces Flight, landing sixty SAS troopers directly into the Argentine air base. It never took place. Why it never took place also forms much of the material that is between these covers.

Then there was the hitherto unknown, submarine-launched, Special Boat Squadron's Operation Kettledrum against the northern naval air base at Puerto Deseado. That the operation was cancelled just a day after HMS *Onyx* sailed from San Carlos is instructive enough; but the circumstances surrounding the decision to execute this attack, made in the United Kingdom some weeks before the executive order was given, remain baffling.

This, therefore, is the account of three mainland assaults that might have changed the nature of the Falklands conflict militarily and diplomatically. The political aftermath of such attacks on the South American continent would, too, have had international consequences. The SAS, and to a lesser extent the SBS, would have struggled to recover from the large loss of life they would inevitably have suffered, while the RAF (and thus the dependent Royal Navy) would have certainly lost the use of the only two heavy-lift, long-range aircraft capable (thanks to hastily fitted air-to-air refuelling apparatus) of supplying the Task Force deep in the South Atlantic ocean. As will be described, this became particularly relevant after the loss of the MV *Atlantic Conveyor*.

Others come into this story: the Secret Intelligence Service (more popularly known as MI6) with its successful 'war within a war' played a crucial part, together with the Royal Navy's aircraft carriers and their embarked helicopter crews, plus the nuclear submarines, destroyers and frigates. Argentine warships and marines defending Rio Grande's air base also appear, as do, most notably, the Super Étendard pilots themselves.

In many respects (and this is not what I was expecting when I embarked on this project) this is also the story of the Hercules aircraft: those who kept them flying and refuelled in the air as well as their would-be 'passengers' on Operation Mikado – the men of B Squadron. Markedly, too, it is the tale of one officer and seven men of 6 Troop during Operation Plum Duff and of the three Fleet Air Arm aircrew that flew their lone Sea King helicopter on a one-way mission into Tierra del Fuego during that austral autumn.

*   *   *

No one is clear when the code words Plum Duff, Mikado and Kettledrum were first used; some people involved in one or the other claim that they did not know the name of 'their' operation at the time. For the sake of clarity I have referred to them by these names from the beginning. For instance, Commodore Alan Bennett, who, as a Royal Navy lieutenant and helicopter pilot played a pivotal role in Operation Plum Duff, was not aware of its name until long after the Falklands campaign was over. At the time he was to regard it as 'Just another sortie – albeit with a dropping point in a different country and a walk home, behind enemy lines – just like all the others we had been doing for special forces since 1 May.'

It might appear that I have occasionally strayed from the central subject – the Exocet 'war' – into the world of submarines and other special forces operations. This has been to add flavour, depth and context to the main theme, so that a feeling for the overall atmosphere might be gained through the use of what a Highland piper would call the 'grace notes'.

While other published accounts have alluded to Operations Plum Duff and Mikado, not one has yet mentioned Kettledrum. As I am privileged to be in contact with primary sources on both sides of the Atlantic (and have visited Buenos Aires, Puerto Madryn, Rio Grande, Rio Gallegos, Ushuaia, Santiago, Punta Arenas and Puerto Montt, and flown across the pampas between these southern towns and cities), the best way forward is to ensure that this account stands on its own. I have therefore not compared my findings with those of others except where significant matters of fact needed to be unpicked and re-examined.

There are, inevitably, criticisms of a few sacred cows ... it would be unrealistic to expect otherwise in any war. There is, though, a culture of 'maintaining the myth' within some sectors of British 'special forces' that is not always conducive to good military practice. The SAS, for instance, are supremely efficient in counter-insurgency operations and, because of that capability, are often asked to attempt near-impossible conventional operations for the wrong reasons: Operations Plum Duff and Mikado are prime examples. As Major General Jeremy

Moore[1] was to comment, 'The SAS's concentration on counter-terrorism and special operations may have developed tendencies which are incompatible with the more conventional roles in support of ground forces that they were tasked with after the landings on 21 May.' [2]

The almost automatic use of special forces, whose primary role is strategic reconnaissance (with counter-revolutionary warfare as an added 'extra'), to support an orthodox campaign needs to be questioned. This was particularly so in a conflict with such a lengthy logistics 'tail', a tail that often stretched resources – especially troop-lift helicopters – beyond breaking point and certainly to a state in which they had to be harboured, nurtured and cosseted more than is usual. This was to ensure that the 'poor bloody infantry' (the three Royal Marines Commandos, the two Parachute Regiment battalions, the two Guards battalions and the Gurkha battalion) – who conducted the bulk of the 'dirty work' – as well as the prima donnas of the battlefield, received their correct and proportionate allocation of scarce assets. The 'urgent' demands of special forces patrols had often to be met with blunt refusals, for there were more critical priorities facing the Task Force commanders than 'dragging a team out of a mess of their own ill-conceived making'.[3]

General Moore emphasized the point in October 1982 when he wrote, 'Although ordered to ensure that communications were maintained with 3 Commando Brigade to coordinate deconfliction, and despite assurances that a SAS Liaison Officer would be deployed to Brigade Headquarters, no link was set up and 3 Commando Brigade had little idea of what was happening on a relatively exposed flank.'

For the British, criticism of the nation's special forces is close to heresy, especially following the SAS's brilliant – and certainly daring and courageous – lifting of the Iranian Embassy siege in London on 5 May 1980. Because this operation was conducted in 'real time' on international television the regiment was, against its wishes, placed on a very public pedestal. Since then, the SAS and SBS can do no wrong, they simply cannot be seen to fail; that is what we are required to think, and it is what influenced those senior decision makers (military and civilian) to believe all they were told, not only by the SAS's hierarchy but, equally significantly, by their RAF liaison officers, in 1982.

Clearly, though, this was unrealistic, for no organization operating in such a risky environment can be trouble-free. The Special Air Service and the Special Boat Service (as it was to become) would argue, rightly, that despite outward appearances of a trigger-happy approach to danger, each operation is planned and trained for down to the most minute detail. And yet ... sometimes their 'special forces capability' is not suited to conventional tasks. Only 47 per cent of all special forces operations are considered fully successful. This may seem a low figure, until the risks involved and the difficulties entailed are taken into account; then it might be seen as a rather high success rate.

So why are these comments necessary? It is so that the SAS's role in both Operation Plum Duff and Operation Mikado, plus the SBS's role in Operation Kettledrum, may be seen in the widest setting within the campaign as a whole.

They may also explain why the SAS command at home felt cheated of a reputation-enhancing operation by the actions of a promising young officer making pragmatic, militarily sensible, on-the-ground decisions – against the expectations of his superiors.

This is not exclusively a story of the risks confronting the United Kingdom's special forces. In many respects, the RAF's 47 Squadron aircrews (including, conspicuously, their ground crews, who in effect made much of the work possible) were more aware of the dangers they were being asked to face than anyone else, while the SAS commanders, erroneously, had a blind faith in the Hercules aircraft always to get them to their targets, and intact. Similarly, therefore, there is harsh comment on the RAF's hierarchy for the myopic vision shown by the air marshals. Prior to 1982, these senior officers could not accept that there should be a 'special' force within the RAF: 'the Hercules will never fly in harm's way' was their extraordinary view, and so this invaluable aircraft was denied (or was delayed receiving) much of the equipment essential for its tasks.

The further I looked behind the scenes and the more I tried to separate myth from reality, the more disturbing became the truths surrounding Operations Plum Duff, Mikado and, briefly, Kettledrum.

* * *

Argentina invaded the Falkland Islands during the night of 1/2 April 1982.[4] Many events led directly to these well-planned, well-conducted amphibious landings. The two most prominent, from which all else would appear to stem, were the coming to power of the military Junta in Buenos Aires in 1976 and (once it had been elected in 1979) the British Conservative Government's military, diplomatic and political antipathy towards both the Royal Navy and the Falkland Islands. These events, literally an ocean apart, seem almost to have run in parallel.

The background to Operación Rosario and Operation Sutton – respectively, the original Argentine assault on Stanley and the subsequent British landings in San Carlos Waters – are well known.[5] Following a military coup in Argentina on 24 March 1976, the Junta led by Lieutenant General Jorge Videla introduced martial law. The 'Dirty War' then began in an attempt to restore order – inflation was running at over 300 per cent – by simply eliminating the opposition, possibly as many as 30,000 of them. With the economy still in turmoil, Videla was ousted by Field Marshal Roberto Viola; yet things did not improve, and on 22 December 1981 General Leopoldo Galtieri assumed control of a third Junta.

At the end of March the next year, with no increase in his popularity, inflation continuing to rise and citizens still 'disappearing', and as a sop to Admiral Anaya who had helped him to power 'on conditions', Galtieri met one of those conditions. He ordered Anaya to execute Operation Rosario.

Meanwhile, and initially unconnected with these events, the newly elected conservative government, under Margaret Thatcher's guidance and through its ill-starred 1981 Defence Review, had begun the destruction of the Royal Navy's amphibious capabilities. (In October 2010 history repeated itself with the equally flawed Strategic Defence and Security Review.) Concurrently, another department, the Foreign Office, conducted its own studies into the future of the Falklands. These unsound reviews together – for both effectively relied on Foreign Office input – provided what was almost certainly the final straw in the Falklands saga by ordering the withdrawal of the Royal Navy's ice patrol ship, HMS *Endurance*. Along with 44 Royal Marines of Naval Party 8901 (the garrison ashore in the Islands), HMS *Endurance* was the United Kingdom's only permanent presence in the South Atlantic. In practice, the ice patrol ship (now HMS *Protector*) was – and still is – only 'on station' for the austral summer months. These two naval 'units' may have been small in numbers of men, but they were vastly important as symbols.

In 1978 NP 8901 had, with the agreement of the Foreign and Commonwealth Office under Jim Callaghan's government, altered its 'standard operating procedures' in case of invasion: from withdrawing into the hills to 'play at guerrilla warfare' to a posture that required it to stay and fight while falling back, under control, to guard the seat of government, Government House. Once bunkered down in GH (as it is colloquially known), the Naval Party was obliged to 'buy three weeks bargaining time' at the United Nations.[6] Only a Foreign Office functionary, with little understanding of real events beyond King Charles Street, could have thought up either of those naive reactions to an invasion. With no increase in numbers, no allocation of defence stores and no replacement for their crumbling 'barracks' (condemned for human habitation three times since 1918), NP 8901 was to remain a toothless symbol.

Argentina was aware of these signs ...

In Buenos Aires, with trouble long brewing at home, and certain that all the diplomatic and military signals reaching the Casa Rosada were true, Galtieri believed that the time was propitious not only in his own country but on the Islands, to retrieve popularity, hide the inflation figure and mask the increasing number of *desaparecidos*. Admiral Anaya was instructed to 'repossess Las Malvinas'.

By the end of 2 April 1982 it was all over on the archipelago. Stanley had fallen and the Governor, Mr Rex Hunt,[7] was deported, along with his family and the Royal Marines. South Georgia fell the next day. Galtieri hoped, too, that apart from a 'slap on the wrist' in the United Nations it would be all over internationally. He was wrong, for he had not reckoned on Britain's Chief of the Naval Staff, the naval Chief of the Defence Staff and, once she was convinced, the resolve of the British Prime Minister herself.

When the shooting stopped, the occupying governor, Brigadier General Mario Menéndez, set about attempting to placate the islanders by attending to civic duties and local affairs while, initially, giving rather less thought to military defence. This posture lasted precisely four days, for once the first ships of the British Task Force had sailed it was clear that serious hostilities could break out, on the assumption that neither side was, in reality, prepared to stand down. Menéndez was now obliged, against his initial inclination, to look to his longer-term defences. On the Argentine mainland, Galtieri's Admiral and his Air Force Commander, Brigadier Lami Dozo, considered their respective armouries. The Brigadier has since claimed that had Argentina succeeded in retaining the

Falkland Islands it would have attacked Chile. Thus the desire to use Stanley as an airbase beyond the range of Chilean fighters – first mooted in 1978 – would have been met.

The initial response of Margaret Thatcher's government was to do nothing – a reaction based on the collective view of ministers and the Chiefs of Staff of the Army and Royal Air Force that 'once lost the Falklands will be unrecoverable'. Indeed, on the face of it, there was little that could be done, for, unlike the case of a few other 'obscure dependencies' around the globe, there were surprisingly (in hindsight, of course) no contingency plans within the Ministry of Defence for retaking the Islands. But maybe this was not such a surprise: over the previous months Britain's amphibious fleet, with its supporting fixed-wing component, had being whittled away. There was not much point in planning an operation for which the essential equipment was being scrapped.

The unexpected had now unexpectedly occurred, and it had occurred a long way from NATO's preoccupation with the Cold War. This was a single-nation, 'out of area' problem far removed from anti-submarine warfare in the North Atlantic or the expected tank battles across the plains of Germany, supported by American-dominated amphibious operations along Europe's northern and southern flanks.

So, could Britain go it alone? Should Britain go it alone? Many believed that the answer to both questions was an unequivocal 'No!' Not so the First Sea Lord, Admiral Sir Henry Leach,[8] acting as Chief of the Defence Staff in the absence, on duty in Australia, of Admiral Sir Terence Lewin.[9] Interestingly, just two months earlier Mrs Thatcher (disgracefully prompted and encouraged by Deputy Prime Minister Willie Whitelaw) had tried to dismiss Leach for undermining Defence Minister John Nott's authority when he, Leach, was quite honourably and correctly 'campaigning against the cuts to the Royal Navy'.

The story of what happened next is well known but in this context bears repeating, for Admiral Leach was not aligned to the defeatist views held by his ministerial, military and air force colleagues. In words that should be heavily embossed (in perpetuity and in gold leaf) on the top of the Prime Minister's dispatch box in the House of Commons, he explained why to Mrs Thatcher:

If we do not [send a Task Force] or if we pussyfoot in our actions and do not achieve complete success, in another few months we shall be living in a different country whose word counts for little.

Later he was to write words that should also be in full and permanent view to every future Prime Minister standing at the same dispatch box:

Since here was a clear, imminent threat to a British overseas territory that could only be reached by sea, what the hell was the point in having a Navy if it was not used for this sort of thing?[10]

The Prime Minister, having listened to these straightforward words of this life-long mariner and Second World War veteran, was persuaded; the Falklands were recoverable and would be recovered.

There were, though, many threats, most of them little known and a good few totally unknown at that moment. First and foremost, to avoid a fiasco, the planned Task Force of a carrier battle group supporting an amphibious group needed the correct ships, aircraft and logistics; but these did not exist in strength, nor were there any airborne early-warning assets available to the fleet. The distance from the British home base to the 'amphibious operating area' was roughly 8,000 nautical miles, whereas for the Argentine forces it was, at the most, 350 miles: a considerable imbalance. Although the approaching austral winter was a determining factor and serious concern, the main body of the ground forces, the Royal Marines' 3rd Commando Brigade, was superbly trained in winter warfare and, having just returned from its annual sojourn in the Arctic, far better prepared and more up-to-date than any others involved or likely to be.

While the known military threats centred around a large occupying force *in situ*, 'dug-in' in defence and supported and supplied by a partially modern navy and air force, the most significant tactical threat was the French-built Exocet missile, of which Argentina possessed at least sixteen afloat and five airborne. These could be launched from the sea, from the air and, as was to be proved unexpectedly, from the back of a lorry.

It might be remembered, too, that the first spilt blood of the campaign to recover the Falklands came with the loss of the cruiser ARA *General Belgrano*, followed shortly by the loss of HMS *Sheffield*. The oldest ship in the conflict (a former American Second World War cruiser) was sunk by the oldest weapon system in the conflict (two British Mark VIII Second World War torpedoes). Conversely, one of the most modern (British) warships in the conflict was destroyed by one of the most modern (French) missiles.

Nor was the balance of forces, as seen by the United Kingdom's press corps, a great morale booster to the home front. Much of the media's reporting before and during the conflict adversely affected those left behind, by so often emphasizing the size, close proximity and ability of the Argentine armed forces. There were, in fact, imbalances on both sides: notably the Royal Navy's nuclear submarines, against which the Argentine Navy had little with which to defend itself, and the Argentine Navy's Exocet-armed Super Étendard fighter-bombers that were to cause the British a similar amount of grief.

Little understood by the British media and still not fully recognized by some sections of the press (even in 2014) was the immediate support of France. While expressing their anger at our neighbour's supplying of the enemy, the British popular press studiously avoided one fact: Britain had itself sold to Argentina two modern Type 42 destroyers, knowing that each would be equipped with Exocets. One was ex-Royal Navy and the other built under licence in Argentina. The relevance of this will become apparent.

France not only voted for United Nations Resolution 502 (calling on Argentina to withdraw from the Islands) but she persuaded two members of the Security Council, Togo and Zaire, to vote in favour as well. Secretary of State for Defence John Nott[11] has recalled that, 'France helped us to win the war'– but so too, in practical terms, did Chile, Spain (in the background), the United States and many Commonwealth countries. Argentina, mindful of the traditional rivalry between France and the United Kingdom, forgot, or chose to ignore, the many similarities between these two 'imperial' nations.

An early and very public pointer to France's support was President Mitterand's persuasion of Germany's Chancellor Helmut Schmidt to postpone the export of four Meko 360 H2 class destroyers to the Argentine Navy. Originally classified as anti-submarine frigates with homing torpedoes and depth charges, each of the slightly larger 'German versions' were also designed to be fitted with eight Aéro-spatiale MM 40 Exocets, each in two quadruple pods. The first ship, *Almirante Brown*, had been laid down at the Blohm and Voss shipyard in Hamburg on 8 September 1980 and launched on 28 May 1981. Her commissioning was delayed until 26 January 1983.

What the French President had been unable to do was to prevent the first five Super Étendards and the first five air-launched Exocets from being loaded into the Argentine 'naval auxiliary' the ARA *Cabo de Hornos* at St Nazaire for shipment to Espora naval air base. Mitterrand was, however, in time to embargo the ten remaining air-launched Exocets that had been part of the original contract signed with Aérospatiale, already paid for and ready for immediate export. Numerous rumours then spread, suggesting that Italy was involved in the undercover export of these missiles and that at some stage the Special Boat Squadron intercepted them while they were on passage in a Peruvian merchant ship as she passed Gibraltar, outward bound from Genoa. As will be emphasized, no Exocet left mainland France, and no such SBS operation took place.

*   *   *

A key figure in this tale is Captain Andy L of 6 Troop, B Squadron, 22 Special Air Service Regiment. It will emerge that he was a young leader, blamed by his senior officers at the time (and a number of authors since) for 'unnecessarily' aborting Operation Plum Duff and thus, indirectly, causing Operation Mikado to be cancelled (although it will be revealed that this latter operation would never have been sanctioned by the Government, despite the powerful influence of the SAS). Until now no one has appreciated his side of the story; no one has been aware that he was launched into the unknown with minimum intelligence, incomplete orders and no maps worthy of the name, during a vicious onslaught of autumnal Tierra del Fuego weather and many miles from his target, with just four days of food and, initially, in a position that was 'crawling with enemy'. No recovery plans were set up in advance, for he and his seven men were, quite simply, 'not expected to survive'.

The SAS – denied a *coup de main* (regardless of whether it would have been a glorious success or, more likely, a glorious failure) – had to have a scapegoat, and Andy L was the obvious, and perhaps only, choice. Whatever the reasons that Operation Mikado did not take place (and they are discussed here in depth), a guaranteed military and diplomatic humiliation (let alone a human disaster on both sides) was avoided.

Acknowledgements

Writing this saga (there is no other appropriate word) would not have been possible without the wholehearted help and encouragement of a large number of old friends and new colleagues.

All have assisted willingly but many have done so on the understanding that they remain anonymous or are only referred to by a *nom de guerre* ... I have respected those requests.

Usually I would leave a 'thank you' to my agent and friend, Robin Wade, until the end, but it was he who first detected the possibility of a story in three operations that never took place! (In the beginning, the third – Special Boat Service – operation was unknown.) It was Robin who suggested that to avoid 'frightening the horses' (my words) in advance I should write the narrative in full before approaching a publisher. Having no legally binding deadline has made research so much easier, while allowing some people to come out of the shadows in their own time and thus with rather more enthusiasm.

In no significant order I must thank all those whose names follow. To avoid clutter I have not included ranks at the time (or decorations, or positions held), since many of these appear in the text. Everyone listed was enthusiastic to the point (and beyond) of showering me with an almost embarrassing amount of detail and first-hand information.

Following my personal thanks, offered individually over the last five years, I can now present a more public acknowledgement ... and, as is conventional (but no less truthful for that), declare that where I have misconstrued or misinterpreted, to the point of culpability, then these errors are mine alone. I must, too, state unequivocally that any criticisms of individuals or organizations (unless clearly stated otherwise) are my personal views and not those of anyone who has helped me chronicle the Exocet story. Where I have felt obliged to comment adversely (mainly in the Epilogue) I have done so with considerable sadness, for some unpalatable facts that have been unearthed were not what I had expected to find; regrettably, there are many more than I have included here.

If there has to be a start, then it must be with the two C-130 pilots, Max Roberts and Harry Burgoyne; their obvious and deep involvement will become apparent. I thank Jeremy Brown for putting us in touch. In this same category come Richard Preston (who also so patiently translated an almost never ending stream of Spanish-language documents), 'Wiggy' Bennett and Charlie Cartwright. The astute reader will realize that without input from these five stalwarts the story would be rather one-sided. My almost daily (certainly weekly) bombardment of them was met throughout with equanimity, humour (masses of humour) – and information.

Without a doubt, Captain Andy L braved yet more unwarranted opprobrium from his former regiment when, unsolicited, he offered his version of events in Hereford, Ascension Island and Tierra del Fuego to (by a most fortuitous co-incidence) the Wade and Docherty Literary Agency. Having read other versions of the story of the aborted Operation Plum Duff (only one of which was written by someone who was there), then being able to authenticate Andy L's with British and Argentine sources, there was no doubt that his first-hand account had to be told. I thank him for his frank and unique story.

Mike Clapp, Julian Thompson, Nick Vaux, Tony Whetstone, Jeremy Larken, Jeremy Sanders, Christopher Wreford-Brown, Sir Peter de la Billière, Robert Tailyour, Bob Tuxford, Jim Cunningham, Colin Stagg, Paddy Long, Pat Fitzgerald, Rob Robinson, Pete Scott, Paul Croasdale, Colin Howard, Jonathan Thomson, David Boyd, 'Ram' Seeger, Clive Grant, Brian Woolvine (plus other SBS colleagues whose 'abbreviated' names appear in the text), Robin Horsfall, Sir Jeremy Black, Sir John Nott, Tim Donkin, Roger Blundell, Sir Robert Woodard, Hugh Bicheno, Mike Page, Michael Shuttleworth, David Chaundler, Simon Argles, David Benest, Nicholas van der Bijl, Tim and Mary Clode and Theodore Almstedt all could not have been more helpful with advice, wise counsel, further contacts ... and priceless snippets from afloat, ashore, in the air and along the 'corridors of military and civilian power'.

Tim Gedge, Bill Covington and Bill Pollock brought me into line over, respectively, a number of Sea Harrier and Sea King issues, reversing some earlier misconceptions.

Tony Bolingbroke told of his ship's near miss from the last air-launched Exocet, while Andy Johnson described, in stark terms, how his submarine (together with an aborted SBS operation) conducted a spot of what I call 'impact hydrography'. I trust the offending rock is now marked on the Admiralty charts ...? Neri Terry has allowed me to quote from his fascinating thesis, 'Selected Intelligence Issues from the Falkland Islands Conflict'.

Mike Barrow's (who died as the manuscript was in its final stages) and Ian Inskip's harrowing accounts of a land-launched Exocet strike against HMS *Glamorgan* are humbling. I am grateful for their input and for permission to quote freely. Concerning MV *Atlantic Conveyor*'s story I thank Sir Michael Layard and his Chief Officer at the time, John Brocklehurst, for their very personal stories. Ian Tyrrell wrote, too, of his rescue attempts as an aircrewman and of his own subsequent status as 'missing presumed dead'. For HMS *Sheffield*'s story I have had to rely on the internet and the Board of Inquiry.

I am grateful to the Disclosure Committees of the Secret Intelligence Service and Headquarters Special Forces for their guidance.

As a balanced account, the Exocet story of 1982 would be incomplete without input from Argentina. George Malcolmson (the Royal Navy's submarine archivist) put me in touch with Mariano Sciaroni, a Buenos Aires lawyer and submarine historian. From that moment I was in good hands, for not only did I become privy to all manner of submarine documents (including, thanks to the Freedom of Information Act, a number of Reports of Proceedings), but I was able to contact the major players on the 'other side' of the conflict. These included, most importantly, Super Étendard pilots Jorge Colombo and Roberto Curilovic. Equally vital has been Miguel Pita's description of his defences at Rio Grande air base. These 'dispositions' were so comprehensive that had a British air-land assault taken place … well, it does not bear further thought, regardless of which side one was on. I thank his son, Alejandro (Alex) Pita, for dealing with (and translating) my interminable requests so diligently.

Afloat, as it were, Washington Barcena kindly referred me to his ship's Report of Proceedings and log. Ashore again, Luis Bonanni, an Argentine Marine officer whose colleagues heard Operation Plum Duff's helicopter landing at Estancia la Sara, offered an account of events during the morning of 18 May; my thanks to them. Mario Menendez sent me a photograph of the damaged Stanley runway (courtesy of the first Operation Black Buck bombing mission) with confirmation of its effect on operations; this helped me assess the value of that still controversial episode.

Alejandro Amendolara allowed me to quote from his paper on the land-launched Exocet, while Pablo Vignolles and Jose Scaglia offered brief vignettes from the land-launch site close to Stanley. Santiago Rivas has been equally supportive in letting me paraphrase from his beautifully presented publication on the Argentine air war, and he also gave me permission to reproduce a number of unique photographs.

Lastly, but certainly not 'leastly', my friend Diego Quiroga sent a fascinating insight into Argentine special forces operations, plus the invaluable publication by Jorge Muñoz from which fundamental information has been culled and verified.

For the maps and charts I am delighted to welcome – for the third book running – my Royal Marines colleague Tim Mitchell of Tim Mitchell Design.

The major editorial work was undertaken patiently and good-naturedly by George Chamier, to whom I am much indebted; however, any errors remain mine!

To everyone mentioned above – and to many more in the shadows – a very serious 'thank you'.

Ewen Southby-Tailyour
South Devon
Spring 2014

Timeline

1916

1 Mar.   47 Squadron RFC forms in the East Riding of Yorkshire.

1949   Rio Grande Naval Air Base established in Tierra del Fuego.

1963

8 Oct.   United States Marine Corps Hercules lands on USS *Forrestal*, then takes off.

1968

25 Feb.   47 Squadron re-forms at RAF Fairford to operate the Lockheed Hercules.

1971

Sep.   47 Squadron moves to RAF Lyneham.

1976

4 July   Israeli forces conduct air-land assault by Hercules on Entebbe Airport, Uganda (Operation Thunderbolt).

1977

Nov.   United Kingdom naval task force in South Atlantic (Operation Journeyman).

1978

24 Apr.   United States forces fail to rescue American hostages in Tehran (Operation Eagle Claw/Desert One).

Jun.   Dassault-Bréguet Étendard enters French naval service.

Dec.   Argentina plans Operation Soberania against Chilean islands in the Beagle Channel.

1979

9 Apr.   Lieutenant Colonel Preston, Royal Marines, as Assistant Director, Operations (Rest of the World) from the Assistant Chief of the Defence Staff (Operations), visits Ascension Island to assess fuel capacity and accommodation.

7 May   Flight Lieutenant Burgoyne joins Special Forces Flight, 47 Squadron RAF.

1980

Nov.	Ten pilots and fifty technicians of the Argentine Navy at the French Rochefort Naval Base for language training. Followed by conversion to the Super Étendard.
	Argentine Navy's Second Fighter and Attack Squadron re-forms, based at Base Aeronaval Commandante Espora.
	Captain Andy L joins the SAS.
Dec.	Squadron Leader Roberts joins 47 Squadron RAF as Flight Commander, Operations and Training.

1981

July	Super Étendard pilots return to Espora from France.
Sep.	Following lessons from Operation Eagle Claw/Desert One, the United States Air Force 'Combat Talon' Hercules conducts an airfield assault demonstration at RAF Hullavington witnessed by Captain C of the SBS.
20 Oct.	ARA *Cabo de Hornos* sails from St Nazaire with five Super Étendards and five Exocet missiles embarked.
10 Nov.	Dassault team led by Hervé Colin arrives at Espora at about this time.
18 Nov.	ARA *Cabo de Hornos* arrives at Espora.

1982

Feb.	Super Étendard/Exocet combination taken into service for French carrier operations.
Mar.	During this month the Argentine Super Étendards and Exocets are married up.
15 Mar.	Squadron Leader Roberts assumes command of 47 Squadron's Special Forces Flight.
	Hercules piloted by Flight Lieutenant Burgoyne conducts air-land assault exercise with R Squadron SAS at RAF Laarbruch, West Germany.
19 Mar.	Argentine scrap metal workers land at Leith, South Georgia.
25 Mar.	Hercules piloted by Flight Lieutenant Norfolk conducts air-land assault exercise at RAF Kinloss. Squadron Leader Roberts embarked as an observer.
26 Mar.	Operation Azul task force sails from Argentina.
31 Mar.	Foreign Office suggests Argentina will invade Falkland Islands on 2 April.
	Argentina's Second Fighter and Attack Squadron ordered to complete its training as quickly as possible.

1 Apr.	HMSs *Hermes* and *Invincible* stood-to.
2 Apr.	Argentina invades the Falkland Islands.
	2 SBS embark in HMS *Conqueror* at Faslane.
3 Apr.	Argentine forces seize King Edward Point and Grytviken, South Georgia.
	President Mitterrand calls Mrs Thatcher and assures her of his full support.
	Squadron Leader Roberts flies to Bradbury Lines for discussion of Hercules capabilities with SAS, orders air-land assault training to begin immediately.
	Capitán de Navío Pita ordered to the mainland from Stanley to prepare his brigade as strategic reserve in the Rio Grande area.
4 Apr.	Lieutenant Colonel Rose at HQ Commando Forces with plan to fly two SAS Squadrons in Hercules to Stanley and capture the airfield.
	Hercules begin training at RAF Colerne (Operation Purple Dragon).
	Flight Lieutenant Burgoyne briefed for covert insertion of G Squadron, SAS, into Falklands via Easter Island. Ten-day training period follows.
	Captain Andy L briefed by Officer Commanding B Squadron, Major Moss, for 'vague' mainland tasks.
	HMS *Conqueror* sails from Faslane Naval Base.
4 Apr.– **7 May**	RAF Hercules and B Squadron, SAS, train for air-land operations.
5 Apr.	HMSs *Hermes* and *Invincible* sail from Portsmouth.
	Rear Admiral Woodward signals Commander-in-Chief Fleet expressing fears of Exocet.
	Around this time Operation Algeciras set up to attack Task Force ships off Gibraltar.
	Portugal indicates willingness to allow British aircraft to use Lajes air base in the Azores.
6 Apr.	French embargo on the provision of arms to Argentina.
	First ships of the British Amphibious Task Force sail.
	British War Cabinet convenes for the first time.
	Special Operations Group forms in London.
7 Apr.	Reports suggest Royal Navy ships over 700 miles from Argentine airfields will be safe from air-to-surface attacks.
9 Apr.	SBS ordered to 'make a bang in the South Atlantic' by this date.

10 Apr.   Hercules conduct first air-land practice at RAF Marham (Operation Purple Dragon).

Argentine Super Étendard pilots begin air-to-air refuelling training.

11 Apr.

Hercules conduct second air-land practice at RAF Marham (Operation Purple Dragon).

Super Étendard/Exocet combination declared operational.

12 Apr.   Argentine Teniente de Fragata Mayora dispatched to ARA *Hercules* to witness Type 42 destroyer's defence tactics against Exocet.

Technical team from Aérospatiale had been planned to fly to Buenos Aires on this day; cancelled on President Mitterrand's orders.

Super Étendards ready to launch Exocets in good weather.

Capitán de Navío Lavezzo and Capitán de Navío Corti, in Paris, ordered to acquire more AM-39 missiles.

200-mile Maritime Exclusion Zone established by British submarines.

Operation Paraquet (retaking of South Georgia) ordered by Commander-in-Chief Fleet.

Capitán de Navío Martini commands communications at Rio Grande, responsible for air operations.

13 Apr.   Two Hercules conduct air-land assault exercise, with SAS embarked, at RAF Kinloss (Operation Purple Dragon).

15 Apr.   Defence Intelligence staff report Argentine aircraft carrier poses major danger if Exocet-armed. Super Étendard aircraft embarked.

Argentine pilots Bedacarratz and Mayora launch a training attack against ARA *Santísima Trinidad*.

15–25 Apr.   RAF Special Forces (Hercules) Flight conducts Operation Grey Mist (night vision goggle training).

16 Apr.   HMS *Fearless* arrives at Ascension.

17 Apr.   Argentine marine brigade prepares to move to Tierra del Fuego.

Argentine pilots conduct full-scale 'mock' attack, including air-to-air refuelling.

18 Apr.   Super Étendards ordered to naval air base Admiral Quijada (Rio Grande).

19 Apr.   First two Super Étendards fly to Rio Grande.

Tank Landing Ship ARA *San Antonio* sails from Stanley to Caleta la Misión (Rio Grande) with vehicles and 600 men.

	Argentine Marine brigade sends an advance party to Rio Grande.
21 Apr.	SBS and SAS land on South Georgia.
	Two Super Étendards fly to Rio Grande.
22 Apr.	SAS rescued from Fortuna Glacier. Two aircraft lost.
	Argentine marine brigade ordered to form strategic reserve for the South Atlantic Theatre of Operations in the Rio Grande area.
23 Apr.	ARA *San Antonio* arrives at Caleta la Misión. Returns to Falkland Islands.
	Three Fleet Air Arm pilots at RAF Coningsby to fly in French Mirage III fighters, witness RAF ground-attack Harriers lose in aerial combat with French.
24 Apr.	Two Buzo Tactico members of Argentine Operation Algeciras fly from Buenos Aires for Paris en route for Spain to attack British ships at Gibraltar.
25 Apr.	South Georgia retaken.
26 Apr.	HMS *Onyx* sails from the United Kingdom.
27 Apr.	War Cabinet approves plans for San Carlos landings.
28 Apr.	Total Exclusion Zone now includes ships and aircraft of all nations.
	SAS tactical satellite link established in HMS *Fearless*.
29 Apr.	ARA *San Antonio* sails from Stanley for Caleta la Misión.
1 May	Captain Woodard, Royal Navy, appointed Special Operations Coordinator on Commander-in-Chief's staff.
	First landings on the Falkland Islands by SBS.
	Vulcan and Harriers bomb Stanley airfield.
	Decision made to extend the range of the British Hercules.
	Argentine Naval Aviation Command orders first Exocet attack.
	HMS *Conqueror* begins tracking Argentine Task Group 79.3.
2 May	ARA *General Belgrano* torpedoed.
	Second Exocet attack attempt.
3 May	Concerns expressed in the War Cabinet over Exocet effectiveness, numbers, delivery and resupply.
	Possible day that the USA changed the orbits of its satellites to cover the Falklands.
3–10 May	Air-to-air refuelling training for British Hercules.
	Ultra low-level Hercules flying training and fighter affiliation.
4 May	Argentine Buzo Tactico team ordered to execute Operation Algeciras.

HMS *Sheffield* hit by one of two air-launched Exocets.

Rear Admiral Woodward calls for action against mainland. Commander-in-Chief requests approval for such an operation, orders Director SAS to draw up plans.

ARA *San Antonio* arrives at Caleta la Misión.

5 May   Joint Intelligence Committee assesses Argentina's ability to fit Exocets to Super Étendards.

First air-to-air capable Hercules arrives at RAF Lyneham.

6 May   Operation Mikado being developed as a two-Hercules assault against Super Étendards based at Rio Grande airbase, following preliminary reconnaissance during Operation Plum Duff

Capitán de Navío Miguel Pita issues first Warning Order for defence of Rio Grande.

7 May   Operation Mikado meetings at Hereford.

Total Exclusion Zone extended to Argentina's 12-mile limit.

Argentina assumes British will attack mainland air bases.

Around this date a British nuclear-powered submarine witnesses an Argentine Hercules conducting night-time, radio-silent approach and landing at Rio Grande.

Second Warning Order for defence of Rio Grande issued.

Main UK Amphibious Task Force sails from Ascension Island.

Two Super Étendards dispersed into Rio Grande town.

8 May   Operation Mikado planning meeting at Hereford.

9 May   Operation Mikado presentation at Hereford. Hercules crews not invited.

Briefing of two four-man Operation Plum Duff patrols; targets – Rio Grande and Rio Gallegos.

10 May   Operation Mikado discussions at Hereford.

RAF Hercules cleared to refuel from Victor tankers.

11 May   Operation Mikado paper presented at Hereford. Hercules crews not invited.

Squadron Leader Roberts and Flight Lieutenant Burgoyne complete air-to-air refuelling training at Boscombe Down.

Operation Plum Duff patrols merged; four-man reconnaissance patrol increased to eight-man fighting patrol. Rio Grande sole target.

SAS Pebble Island reconnaissance inserted by Sea King.

Rio Grande air base commander delivers new defence plan.

12 May	Amphibious Task Force ordered to 'repossess the Falklands as quickly as possible'.
13 May	Reports from mainland indicate Argentina has three Exocets left.
	Chief of the Defence Staff officially orders detailed planning for Operations Plum Duff and Mikado to go ahead.
	Plans for Operation Mikado presented at Northwood.
	Flight Lieutenant Burgoyne and crew arrive at Ascension Island.
14 May	Discussions on Operation Mikado at Hereford.
	Orders delivered to 6 Troop for Operation Plum Duff.
	War Cabinet approve Admiral Lewin's plan for Operations Plum Duff and Mikado.
	Pebble Island raid by SAS.
	Major Moss relieved of command of B Squadron SAS by Major Crooke.
15 May	B Squadron (less 6 Troop) training for Operation Mikado.
	6 Troop flies to Ascension Island.
	846 Naval Air Squadron Sea King aircrew chosen for Operation Plum Duff.
	ARA *Hipolito Bouchard* and ARA *Piedra Buena* anchor off Cabo Domingo.
16 May	6 Troop parachutes into South Atlantic. Embark in HMS *Hermes*, meet aircrew.
	B Squadron flies to Ascension Island.
	HMS *Onyx* sails south from Ascension Island with 'sealed' orders for the SBS to attack Puerto Deseado.
17 May	Argentine Navy Day.
	Squadron Leader Roberts at Northwood for Mikado discussions.
	Spanish police arrest Operation Algeciras team.
	6 Troop to HMS *Invincible*.
	Operation Mikado talks at Hereford.
	Messages of support are received in London from the Dominican Republic, Sri Lanka, Belize, Nepal and Mauritius. New Zealand breaks off diplomatic relations with Argentina, Australia and Canada recall their ambassadors. Canada imposes an arms embargo on Argentina. Chile condemns Argentina's use of force.
	Chiefs of Staff told 'quite categorically' (but erroneously) that 'the Argentines now have ten air-launched Exocets'.
18 May	6 Troop flown to Argentina and then Chile by Sea King from HMS *Invincible*.

Argentine marines alerted by helicopter noises.

Blackout imposed in Rio Grande, vehicles to show only sidelights.

6 Troop walk eastwards. Radio call to Hereford. Told to push on.

19 May   Reuters reports seven men captured at Rio Gallegos.

Cabinet approves landings at San Carlos.

Sea King ditches in South Atlantic.

6 Troop sends out night patrol then continue eastwards. Hereford believes patrol captured.

Squadron Leader Roberts flies to Ascension Island. Ordered to conduct 'two-ship' assault on Rio Grande. Meets Major Crooke.

Secret Intelligence Service officer tasked to track down missiles for sale on black market.

20–23 May Only possible dates for Operation Mikado.

20 May   Meeting at Hereford agrees Operation Mikado will continue without prior reconnaissance.

Chilean government informs Argentina of 'crashed' Sea King.

21 May   3 Commando Brigade establishes beachhead in San Carlos Water.

6 Troop informs Hereford they need food. Ordered to emergency rendezvous.

Operation Mikado 'on hold' for Drop Julie to HMS *Alacrity* by Hercules.

Flight Lieutenant Burgoyne sees SAS model of Rio Grande. Beginning of plans for Operation Plum Duff Mark Two.

21–22 May 6 Troop march towards emergency rendezvous. No communications with Hereford.

22 May   No one at 6 Troop's emergency rendezvous.

23 May   No one at 6 Troop's emergency rendezvous.

Operation Mikado 'on hold' while Flight Lieutenant Burgoyne executes Drop Katie.

Flight Lieutenant Robinson flies to Ascension from Dakar. Briefed to fly B Squadron to Belize in a VC 10.

24 May   No one at 6 Troop's emergency rendezvous.

Operation Mikado 'on hold' for supply drop.

Argentine attempts to move Exocets to Falkland Islands thwarted by British air activity.

Flight Lieutenant Robinson loads his VC 10 with ammunition – and is then stood-down.

25 May	Operation Plum Duff's Sea King aircrew picked up by Chilean authorities. Eventually fly to United Kingdom.
	MV *Atlantic Conveyor* hit by two Exocets.
	No one at 6 Troop's emergency rendezvous.
	Portugal allows British Nimrods to refuel at its Lajes air base in the Azores.
	New Zealand's offer of HMNZS *Canterbury* is accepted by Mrs Thatcher.
26 May	Four Exocets, ordered by Peru, ready to leave Aérospatiale factory for Peruvian ship at Toulon. Commander-in-Chief alerted.
	Operation Mikado 'on hold' for supply drop.
	B Squadron commander 'champing at the bit'. Discussions with RAF about alternative landing sites.
	6 Troop commander hitches lift into Porvenir and telephones British Consul in Punta Arenas. Remainder wait at emergency rendezvous, find SAS 'rendezvous team' in a restaurant.
	Operation Mikado 'on hold' for supply drop.
27 May	HMS *Avenger* believed to be overflown by land-launched Exocet.
26–27 May	6 Troop commander collects remainder of patrol and returns to safe house.
27–29 May	6 Troop told they may be ordered back to Argentina.
28 May	RAF and SAS at Ascension Island told that Operation Mikado is cancelled.
	Operation Mikado back 'on' less than twelve hours later.
	Operation Mikado 'on hold' for supply drop.
29 May	Operation Mikado 'on hold' for supply drop.
30 May	Last air-launched Exocet misses HMS *Avenger*.
	6 Troop fly to Santiago.
	Operation Mikado 'off' at Ascension Island. In London it is merely 'put on ice'.
30 May– 8 Jun.	6 Troop team in Santiago safe house.
31 May	HMS *Onyx* arrives San Carlos carrying orders for SBS Commanding Officer. Rehearsals for Operation Kettledrum against Puerto Deseado.
Jun.	Early in month three Exocets arrive Stanley in Argentine Hercules.
1 Jun.	Squadron Leader Roberts recalled to Lyneham. Operation Mikado cancelled (on Ascension Island).

	Super Étendards withdrawn from Rio Grande to Espora.
2 Jun.	HMS *Onyx* sails for Operation Kettledrum.
	Operation Mikado 'on hold' for supply drop.
	HMS *Fearless* concerned about Exocets on Pebble Island.
3 Jun.	Operation Mikado 'officially' cancelled.
	Flight Lieutenant Burgoyne and crew return to United Kingdom.
	Operation Kettledrum aborted. HMS *Onyx* returns to San Carlos.
5 Jun.	HMS *Onyx* hits an uncharted rock.
	Four Exocets arrive in Stanley by Hercules.
6 Jun.	2 Battalion Scots Guards land at Bluff Cove – late, due to fear of land-launched Exocets.
8 Jun.	6 Troop flies to United Kingdom.
	Royal Fleet Auxiliary ships *Sir Galahad* and *Sir Tristram* bombed at Fitzroy.
11 Jun.	Final battles for Stanley begin.
12 Jun.	HMS *Glamorgan* hit by land-launched Exocet.
13 Jun.	Super Étendards ordered back to Rio Grande, fitted with iron bombs.
14 Jun.	All land objectives taken by British. Argentine forces surrender.
21 Jun.	One Exocet discovered at Stanley.

Operation Thunderbolt, Entebbe

On 27 June 1976 an Air France Airbus A300 flying from Ben Gurion airport, Tel Aviv, to Charles de Gaulle, Paris, with 248 passengers and 12 crew on board, was hijacked in Greek airspace then forced to land – via Benghazi for fuel – at Entebbe in Uganda. A week of intense diplomatic negotiations followed, during which a military option was planned. Following the collapse of negotiations and Israeli patience, on 4 July 100 'special forces' from Israel's Sayeret Matkal, Sayeret Tzanhanim and Sayeret Golan flew 2,500 miles overnight at very low level in four Hercules to land, unopposed, at Entebbe's civilian airport.

The operation to free the hostages took ninety minutes, at the end of which 102 of the 106 Jewish hostages were rescued, with four killed and ten wounded. All seven hijackers, who had been demanding the release of forty Palestinians held in Israel and thirteen more held in other prisons, were killed, for the loss of one dead Israeli – the raid commander – and five wounded. Forty-five Ugandan soldiers were killed, while thirty Soviet MiG-17s and MiG-21s were destroyed on the ground to prevent them counter-attacking the returning Hercules.

The undoubted success of Israel's Operation Thunderbolt gave the United States confidence that it could carry out a similar incursion into Iran to rescue fifty-three American embassy personnel held hostage in Tehran in April 1980. From every military and diplomatic aspect, and for many operational reasons, Operation Eagle Claw on 24 April was a total disaster.

A few months after the Entebbe raid, the Royal Air Force and the Special Air Service, recognizing the advantages of surprise and shock that such an un-announced landing by large transport aircraft could achieve, rehearsed at an RAF airfield the first of what later would be known as Tactical Air-Land Operations. While the ground troops were successful in their part of the exercise, the pilots were doubtful that they had remained undetected during their approach, despite taking evading action.

It might have been better if the ghosts of Operation Thunderbolt had never been resurrected ...

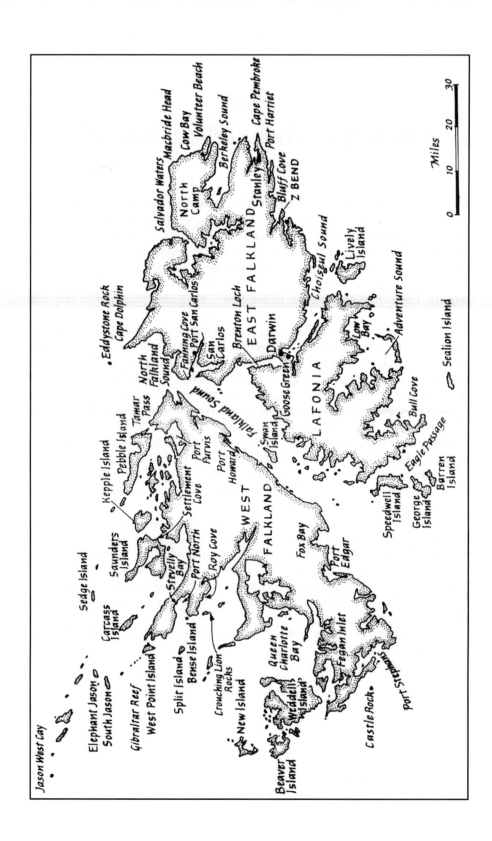

Jason West Cay

Elephant Jason
South Jason

Sedge Island

Gibraltar Reef
West Point Island

Carcass
Island

Saunders
Island

Split Island
Bense Island

Crouching Lion
Rocks

Strehly
Bay

Port North
Roy Cove

Kepple Island

Pebble Island

Tamar
Pass

North
Falkland
Sound

Eddystone Rock
Cape Dolphin

Salvador Waters

Macbride Head

Low Bay
Volunteer Beach

North
Camp

Berkeley Sound

Stanley
Cape Pembroke
Port Harriet
Bluff Cove
Z BEND

EAST FALKLAND

Choiseul Sound

Lively
Island

Adventure Sound

Fanning Cove
Port San Carlos

San
Carlos

Brenton Loch

Darwin

Goose Green

Swan
Island

Settlement
Cove

Port
Purvis

Port
Howard

WEST FALKLAND

Fox Bay

LAFONIA

Low
Bay

Bull Cove

Eagle Passage

Barren
Island

Speedwell
Island

George
Island

Sealion Island

Beaver
Island

New Island

Weddell
Island

Queen
Charlotte
Bay

Port
Edgar

Fagan Inlet

Castle Rock

Port Stephens

Falkland Sound

Miles

0   10   20   30

Chapter 1

RAF Laarbruch, West Germany

15 March 1982, 2030 hours GMT – RAF Lyneham, Wiltshire, England
Flight Lieutenant 'Harry' Burgoyne[1] glanced out of the port cockpit window of
his four-engined Hercules C Mk 1, known worldwide as the RAF C-130 K.
Although Burgoyne was a member of Special Forces Flight, 47 Squadron RAF,
his aircraft 'belonged' officially to the Royal Air Force's Hercules Transport
Wing of RAF Lyneham. 47 Squadron's Special Forces Flight did not 'own'
aircraft, and if the air marshals could have had their way the Flight itself would
not have existed.

The Squadron has enjoyed a distinguished history, starting with its formation
in the East Riding of Yorkshire on 1 March 1916 as a home defence unit of the
Royal Flying Corps, attacking marauding German Zeppelins. In early 1919 the
Squadron moved to southern Russia in support of White Russian forces facing
the Bolsheviks. On return it was disbanded, only to be re-formed in Egypt twelve
months later. Perhaps with a nod to the future, in 1925 the Squadron carried out
the first of many long-distance flights, when three aircraft pioneered the route
between Egypt and Nigeria. During the Second World War, and following
peacetime operational service with, among others, the Sudan Defence Force, the
Squadron supported Field Marshal Slim's 14th Army (including Orde Wingate's
Chindits), until it was disbanded at Butterworth in March 1946.

Following its re-formation in September of that year, and equipped with the
Blackburn Beverley for the Berlin Airlift, the Squadron embraced the role of air
transport, but was disbanded again in 1947. Its final metamorphosis occurred at
RAF Fairford on 25 February 1968, when it was re-formed to fly the Lockheed
Hercules, which since September 1971 had been based at RAF Lyneham.
Pending the closure of Lyneham, 47 Squadron moved to Brize Norton in 2011.

Apart from the hazy blue glow from the lines of taxiway lights that led from the
floodlit apron, RAF Lyneham was dark on that March evening in 1982. Brief
wintry squalls were fading away, leaving a few last wisps of snow to eddy across
the tarmac. Above the cockpit's upper windows the unseen cloud base was
reported at 2,000 feet. A 10-knot wind was blowing from the west, and the
temperature, already a chilly 5°C, was forecast to drop three more degrees by the
time Burgoyne turned his aircraft on to Lyneham's 7,000-foot 'Runway 25' for
take-off. There were less than twenty minutes to go.

Burgoyne had always wanted to fly. Now aged thirty-one and a C-130 pilot
since 1973, he was the longest serving pilot in the RAF's Special Forces Flight.
Despite knowing that it was rare for a transport pilot to reach the higher ranks, he
had volunteered to fly the Hercules. (Not until January 2013 was it announced

that a former helicopter pilot, the first non-fighter pilot in the RAF's 95-year existence to reach the top, would become Chief of the Air Staff.) Burgoyne's 'boss', Squadron Leader Max Roberts,[2] who was joining the Special Forces Flight as its new Commanding Officer that very day, had not always wanted to fly trans-port aircraft, but had taken the practical view that one should 'never fly in an aeroplane without a loo!'

Unusually, the aircrew had been cleared to fly through Germany and Holland 'at low level if required', so Burgoyne was determined not to miss this unique opportunity. From the Dutch coast inland the weather would be as cold as in southern England, sharpened by the same 10-knot wind. It was probable that Hercules XV196 would be overtaking the light showers that had just moved on from the Wiltshire countryside. Thus visibility could be a problem, especially once they had 'coasted in' over Holland. Lovely, flat Holland with nothing solid above 1,059 feet, nothing to force XV196 up into the low cloud. The moon, if it could be seen at all, would be in its last quarter. The sun had long since set. It was a Monday.

Burgoyne's mission, in conjunction with the troopers from 'R' Squadron, SAS (later, renamed L Detachment, SAS) now settling into the cargo bay, was to conduct an airfield assault against RAF Laarbruch[3] as part of the station's work-up for its annual NATO Tactical Evaluation or TACEVAL. (Since the 1990s these exercises/operations have been known as a Tactical Air-land Operation or TALO.) But Laarbruch was no run-of-the-mill air base, for it was a major con-tributor to Britain's Cold War fighter-bomber force. Central to NATO's air defence of Europe, it was host to a number of RAF squadrons, two of which possessed a nuclear capability. Thus it was essential that this RAF station should be alert for the unexpected, 24 hours of every day of every year. Annual TACEVALs were designed to test this vigilance and the station's ability to conduct wartime operations. A station-generated exercise was vital to ensure that when the real test came no aspect would be found wanting. To ensure surprise, and for safety and deconfliction reasons, only a handful of Laarbruch's staff were 'in the know regarding the evening's activities'.

No. 15 Squadron, assigned to the Supreme Allied Commander Europe, had been stationed in Laarbruch since 1970. Equipped with twelve Blackburn Buccaneer S.2B bombers, the Squadron's role was to support the British Army against a Russian advance. If subsequent events so dictated, the Squadron would deploy WE.177 tactical nuclear weapons, two of which could be carried by each aircraft. Number 2 Squadron, flying Jaguar GR1s in the ground attack and reconnaissance roles was at a similar state of readiness.

Each squadron's ground crew worked alongside their aeroplanes, which were housed in hardened aircraft shelters (HASs): 2 Squadron to the south and east of the centre of the runway and 15 Squadron to the south and west. Positioned close to the HASs, the squadrons' pilots lived in their own equally-hardened Pilot Briefing Facilities. Here lay the operation rooms and administration offices, the planning rooms and limited sleeping accommodation for those duty pilots waiting to fly. The PBFs, as they were known, were proofed against nuclear, chemical and biological attack, and thus pressurized through an air conditioning and ventilation system. To the SAS this was their Achilles heel. The shelters' air conditioning and air filtration systems, protecting the inmates from a chemical attack, were precisely the weak points that had been sought by the attackers' inventive minds and had then become the subject of many realistic rehearsals at Hereford. In the real thing, petrol would have been poured into the systems' intake vents, followed by a phosphorous grenade; but this time it was going to be fresh water and a stun grenade. Had this been a genuine attack, no one in either of the PBFs would have survived.

Although Burgoyne had never conducted an airfield assault, the principle was similar to the numerous strip-landing operations, on to and from unprepared landing zones, that he had flown in many of the world's trouble spots: work that was central to the Special Forces Flight's existence. Up to the moment he brought his aircraft to a stop 3,000 feet down Laarbruch's runway it was to be a normal night 'strip-landing' practice, albeit on to a lit and hard surface. After that it would not be quite so 'normal'.

If his passengers (known affectionately and with justified admiration by the Special Forces Flight as 'The Hooligans') succeeded in 'killing' the fighter pilots, then not only would the SAS and the Flight have proved the effectiveness of their embryo procedures but, conversely, the air base would have failed its pre-TACEVAL practice and lessons would need to be re-learned very quickly. If, later, it failed the real test, then senior RAF heads would be scalped. In NATO's ideal world it would, of course, be better if the air base 'won'; indeed, the air base simply had to win. Yet if the SAS failed ... well, that option was not considered by the 'ground troops'.

There was, though, a real possibility that the aircraft would be 'shot down' by the base's air defence unit, and Burgoyne was well aware that this was the weak point of the plan; if the Hercules went down then the SAS, rather obviously, went with it. The success of this mission relied entirely on the survival of Hercules XV196 – either in the air or on the ground – until after the troops had disembarked. If Laarbruch's radars managed to pick him up on the way in, then the ground defences would be alerted, and that, too, would be just as fatal.

Somebody had to lose, but the SAS and the Special Forces aircrew were determined it wasn't going to be them ...

Two days earlier (Saturday), the SAS troopers had arrived at Lyneham for rehearsals with Burgoyne and his crew. The aircraft had been taxied to a position away from the runway for slow-time drills, followed by more taxiing and faster drills, until the SAS Squadron Commander and the RAF Flight Lieutenant were happy to undertake a full night-time dress rehearsal.

After supper in the airmen's mess everyone met again by the rear of Hercules XV196. The sun had set at one minute past six, and with low cloud and fine, near-freezing rain it was already dark. Harry Burgoyne and Master Air Loadmaster, Pete Scott, conducted a confirmatory brief that emphasized the precise stopping point of the aircraft in relation to the targets. This was followed by comprehensive orders from the SAS officer commanding R Squadron, who pointed out the simulated targets at Lyneham that mirrored the real ones at Laarbruch. The drills on reaching 15 and 2 Squadron's Pilot's Briefing Facilities had been practised, rehearsed and perfected at Hereford, where, understandably, there was less concern about the apparently indiscriminate spraying of petrol into mocked-up copies of Laarbruch's air conditioning units and ventilation systems.

With the night rehearsal a success, Burgoyne brought XV196 back to its stand, allowing everyone to disperse for what was left of the weekend. In R Squadron's case this involved a second night at RAF Lyneham's familiar Route Hotel.

The weather was no better when, on Monday afternoon, Burgoyne rejoined his co-pilot, Flight Lieutenant Don Macintosh,[4] and navigator, Flight Lieutenant Jim Cunningham,[5] in Lyneham's flight planning room. Although this was regarded as an exercise, it was being conducted as an 'operational' sortie, so the team had arrived four hours before the estimated time for 'brake release' rather than the more usual ninety minutes.

Knowing that the SAS needed to be on the ground at Laarbruch at 2315 GMT, or 0015 local, the time that the SAS felt was best to begin their nefarious deeds at Laarbruch, the pilots and navigator needed to work their flight plan backwards from then in order to calculate precisely when to take off.

Burgoyne, Macintosh and Cunningham had discussed all aspects of the mission some days earlier with Hereford's counter-terrorism wing, and from this an outline plan had evolved. With the help of a squadron leader who had recently left Laarbruch, the SAS identified the two PBFs that they needed to attack, then decided that the best way to reach those targets was with their specially adapted, 'desert-pink' Land Rovers.

The Hercules would stop at a specific point on the runway that not only suited the SAS but would ensure enough room ahead to take off without having to turn through 180 degrees in order to return to the beginning of the runway. The precise stopping point was alongside the 5,000-foot 'distance to go' marker, one of seven such boards on the side of the 8,000-foot runway. When the SAS troopers drove out of the aircraft they would know exactly where their starting point was and thus the direction of and distance to their targets, one of which was at ten o'clock to the aircraft south of the runway, the other, also south of the runway, at seven o'clock.

By consulting the aircraft's performance graphs Burgoyne knew that if he approached the runway's threshold at the tactical landing speed of 96 knots, about 15 knots below a normal approach speed, he could stop at the required spot comfortably. He often landed in far shorter distances, but that involved putting the four-bladed Hamilton Standard 54H60 propellers into reverse thrust, and if his aircraft had not been heard before its arrival it certainly would be then. This time, with 3,000 feet in which to stop, he had plenty of distance to use just his brakes. Things would be pretty quiet at Laarbruch at that time of night, and they wanted to keep it that way for as long as possible. A westerly wind was forecast, so Burgoyne's stopping point would leave him a clear 5,000 feet to take off on completion of the 'dirty work'.

To add realism, the plan was for the Hercules to remain on the ground with engines running while the men carried out their attack. On their return, the 'Pink Panthers' (as the Land Rovers were known) would (for real) be dumped and the men, in Burgoyne's words, 'would trot up the ramp so we could eff off in fine pitch within five seconds of the last person running on board'. There was to be no time for the returning troopers to strap in, for the final part of this Laarbruch exercise was a fast exfiltration. As soon as the ramp was closed, the brakes would be released. The door that comes down out of the Hercules' roof did not need to be shut, and often was not, but the ramp had to be raised, since it formed part of the 'tail plane's structural integrity'. Nor was it a good idea to allow it to scrape along the runway when the control column was pulled very firmly – almost wrenched – back into the pilot's stomach to 'rotate' the aircraft into the night air.

Now that they knew where and when they were aiming to stop, Burgoyne's team moved back a few minutes in time to consider their final approach. It was this that concerned the crew most, for they had to take into account Laarbruch's three radar systems, detection by only one of which would give the game away.

The first electronic hurdle was the Precision Approach Radar. This radar looked up the runway centre line to guide aircraft down in poor visibility. It 'saw' out to about 15 miles and normally swept 10–15 degrees either side of the centre line. Providing XV196 kept outside that sweep area it would not be seen until the last moment, by which time the pilot had to be lined up. Burgoyne needed to keep XV196 clear of the runway's centre line until he was less than one mile out.

Of greater concern was the Area Search Radar used by the air traffic controllers to identify and control aircraft within the airfield's surrounds, since it was also able to identify low-level targets at less than 500 feet above the ground up to ten miles out. This range, though, could be reduced by ground clutter, hills and buildings or, quite simply, by bad weather. It could also be reduced further if Burgoyne conducted a 'terrain flying' approach at a 'seriously' low level. To minimize his exposure he planned to come in as low as possible, yet still expected to be spotted 8 miles away. His success would then depend on the speed of reaction at the airfield.

The third system was the one that worried the crew most, for in a real war it could literally be fatal. Specifically designed to detect, track and destroy low-flying aircraft, the British manufactured Rapier Air Defence System was, and remains, a world leader and is considered virtually impossible to defeat.

The Rapier's radar acquired targets much as the Area Search Radar did, but then used its missile fire-control element to remain 'locked on' while measuring the height, speed and direction needed to provide a firing solution. The Rapier could kill virtually any threat within 3 miles of it. If detected, an attacker had two options: take immediate evading action, or abort the mission. Yet the only really effective evading actions were either to turn hard away or to fly at an even lower level, maybe as low as fifty feet, in the dark, over land. The Rapier was also designed to resist Electronic Counter Measures, but for Burgoyne and his crew this was not a consideration. Thanks to their 'underdog' status when compared with the fast jet fraternity, the Hercules of 47 Squadron's Special Forces Flight did not even have a Radar Warning Receiver or any Electronic Counter Measures. They would never know if they had been seen, electronically, by anything. If they were targeted by the RAF Regiment's 26 Squadron's surface-to-air missile teams when 3 miles out, then that would be the end of the mission. If the missiles missed, and someone was thinking quickly enough, the runway would be blocked by the defending forces.

This was an approach to an airfield whose defences Burgoyne knew, yet he doubted that, despite meticulous planning, he would arrive at Laarbruch unannounced. The need to fly low, especially at night, was vital to avoid detection and so was practised as often as possible with the best aeronautical charts available. Such an approach helped to ensure, but could not guarantee, that the elements of shock and surprise were exercised to the full.

For general navigation, the standard 1:1,000,000 aeronautical chart[6] sufficed but, with a lack of detail, these publications were unsuitable for low-flying sorties. For the en route section of a normal, low-level flight the crews used 1:250,000 or even 1:500,000 charts. However, for the final run in to a Dropping Zone or Landing Zone, where pinpoint accuracy was essential, they would shift to a 1:50,000 chart or an even larger scale if such existed.

Under the RAF's 38 Group regulations, the legal minimum height for a RAF C-130 to fly at night was 500 feet above the highest obstacle within 3 nautical miles either side of the proposed track. To calculate the height to fly, the navigator needed to divide the route into 10-mile sections, identify the highest obstacles – hill, tower, mast – within this 6-mile-wide corridor and add 500 feet to the height of that obstacle. The aircraft would then be flown at that combined height for that portion of the route.

This produced limitations that either needed to be circumvented or ignored. Burgoyne's view was straightforward:

> If you have a 600-feet-high TV mast at the end of your 10-mile sector that is 2½ miles off the main track's centre line, then the aircraft will end up flying 1,100 feet above the ground for the whole of that sector. This is hardly flying at low-level. You can improve things by choosing a route that avoids the mast, narrowing the width of the corridor or, if operationally essential, by reducing your clearance height from 500 feet down to 250 which is an absolute peacetime minimum at night. The navigator can also reduce each sector's length to, maybe, 5 miles, thus allowing the aircraft to follow the ground contours more closely.

For this near-experimental raid the crew used a combination of 1:50,000 and 1:250,000 aeronautical charts and the airfield's own instrument approach charts (large-scale and containing extremely accurate information about all the obstacles and high terrain surrounding the airfield) to scrutinize the approach to Laarbruch. Armed with this information, Burgoyne decided that it would be safe – and would certainly offer a greater chance of his aircraft being undetected – to reduce the width of the corridor to 2 miles and his clearance height to 350 feet for the last 3 miles.

In 1982 the navigation equipment in the RAF's C-130 fleet was basic, thanks to most procurement money being channelled elsewhere. Despite its often operating in extreme conditions, and occasionally under fire, the air marshals had refused to accept that the Special Forces Flight was 'special'. It may have carried special forces but, they argued, the Special Forces Flight itself was not 'special'.

The Flight had remained undaunted and had attempted to procure equipment that they had seen used in the USAF's Special Operations C-130s, such as Radar Warning Receivers, chaff and flare dispensers, fuel tank protection, Inertial Navigation Systems, Terrain Following Radar and Forward Looking Infra-Red Television. All had been part of a 'wish list' submitted following exercises in America the previous year. By March 1982 the aircrew had still heard nothing, as the RAF hierarchy continued studiously to avoid recognizing the truth. The air marshals' mantra every time a request for something special was made by the Flight was, 'The Hercules will never be sent anywhere where it might come under fire' … and yet the Hercules force had been deployed on numerous operations such as evacuating refugees from Cyprus and Tehran and flying ultra-low-level missions in Rhodesia during the transition to independence, the latter tasks flown under direct threat from small arms, Triple A and surface-to-air missiles. Indeed, on the first day of the Rhodesia operation, an AK 47 round had entered the lower window of an aircraft, only just missing the co-pilot. After this incident, all flight deck crew placed their flak jackets over the bottom windows or used them as rudimentary seat armour.

Planning their covert route from Lyneham to Laarbruch in the dark at low level was one thing; actually navigating it was another problem altogether, for the equipment was already old. Navigation was by map reading, dead-reckoning and Doppler. The Doppler Computer Navigation System transmitted radio beams from an aerial on the underside of the aircraft to the earth's surface, from where they were bounced back. These reflected beams had their frequency altered by the Doppler Effect that was then used to calculate the aircraft's ground speed and drift. By combining these with the aircraft's heading, the aircraft's position could be plotted and shown as either latitude and longitude or as distance travelled along a desired track, plus any deviation to right or left.

The Doppler fitted into the Hercules was not only old and limited in its capability, but it was regularly unserviceable. It was also susceptible to 'drifting' and so, even at its best, was frequently inaccurate. Consequently, it had to be updated regularly, a process that required the co-pilot to identify geographical features and then tell the navigator where they were so that the Doppler could be 'rationalized'. That was not easy over some of the featureless terrain they crossed, or over the sea, and was especially challenging at night. By early 1982 night vision goggles for pilots were undergoing trials at Farnborough, but were not expected to be cleared for use for some years.

To help the co-pilots see navigation checkpoints, two sets of 'old, bi-focal, hand-held, binocular' night vision goggles (manufactured by the American ITT company) had been acquired, but this fact was kept strictly within the Flight. More often than not, this first generation of night vision goggles were affected by lack of moonlight, cockpit and external light sources, by moisture in the atmosphere or by clouds ... and, just occasionally, they did not work at all.

The Doppler had another drawback. As an 'active' system it could be detected by enemy electronic warfare sensors if, as the pilots had calculated, they banked their aircraft over 15 degrees. Beyond that limit the radio beams were emitted away from the aircraft, so routes to avoid excessive banking were chosen.

To ensure that they could find Laarbruch's runway the navigator and co-pilot needed to select an easily identifiable final point to update the navigation equipment before beginning the final run-in. This had to be unique enough to guarantee that the co-pilot could see and, crucially, identify it at night, with or without the night vision goggles. In Lyneham's flight planning room Cunningham and Macintosh selected the northern end of a bridge 8 nautical miles northeast of Laarbruch for their final Doppler re-alignment point, and a line was drawn on their charts from this bridge to the '1 mile to go' point on the extended centre line of the runway. By design, this line was offset by 45 degrees to the north of the normal approach path and thus would offer a course that avoided the sweep of the Precision Approach Radar. Two more lines were drawn, with each line 1 nautical mile either side of the primary track from the bridge. This would delineate their 'safety lane' for the final approach and would be used to calculate the correct height to fly and when to descend. At the '1 mile to go' position the aircraft would be 350 feet above ground level and this, they hoped, would avoid their being spotted until the last few moments.

With his outward leg planned for two hours and twenty minutes, Cunningham could now deduce the take-off time that would, with a little margin for the unexpected, meet the required landing time: 'brake release' was to be at 2054 hours GMT. Precisely.

As captain, Burgoyne needed to make his own calculations for the take-off and landing speeds based on the weight of the load and the required fuel states. He also had to assess his 'immediate action' in case of emergencies immediately after becoming airborne. With all to his satisfaction and everyone ready, Burgoyne called his cockpit crew for a final brief before walking out to their aircraft. Here they met the Flight Engineer and Air Loadmaster, who, for the previous two hours, had been carrying out their own checks.

The thirty SAS troopers waiting on the grass were huddled in small, penguin-like groups with their backs against the wind. Some were drinking coffee, some drew on last-minute cigarettes, while their breaths, tobacco smoke and coffee steam mingled near-horizontally in the cold breeze, a ghostly swirl lit eerily by the blue taxi-way lights. Short bursts of laughter carried across the tarmac as individuals joked and teased. Burgoyne was familiar with such pre-flight scenes, from the Arctic's ice-bound strips to the dusty plains of Equatorial East Africa. Now, with fewer individual pre-flight checks to complete than his crew, he made four cups of tea, handed three around the flight deck, then took his outside to join the troops for his own last nicotine fix. He left his co-pilot, navigator and flight engineer settling into their seats, tidying away their personal equipment, checking that their oxygen masks were connected and their headsets were plugged in.

One final pee completed the aircraft's captain's own pre-flight routine, before he returned to the cockpit, buckled himself into the left-hand seat and pulled the restraining straps tight over his shoulders.

In the cargo bay the last members of R Squadron settled into the two rows of red, parachute-webbing seats, facing inwards to the two Land Rovers. Flight Sergeant Pete Scott – the Air Loadmaster – called the cockpit to confirm that all were strapped in and that the rear ramp and door were both 'closed and locked'.

Burgoyne turned to his co-pilot and nodded. He twisted round further to face Flight Sergeant A, XV196's Flight Engineer. The pilot nodded once more. With twenty minutes to go before 'brake-release', the team understood that it was time to 'coax the Hercules into life', starting with the starboard, inner engine.

The navigator read through the complex checklist, and the other crew members responded accordingly.

Cunningham spoke sharply into his headset, 'Clear number three?'

Master Air Loadmaster Scott was outside the aircraft, 'attached' by a long 'intercom' lead. 'Clear number three,' he confirmed.

'Start number three engine,' Cunningham responded.

'Roger,' called the pilot, 'Turning number three … Now!'

His right hand moved the number three engine 'condition' lever forward from the 'ground stop' position and dropped it into the 'run' détente, then with his left index finger and thumb he pressed the starter button above his head. Normally, the 'condition' of the propellers was altered automatically depending on the power settings, but these could be overridden in an emergency. If anything went wrong during the start, Burgoyne would retard the condition lever fully aft to the 'feather' position and shut down the engine.

On the cue of 'Now!' Macintosh started a stopwatch.

The Flight Engineer joined the process by announcing, not from a checklist but from memory, the various key points in the start process: 'Fuel flow … Oil pressure … Hydraulic pressure …'

As 'Number Three' wound up past 60 per cent to become self-sustaining – accelerating on its own – Burgoyne released the starter button. 'Button … out!' he called.

In the cold temperature it had taken a comfortable twelve seconds less than the sixty-second limit. In quick succession numbers 4, 2 and 1 engines were brought to life until the gauges of each of the Allison T56-15 turbo prop engines – known in the Hercules family as the Dash Fifteen – were indicating '100 per cent', each developing only a fraction of the 4,350 shaft horsepower that would be available at full throttle.

With his engines running smoothly, Burgoyne called the Air Loadmaster back on board and began running the Pre-Taxi Checks. He then released the parking brake by his right knee and slowly manoeuvred XV196 between the taxiway lights towards Runway 25. As the Hercules approached the threshold, the crew actioned the 'take-off checks.'

'Flaps.'

'Set 50 per cent.'

Cunningham continued with other cross-checks until he could announce, 'Take-off checks complete.'

Burgoyne lined up his aircraft facing south-west, almost directly into the breeze, and at precisely 2054 hours he pushed the four throttles 12 inches forward, and his 57-ton aircraft began its take-off roll. The fully-laden, fully-fuelled weight of a C-130 is in the region of 70 tons, but on this occasion XV196 was not fully fuelled and would weigh about 52 tons on landing at Laarbruch.

Shortly after crossing the Dutch coast, on time and on track at 'L Hour minus 30 minutes' (2245 hours GMT), it was the moment for the crew of XV196 to begin their final checks for a 'strip landing', albeit a strip landing on to a long, lit, hard-surface runway. For realism, the drills were the same as those used for a grass or sand surface and were strictly adhered to in order that the aircraft landed safely, as far as any 'enemy' might allow. Timely and accurate touch-downs ensured that the assaulting troops were presented with the best possible start for their phase of the operation. If the aircraft stopped in the wrong position or even facing the wrong way there could be a disaster.

The navigator called, 'Thirty minutes,' over the intercom.

This half-hour warning was largely for the benefit of Pete Scott in the cargo bay, who now roused the troops to begin preparing the large, cluttered cargo compartment.

'Twenty minutes,' called the navigator.

Burgoyne, concentrating hard on flying at 500 feet across the darkened Dutch countryside, replied, 'Twenty minutes. Prepare for action. Prepare the load.'

Scott's response from aft was immediate: 'Roger. Prepare for action.'

His duties, well honed, now focussed on ensuring that there were no loose items to fly around should the landing be rough. The embarked troops, black-faced, camouflaged, fully armed and menacing, knew the drill. They stood to fold back their canvas seat bottoms so that nothing could snag the Land Rovers. Each trooper checked his buddy.

Forward, the Flight Engineer began de-pressurizing the aircraft. He also turned down the cargo bay heating to give the troops a brief period of acclimatisation before they drove off into the night air of northern Germany in March.

A few moments later, he called, 'No pressure.'

The countdown continued: 'Ten minutes.'

The familiar Strip Approach Checks were called for and actioned. On cue, the Air Loadmaster was cleared by the captain to open the cargo door, and as the heavy flap swung upwards and inwards to be locked into the aircraft's roof, a sharp gust of refreshing cold air was sucked back into the cargo bay.

Throughout the flight, Burgoyne's Radar Altimeter alarm had been set at 450 feet to avoid the shrill warning bleeps if he inadvertently descended below his 500 feet limit. Now it was altered to 17 feet.

The heavy restraining chains were removed from the Land Rovers' wheels, leaving light, quick release tie-downs attached to each axle, with kneeling troopers ready to slip them on the Air Loadmaster's orders. Two other troopers moved to the two 70-pound toe ramps that would bridge the 12-inch drop once the rear ramp had been lowered to the ground. These mini-ramps had been hooked into the main ramp prior to take-off and would be dropped the moment the Hercules stopped. It was perfectly possible for the Land Rovers to shoot straight across this gap, but the opening phase of such an operation was not the time or place to risk a delaying accident.

The Hercules' captain, visualizing the scene behind him, was conscious that any violent manoeuvre now could break the light chains that secured each vehicle, and the very last thing he needed was a loose vehicle sliding about as he steadied up for the final run-in. Men not involved with releasing restraints or lowering ramps clambered aboard their vehicles.

While all was made ready in the cargo bay, the flight deck crew were concentrating hard on keeping the Hercules unseen by flying as low as they dared, the navigator and co-pilot confirming and updating their position to their captain as they continued towards their final approach fix, the bridge north-east of the field.

Co-pilot Macintosh, with the bridge in sight through the night vision goggles announced, 'Stand by for the overhead ... ready ... ready ... NOW!'

As he confirmed the 'overhead', Cunningham updated the Doppler and called his captain, 'Captain, Nav. Make your heading 225. 140 knots ... 140 knots ... GO!'

'Roger, 140 knots', Burgoyne replied, banking the aircraft gently on to the new heading and pulling the four throttle levers back to zero thrust to reduce the speed.

As the Hercules decelerated Burgoyne called, 'Flaps 50', and as they began extending he pulled gently back on the control column to prevent the aircraft dipping downwards. Flicking the trim switches with his left thumb, he kept the Hercules at the required height but with a slight nose-up angle. As the aircraft's speed dropped past 160 knots Burgoyne called, 'Gear down.'

An immediate increase in noise indicated that the four large, main undercarriage wheels and the two smaller nose wheels were extending into the airflow. Ten seconds later three wheel symbols appeared in the indicator immediately above the gear lever itself to confirm that all were 'down and locked'.

As their speed 'bled off' past 150 Burgoyne advanced the throttles to stabilize XV196 at 140 knots. 'Strip-landing checks,' he demanded.

Within ten seconds all checks were complete, ensuring that the aircraft was finally in the correct configuration for landing. The only outstanding pre-landing action was the selection of the flaps to 100 per cent and a further speed reduction to the required 'threshold' or touchdown speed.

Although this was RAF Laarbruch's annual tactical evaluation practice and was an unannounced landing, there was a genuine safety need to deconflict with any 'normal' flights. One single call to their 'agent' in air traffic control was sufficient. Using a secure 'trigraph' call sign rather than 38 Group's 'Ascot' system, Macintosh selected the appropriate ultra-high frequency channel and called, 'Laarbruch tower. Delta Foxtrot Romeo Six Four. Six miles ... Finals, Gear down. Land.'

In the control tower the C-130's 'agent' replied instantly, 'Delta Six Four. Laarbruch tower. Roger. Clear to land.'

The navigator and co-pilot continued their course-plotting.

'Six miles to run, five miles right of the centre line ... good heading, good speed ... five miles to run, four miles right of centre line ... height and speed good ... timing good ... TWO MINUTES!'

Cunningham's strident call of 'two minutes' was the cue for Pete Scott to signal 'start the vehicles'. If nothing happened, jump leads and a spare battery were ready. If the first vehicle off did not start, a swift decision would be made either to abort instantly or, once the aircraft had stopped, to bump start the vehicle down the ramp. If the former, the Air Loadmaster was ready to shout, 'Abort, Abort.' The aircraft would climb back into the night air almost before the flaps had had time to be re-set to 50 per cent. If the 'flat' vehicle was the second one off, then the mission would almost certainly be aborted and, in Burgoyne's words, 'We would run away bravely as fast as we could.'

'Three miles to run, two miles right of centre line ... cleared to descend to 350 feet. Slow down ... slow down ... GO!'

This was the navigator's last opportunity to advise his captain on any speed adjustment to ensure that he landed XV196 on time. Seconds counted. On a genuine strip-landing operation, if the Hercules was two minutes early or two minutes late (or one minute either way for a drop) the ground party would not illuminate the landing zone. Even if the flight had been across 4,000 miles, the timing would still have been as tight. All the Special Forces Flight's navigators prided themselves on never being more than ten seconds early or late.

Burgoyne retarded the throttles to reduce XV196 to the target threshold speed of 96 knots and called, 'Flaps 100', and 'Lights Off'. With all external lights now extinguished and the aircraft under minimal power, an observer on the ground immediately below would only have been aware of a fleeting dark shadow and a thundering 'whooooosh'. As the flaps slid into the fully extended position, XV196 descended further into the darkness.

Outside, the shadowy German farmland was flat and featureless. With no-where to hide his 52-ton aircraft, Burgoyne was approaching the 'one mile to go point' and, at a horizontal angle of 45 degrees to the runway's centre line, well out of the Precision Approach Radar's narrow 'line of sight'. While certain that he was not being pinpointed by that radar, he had no way of knowing whether the other two had 'pinged' him further out and that consequently even now the Rapier Air Defence System had acquired XV196 as a firm target.

'Two miles to run. One mile right of centre line ... Commence right turn to 270 degrees. Runway is at your one o'clock. Two miles.'

The captain looked to his right, then spoke into his microphone: 'Visual with the runway. Happy with the height.'

In that one glance he could see that he was approaching the ideal glide slope and that the turn was bringing him gently on to the runway's centre line. 'I have the runway. Action stations. No further calls.'

The final call – but only to the troops – came as the aircraft lined up on the centre line of Laarbruch's Runway 27. Fifteen seconds before touch-down, Cunningham selected 'PA' on his intercom box and keyed his microphone. In the cargo bay the public address tannoy barked, 'Brace, Brace, Brace.'

Burgoyne continued the deceleration towards the threshold speed; then, as they crossed the very end of the runway and a mere 17 feet above it, the radar altimeter warning bleeper, pleasingly on cue, sounded shrilly in everyone's head-sets. The pilot closed the throttles, eased smoothly back on the control column to cushion the landing and touched XV196's main undercarriage down at exactly the right speed, at exactly the right spot ... and exactly three seconds early! He lowered the nose wheel to the tarmac and began braking towards the off-load point.

Confident that he had the aircraft under control and that he would make the desired stop point, Burgoyne called, 'Red on!'

In the right-hand seat, Don Macintosh switched the parachute jump lights to red. Standing by the ramp hinge in the cargo bay, Pete Scott, noting that both lights had illuminated, responded, 'Red on', then began lowering the ramp to the horizontal position, using the control panel on the port side of the aircraft.

The Land Rover drivers each applied their brakes and raised a fist. The troopers by the wheels released the remaining chains.

With the throttles in the 'flight idle' position to minimize noise, Burgoyne counted over the intercom the 'distance to go' markers spread down the side of the 8,000-foot runway: 'Seven ... braking! Six ... braking. Speed decreasing. Approaching the Five marker and ... brakes fully on and ... stopped! Green on!'

Scott replied 'Green on', and lowered the ramp to the ground, but remained facing the vehicles with one arm outstretched horizontally. 'Do not exit!'

The toe ramps were lowered, the Air Loadmaster raised his forearm vertically and called on the intercom, 'Troops Moving!'

On the flight deck the noise of the Land Rover engines revving was heard clearly and their movement aft felt, until, only forty-five seconds after touch-down, the call came, 'Troops and vehicles gone.' The crew relaxed and smiled at each other. The captain waited for his navigator to ask why he had landed so early.[7]

If this assault landing had been 'for real', Harry Burgoyne would have had two choices: remain on the ground with engines running waiting for the men to return, or set the flaps to 50 per cent, call for the 'Strip Take-Off Checks', then, as soon as the Air Loadmaster reported that the ramp was closed, slide the throttles forward and accelerate down the runaway.

This time, though, XV196's part in Laarbruch's exercise was over, and the exfiltration departure cancelled in favour of waiting to fly R Squadron home. All the crew of XV196 had to do was enjoy a cup of coffee and wait for the 'end of exercise' call. A short debrief would follow with the SAS, the base staff, the RAF Regiment and the RAF police. Only on the completion of that 'hot wash-up' could Burgoyne ferry the team back to Lyneham in time for, in his own words, 'Tea and medals!'

Waiting for the formal end to the night's activities, Burgoyne pulled the throttles back to the 'ground idle détente' and listened to the familiar increase in volume as the propellers adjusted their pitch towards reverse. He applied the parking brake before expressing his pleasure at how well the flight had gone.

Outside, the Land Rovers split into two assault teams that sped along the tarmac and across the grass towards their targets, the troops holding their fire. There was no sign of the RAF Regiment's No. 1 Squadron, tasked with the airfield security, so, with nothing to shoot at, there was no point in alerting the base unnecessarily. Perhaps the Hercules, idling in the middle of the runway, was a planned arrival of which the defenders had simply been given no prior warning. The SAS wanted the pilots of 15 and 2 Squadrons to remain secure in their hardened pilots' briefing facilities so they could be burned alive or suffocated; they did not want them running into the fresh air to see what all the fuss was about.

Each hardened bunker was just under 1,000 yards away. Unaware of what lay in store, their inhabitants were enjoying the warm air-conditioning that cosseted them from the cold, damp outdoors.

Ninety seconds after the Hercules' ramp had been lowered to the tarmac the defenders 'woke up' to the assault. At last the RAF Regiment's 'Rock Apes' and the RAF Police's 'Snowdrops' (as the men of these two are respectively known) homed quickly on to the two PBFs, but from this point onwards no one was quite sure what happened next. As far as the SAS were concerned they had successfully fried alive or suffocated a significant number of pilots from two British front line squadrons. Now, had it been for real, all they needed to do was either fight their way back to their C-130 taxi home, assuming it was not riddled with bullets, or melt into the surrounding countryside to execute a pre-planned escape and evasion programme.

The RAF Regiment – for obvious reasons aware that that this was indeed an exercise – deployed, as they had so often practised, to prevent the aircraft from taking off, prepared (had it been real) to destroy it. Unfortunately, the RAF police, not quite so alert to the reality of the situation, set their Alsatian dogs on to the attacking troops. A man with a rifle and blank ammunition can do little damage on an exercise, but a dog has no 'blank firing attachment' other than its handler's commands. After a brief, snarling skirmish one SAS trooper was obliged to kill his assailant with a swift knife-thrust to the heart. The dog died quickly, silently, efficiently, but bloodily.

The Station Commander was far from happy, understandably, for the failure of a TACEVAL, even a practice TACEVAL was not a key to swift promotion. Of considerably more importance than the Group Captain's future was the RAF's reputation within NATO. What if instead of Burgoyne landing his Hercules with blank-ammunition-carrying SAS soldiers, it had been Russian Spetsnaz that were now occupying RAF Laarbruch? It did not bear further thought. RAF Laarbruch air base's motto was 'Ein feste Burg' [A Fortress Sure], and now 'R' Squadron SAS and Hercules XV196 had, in less than two minutes, dented that proud boast.

That, of course, was the initial perception. During the exercise debrief, at which Burgoyne and his crew were represented by the SAS, it was confirmed by Laarbruch's staff that, as suspected, the approaching Hercules had been spotted and 'engaged'. It had been picked up on the station's search radar when 7 miles out, then successfully 'shot down' by the Rapier at 3 miles. The missile teams, for that night alone, had been notified that up to the actual firing of the missile this was not an exercise. The Royal Artillery (and naval gunfire) equivalent order of 'guns tight' had been issued.

On his return to the United Kingdom, Burgoyne was verbally debriefed by Squadron Leader Graham Young[8] (the departing Commanding Officer Special Forces Flight, who had initiated the exercise in the first place and who was to be killed in a Hercules crash in Scotland in 1993) but was not invited to raise a post-exercise report; it was presumed that the SAS, as the prime participants, would do so in due course.

For Laarbruch, the 'exercise' might have looked a failure, but that would be too harsh, for considerable good came out of the evening's events. The Station Commander and his team accepted that they were vulnerable and immediately changed many of their procedures to ensure that, had this been an authentic assault, and the attacking aircraft a brace of Russian Mi-24 Hind helicopters or even one AN-12 Cub (the Hercules' near-equivalent) they would, too, have been dealt with swiftly and efficiently by the Station's defence systems.

For the Hercules crew there were mixed feelings. At best, their performance might have been seen as a form of pyrrhic victory for, despite all their careful flight planning, radar avoidance techniques and low flying skills against an unalerted target, there remained no doubt that they had been 'shot down'. This awkward fact, from the Hercules' point of view, was accepted by those in Headquarters, RAF Germany whose task it was to assess all the results in great and measured detail. While RAF Laarbruch may have 'failed', invaluable lessons were learned by both 'sides'.

Ten days after Laarbruch, on 25 March, a similarly successful raid – again, only as far as the SAS were concerned – took place against RAF Kinloss. This time the aircraft was piloted by Flight Lieutenant Jim Norfolk, with Jim Cunningham as his navigator and their new Commanding Officer, Squadron Leader Max Roberts, embarked as an observer. On their way to the tactical landing they had dispatched a team of SAS parachutists in a High Altitude/Low Opening free-fall exercise.

The lessons from Laarbruch might already have been implemented in Germany but they had yet to reach Scotland, where the Station Commander's own quarters were surrounded and considered 'captured'.

The fact that Hercules C-130s had conducted two 'apparently successful' airfield assaults was viewed with well and widely voiced scepticism among the aircrew of the Special Forces Flight, and especially by their new Commanding Officer. In harsh reality, their part in the operation would certainly have failed; indeed, it most certainly should have failed, for on each occasion the aircraft had been picked up on radar well before touchdown. This unpalatable fact was to weigh heavily on the C-130 crews over the next months, and yet this was an aspect of the operation that many senior officers in both the RAF and SAS seemed unable to grasp. Soon this short-sightedness among some of the country's top-level decision makers was to come very close indeed to sending two Hercules aircraft and one SAS Sabre Squadron to their deaths.

By a remarkably timely coincidence, just seven days after the Kinloss raid Argentina invaded the Falkland Islands. At very short notice everyone at Hereford and Lyneham was forced to come to terms with this unplanned situation. In the fast escalating crisis, the task with which British Special Forces were about to be faced was not a short hop across the North Sea to practise against British Buccaneer nuclear-armed, fighter bombers, but a confrontation with Argentine Exocet-armed Super Étendards over 8,000 miles away from the United Kingdom.

On 3 April and almost immediately following the landing by Argentine maritime special forces at Mullet Creek, south of Stanley, the new Commanding Officer of the Special Forces Flight was invited by the SAS to Bradbury Lines, Hereford. The SAS's senior officers had not forgotten their recent experiences with C-130s and were searching for a role in this latest crisis, no matter how outlandish. Squadron Leader Roberts had been summoned to answer questions and comment on a selection of ideas. Almost clandestinely, he was lifted by helicopter from behind 47 Squadron's buildings to meet the SAS team led by the Director of the SAS himself, Brigadier Peter de la Billière.[9] Among others present were the Officer Commanding B Squadron, Major John Moss, and 22 Regiment's Second in Command (and recently the Operations Officer), Major Ian Crooke.

The first two questions put to the airman by Hereford's imaginative minds were: 'Can you land a Hercules on HMS *Ark Royal*?'[10] and 'Can you parachute a recce team into the Falklands? Now!'

At that stage of the campaign the first request was marginally more feasible than the second, although no one, and certainly no one in the Royal Navy outside Whitehall, knew which ships were being earmarked. The SAS had read of a USMC C-130 landing on USS *Forrestal* on 8 October 1963 and had talked to 47 Squadron about it several times; yet they seemed unable to appreciate that *Forrestal*'s flight deck was 1,063 feet long and 250 feet wide, whereas *Ark Royal*'s was 550 feet long and just 44 feet wide; the C-130's wingspan is in the order of 132 feet. HMS *Ark Royal* was not due to sail south but her sister ship HMS *Invincible* was, along with the larger aircraft carrier HMS *Hermes*.

Having given negative responses to both questions, Roberts felt it necessary to highlight to the assembled team the advantages of the Hercules.

It may not be able to land on an aircraft carrier nor fly to the Falklands and back on one load of fuel but it does have some remarkable properties that it might be useful to bear in mind. As you all know, we can land on 2,500 feet long roughly prepared strips in the dark and take off in less. Depending on freight the aircraft has an endurance of between twelve and thirteen hours.

Despite its size the C-130K is very agile. We can throw it around and turn inside most western fighters that are operational now, in 1982; except perhaps the Harrier and the F16, neither of which are operated by the Argentines. We practise fighter evasion as part of our normal training. Indeed, the comedian Jimmy Edwards, one of our forebears who earned a DFC during the Arnhem campaign, performed evasion tactics in his Dakota DC3 against an attacking Focke-Wulfe. Those wartime transport pilots would turn their surprisingly manoeuvrable DC3s in towards attacking fighters so that their aggressors couldn't get a shot at them and that still forms the basis for what we do today.

With half flaps and at about 150 knots we just go round in tight circles or use terrain masking until the opposition runs out of petrol. At such slow speeds we are particularly manoeuvrable in the mountains. More so than many smaller aircraft. Manoeuvring against fighters is practised regularly.

Reading between the lines of the conversation that followed, Roberts gathered that the outline plans had something to do with retaking the Falkland Islands through an air-land operation, and at this stage he presumed the target had to be Stanley airport. At the end of the afternoon Roberts came away knowing that his Special Forces Flight needed, right away, to start practising for such landings; yet there had been no mention of specific targets and certainly no talk about the mainland, or of air-launched Exocet missiles.

Back at Lyneham, Roberts concluded his first 'crew brief' with the observation, 'This most certainly is not going to be a 'Bring a Bottle War'.' He was referring to all the previous post-Second World War actions where, apart from the odd bullet being fired at them during 'confrontation' in Indonesia as well as in Aden and Rhodesia, most Air Transport operations took place in benign environments where 'a good drink was always available'.

In the early days of the Falklands conflict both RAF Special Forces aircrew and the SAS were worried that they would be left out of any impending 'excitement'. They might have been right, for at a Chiefs of Staff meeting the day after the Islands had been invaded, both the Chief of the General Staff and the Chief of the Air Staff expressed reluctance for their individual services to become involved in what the Army, in particular, saw as a 'potential bloody nose' for the Royal Navy. As though to add emphasis to this view, as early as 2 April the Chiefs of Staff warned the Commanding Officer of HMS *Endurance* (in a signal relating to the offer of assistance to the Royal Marines ashore on South Georgia), 'To bear in mind the potential of the Argentine corvette armed with Exocet'.

So, both 'Chiefs' were convinced that their own service should stay well clear, while Defence Secretary John Nott helped them in their views by declaring that, 'the Falklands once taken could not be retaken'.

From the very first days of the emergency, however, neither the SAS nor the RAF's Special Forces Flight were following the party line peddled by their respective Chiefs of Staff. Thank goodness.

Chapter 2

Opening Shots

During the night and into the day of 2 April 1982 Argentine amphibious and special forces occupied the Falkland Islands. Twenty-four hours later they followed this undoubted military success with the slightly bloodier capture of South Georgia, 800 nautical miles to the east.

At Stanley, the capital of the Falklands, the British garrison – Naval Party 8901 momentarily doubled in size from forty to eighty Royal Marines due to its annual changeover – had been swiftly and predictably overcome, despite the unrealistic orders to 'buy three weeks bargaining time in the United Nations'.[1] General Galtieri, Argentina's unelected president and head of the military Junta, expected no more than a mere 'slap on the wrist' from that international forum, accompanied by a boost to his personal popularity at home that would divert attention from the very real economic and civil problems that his administration faced. After all, he and his colleagues reasoned, all the signs indicated that once the Islands were lost, the British Foreign and Commonwealth Office would not only breathe a sigh of relief but would, in cahoots with the Ministry of Defence, persuade the Government that not only were Las Malvinas, as the Argentines call them, unrecoverable but that no attempt should be made to recover them. Galtieri was to be disappointed on all counts, thanks largely and initially to two people: Britain's Prime Minister and her First Sea Lord.

Despite well voiced misgivings from the Foreign and Defence Secretaries, along with those of the Chief of the General Staff supported by the Chief of the Air Staff, Mrs Thatcher followed the First Sea Lord's advice and instructed Admiral Sir Henry Leach to dispatch a large naval Task Force as soon as possible. The bulk of that armada sailed within six days, carrying its associated Royal Marines Commando Brigade, boosted by two battalions of the Army's Parachute Regiment, supported by Sea Harrier jump jets and helicopters of the Fleet Air Arm, plus a then unknown number of submarines, two aircraft carriers, destroyers, frigates and (later) minesweepers, all supplied and supported by ships of the Royal Fleet Auxiliary and Merchant Navy.

Over the coming weeks this reinvasion force was to be augmented by more merchant ships 'taken up from trade' and by a brigade of infantry. The RAF began basing at Ascension Island a number of Nimrod maritime reconnaissance aircraft, Vulcan long-range bombers, Victor 'tankers' and, of the utmost significance to this tale, two air-to-air-refuelling-capable Hercules C-130s.

On Sunday 4 April Brigadier Julian Thompson,[2] and Colonel Richard Preston,[3] Chief of Staff to the Major General, Royal Marines Commando Forces, were in the conference room of Hamoaze House, Devonport (the Headquarters of Commando Forces) discussing the mobilization of Thompson's 3rd Commando Brigade. Suddenly, the Commanding Officer of the 22 Special Air Service Regiment, Lieutenant Colonel Mike Rose,[4] was standing in the door clutching a *Daily Telegraph* map of the world on which he had marked, within a blue circle, the Falkland Islands. Despite the more pressing matters occupying them, the two Royal Marines were then deluged by Rose with a series of eccentric ideas for his regiment to win the campaign before it began.

The most outlandish of his 'plans' was to fly two SAS squadrons equipped with armed Land Rovers direct to Stanley in two C-130s and take the airport by *coup de main*. Clearly, he had already forgotten his brief from Squadron Leader Max Roberts at Hereford the day before. No such aircraft could fly that far, even empty, and it was known that the airport was already guarded by radar and anti-aircraft weapons; it was, too, within range of Argentine fighters.

The SAS officer had chosen the wrong audience. Preston, who had once been the Assistant Director Operations (Rest of the World) on the Assistant Chief of Defence Staff (Operations) staff, responsible for contingency planning and operations outside NATO, knew better than most the problems of reinforcing the Falklands when threatened by Argentina. Now the sword had actually been drawn, those problems were multiplied, and Thompson and Preston had more realistic solutions to discuss and assess.

Rose was not the only one to speak before appreciating the reality of the situation. The Officer Commanding the SBS, Major Jonathan Thomson,[5] a calm, steady officer, had already volunteered to lead the first team into the Falkland Islands either by parachute from a C-130 or by rubber assault craft launched from a nuclear submarine. This offer had followed a request by an unnamed minister within the Ministry of Defence demanding of Colonel Martin Garrod,[6] on the staff of the Commandant General, Royal Marines, that the SBS 'make a bang in the South Atlantic by 9 April'.[7] It would appear that the minister had no more idea of the difficulties of reaching the Falklands than had Rose.

On arrival in Ascension Island Thomson was ordered by Colonel Garrod to 'stay put', for it had dawned on the command that neither method of transport – air or sub-surface – was feasible. The South Atlantic 'bang' was cancelled. It was never a starter, for the nuclear submarines were not suitable for landing special forces in shallow waters and, as yet, no Hercules had been fitted with air-to-air refuelling equipment; although a one-way option was, briefly, mooted. Determined voices, however, persisted in suggesting far-fetched schemes, since, as will be detailed, one lone RAF C-130 would be earmarked to fly to Easter Island in the Pacific and from there – via a subterfuge flight to Chile – it would drop parachutists on to Bombilla Flats in the middle of East Falkland. The significance of this far-fetched plan to the Exocet saga will unfurl.

On the Falkland Islands throughout April the initially planned figure of 800 Argentine personnel detailed to form the occupying force was, once the Junta had analysed Britain's response, steadily expanded to over 10,000. These men, with more to come, would have to face an eventual reinvasion. Largely conscripts, but with a significant smattering of well trained professionals including marines and gunners, their limited capabilities might have been considered predictable. Their degree of resolve and fortitude was, though, a 'known unknown'. The reason for such a small initial figure was the Argentine expectation that the greatest obstacle facing General de Brigada Mario Menéndez would be civil disorder, not a powerful, all-arms, British Amphibious Task Force.

For the British, the prime threat, initially at sea and eventually in the skies above it, that the commanders and to a certain extent the politicians who had sent them south had to ponder was the effectiveness of the Argentine naval air arm. Elements were stationed not only at a number of naval air bases along the length of the Atlantic coast but also on the navy's one aircraft carrier, ARA *Veinticinco de Mayo*. The British admirals, generals and air marshals at home, and a Rear Admiral, Commodore and Brigadier at sea, could gauge, numerically, what they were up against: the swiftest of glances at *Jane's Fighting Ships* and *Jane's All the World's Aircraft* provided much of the vital information. Yet there were gaps in everyone's knowledge of Argentina's potential, and the air-launched, anti-ship Exocet definitely fell into that category. It was understood that the Argentine surface fleet operated them, but it was not known whether or not the naval air arm had taken delivery of them and their associated aircraft, the Super Étendard. If they had, had they been able to fathom out, technically and practically, how to use them?

During the journey south the amphibious commanders, most notably Commodore Michael Clapp,[8] a vastly experienced naval aviator of the Amphibious Task Group, and Brigadier Julian Thompson,[9] an equally experienced Royal Marines commando officer of the Amphibious Landing Force (both embarked in the Landing Platform Dock, HMS *Fearless*, commanded by Captain Jeremy Larken[10]) studied and assessed the likely opposition they could expect to meet once 'in theatre'. The Royal Navy's Battle Group Commander, Rear Admiral John 'Sandy' Woodward,[11] a submariner of renown and now flying his flag in the aircraft carrier HMS *Hermes*, with his intelligence, air, surface and underwater specialists, did likewise. Pure numbers were not the problem, for numerically the British Task Force was superior to anything that might be ranged against it on the sea's surface and beneath it. The Argentine capability in the air was the real British worry, a worry that persisted until the last day of the campaign despite Woodward having moved his carrier battle group beyond the supposed range of the land-based Super Étendard. Here, as events on 30 May showed, it still did not enjoy 'local air superiority' for, until it was too late, none knew of the Argentine air-to-air refuelling capability.

On paper, any losses suffered by Argentina could be replaced swiftly, while the British, to a certain extent, would be stuck with what they took; and what they took would be transported in very lightly armed Royal Fleet Auxiliary and merchant ships, the latter having nothing in the way of 'damage control' in their construction. This lack of follow-on materiel was particularly true of fixed-wing air defence and ground-attack aircraft (although some were, quite remarkably, to fly direct to the Task Force from the United Kingdom, via Ascension Island) as well as for troop-lift helicopters. Every aircraft lost and every ship sunk, merchant or war, would be well nigh irreplaceable and thus another step towards possible failure.

A second infantry brigade was to be deployed south, but had a third been needed it was difficult to know from where it would be found and how it would have been transported in time. As it was, the one army brigade that was dispatched – late, thanks to the Army's earlier concerns – was poorly prepared for the task it faced. The Chief of the Air Staff was equally cautious to begin with, but he had a more understandable excuse: with the area of operations at such a distance from any secure base it was, initially, not easy to see how his service could help in any constructive manner 8,000 miles from the action at the worst, or (from Ascension Island) 4,000 miles at best.

The most significant and vital gap in British intelligence was the status of Argentina's Aérospatiale-manufactured Exocet missiles. It was understood that the first five of fourteen Dassault Super Étendard fighter-bombers, nicknamed 'Sue' by their naval pilots,[12] might have arrived in Argentina in November 1981 along with five out of a planned total of fifteen AM 39 air-to-surface missiles.[13] The second and final tranche of this order was due to arrive in Argentina in September 1982. A technical team from Aérospatiale that had been earmarked to fly to Buenos Aires on 12 April was prevented from doing so by President Mitterrand, following his decision on 6 April to place an embargo on further arms exports. There was already a team of eight technicians in the Espora naval air base at Bahia Blanca helping to 'integrate' the missiles with their aircraft, but how far that 'integration' had progressed was not known by the Task Force. They would soon find out.

Nor did the Super Étendard pilots themselves know how successful the integration was likely to be, for there were no spares to be wasted on tests; the first firing would be a live shot against a live – British – target. One of the Super Étendards was to remain non-operational for spares and tests, but all five Exocets would be destined for use.

Despite deliberately misleading statements from the Argentine military at the time, and the opinions of a number of British historians since, the threat of an air-launched Exocet attack against the major warships of the Task Force was, from the beginning, considered very real and worthy of substantial study as soon as the Task Force left the English Channel. For instance, as early as 5 April Rear Admiral Woodward signalled Admiral Sir John Fieldhouse,[14] the overall commander of the Task Force and Commander-in-Chief at Northwood, from his then flagship (the MM-38 Exocet-armed, guided missile destroyer HMS *Glamorgan*):

> My operational plans will be critically dependent on top grade information from manufacturers, delicate sources, whatever on the following … USA and German built submarines [plus] their anti-ship torpedo capability. Exocet: ship fitting … numbers … and any details of any Exocet air launch capability and their radar parameters'[15]

Furthermore, he asked to be told if the Argentine aircraft carrier could operate the Super Étendard and, if so, what their radius of action was and whether they had any night flying/all weather experience.

In his *Official History of the Falklands Campaign* Professor Freedman describes the naval position at that stage of the conflict thus:

> Against the Argentine air threat, the Naval Staff were reasonably confident that there was sufficient defensive capability, provided the Task Force was not too widely scattered. Exocet was the most serious prospect, although that was vulnerable to chaff which was readily available ... [Chaff is a radar countermeasure in which aircraft or ships fire clouds of small, thin pieces of aluminium into the air from a rocket. This can appear as a confusing mass of secondary targets on radar screens.] Given that it was difficult at the best of times to detect and attack surface ships, the Chiefs' [of Staff] initial assessment was that the Falkland Islands themselves were comfortably within the radius of action of Argentine land-based offensive aircraft, but that a combination of range limitations and inadequate navigational aids would leave British ships reasonably secure so long as they kept their distance. This view was supported by the first Naval Staff study, produced on 7 April, which reported that so long as Royal Navy units remained over 700 nautical miles from Argentine-held airfields, the air-to-surface threat would be negligible. It was only as RN ships moved to within 300 nautical miles that the threat increased greatly, notably from the Super Étendard/AM 39 Exocet combination.

On 15 April the Defence Intelligence Staff, who supplied the background to War Cabinet briefings, believed, again according to Freedman, that, 'The Argentine carrier posed the major danger, especially if it had Exocet-armed Super Étendard aircraft ...'

Freedman concludes with this statement:

> The assessment of the air threat was seriously contested at the time, especially by those thinking about an amphibious landing [most strongly by Commodore Clapp and Brigadier Thompson, who felt that their concerns were being brushed aside]. One factor, to which not enough attention had been paid, was Argentine aerial refuelling, using KC-130s. In the event, these made a significant difference to the Argentine campaign, most notably in permitting the Super Étendard to reach the British ships.

The Royal Marines officer appointed to Admiral Woodward's Battle Group staff, Colonel Richard Preston, has stated:

> It was quite clear when I joined Sandy Woodward on board HMS *Glamorgan* at Ascension Island on Easter Day that he and his staff were only too aware of the threat ... Once the Admiral moved to *Hermes* we practised Action Stations frequently when I was conscious that in the event of an Exocet attack the ship would turn her stern towards the threat. One of my two action stations was the Admiral's dining room and that was just below the quarterdeck and so where the missile would probably hit. Sandy was confident that *Hermes* would survive, albeit restricted to a significant degree, but he thought that *Invincible* would not.[16]

Opinions varied then and do so now, with the majority believing that the admiral was unduly pessimistic.

Those who needed to know at that stage knew that Argentina had procured the Super Étendard/Exocet combination; what was not so certain in the early days was how many had actually been delivered before the French embargo was announced. When that figure was revealed, uncertainty shifted to the level of expertise of the Argentine naval pilots and technicians at marrying aircraft and missile, and whether or not the global black market was capable of providing replacements from outside France.

At the time the Argentine technical literature mentioned only 'the possibility' of a successful combination of Super Étendard and Exocet, because technical support staff from Aérospatiale had been prevented from flying to Espora. Therefore, it was believed in Buenos Aires, British intelligence would have advised its own government that the Argentine Navy had not yet successfully married up this dangerous combination. In the Argentine capital it was important that the British were given every reason to continue thinking that.

The pre-campaign procurement of such a lethal anti-ship weapon system, against which – with no airborne early warning – the British Task Force was vulnerable, produced considerable 'rantings about the perfidious Frogs' from the British tabloids. As the French press noted, these British editors were ignoring the unpalatable fact that Britain herself had sold the Argentine navy two modern Type 42 destroyers, well aware that they were to be fitted with the surface-to-surface version of the missiles, the MM 38. Four older Argentine ex-US Navy destroyers of the Gearing and Sumner classes had also been retrofitted with four Exocets each.

It is certain that the London press were also unaware that French pilots had, by British invitation and early on in the conflict, conducted several missions against British aircraft with the aim of training the Royal Navy's Fleet Air Arm to thwart similar Argentine attacks. Above the English Channel French pilots, in their view, produced enough evidence to convince the British Admiralty that, 'Their own formidable efficiency with the Super Étendard/Exocet combination would be a real hazard to the British.'[17]

Nor did many know at the time that in April 1982 a freak accident had occurred when one of the Royal Navy's MM 38 missiles was 'inadvertently' dropped and broken in two. In the course of putting the pieces back together, before returning it to Aérospatiale for repair, the Royal Navy gleaned a considerable amount of information, much of which was previously unknown. Based on this fortuitous intelligence, the decoy carried by the Lynx helicopters was developed; but further information was still needed.

Lieutenant Commander Tim Gedge,[18] then the Commanding Officer of 809 Naval Air Squadron equipped with Sea Harriers, remembers:

The Super Étendard and Exocet missile combination was always going to be a deadly weapon. From everything I knew about the Super Étendard attack profiles, without 'airborne early warning' it would have been well-nigh impossible to counter the attacks other than to kill – or decoy – the incoming missile.

The questions uppermost in my mind at the time were: what was the radius of action of the Super Étendard? What in-flight refuelling capability did the Argentines have for these aircraft and what was their state of training? In earlier discussions with the French I recalled that the Super Étendard radar had, at the time, a surface search capability very similar to the Blue Fox radar in the Sea Harrier. Without airborne early warning coverage – and with the Super Étendard/Exocet capability and the expected low level tactics of the Argentine Navy pilots – the Sea Harrier with its relatively short-range pulse radar would not be able to guarantee the safety of the carriers from Exocet attack.

During the April 1982 three-week work-up of 809 Squadron at Yeovilton prior to deploying to Ascension and *Atlantic Conveyor*, I specifically asked for a liaison visit to Landivisiau to talk personally to the Super Étendard squadron there. This was refused by the Ministry of Defence, when I was told that, diplomatically, the French had turned down the request.[19]

This request was not passed through the British Naval Attaché in Paris, Captain Simon Argles. Thus it is questionable whether the French government knew of it, especially as a Mirage and a Super Étendard were actually flown across the Channel. John Nott states in his memoirs that M Hernou, the French Minister of Defence, offered these two aircraft as soon as the conflict began. The Ministry of Defence's naïve error was to have them flown to a RAF airfield and not to a naval air station; thus the wrong comparison was made when the French aircraft flew in aerial combat against only the RAF ground-attack Harrier and not the naval air defence fighter, the Sea Harrier. Gedge further recalls:

It would have been very useful to have spoken face-to-face with the French to confirm our thoughts. The Argentines, along with the RAF's Harrier ground-attack pilots, did not have what I saw as this very significant advantage, nevertheless the Super Étendard attacks were in my view inspired, well planned and very effectively executed.

The Sea Harrier pilots were also much concerned about the Argentine fighters that might be tasked against them; in particular, the French-built Mirage. On 23 April, while the eight pilots of 809 Naval Air Squadron were working up their eight Sea Harriers, three of those pilots – Lieutenant Commanders Dave Braithwaite and Hugh Slade and Lieutenant Bill Covington[20] – were dispatched to RAF Coningsby in the Flag Officer Naval Air Command's Sea Heron (known, inevitably, as 'the Admiral's Barge'). There they met a French test pilot who flew each of them in his two-seat Mirage III. Covington recalls:

There was also one Super Étendard flown by a French Navy pilot but as this was a single-seat aircraft it was not available for the Fleet Air Arm. However, the French talked fairly freely on the performance of their aircraft and weapon capabilities.

In particular, we were interested in the air-to-air capability of the Mirage armed with Matra 530 and Magic 550 missiles, as well as the Super Étendard/ Exocet capability. We concluded that the Mirage was a formidable threat at medium to high level. Capable of flying supersonic with a missile fit, it had good turning and vertical performance and a radar similar in capability to that of the Sea Harrier. In a head-on engagement, the Sea Harrier pilot could expect to be engaged by the semi-active radar guided Matra 530 before he was in range to fire his Sidewinder air-to-air missiles. Also, in a dog fight, the Magic 550 had a good rear hemisphere capability. None of this was completely new information but it was first-hand and therefore helpful.

This was borne out in my forty-minute flight in the Mirage from which I witnessed air-to-air combat with RAF Harrier GR3s of No. 1 (Fighter) Squadron. This highlighted, not surprisingly, the poor capability of the ground-attack Harrier in combat with a radar-equipped fighter at medium altitude. We reported our findings to the Admiral, Ted Anson,[21] who agreed our assessment. We also advised that Sea Harriers of 809 Naval Air Squadron were likely to be needed as attrition replacements and that the six GR3s of 1 Squadron should be used as air-to-ground assets, thus freeing up the far more capable Sea Harriers for air-defence of the fleet and the ground troops.

The RAF pilots were operating out of Wittering and so we in the Fleet Air Arm were not involved in the brief or debrief between them and the French. As a result, it is possible that the Super Étendard and Mirage pilots could easily have returned to their French bases with a mistaken view of what had taken place. The French pilots would have reported that they had overwhelmed the ground-attack Harriers they had met in mock combat but mistakenly believed that they were Sea Harriers flown by air combat-trained pilots.

Tim Gedge continues:

After welcoming my 809 Squadron pilots back from taking part in those simulated engagements between RAF Harrier GR3s and the French Mirage, I was told that the Harriers had lost every single time. I asked who had been at the controls and was told that the Royal Navy pilots were simply passengers in the French aircraft and that the Harrier pilots were RAF.

However, the Commanding Officer of 801 Squadron at the time, Lieutenant Commander Nigel 'Sharkey' Ward[22] in his book *Sea Harrier over the Falklands*[23] incorrectly and confusingly states that it was Fleet Air Arm Sea Harriers against which the Mirages had been flown. Thus it is possible that Maisonneuve and Razoux, having read Ward's erroneous account, repeated it in their own book ten years later. The signal that Ward misquotes, received on board HMS *Invincible*, had been sent by the Flag Officer Naval Air Command (FONAC) himself. According to Ward's version, the admiral (Ward's ultimate aviation authority) 'was no aviator and probably not therefore able to judge the issue'. This, too, is not correct, for FONAC was Rear Admiral Ted Anson, who had not only been a

Buccaneer pilot but had, in 1962, commanded Ward's 801 Squadron. The admiral had also made it clear in his signal that it was RAF Harriers that had been involved. So why Ward refers to Sea Harriers (thus allowing him to make disparaging and unwarranted criticisms about his brother Fleet Air Arm pilots' abilities as fighter pilots) is difficult to fathom.

Gedge goes on to say:

> However, I would not denigrate the RAF Harrier pilots as they were well trained and very good in their ground-attack role, but few had any air defence background at the time of the Falklands. So I was not surprised. All the Royal Navy pilots had current experience of fighting the Sea Harrier against other fighter aircraft. In the two years I had commanded 800 Squadron between 1980 and 1982 we had fought the Sea Harrier in practice air combat against virtually every fighter aircraft in the western world with, as it happened, the exception of the Mirage III. These included the F-16, F-15, F-14, A-4, F-4, F-8 Crusader, with much of this on the instrumented ranges in the United States. We knew what we could do and more particularly what we could not do against modern aircraft and their sophisticated weapons systems. On that basis I believe the 'trial' had been a success but as a morale booster it certainly had not been, especially for 1 (Fighter) Squadron RAF, and I don't recall any more mention of them being an air defence asset.

Commander Gedge offers an interesting climax to this episode:

> Following my request for a brief on the air capability of the Argentine forces, a senior civil servant visited from the Defence Operational Analysis Centre at West Byfleet. Before he addressed us, I spoke to him in my office where he said that their analysis had shown that we would lose all twenty Sea Harriers within two and a half days after the first engagement. Based on my experience in 800 Squadron I was adamant that this was unhelpful information and in my view totally incorrect. I asked him to return to London without giving his talk and told the Commanding Officer of Yeovilton, Captain Peter Williams, that an irate senior research civil servant was on his way to complain (at his dismissal)!

After the conflict the French flew a Super Étendard to Yeovilton Naval Air Station, but this was not made public at the time either.

While there is certainly anecdotal evidence that some French organizations, below government level, were hesitant to assist the British, the majority were happy to do so. Commander William Alexander,[24] a Royal Navy weapons engineer responsible for Sea Wolf trials at the Admiralty Surface Weapons Establishment in early 1982, asked the Ministry of Defence for the frequencies of those Exocets that had been sold to Argentina. The reply from the French was on his desk within four hours and showed that their missiles could disrupt a British Sea Wolf counter-attack. Revised circuit boards were immediately flown to Ascension Island and dropped to HMSs *Andromeda*, *Brilliant* and *Broadsword* by a Hercules.

Back in diplomatic circles, President Mitterrand had been quick to reassure Mrs Thatcher that she could expect help, a point Margaret Thatcher stressed in her memoirs.[25] John Nott in his own autobiography[26] recalled, rather loosely, that in many respects President Mitterrand and the French 'were our greatest allies'. In effect, France was one of many allies, and while Mitterrand certainly prevented the export of Exocets, another nation that assisted in practical terms was the United States. Nor should the help from many Commonwealth countries be subsumed by a desire to 'be nice to the French'.[27]

This evidence of French 'help' was made clear when on 3 April 1982 Mitterrand, immediately following the capture of South Georgia, telephoned the Prime Minister to pledge the full support of his government. According to Thatcher, Mitterrand was the first head of state to offer support, and in convincing words:[28]

> I am ringing to express my sympathy with you. I wouldn't wish you to think that France, as a very close friend and neighbour, was not absolutely with you in thought and freedom ... Of course I quite realize that Britain is quite big enough to find its own solution to this problem. But it is important that you should realize that others share your opposition to this kind of aggression ... Please accept my very best wishes and I hope that we can be in touch again if there's anything that we can usefully do.

That, though, did not prevent a continual British worry that Exocets would leave France, despite Mitterrand later telling Thatcher that she was to 'brush aside the pro-Argentine statements from his Foreign Minister, Claude Cheysson'.[29]

During April, France voted for United Nations Resolution 502, persuading her African allies on the Security Council to do likewise. Resolution 502 was adopted on 3 April 1982 by 10 votes to 1 against (Panama) and four abstentions (China, Poland, Spain and the Soviet Union). Among other clauses, the Resolution demanded an immediate cessation of hostilities between Argentina and the United Kingdom and a complete withdrawal of Argentine forces. The UK was also given the option to invoke Article 51 of the United Nations Charter, allowing it to claim the right of self-defence. The Resolution was supported by members of the Commonwealth, and by the European Economic Community, which later imposed sanctions on Argentina. Closer to home, President Mitterrand influenced Chancellor Helmut Schmidt to freeze contracts under the Meko 360 H2 programme.[30]

None of this *entente cordiale* should perhaps have been surprising, even to the xenophobic British newspapers, for France and the United Kingdom shared, as they continue to share, considerable international interests: permanent membership of the United Nation's Security Council, nuclear-armed submarines, responsibility for overseas territories and a blue-water, amphibious capability.

Nor was French support for Britain entirely altruistic. While Mrs Thatcher was not popular in France, that did not influence the view in Paris that were Britain to lose the forthcoming 'colonial war' as a direct result of French indifference or worse, the wrong message might be sent to the Soviet Union, a nation already taking an interest in a number of French overseas territories, especially those in the Caribbean. Faced with the possibility of a similar challenge to her own sovereignty, it was necessary that France declared, in advance as it were, her hand. Presumably, under such circumstances France would expect similar support from Great Britain. Indeed, an example might be found in the British support for French operations in Mali in January 2013.

Contrary to the accusation by London's tabloids that Paris was continuing to deliver sensitive military equipment to the Junta, the French President immediately froze all deliveries of weapons whose destination was Argentina, including several batteries of Roland anti-aircraft missiles. He ordered the Chief Executive Officer of Aérospatiale to halt the export of the remaining ten Exocets[31] that were ready for imminent delivery. The company's technical mission, due to arrive in Argentina on 12 April to 'integrate' the five Exocets with the five Dassault-Breguét Super Étendards (which had arrived in Argentina in November 1981), was cancelled.

This marrying-up of the two weapon systems was already being assisted by a team of eight technicians from Dassault led by Hervé Colin who were *in situ* when hostilities broke out. According to the semi-official Argentine account in *¡Ataquen Rio Grande! Operación Mikado*, the fact that they had been there since before hostilities was initially 'forgotten' in Paris. When eventually summoned back to Europe, Colin and his team were able to reveal a number of vital snippets to the French and British, one of which was the redeployment of four of the five Super Étendards[32] and their five missiles to the Rio Grande air base in Tierra del Fuego. They were also able to confirm that one aircraft had remained at Espora naval air base to be cannibalized for spares. Another worrying snippet, seized upon by British intelligence, is emphasized in the same publication:

> Those responsible in the National Society of the Aerospace Industry (SNIAS) admitted that the provision of arms to [Argentina] happened just at the time when the [French] were prevented from sending advisers to Buenos Aires to help in the final fit of the missile to the SUE. But they [in SNIAS] also thought that this was not essential because 'the Argentines are certainly capable of doing this on their own'.

A further indication of French support came with the agreement (following diplomatic demands from Paris) that both Dakar's port and airport in the former French colony of Senegal would be declared 'open' to the British military. This would ease a number of logistical problems such as supplying fuel to ships and aircraft, particularly the latter along the otherwise tenuous 'air bridge' between the RAF airfields at Brize Norton and Lyneham and Wideawake airfield on Ascension Island. Aviation fuel on Ascension had to be strictly controlled, thus it was an enormous help that most 'regular' flights staging through Wideawake arrived via Dakar, with enough fuel to return whence they came.

Cooperation between the French and the British 'secret services', respectively the Direction Générale de la Sécurité Extérieure and the Secret Intelligence

Service, was not obvious but was, as will be seen, much in evidence to those involved with the prevention of Exocet replacements reaching Argentina.

In Spain, government support for the United Kingdom was strong but outwardly muted. Spain's dilemma was that while they felt it necessary to support Argentina, the government was also anxious for Britain's approval of its application to join the European Community, which Spain was to do in 1986. Public opinion, however, was not mute. The British Ambassador to Madrid at the time, Sir Richard Parsons, commented in an interview with Malcolm McBain:

> Public opinion was very much against us in Spain because they saw themselves as the mother country of Argentina, although more Argentines are Italian than Spanish. Calvo Sotelo, the prime minister, told me that actually they were on our side. I said, 'Why are you on our side?' He said, 'Well, because if the generals win in Argentina that will be a great boost for the right-wing generals here. That's the last thing we want, so we are secretly on your side.' I said, jokingly, 'Would you mind saying that in public?' 'No,' he said, 'I'd rather not.'[33]

The Spanish government's support is illustrated by two events. On one occasion the Foreign Minister, Señor José Perez-Llorca, telephoned Sir Richard shortly after the *General Belgrano* had been sunk to ask if he thought that Gibraltar 'was all right?' As the Ambassador had no reason to think otherwise he replied 'Yes ... [unless] you have any special reason for asking?' 'Oh no', was the Foreign Minister's reply. Sir Richard, knowing this was 'diplomatic code' for alerting ambassadors, immediately reported the conversation to his own Foreign Office, and Gibraltar was placed on high alert. Shortly afterwards, as will be seen, the members of an Argentine assault team sent to sink a British ship in Gibraltar were arrested by the Spanish police in an operation that was almost entirely a Franco-Spanish intelligence success.

The second example of practical Spanish help occurred when Sir Richard heard that one Exocet had managed to escape the French embargo, through, it is believed, a third country. The aircraft carrying it had reached Las Palmas airport in the Canaries en route to an intermediate South American country. It had to be stopped. Sir Richard, in his interview, takes up the story:

> It was the middle of the night. But when you are an ambassador you have always to know the telephone number of some person, male or female, who has access to the number that rings beside the bed of the prime minister. I was able to get through to the prime minister and we did get it stopped. All [these things] really played a great part. It made the Thatcher government conceive the idea that the Spanish were our allies in a secret way. And whatever one may say about Mrs Thatcher she was very loyal to her allies.

So France was not alone among European nations to offer practical support, even if the Spanish often remained in the background for the sake of diplomatic tact. Despite abstaining in the United Nations debate on Resolution 502, Spain was, according to Sir Richard, helping 'in the shadows'.

Reference has already been made to Gibraltar. In early April, as soon as it became clear to the Junta that Britain was intent on military action, an operation to show that Argentina could act outside South America was set in train. Under the personal control of Admiral Jorge Anaya, the Commander-in-Chief of the Argentine Navy and member of the ruling Junta, the aim of Operation Algeciras was, quite simply, to sink a British ship at Gibraltar. A secondary aim, though not publically declared, was to highlight to other European countries the 'folly' of having sent a major NATO maritime force 'so far from its natural theatre, thus opening the opportunity for unfriendly powers to strike with ease close to home'. For many years this operation was regarded with such delicacy in Argentina that even to hint at knowledge of its existence 'was to look for trouble'.[34]

At this stage in the conflict there was already much bad blood between the members of the Junta, with each trying to gain every ounce of political advantage. As Anaya knew that he had to 'go it alone' it was necessary to exercise direct control of this operation through his Chief of Naval Intelligence, Vicealmirante Eduardo Guirling.

Three combat swimmers from the Buzos Tacticos (tactical divers) were ordered to target at least one British warship anchored in Gibraltar Bay. Such an attack would obviously not affect British military decision making, but it would have a strong symbolic value in highlighting the vulnerability of the Royal Navy. Thus, it was hoped in Buenos Aires, the sinking of a Task Force ship would undermine British public opinion as well as indirectly involving two European states in the conflict. An attack in mainland Great Britain was ruled out, as the 'Latin appearances' of the team members would be more obvious than in southern Spain.

One member of this team, all of whom were 'retired' Montoneros guerrillas ('taken in' by the navy after deserting their terrorist organizations following their capture) was Máximo Nicoletti, better known as Bruno, and the man credited with leading an attack on ARA *Santísima Trinidad* in Rio Santiago in 1975. Later, Nicoletti was appointed to command a MEKO 140 corvette as well as pioneering the navy's 'swimmer delivery vessels'. The son of an Italian Second World War naval diver, he had been brought up in Puerto Madryn diving with the southern right whales that come there to breed and suckle their young.

The second was Nelson Latorre, known as the 'Bald Diego'; while the third was called simply 'el Marciano' (the Martian). Nicoletti and Latorre left Buenos Aires on 24 April for Paris, using false passports so that if they were caught the Argentine government could deny any knowledge of them. On their arrival in France, en route for Madrid, the French Direction de la Surveillance du Territoire, meticulously scrutinizing all passports from South America (and alerted by a brief discussion about those of Nicoletti and Latorre at the airport) warned their Spanish counterparts in the Centro Superior de Información de la Defensa of the imminent presence of a 'commando team' on Argentine soil, in other words in the Argentine Embassy in Madrid. The French intelligence service was able to offer a hint at the possible reasons for their presence as the Argentines had with them 'very overweight luggage'. These were two Oxyger 35 closed-circuit underwater breathing sets then in use by combat divers of many countries, although one set may have been the Oxyger 57, a later model. The 35 had a stated 'endurance' of three hours, but in practice it was more like ninety minutes. Had the potential saboteurs been quizzed carefully (a procedure that was wisely avoided in order not to warn them off until fully implicated), this equipment would not have fitted their alibi of being underwater spear-fishing enthusiasts – who would have used civilian, bubble-emitting air bottles.

The surveillance operation was being conducted in France by Pierre Marion, the director of the new Direction Générale De La Sécurité Extérieure (until early 1982 the Service de Documentation Extérieure et de Contre-Espionage) in collaboration with Alexis Forter[35] of the British Secret Intelligence Service in France. Forter was a longstanding career SIS officer on a last 'peaceful' assignment after many years in the Middle East. As First Secretary in the British Embassy in Tehran he had been awarded the OBE in June 1962.

Nicoletti and Latorre were allowed to continue their journey, believing themselves to be unobserved. In Madrid they met 'el Marciano' and an 'Argentine naval intelligence officer' named, apparently, Teniente de Navío Héctor Rosales, who would not take part in the raid but who would orchestrate it from within the embassy. While Rosales is not an unusual surname in Argentina, the only Hector Rosales in the navy list at the time was a Lieutenant Commander in the Infanteria de Marina, who was 'certainly not a diver or an intelligence officer'.

Here the four were now joined by two magnetic limpet mines that had arrived in the diplomatic bag from Italy. These were 'swimmer-portable' devices perfected over the years by the Italian Navy's Gruppo Navale Speciale and were, as they always have been, superior to any used by other nations. These, and the Italian self-contained vintage underwater breathing apparatus with which the Argentine Navy was then equipped, were still in use despite their provenance and age. Later, when asked by Captain C of the Royal Marines why the Italian Incorsi at La Spezia used such apparently out-of-date equipment, their Commanding Officer, Roberto Vassali, replied, without fear of contradiction, 'Because they work!' Whether these 'elderly-designed' limpets would have been effective against modern double-hulled ships is, perhaps, a moot point.

All the while, radio traffic in and out of the Argentine Embassy in Madrid was being monitored in the UK by the Government Communications Headquarters at Cheltenham. Thus it is interesting to note that the British Ambassador in Madrid had been alerted to Operation Algeciras – and that in a roundabout manner – by the Spanish Foreign Minister.

In due course the four Argentines moved in a series of hired cars to small hotels and guest houses, first at Algeciras (west across the bay from Gibraltar), and subsequently at La Linea (just over the border). Their cover was that they were tourists intent on underwater fishing, for which they had rented 'all the right kit', including a small inflatable dinghy with an outboard engine.

Although the original aim of Operation Algeciras had been simply to show that Argentina could, geographically, cast a long shadow, the sinking of the Argentine cruiser ARA *General Belgrano* on 2 May gave Admiral Anaya a stronger reason for retaliation, even revenge. On 4 May orders to attack as soon as possible were issued. After two or three false starts, all vetoed personally by their naval Commander-in-Chief, clearance was obtained to attack the 25,000-ton BP tanker *British Tamar*, requisitioned as part of the Task Force and on her way south.

The team had, however, quite apart from alerting the various intelligence agencies, roused local suspicions through their use of cash for all transactions and the number of times that they changed rental cars from the same garage; indeed, it was the garage proprietor who tipped off the police. On the evening of the day chosen for the attack, 17 May, and while filling their outboard engine with petrol on the La Linea beach, they were arrested by the Guardia Civil for the less than exotic crime of bank robbery, of which there had been a spate locally. Another version of these events suggests that they were arrested as suspected smugglers. Either way, they were soon in the clutches of the Spanish security services.

According to French accounts, the presence of this team was kept secret by the Spanish government until the end of hostilities; only then were its members discreetly returned to Argentina. Other sources advocate, unconvincingly, that British Intelligence was involved in their capture. However, the main effort was initiated by France with certainly Spanish, but only a modicum of British, involvement.

While the operation has never been officially acknowledged by Argentina, the unofficial line remains that the group were detained through an unlucky co-incidence. Once arrested, their original story – undermined by the equipment with which they were 'armed' – did not stand up to scrutiny, and they confessed, on the assumption that they would be treated sympathetically by Spain. After two days of interrogation they were quietly shipped home in a civilian aeroplane and 'forgotten' by the Argentine authorities. They were now known men and so out of the war. Thus Spain can claim to have been the second European nation to have aided the British cause.

Earlier, back in the United Kingdom, two committees relevant to the Exocet saga were being established. In London the Special Operations Group was formed on the 6 April, with Captain C[36] of the Royal Marines representing the Special Boat Squadron (it became the Special Boat Service in 1987) while acting as the committee's secretary. The RAF representative was Squadron Leader Jerry King, a C-130 pilot, while the Army's man was Major David Roberts of the SAS. Rear Admiral Tony Whetstone,[37] employed as the Assistant Chief of Naval Staff (Operations), was an additional member, as was a diplomat from the Foreign and Commonwealth Office. Moray Stewart, an Assistant Under Secretary on the Defence staff completed the team, while the Assistant Chief of the Air Staff (Operations) also attended. Civil servants from Defence Secretariats 5 and 6 also attended for their immediate access to the War Cabinet. Interestingly, the intelligence services (both military and civilian) were unrepresented.

The prime remit of the Special Operations Group has always been difficult to pin down. Some of its members, even with the benefit of hindsight, remain unclear about its purpose. Tony Whetstone, a submariner with 'a front row seat', was a witness to the twice-daily conversations on a secure telephone between Vice

Admiral David Halifax (Chief of Staff to Admiral Fieldhouse) and the First Sea Lord, before the daily Chiefs of Staff meetings in the Ministry of Defence. He wrote:

> I am not sure why the SOG was set up but my conclusion is that it was designed to act as a means of assessing the 'bright ideas' which various bodies were hatching. It did not in itself initiate plans for operations but considered proposals which came to it from other sources as well as those put up by its members of whom Peter de la Billière was most active. The proposals from those in the front line, wishing to get more involved, quite understandably, did not always give enough weight to the need to ensure international, and especially United States, support for our actions. The SOG enabled these factors to be considered as well as the military practicability of the sug- gestions.[38]

The second committee of significance was formed in Northwood: not so much a committee, rather a loose collection of officers with more than a passing interest in special operations and their deconfliction. At Fleet Headquarters on 1 May Vice Admiral Halifax,[39] concerned that special operations were likely to con- flict not only with each other but with mainstream, conventional operations, appointed Captain Robert Woodard[40] to be the Special Operations Coordinator or SOCO. This was at the insistence of the Commander-in-Chief (and Task Force Commander) himself, who was determined that all operations, special and conventional, should be dovetailed and deconflicted rather than be conducted in isolation, for that way lay dangers of 'blue on blue' (or friendly fire) tragedies.

As Halifax stated in his memo establishing Woodard's appointment:

> In order to avoid confliction of tasks and duplication of message traffic and to ensure the safety of all forces taking part the Special Operations Coordi- nator is to be shown drafts of all signals pertinent to special operations *before* release. Naturally I would expect him to be consulted during the planning stages of Special Operations. The operations referred to are those organized by Tactical HQ of the Major General Royal Marines at Northwood [then still Major General Jeremy Moore before he moved south in RMS *Queen Elizabeth II*], the Special Forces Liaison Officer and 18 Group.[41]

The need for such an appointment was not without precedent. Lord Ashdown describes as 'a Whitehall cock-up of major proportions' the fact that in December 1942 there were two missions to sink German blockade runners to Japan while they were moored in Bordeaux.[42] One such was Operation Frankton led by Major Blondie Hasler[43] of the Royal Marines. At the same time a second attack was being orchestrated by the Special Operations Executive. This lack of co- operation (largely caused by the SOE's over-tight 'bubbles of security') led to the 'setting up of a Controlling Officer at Whitehall, responsible for avoiding inter- departmental rivalry, duplication or even conflict'.

Woodard's appointment was to be pointless as far as the integration of SAS operations were concerned, for the regiment's representative, Lieutenant

Colonel Neville Howard, who might have ensured that the Commander-in-Chief's wishes were met in full, was dispatched, without replacement, to Santiago to speak to the Air Attaché in Chile, Group Captain Sid Edwards. Howard, who was to stay in South America, had been appointed Commanding Officer of 22 SAS, but, in the words of a senior staff officer at Northwood, 'Rose wasn't going to give up and dashed off before Howard could take over'.

Therefore the SAS were de facto no longer part of the Special Operations Coordinator's team and thus could continue operating as they preferred, referring little to anyone else. There was another SAS officer at Northwood who should have supplied the required SAS input (and thus helped guarantee deconfliction) into overall planning within the Task Force Commander's organization; but Lieutenant Colonel Andy Massey[44] was regarded as an unfortunate choice by his colleagues, for he viewed everything only from an SAS standpoint and not 'in the whole' – precisely what Woodard's appointment was intended to prevent.

Other members who would be co-opted on to Woodard's team with responsibility for overseeing, and in particular deconflicting, special operations by land, sea and air included Lieutenant Colonel Tim Donkin[45] of the Royal Marines and Wing Commander Peaker of the RAF.

Further French help may best be illustrated by an incident that began with a British agent in France 'watching' the Aérospatiale factory at Toulouse and noticing that six Exocets 'were ready to leave on the morrow'.[46] But whither bound – Argentina or Peru? It was unclear, but at that moment a Peruvian Government 'service forces' freighter, the 18,000 ton *Ilo*, was lying in Toulon harbour; and Peru had purchased, but not yet received, up to six Exocets. This information was passed via Headquarters, Secret Intelligence Service direct to the Commander-in-Chief's staff.

Robert Woodard, by coincidence the duty staff officer that night, was summoned at 0300 on the morning of 26 May to the Fleet Communications Centre. As Woodard knew that the President had decreed no weapons would be dispatched from France – not even those under contract and paid for – he felt that either M Mitterrand was not keeping his promise or that something was taking place behind his back. Woodard explained:

> It was vital that I personally woke John Fieldhouse in Admiralty House as he was not in his cabin 'down the Hole' (the nuclear bomb-proof Fleet Headquarters dug deep into the Middlesex countryside at Northwood). His absence was such a rare event that he was only woken at home on the very strongest of pretexts. So it was up the hill and across the road – in the dark. Very frightening! But much more frightening was that he slept with Midge, Lady Fieldhouse.

Her ladyship was an entertaining but formidable woman, and although most affable and approachable to junior officers, she was nevertheless regarded as 'awesome', in the proper sense of the word. Woodard continued:

> Midge did not agree that the Admiral should be disturbed by anyone other than his Chief of Staff, but reluctantly woke the great man, who must have

known it was a priority because of the job I was doing. He sat bolt upright, and I said, 'Sir, six Exocets are on their way to a ship in Toulon ready to take them to Peru or perhaps direct to Argentina ... We should let the Prime Minister know immediately as there was an undertaking that this would not happen. As soon as I was out of the room Admiral Fieldhouse telephoned Mrs Thatcher, who then spoke to M Mitterrand. The ship sailed at dawn without the missiles.[47]

Lieutenant Colonel David Chaundler (who would shortly parachute into the South Atlantic to take command of 2nd Battalion the Parachute Regiment after Lieutenant Colonel 'H' Jones was killed at Goose Green) casts additional light on the *Ilo* saga:

It was probably on the night of 25/26 May that I had left my office to go to the National Liberal Club, which MOD was using as a sleeping annex. At about 2200 I got a message to return to my office where I learned that Aérospatiale were about to load Exocets into the *Ilo*. I rang the Foreign Office Duty Officer and told him that our Ambassador in Paris must be told immediately. 'My dear chap I could not possibly disturb the Ambassador, won't the Defence Attaché do?' The Defence Attaché was Roger Southurst from my Regiment, and I knew that he was carrying out a recce for the D Day celebrations in Normandy. Fortunately, Sir Anthony Acland, the Permanent Under Secretary of State came in after a dinner. I explained what was going on. 'Of course the Ambassador must be told', he said, and he instructed the Duty Officer to get on with it. Well before dawn not only had the Ambassador been informed, but the French Chef de Cabinet had been summoned. The lights burned in the Quai d'Orsay that night.[48]

Many myths have grown up around this incident, some of which were encouraged at the time, and yet there were never any Exocets on the high seas heading for Argentina. Only once was Mrs Thatcher alerted to call Mitterrand to stop missiles leaving Aérospatiale, and those were the ones due to board the *Ilo*. What was rumoured to have happened has been the subject of much inaccurate speculation. To scotch those rumours it might be useful to explain what they were.

The first myth is this: denied her cargo in Toulon, the *Ilo* then sailed to the Italian port of Genoa, whence the missiles had by then been diverted and where they were loaded, safely outside France. According to this story, the SBS then boarded the *Ilo* as she passed Gibraltar in the dark. Once on board they altered the altimeter settings on the six missiles so that on release from their parent aircraft they would crash into the sea. The Royal Marines then returned, still undetected, to Gibraltar. Dramatic though this operation would have been, it never took place. The SBS were 'stood-to for a maritime operation in the Gibraltar area' at that time, but in the event never left their base at Poole.

A similar myth involved a C-130 of the Special Forces Flight that was also 'stood-to'. This time the SBS team, with their Rigid Inflatable Craft, were to be parachuted ahead of a ship, again rumoured to be the persevering *Ilo* that had, apparently, left St Nazaire with the Peruvian Exocets on board. But again, it must be emphasized, no Exocets left French soil.

It was known that Iraq had received sixty Exocets, and those that she had left (they had been used prodigally against Iran) she was not going to sell to anyone. South Africa and Qatar had ordered forty between them, but none had been delivered. Pakistan had received twelve but it was inconceivable, according to the Pakistani Foreign Ministry, that they would deliver any to a third party. Six, as has been described, had been ordered by Peru and were due to be delivered as events were unfolding. France, not wishing to be seen openly reneging on the contractual terms of Peru's procurement order, had the *Ilo* shifted from port to port and from excuse to excuse until it was 'understood by the Peruvians' that the missiles were not, yet, available for export. Eventually, the freighter sailed empty – possibly thanks to Woodard braving Lady Fieldhouse and waking his Admiral.

President Mitterrand had been under considerable pressure to appease countries in South America, but he remained true to his original promise of 3 April, despite explaining to Mrs Thatcher on 29 May (while the *Ilo* was being shunted around various French ports) that, 'Peru has made it known to other Latin American countries that France is declining to execute the contract. Consequently, France's contracts with other Latin American countries are in danger.'

The next day, the Prime Minister, perhaps unaware of what was actually happening to the Peruvian missiles and the *Ilo*, sent a telegram to President Mitterrand:

> All [my Cabinet colleagues] are dismayed by the prospect of France supply-ing these missiles to Peru when, as you yourself agreed, there can be no doubt that Peru will pass them on to Argentina ... It would have a disastrous effect on the alliance as a whole. This is the last thing that either of us would wish. I hope therefore that for the time being you will be able to find some way of keeping those missiles in France.

Mitterrand found a way.

The need for Robert Woodard's temporary post was becoming daily more obvious and stemmed, in part, from the SAS establishing their own satellite communications on board HMS *Fearless*. The Tactical Headquarters of 22 SAS, at sea in the South Atlantic, was now in direct contact with Hereford and, via Headquarters SAS at Duke of York Barracks, Chelsea, with the Assistant Chief of the General Staff in the Ministry of Defence. Not only was this bypassing every established chain of command, but a number of outlandish ideas for the conduct of the campaign were being distributed to SAS colleagues attached to the Cabinet Office Briefing Room from a team that knew little of amphibious warfare and of the campaign as a whole. This might have been normal for a counter-terrorism operation, but in a conventional campaign it was dangerous, especially as some of the signals dispatched from the South Atlantic by comparatively junior officers were critical of those conducting and commanding the amphibious campaign.

Luckily, through methods best left unaired, copies of these messages were seen by the Royal Marines officer in the Special Operations Group, who passed them to Colonel Martin Garrod. When forwarding these signals to the Commander-in-Chief's staff, Garrod was able to soften the blow by either heading them off altogether or by pre-empting their contents and briefing the Northwood staff accordingly. Thankfully, common sense prevailed, and the signals were to be seen for what they were.

The Commander Land Forces, Falkland Islands, Major General Jeremy Moore, was still in Northwood when these 'disloyal and contemptible signals' began to arrive. At the end of hostilities the General was moved to report, with restrained tact:[49]

> Requests for special forces missions should have been made through the command chain from Commodore Amphibious Warfare as Commander Amphibious Task Force to the Commander Task Force Battle Group. The system was followed for all SBS tasks but was short-circuited by the SAS using their own communications and taking orders from the Commanding Officer 22 SAS based in HMS *Fearless* ...

One of the most – if not *the* most – important aspects of Captain Woodard's task as Special Operations Coordinator was the dovetailing of special forces tasks, made more difficult by everyone (not just the SAS and SBS) living within their own 'security bubble'; this insularity included not telling the central coordinating officer what was being planned, despite the Admiral's wishes. Woodard cites an amusing but far from trite example:[50]

> A major worry of managing the special forces operations was that the RAF might start using radar-homing missiles without telling anyone ... The RAF were planning to knock out Stanley's radars but they wouldn't say when. My response was to state that, 'You mustn't do that without telling me'. They said, 'We are not going to tell you'. Eventually Fieldhouse asked me what all the fuss was about and I said, 'The Air Commander won't tell me their plans and that is dangerous'. The Admiral asked, 'Why was it dangerous'. He knew full well the implications of people dashing around the war doing their own thing unannounced, which is why I was appointed Special Operations Coordinator in the first place. I replied, 'Here is a typical example. Suppose the SBS decide that they want to climb up a radar aerial to disable it, then the enemy won't know why it doesn't work and the Argentines in Stanley won't get another one flown out. They'll try and mend it and so for days they won't have one. And that's a more clever way. But its Sod's Law that the Royal Marines' SBS will be up there in the dark wielding a spanner when a bloody great "crab"[51] missile comes hurtling in!' It was my job to stop this sort of thing happening. The Commander-in-Chief called in his Air Commander who muttered and said, 'Well of course ...'

Special forces did not have a monopoly on outlandish ideas. A plan that originated from within Fleet Headquarters (and was considered for almost three days) was to parachute a team directly on to the Argentine aircraft carrier that was known (thanks to 'a man in the dockyard') to be unguarded. The assault party of a seaman officer, an engineer officer and two naval mechanics, escorted by a small special forces team, would land on the carrier or, failing that, in the water close by, to 'unbuckle the ship and sail it out of its harbour!' Woodard thought, 'What an absolutely wonderful moment, for the Argentines to wake up and find her gone. We'd pinched it! That was how widely out of the box we were thinking.'

Chapter 3

Super Étendard fighter-bombers and Exocet missiles

In 1969 the Argentine Navy had procured its second aircraft carrier, ARA *Veinticinco de Mayo*, this time from the Netherlands. Originally she was the British 19,000-ton HMS *Venerable*, built in 1945 and sold to the Royal Netherlands Navy as HrMs *Karel Doorman* in 1948. During her voyage to Argentina without aircraft on board the British company Hawker Siddeley demonstrated its Harrier GR1, but the Argentines eventually opted to embark the A4-4Q Skyhawk instead.

Alouette III and SH-3 Sea King helicopters were also incorporated into the ship, while Fokker F-28s and L-188 Electras were modified for maritime patrol. Modernization of the Argentine surface fleet in the 1970s included the purchase of Exocet-armed British destroyers, but their use in 1982 would be limited following the sinking of ARA *General Belgrano*.

In 1982 Argentine naval aviation operated out of four naval air bases (Bases Aeronaval). These were Punta Indio (BAPI) in Buenos Aires province, Comandante Espora (BACE) at Bahía Blanca, Almirante Zar (BAAZ) in Trelew, Patagonia and Almirante Quijada (BAAQ) at Rio Grande in Tierra del Fuego. The navy also operated a few Estaciones Aeronaval with smaller staffs and usually no permanent aircraft; included in this number was the air base at Rio Gallegos.

During Argentina's 'Dirty War' (1976–83) the US refused to supply spares for the primary aircraft then operated by the Argentine Navy, the A4Q Skyhawk. It was this embargo that forced Argentina to turn, in 1980, to a less fussy partner, France, for their next generation of sea-based aircraft.

The original Dassault-Bréguet Étendard was designed in the early 1970s as a carrier-launched aircraft for the French Navy and entered service in June 1978. The 'Super' version, a natural development, was to have been replaced by the SEPECAT Jaguar. However, as those aircraft were proving unsuitable for carrier operations the manufacturers proposed a more powerful version of their own original. In due course the French bought 71 Super Étendards, reduced from an initial order of 80 because of budget constraints.

The Super Étendard is a single-engined, single-seat, swept-wing fighter capable of flying at 637 knots at low level. Armed with 30mm cannon, the Super Étendard can also deliver AM-39 air-to-surface missiles or iron bombs. With a ceiling of 45,000 feet (13,700 metres) it has a range of 920 nautical miles. In time, the French Marine Nationale gave the aircraft a nuclear strike capability.

This aircraft remains in service with the French navy, and in 2014 there were still five operational Super Étendards with the Argentine Navy out of a remaining total of eleven. There are plans to upgrade ten of these to modern operational standards. As Argentina no longer has an aircraft carrier – *Veinticinco de Mayo* was taken out of service in June 1986 and eventually scrapped in Italy – since 1986 carrier operations have been practised occasionally with Brazilian and US ships.

A prime example of the 'fire and forget' principle, the AM-39 Exocet missile flies at Mach 0.93 in level flight, usually between 6 and 16 feet above the sea. Designed to detonate on impact (or immediately afterwards) it can be launched at a range of up to 37 nautical miles, depending on the altitude and speed of the launching aircraft. In 2014 at least thirty-one countries were still operating the missile in one of its various forms: air launched (AM-39), surface launched (MM-38) or submarine launched (SM-39). The MM-40s were to be fitted to Argentina's German-built Meko 360 destroyers after the conflict, while the Royal Navy decommissioned its last MM-40 Exocets in 2002.

The airborne version, only one of which can be carried by each Super Étendard beneath the starboard wing, with a fuel pod beneath the port, is 17 feet long with a breadth over the stabilizing fins of 3 feet 4 inches and a weight of 1,444lb (655kg). It is fuelled by a solid propellant and, thanks to its low altitude, flies below the radar horizon of any target until the last few seconds, during which time the target (once visual contact has been made) must take avoiding action. This is usually effected by a ship presenting the smallest radar echo to the approaching missile – bow or stern. The Exocet's inbuilt radar continually sweeps from left to right, and if a larger radar echo (such as that produced by chaff) is seen to the left of the real target by the Exocet's radar, the missile will alter course accordingly. That is the theory.

Another method of decoying an incoming Exocet is to position a helicopter 'up-threat' and to the right, again as seen from the target. The aim is for the helicopter to seduce the missile away from its parent ship and then – at the last moment – climb rapidly with, hopefully, the missile passing harmlessly below until it runs out of fuel and stalls into the ocean. Prince Andrew, flying from HMS *Invincible*, was one of a number of Sea King helicopter pilots employed on such decoy missions.

From the Super Étendard pilot's point of view, attacking a ship with the AM-39 Exocet is conducted in a number of stages. The aircraft is flown as normal at altitude until just outside a suspected target's radar range, at which point it drops to sea level. Before the target is calculated to be within range of the missile the aircraft climbs momentarily, then, having sighted the target on his Agave radar, the pilot enters the coordinates into the missile's 'brain' and descends to 100 feet, where the release button is triggered.

Exocets navigate by taking their initial direction from the aircraft that delivers them to the release point. Once launched, their own guidance system flies them at about 8 feet (depending on the sea state) above the surface and thus, thanks to the curvature of the Earth, well below any radar. It is only during the last few seconds of flight, the final 6,500 yards as it comes into the radar coverage (and visual range) of the intended target, that the Exocet's own radar system takes over to guide the missile to its destination. If the intended target has not picked up the initial Agave radar emission as a warning that such an attack is likely, then this last, very brief visual window is all the time a defender has to take avoiding action.

By February 1982 the French were bringing their own Super Étendard and Exocet combination into service for carrier operations. Prior to that, the missiles had only been fitted in helicopters such as Sea Kings operated by Pakistan in 1978.

The Argentine Navy was not entirely unused to the Exocet, for it had also purchased, or agreed to purchase, in previous years forty-eight surface-to-surface MM-40 missiles in order to equip ten ships with a total of forty launchers and eight sets of spares. Of these the French factory had actually delivered sixteen before the conflict. Marcel Dassault had been contracted to equip the Argentine Navy with fourteen Super Étendard and fifteen Exocet AM-39, all to have been delivered by September 1982. When hostilities began in April only five aircraft and five missiles had arrived. The delay to the Argentine shipment, which had been paid for in full, was due to Iraq's massive order (worth in the region of $650 million) for use against Iran. A technical team from Dassault, led by Hervé Colin, had arrived at Espora around 10 November 1981 – a week before the first aircraft and missiles were due from France – to oversee the Super Étendard/ Exocet combination. At this time the French confirmed that they had cancelled the departure of another team, this one from Aérospatiale, that should have flown on 12 April 1982 to advise on the installation of Exocets to the Super Étendards at Base Aeronaval Commandante Espora. That help was terminated following the French President's embargo. Nevertheless it was initially 'forgotten' that the engineer, Hervé Colin, and his seven technicians were still working at the air base outside Bahia Blanca; they were eventually summoned home, but not before at least one of their number (possibly Colin himself) was made privy to the final, wartime, destination of the 2da Escuadrilla Aeronaval de Caza y Ataque.

There remains ambiguity over whether or not this French team's presence in Argentina was, in fact, known in Paris. The Chief of Staff to the Direction Générale de la Sécurité Extérieure at the time was adamant that the close co-operation between the French and the British was absolute and never compromised by the activities of Hervé Colin's men, only seven of whom were actually employed by Dassault. The Chief of Staff later stated that the French team did not help fit the missiles to the Super Étendards, while one of the members was actually a member of the Direction Générale de la Sécurité Extérieure. Unsurprisingly, the French government was keen to keep their man (and thus the whole Dassault team) in Argentina for as long as possible 'to see what was going on'. That on their return to France a 'member' of the team was able to pass on the dates and destination of the planned move south of the aircraft and missiles would support this view. Additionally, Hervé Colin is believed to have reported that when his team met the missiles at Espora three out of the five did not work, although this revelation is not mentioned by Jorge Muñoz in his semi-official publication on the operation,[1] by Charles Maisonneuve and Pierre Razoux in their work[2] or by the pilots themselves.

Before the aircraft and missiles left their country of origin it was necessary for the Argentine naval pilots to become acquainted with their new steeds and the weapons they would deliver. In the beginning, though, they and their ground crews had to learn French. The man considered by the Junta to be the most suitable to lead this 'foreign training expedition' was a naval pilot, Capitán de Navío Julio Italo Lavezzo.[3] In November 1980, accompanied by ten pilots with experience of carrier operations and all with over 1,000 hours on fast jets, Lavezzo and his team flew to the French school at Rochefort on the Biscay coast for intensive language training. This lasted one month for those with some knowledge and two for those learning from scratch.

The pilots chosen to fly the Super Étendards were led by their future Commanding Officer, Capitán de Corbeta (Lieutenant Commander) Jorge Luis Colombo, with Capitán de Corbeta Augusto Bedacarratz as his second-in-command. Three other Capitánes de Corbeta made up the squadron's senior officers: Roberto Agotegaray, Roberto Curilovic and Alejandro Amadeo Francisco, along with two Tenientes de Navío (Lieutenants), Luis Antonio Collavino and Julio Hector Barraza. The final three pilots were Tenientes de Fragata (Sub Lieutenants) Juan Jose Rodriguez Mariani, Armando Raul Mayora and Carlos Rodolfo Machetanz.

These officers were accompanied by an air engineer named Garcia, an electronics engineer, Frontero, and forty-eight petty officers of various specialisations relevant to servicing and maintaining the aircraft and their weapon systems. The last of the language students was finally proficient by January 1981, when the full team came together at the French Fleet Air Arm base at Landivisiau in Brittany, about 20 miles north-east of the naval dockyard at Brest. Here they were taken under the wing of a French training team (Société Navale de Formation et de Conseil) from 57S Training and Support Squadron led by a French pilot, Capitaine de Corvette Paul Habert.[4]

Training on the aircraft was intense. Learning to fly their Super Étendards for these pilots was not difficult but, once qualified, there was no Exocet training other than in elementary simulators, although there were a few carrier-borne exercises with FS *Clemenceau*. The pilots conducted no 'tactical' flying, but in fifty hours they practised basic procedures, instrument flying, formation flying and navigation. This is not surprising, for live fixed-wing firings of the missiles were unknown even to the French pilots; the only two known live launches had been conducted by Iraqi Super Pumas against Iranian targets, and during the manufacturer's initial trials. Although it was believed that Iraq had 'expended' forty-five of their sixty missiles, no useful technical data had been submitted.

The programme was nearly brought to a halt during a few genuinely anxious weeks following the elections on 10 May 1981, when the new French President called for a re-examination of all foreign arms contracts, including the training of Argentine pilots. One other 'complication' was the Argentine mechanics' grasp of French 'technical' vocabulary, for the Rochefort language school had taught little beyond the colloquial!

By April 1982 the AM-39 had not been fired at long range against a naval target and certainly not from a high-speed aircraft. As the literature of the day mentioned the 'possibility' of such a combination being taken up by Argentina it was entirely feasible that the pilots and their leaders, not only in Buenos Aires but also at Espora, hoped the British believed that the Argentine Navy could not, without French assistance, make this amalgamation in time.

The Argentine pilots and technicians returned to Base Aeronaval Comandante Espora in July 1981 and on 18 November they were reunited with their aircraft and missiles when they arrived at Bahia Blanca's Puerto Galván, 6 miles from Espora air base. They had been shipped across the Atlantic on board the 5,235-ton ARA *Cabo de Hornos*, an Argentine transport vessel that had sailed from St Nazaire on 20 October 1981 with the aircraft, plus their missiles, carried 'fully assembled' in her hold.[5]

On their return to Espora the Super Étendard aircrew, now under the full command of Jorge Colombo, had re-formed the Segunda Escuadrilla Aeronaval de Caza y Ataque (Second Fighter and Attack Squadron) of the Comando de Aviación Naval Argentina (Argentine Naval Aviation Command or COAN),[6] having converted their considerable Skyhawk experience into that needed to master and operate the vastly superior Super Étendard. The pilots did not know it, of course, but they had just over four months to marry up and test the two weapon systems. Work started immediately.

Then, on 31 March 1982, Colombo was ordered to have his five aircraft, designated 3-A-201/2/3/4/5, ready for deployment 'as soon as possible'. This was an optimistic instruction, for at least 30 more days were needed to train the pilots in a combination that they had not used before, other than briefly in a foreign simulator. But the optimism was well founded, for the detractors and the pessimists had failed to take into account that the Argentines had learned a great deal about French avionics since the purchase of 20 Mirage IIIs in 1970. As their aircraft industry was one of the oldest in South America – dating from 1927 – it had attracted specialists in electronics, particularly from Israel and Germany. The Squadron's pilots, engineers and technicians, together with those of No. 2 Arsenal Aeronaval, confronted the challenge 'on their own and without outside help'.[7]

By 1 April the physical marrying of the aircraft with their missiles had begun. In practice, this was the easier problem; far more complicated was the integration of the inertial navigation system, the digital calculators, the Agave radar system and the software for exchanging data, plus, vitally, the physical coupling of the missile and, equally vitally, the coupling and decoupling during air-to-air refuelling (although this last procedure was yet to be practised).

The decision by the French government on 6 April to enforce the arms embargo ensured, theoretically, that the Argentine aviators and technicians were deprived of further experienced assistance. As if to compensate for this setback, Argentine naval personnel who had remained for a little longer working at Dassault-Breguét received some unexpected help when a French technician, coming to the end of his contract and 'disgusted at his country's embargo', passed to Capitán de Navío Lavezzo the technical specifications for the installation of the missiles (or in Spanish, 'los cosenos directores'). These were, in fact, the 'algorithms and mathematic formulae for the missile's inertial guidance system during the first stage of flight, together with the complete circuit diagram of the weapon system'.

Knowing well that without these figures and formulae back at Espora the Super Étendard/Exocet combination would be dead, Lavezzo rushed this information to an Aerolineas Argentinas captain, who, flying to Buenos Aires on a scheduled flight, was able to deliver it to the naval aviation authorities in person. As the Argentine semi-official history of this phase of the conflict points out, 'Through this providential help and native cunning it was possible to obtain valuable information that led to the subsequent achievements of our naval fliers.'[8]

Meanwhile, and as an unintended counterweight to this 'bad news', the French Direction Générale de la Sécurité Extérieure told their Secret Intelligence Service counterparts in Paris the precise number of aircraft and missiles that had left for Argentina before the embargo.[9] While this was a bonus to the Royal Navy, there remained a worry that others would sneak through the net. Nor did this invaluable news confirm whether or not those that had arrived in South America were or were not capable of becoming operational without French assistance.

Adding urgent impetus to their work, the invasion of the Falklands on 2 April had the officers and men, the pilots, engineers and technicians, of the 2da Escuadrilla Aeronaval de Caza y Ataque working long hours developing, now largely unaided, their combined weapon system to the point that it could penetrate the British Task Force's defences without being detected until too late.

Meanwhile, on board HMS *Hermes*, and clearly unknown at Espora naval air base, the only chance the British had, without any form of 'airborne early warning', of detecting an approaching Exocet-armed Super Étendard was, simply, to hope that the aircraft's Agave radar emissions would be spotted by an alert radar operator as the aircraft popped up momentarily from sea level before re-descending to launch its missile.

The ideal base for the emerging Super Étendard/Exocet combination had to be as close to the British Task Force ships as possible. Unaware yet of the Argentines' ability to merge the two weapon systems – or at best uncertain of their progress but not wishing to take any risks – the various elements of the Task Force steamed south from Ascension Island on a route that took them as far away from South America as was sensible. Nevertheless, there was to come a phase of the journey where ships of all types – battle group, amphibious group, 'up-threat' escorts and supply ships – would need to turn westwards towards the Islands and thus come within range.

One of three possible bases for Argentine fighters and bombers was the only paved runway in the Falkland Islands, 3 miles east-north-east of the outskirts of Stanley and named by the Argentine forces, post-2 April, as 'Puerto Argentino'. This 4,000-feet runway had been operational since the beginning of 1978, although it was not officially opened until 1 May 1979 by Sir Vivian Fuchs, the old aluminium-planked landing strip having blown away in a storm during the early hours of 1 November 1978. This option, though, was ruled out by the Argentines, as even with a dry surface the take-off and landing length would be at the very limits of safety for a 'fast jet', with no margin whatsoever for error. With a wet runway it would be impossible. Added to this, the runway did not possess what the Argentines called 'cables de frenado', or braking cables, with which to arrest a landing aircraft, much as on an aircraft carrier.

The second option was the aircraft carrier herself, the *Veinticinco de Mayo*. She was old, and although capable of operating the Super Étendard (despite possible catapult limitations) there were considerable reservations among the pilots. As it happened, the carrier option was to become academic once the ARA *General Belgrano* was torpedoed on the 2 May. The third option was the one that found the most favour with the Argentine naval air arm: operating out of a southern air base and using a KC-130 tanker of the Argentine Air Force to give the Super Étendard a radius of action beyond its nominal 460 nautical miles.

In Fleet Headquarters at Northwood, in the Ministry of Defence in Whitehall and on board HMS *Hermes*, speculation on Argentina's capability in the air was tossed 'backwards and forwards' and 'in and between' those various corridors of military power. In his *Official History* Professor Freedman states:

> Information obtained in early April tended to confirm that the Exocets were operational. It appeared that the original American inertial guidance system fitted to the missiles had not worked properly but a new system developed by the French had been supplied for the Super Étendard. There was evidence that the French firm Société Nationale Industrielle Aérospatiale was helping ... and that five Super Étendard had been modified ... Initially the Defence Intelligence Service was inclined to the view that the Super Étendard could not reach the Falklands area with any effective weapons load; the [British] Naval Staff also argued that the aircraft's operation and effectiveness would be limited by its targeting capability and also its vulnerability to chaff.

Yet these outwardly reassuring views were contradicted by a US Navy assessment, as reported by Freedman:

> It should be assumed that when operating from land the aircraft would have full Exocet capability and that they could also operate from the carrier although limitations in the alignment of inertial platforms would probably rule out effective use of the Exocet in this role.

On 8 April the Ministry of Defence's advice to the Fleet was based on these American assessments and confirmed by the French on 12 April. The encouraging news for the British that the Super Étendards were most unlikely to operate from ARA *Veinticinco de Mayo* was dashed by the French warning that, instead, the aircraft could be refuelled by Argentina's two C-130 tanker aircraft, although there was no evidence that this had yet happened. Despite these conflicting views it was assumed by the Ministry of Defence in consultation with their counterparts in the Pentagon that the *Veinticinco de Mayo*/Super Étendard option was still extant, and operational planning had to take this into account.

The fear that the loss of either *Hermes* or *Invincible* would 'almost automatically' bring the conflict to an end was giving the missile a reputation for destructive power that it had not yet earned. There was certainly a body of opinion which felt that with the Royal Navy's ships at full 'action stations' (State 1, Condition Zulu, with all hatches and vents closed) it would need more than a single Exocet to incapacitate a 'fully-worked-up' ship's – especially a capital ship's – survival and fighting ability. In this regard it is interesting to note that Hugh Bicheno[10] claims the Royal Navy was in a 'blue funk' throughout the campaign over (only) five missiles, an attitude that 'almost caused a squadron of SAS to be sent on a suicide mission to destroy the missile-carrying Super Étendard at the mainland base'. To those at sea, though, the threat was real, as was to be witnessed by HMS *Sheffield*, HMS *Glamorgan* and MV *Atlantic Conveyor*. Yet on 30 May HMS *Avenger* proved that the air-launched missile was not unbeatable when she decoyed with chaff the last one to be launched against the Task Force, before 'claiming' to have destroyed it with her 4.5-inch gun.[11]

At Espora naval air base the pilots of the 2da Escuadrilla Aeronaval de Caza y Ataque were, together with their own engineers and technicians, continuing to marry the aircraft with their missiles. Two days before the Argentine landings at Yorke Bay on East Falkland, the squadron's Commanding Officer had been asked by the naval high command how much more time he needed before being available for 'a mission'.[12] The reply was, 'One month'. As the Argentine aviation and defence journalist, Santiago Rivas, explains:

> On 1 April the squadron was notified of Operatión Rosario and began to study tactics and the different flight profiles possible, both with and without in-flight refuelling. Landing and take-off tests were flown with likely loads on short runways, evaluating the possibility of operating off the Puerto Argentino/Stanley runway. It was decided that this runway would only be used in emergency.

To make communications and training easier the squadron pilots would operate in pairs. These were: No. One – Colombo and Machetanz; Two – Bedacarratz and Mayora; Three – Agotegaray and Mariani; Four – Curilovic and Barraza; and Five – Francisco and Collavino.

On 10 April, knowing, even if the British did not, that the use of the Argentine aircraft carrier was out of the question, these pilots began a short, in fact a very short, intensive training package in air-to-air refuelling using a KC-130H tanker of the Argentine Air Force, many miles offshore and in electronic silence. All went well, and the next day the squadron's armaments and navigational specialists declared that the Super Étendard/Exocet combination was close to being operational.

The following day, 12 April, Sub Lieutenant Armado Mayora was dispatched to ARA *Hercules* to witness this British-built destroyer's defence tactics against an Exocet attack. Not only could the young pilot then debrief his colleagues but, as an unexpected bonus, *Hercules* was a 'sister' to the Royal Navy's Type 42 destroyers then en route for the South Atlantic: HMSs *Cardiff*, *Coventry*, *Exeter*, *Glasgow* and, significantly, the ill-fated *Sheffield*.

At Espora the final integration took fifteen days, by which time the engineers and technicians had managed to obtain what they termed 'el top de misil', confirming that they could guarantee the aircraft/missile combination would be effective. This 'guarantee', however, came with a serious reservation: 'the conditions had to be good', by which it was assumed by those involved that the weather had to be fine, although the pilots would have preferred bad weather to help prevent detection. The announcement of this surprising leap forward, for it had been against the odds, was followed by intensive simulation exercises and sorties against targets at sea consisting of all types of warships and merchant vessels. The launch procedures were repeated dozens of times until an acceptable standard was achieved.

On 15 April No. Two pilots, Bedacarratz and Mayora, launched an 'exploratory' attack against another of the 'sisters', ARA *Santísima Trinidad*. Two days later, the same pair conducted a full-scale 'mock' attack. Flying from Espora in radio silence they refuelled from a KC-130H tanker 300 nautical miles after take-off before homing on to their victim – again, the *Santísima Trinidad* – whose position was being monitored by a Grumman S-2E Tracker. This 'attack' was rated a success, and the 2da Escuadrilla Aeronaval de Caza y Ataque declared itself fully operational, with the pilots having clocked up a further forty-five or so hours since their training in France. One proviso remained: the squadron was still only cleared for operations in 'good weather'.

On 18 April came the orders the Argentine pilots were expecting and for which they had been praying, advance notice of which had been brought back to France (and thus to the UK) by a member of Hervé Colin's team. The Commander of Argentine Naval Aviation ordered four Super Étendards to fly the 900 nautical miles south to Base Aeronaval Admiral Quijada, close to Rio Grande town. The fifth aircraft (with the first of the registration numbers, 3-A-201) was to be left behind for spares. The Exocets and six pilots not involved in this ferrying would be carried south in due course. The choice was an obvious one, for at 380 nautical miles' distance Rio Grande is the closest mainland airfield to Stanley. The Argentine commanders knew that the British would have worked that out as well.

On 19 April Super Étendards 3-A-202 and 204 took off from Espora. Under two hours later they were coasting in just north of Rio Grande, slowly turning into a steady north-westerly wind while lining up for the final approach to 'Runway 25'. At the end of the landing run they turned south on to the taxiway to park in front of the single hangar, 400 yards from the runway. Two days later the second pair of aircraft, 203 and 205, followed. The remaining pilots, maintenance personnel and spare parts – many stripped from Super Étendard 201 – flew south in a transport aircraft. This is believed to be the only occasion when there were, briefly, more than two missiles at Rio Grande.[13]

The Argentine assessment was that the British would doubt there had been enough expertise to instal and fire the Exocet from a Super Étendard without the technical assistance from the French that they knew was lacking. They were not far wrong, for although the British were taking the Exocet threat very seriously indeed there remained, in the Fleet, at Northwood and in Whitehall, an under-lying hope that there had not been enough time to ensure that the avionics of the two systems were integrated satisfactorily. It was further assumed that the Super Étendards would not be able to engage targets further away from their home base than 460 nautical miles, since it was hoped by the British that the inter-service rivalries and jealousies known to exist between the Argentine Navy and Air Force might preclude any 'light blue' help from the latter's Hercules KC-130 tankers. What the Royal Navy did not have, thanks to successive defence cuts, was any form of airborne early warning until the three nuclear submarines were 'in theatre', and even then these submarines could only report when an aircraft took off but not its destination (the use of a Nimrod R1 is discussed later). The Royal Navy also assumed that the Exocet would only be fired against one of the two aircraft carriers. The Argentine Navy surely would not waste one of only five on a 'replaceable escort'?

That was all in the South Atlantic. Elsewhere, a campaign against the Exocets of an entirely different nature was about to be waged, one that would last until months after hostilities had ceased. That battle of wits and subterfuge was between the British intelligence services and those who had Argentina's interest closer to their hearts. The British were determined that Exocet missiles should not reach Buenos Aires through either the black market or via states that were less than sympathetic to the United Kingdom – countries such as, Israel, Iran, Iraq . . . and even Pakistan if the price was right.

Meanwhile, the French service had given British intelligence a copy of the sales contracts for the aircraft and missiles, while confirming that all flying training had taken place only in good weather. This reinforced the assumption (by the British) that the Argentine ability to both fly the aircraft and deliver the weapon was limited to fair meteorological conditions.

Capitán de Navío Carlos Corti (responsible for the original procurement of aircraft and missiles from the French) now joined forces with Julio Lavezzo to break the French embargo and acquire more AM-39s through non-European countries. Expecting the attrition rate to be high, the Junta entrusted Corti with the task of obtaining new air-launched Exocets 'by any means'. Seeing an oppor-tunity to redress the disastrous finances of the Ambrosiano Bank, of which he was a director, the Italian Roberto Calvi now offered 'unlimited funds'. Calvi, and a subsidiary of his bank in Peru – the Banco Andin – had already been involved in the saga of Peru's convoluted payments system. Now equipped with funds, Corti established an office in Paris, from where he could count on a vast network of influence and also from where it would be easier to contact the original 'approved' customers to whom Aérospatiale had sold missiles.

From the beginning, the actions of the Argentines did not escape the French intelligence services. This was perhaps hardly surprising, bearing in mind Corti's earlier duties and the fact that the offices he now rented were at 58 Avenue Marceau. Sharing this building, and its telephone switchboard, was the French government-run Office Francais d'Exportation de Material Aeronautique. Equally unsurprisingly, therefore, the Argentine telephones and telexes were listened to and read twenty-four hours a day by the French, who passed on what they gleaned to the British Government's Communications Headquarters at Cheltenham.

In due course, and on his President's orders, Pierre Marion, the Director of the Direction Générale de la Sécurité Extérieure, warned Alexis Forter, the British Secret Intelligence Service's representative in Paris (who had been involved in Operation Algeciras) of disturbing developments stemming from Avenue Marceau.[14]Already on the lookout for such an operation, the Secret Intelligence Service was aware of Corti's and Lavezzo's mission and had begun coordinating its own activities with its French counterparts. The Direction Générale de la Sécurité Extérieure took on the responsibility for monitoring and deciphering communications between Corti and his contacts, then passed this information back to Cheltenham. The perseverance and efforts of this energetic and determined Argentine duo caused the British to believe that Argentina could, and just might, obtain more Exocets.

Lavezzo always admitted that he had sent the mathematical formulae to Buenos Aires while knowing that his calls in France were being monitored. He knew, too, that it was his duty to do so, and that by passing precise information he would enable the missiles to hit their targets through a modicum of 'double bluff'. Speaking in clear over 'knowingly-bugged' telephones, he hoped that the Secret Intelligence Service would regard what he had to say as typical Argentine boasting and thus to be disbelieved.[15]

A covert battle of intrigue and wits was now in progress and had already become unveiled ('develado' according to the Argentines) when HMS *Sheffield* was hit on 4 May. Ultimately, the British strategy and 'buying mission' proved effective, with Argentina unable to achieve any purchases on the world market before the end of the conflict.

Tracking down 'new' missiles should not have been impossible, as 2,000 AM-39s had been sold to twenty-six nations on the open market. However, because of legally binding 'end user certificates', buying second hand missiles was not to be quite so simple. Corti was going to meet firm refusals at all levels of the world's markets, where a missile, even if he managed to find one, would cost millions of dollars. Israel's Prime Minister, Menachem Begin – a known Anglophobe – was approached, and while he certainly offered to (and did) supply all manner of useful equipment he did not have any Exocets to give or sell. In Peru there was strong pressure from the British government, boosted by the intelligence agencies, to prevent that country acting as a 'middle man' within the black market, its own bona fide supply having been blocked.[16]

Assisted by Lavezzo, Corti tried to convince many of Aérospatiale's clients that the company wanted to purchase back a number of missiles. Iraq and Libya were approached but refused to co-operate, considering their own need for Exocets to be greater. Several arms dealers were also contacted. One of them, Marcus Stone, agreed to deliver four AM-39s but at three times their normal price. For various reasons the second-hand Exocet market failed to materialize because, according to semi-official Argentine accounts, Stone was proving to be 'less than honest'.

At the start of hostilities the British Ministry of Defence believed that the Argentines had only five Super Étendard aircraft and five Exocet AM-39 missiles.[17] When HMS *Sheffield* foundered, suspicions were confirmed that this was the weapons system that most threatened the Task Force. It therefore became an urgent priority for the Ministry of Defence to discover whether the Argentines would be able to acquire more of these missiles and, if possible, to prevent them from doing so. There were only two sources from which Argentina could expect to secure resupply of AM-39s: directly from the makers, or from a country that had received or was about to take delivery of them.

The President of France (whose brother, Général Jacques Mitterrand, was a director of Aérospatiale) had already assured Mrs Thatcher that he had forbidden the supply of further missiles to Argentina. British defence attachés and ambassadors in countries that had taken delivery of Exocets sought and received guarantees from their hosts that they would not be sold on to Argentina.[18] Qatar and Peru were the only new customers due to receive orders of AM-39s, and although Qatar had given assurances, as mentioned earlier, there were persistent rumours that the Peruvian order would be diverted to Argentina once on the high seas and outside European jurisdiction.

Nevertheless, there always remained a real possibility that missiles could find their way to Argentina through the arms black market, in which dealers were known to exploit the 'end-user certificates' for third countries (particularly some African states who were less than diligent about such niceties) to supply embargoed clients. As the task of monitoring the Argentine resupply system, and of preventing any missiles reaching them, was outside the competence of the Ministry of Defence, it fell to the Government Communications Headquarters and the Secret Intelligence Service. Both organizations were then required by the Ministry of Defence to submit appropriate plans, and under established procedures those plans would need to be authorized by a Secretary of State.

It was the Secretary of State for Defence, John Nott, who gave that authorization, thus allowing the Secret Intelligence Service to deploy agents acting as bona fide dealers to prevent any missiles reaching the Argentines. If necessary, these 'dealers' would outbid everyone else on the black market, then either hold the missiles or, with technical advice provided by the French, covertly render them inert before delivery. An important objective of these operations was to provide timely intelligence on the progress of Argentine resupply efforts. This would serve to keep the Task Force reassured that, once the Argentines had launched their stock of five missiles, there could be no further threat of Exocet attack.

The main part of the operational plan, supervised (indeed, masterminded) by a Secret Intelligence Service officer known as 'Anthony Baynham', was to monitor the arms market using Tony Divall, a wartime Royal Marines non commissioned officer with previous associations to the SIS, who had established himself as an arms dealer in Germany. Divall was backed by £16m of government money lodged with Williams & Glyn's Bank that was later returned with accrued interest![19] John Dutcher, an American dealer based in Milan, was employed by

Divall to offer his services to Captain Carlos Corti, the central figure in the Argentine resupply effort in Paris where, as Head of the Argentine Naval Aviation Sub-Commission, he enjoyed diplomatic status. Very early on in his quest, Corti had lost $6.3m to a fraud perpetrated in Amsterdam, when the 'less than honest' Marcus Stone[20] and a Dutch accomplice had taken a substantial forward fee for an imaginary deal and then disappeared. Paradoxically, this set-back encouraged Corti to employ a professional dealer who understood and could untangle the complexities of the private arms market in his attempt to secure more missiles. So Dutcher's approach was perfectly timed and imme-diately welcomed by Corti.

The Secret Intelligence Service now held the reins of the Argentine procure-ment operation, allowing its agents, over the next few weeks, to brief Baynham on what Captain Corti was up to, as well as on all the proposals that were emerging from the private arms network across Europe. As Baynham and his team followed these up none proved credible, until Dutcher identified a deal, codenamed 'Project Wallis', through a bank in Lugarno, which was offering twenty missiles at $1.5m each. As this was the first chance to take control of a potential deal that would attract Captain Corti, Dutcher was ordered to proceed as if acting for Corti as the 'undeclared principal'.

In deals such as these the buyer is required to show that sufficient funds are available, through a letter of credit, while the seller has to put up a performance bond in order to prove intent. Both sums are held in escrow until the buyer's bank is instructed to make payment. In this case the buyers, under the code name 'Repa', lodged a letter of credit for $27m with a bank in Zurich at the same time as the sellers were to provide a performance bond of $10m with the Credit and Trade Bank in Lugarno. On enquiring when the bond was to be lodged, Dutcher made contact with the seller, a Swiss dealer called Gerard Hallauer. Dutcher informed him that his principal required the performance bond and documents on the missiles to be available within seven days. Hallauer now suggested that credit should be shown in Frankfurt, while the buyers opted to show credit and inspect documentation in Hamburg. The seven days passed, but no performance bond was lodged in Frankfurt and no documents had arrived in Hamburg.

Following hectic negotiations, Hallauer requested an urgent meeting at Orly Airport, claiming that the missiles were on a Zairean 'end user certificate' and awaiting inspection. Dutcher now made it clear that Hallauer was to bring evidence that the performance bond had been lodged, that all the necessary documentation was in order and the missiles were indeed ready for examination at Orly.

Two days later, a meeting in the Orly Hilton included an Italian arms and rocket expert, Glauco Partel, to verify the missiles. However, it soon became apparent that his expertise would not be required, for Hallauer had not brought any of the evidence or documentation demanded and was instead asking for a substantial advance payment before doing so. In a rather theatrical move, the 'buyers', including one acting the part of an Ulsterman, stormed out, and Corti was withdrawn by his government before the bogus deal went any further and yet more money was lost. More importantly, the British knew, and could identify and monitor from now onwards, all the main Argentine players and their associates.

In October 1982 the *Sunday Times* Insight Team published a front page article under the headline 'Secret Service Mole Foils Exocet Black Market Deal'. In it they confirmed from 'other sources' that an ingenious British operation had been mounted to infiltrate arms deals, although no one could identify the mole. Glauco Partel is quoted as saying, 'It went off the rails through the intervention of British Intelligence. The organizers were as stupid as British Security were clever.' The article concluded: 'The remaining mystery was whether there were ever any missiles for sale on the black market. In the world of arms dealing a clear answer is hard to find, though one fact is evident. If there were black market Exocets for sale, Britain did not intend to let the Argentines buy them.'

At the end of hostilities, against the background of various countries, particularly Israel and South Africa, trying (and in Israel's case succeeding) to help the Argentines with military supplies, the Minister of Defence considered that the SIS operations had been remarkably successful, an accurate summary that would appear contrary to the view of the then Attorney General, Sir Michael Havers. Without knowing what was actually going on at the time, Havers had placed a scheme before the Prime Minister, thinking that it would do his reputation with her some good; well aware of the Secret Intelligence Service's remarkable efforts, she simply dismissed it.

Havers' idea (in fact it had been dreamed up by a friend of his who ran an air freight company), explained to the Prime Minister in a handwritten note on 1 June 1982, was to hijack missiles being transported through South America:

> The risk of resupply to the Argentines of further air-to-sea missiles justified consideration of all options to prevent this – even the most way-out, which may be thought to be more appropriate to a James Bond movie. [The idea was to tender for the cargo contract] . . . where the exporting country will not want to risk its own aircraft for publicity reasons. The loadmaster has total control over the flight [*sic*] and therefore could redirect the aircraft, in transit, to (for example) Bermuda. This will cost money (this is an expensive, dirty business) but would, in my view, be cheap at the price.

Havers' unlikely plan never reached those who were responsible for operations of this nature. If it had, the SIS would (it has been explained) have quietly thanked him for his enthusiasm while politely implying that that aspect was already being well covered. As indeed it was, most successfully.

On 18 June 1982, three days after the end of hostilities, Roberto Calvi's body was found hanging beneath Blackfriars Bridge in London. The circumstances of his death were believed at the time to have been related to the Ambrosiano Bank scandal, but they were never made public.[21] On 27 November 2012 the *Daily Telegraph* revealed a far more plausible explanation: he had been laundering drug cartel money for Pablo Escobar (which he had not returned) through a bank in Nassau.

How close the Argentines came to beating the British with those missiles that they did have was revealed in an article in the Buenos Aires newspaper *Clarín*. In September 1996 the then retired Vicealmirante Lavezzo confirmed, among other snippets, that he and Corti:

Conscious of the British game, had attempted to mislead the enemy intelligence up until the first Exocet was fired, by encouraging them to underestimate our pilots and technicians, making them believe that 'they would not have the necessary experience to install, navigate and deliver tactically the missiles'.

Chapter 4

Base Aeronaval Almirante Quijada, Rio Grande, Tierra del Fuego

The Tierra del Fuego town of Rio Grande lies 130 nautical miles north of Cape Horn; it is 33 miles due east of the Chilean border and precisely 258 miles west-south-west from the nearest of the Falkland Islands (Beaver Island), with San Carlos Water 80 miles further away towards the north-east. Of the greatest significance, Rio Grande is 3,790 nautical miles south-west from Ascension Island. Base Aeronaval Almirante Quijada (now renamed Hermes Quijada International Airport), on the north-western outskirts of the town, was not the only Argentine mainland air base during the Falklands conflict, but it was the one that received most British attention.

Straddling the mouth of the River Grande and astride the north-south highway, Ruta Nacional No. 3 (part of the Pan American highway that continues south to its terminus at Ushuaia, the area's provincial capital), the town enjoys a central position that underlines its status as the industrial capital. It does not, however, have a deep-water port, although a jetty 6 miles to the north at the Caleta la Misión serves as such, while another two are situated just within and either side of the river entrance. The British Admiralty Sailing Directions current at the time were (and remain) far from flattering:

> Since 1979 the port has been closed to commercial traffic and no dredging has been carried out ... The river is approached through a gap in the reef which fringes the coast between Cabo Domingo[1] and Cabo Peñas. From this gap, 1½ miles offshore, a tortuous channel leads between drying reefs and banks each side.[2]

The local beaches are not ideal for amphibious operations, with an average tidal range during springs of over 20 feet, exposing, at low water, a rough surface of reefs and rocky outcrops. Landing ships can beach, but probably best only at high water and only in the Caleta la Misión area.

The weather is influenced not so much by the South Atlantic Ocean that lies downwind to the east as by the South Pacific Ocean, the Drake Passage and the Antarctic continent to the west and south. The climate is generally considered damp and cool; frost and snow have been recorded in every month, and the wind blows almost unceasingly from the south-west to north-west quadrant, keeping the austral winter's average daily temperatures in the low 30°s Fahrenheit (0° to +2°C). During April and May 1982 the temperatures were unusually low, with the ground remaining 'completely frozen'[3] for much of the time. The coast is also notable for fog. Jorge Colombo reported:

> May, June, July, August and even September are the worst months of the year in Rio Grande as far as flying is concerned: 90 per cent of the time it is cloudy, rainy, foggy and icy with a low or very low cloud base and visibility usually below 100 feet or (at the best) a quarter of a mile, not to speak of strong crosswinds that were always present in Rio Grande.[4]

It is not, and never was, considered a prime military posting, yet from a civilian entrepreneur's point of view a most advantageous tax regime may now override such climatic inconveniences. For instance, Argentina's portion of Tierra del Fuego is exempt from VAT duties.

Base Aeronaval Almirante Quijada, with its single 6,561-foot runway, was established in 1949 on a bare, grassy plain five kilometres north of the 'city' of Rio Grande. Since then, houses, light industry and the normal infrastructure for the current 55,000 inhabitants have crept closer. In 1982 the nearest civilian buildings were nearby, now they encircle the eastern end of the runway. In his book *The Secret War for the Falklands* Nigel West states, wrongly, that the runway was 10,000 feet long. Prior to 1982 there had, it is true, been plans to extend the runway in a westerly direction by a further 1,500 feet, and the land was levelled; the total length would then have been in the region of 8,000 feet, but this extension remains unpaved to this day.

The naval air base's first brush with 'war' was earlier than 1982. In 1978 it had been particularly active during Argentina's brief skirmish with Chile, largely over islands in the Beagle Channel. As Rio Grande was then considered too close for comfort to the adversary, the Junta were presented with an added spur to re-possess the 'Malvinas', whose brand new runway of 4,000 feet was at the extreme limit of many of Chile's military aircraft. However, a report by the United Kingdom's beach intelligence officer with Defence Intelligence Branch Four (DI4) suggested at the time:

> While Argentina and Chile are at each other's throats the last thing the Argentines will want to do is to involve themselves in warlike activity against the Falkland Islands. This will not necessarily stop them encroaching further into unoccupied Falkland Island Dependencies next season.[5]

In 1982 much of Rio Grande's defences were the result of Argentina's planned Operación Soberania[6] against those Chilean islands in the Beagle Channel in December 1978, when a counter-attack might have been expected from across the western border. Nevertheless, DI4's assessment proved correct. There would be no 'invasion' until that internecine South American spat was over, at which point the Falklands would, once more, be on the Junta's military agenda. This is what happened, although the whys and wherefores of Operación Rosario (taking the Falklands) and Operation Corporate (retaking the Falklands) have been well documented elsewhere.

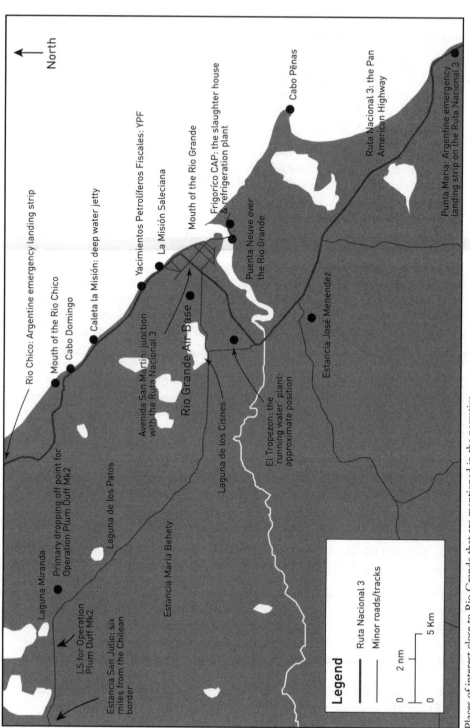

North

Rio Chico: Argentine emergency landing strip

Mouth of the Rio Chico

Cabo Domingo

Caleta la Misión: deep water jetty

Yacimientos Petrolíferos Fiscales: YPF

La Misión Saleciana

Mouth of the Rio Grande

Frigorico CAP: the slaughter house & refrigeration plant

Cabo Pēnas

Puenta Neuve over the Rio Grande

Ruta Nacional 3: the Pan American Highway

Punta Maria: Argentine emergency landing strip on the Ruta Nacional 3

Avenida San Martin: junction with the Ruta Nacional 3

Rio Grande Air Base

El Tropezon: the 'running water' plant: approximate position

Estancia José Menendez

Laguna de los Cisnes

Estancia Maria Behety

Laguna de los Patos

Primary dropping off point for Operation Plum Duff Mk2

Laguna Miranda

LS for Operation Plum Duff Mk2

Estancia San Julio; six miles from the Chilean border

Legend

Ruta Nacional 3

Minor roads/tracks

0   2 nm
0   5 Km

Places of interest close to Rio Grande that are mentioned in the narrative.

An earlier and perhaps more definite threat to the Falkland Islands, and thus one that would have involved Rio Grande's air base, occurred in November 1977, when Argentina landed fifty 'scientists' on Southern Thule in Antarctica to establish a military base. This coincided with reports of 'troop movements' in the south of Argentina, the 'possibility' of an expeditionary landing on South Georgia, the capture by Argentina of six Soviet trawlers and a factory ship 'on the high seas' and finally, closer to home, Argentina's termination of the fuel supply to the Islands coupled with the announcement that Argentine vessels would no longer wear the British courtesy ensign while in Falklands waters. Added together, these perceived threats were neatly pre-empted by the UK's then Labour Prime Minister, Jim Callaghan. A nuclear submarine, HMS *Dreadnought*, with two frigates, HMSs *Alacrity* and *Phoebe*, supported by the Royal Fleet Auxiliaries *Resource* and *Olwen*, were dispatched on what was codenamed Operation Journeyman. The flotilla's crew were not told of their destination, although it was revealed to the Junta via the 'normal diplomatic channels'– unsurprisingly, since there is not much point in sending a deterrent if the people you wish to deter are kept in the dark. Neither the British public nor the Falkland Islanders were aware of the occupation of Southern Thule, or of the presence of the British mini-task force, until over a year later. No invasion of the islands took place, and thus Rio Grande and not Stanley remained the primary anti-Chile air base in the area.

According to Roberto Curilovic,[7] Rio Grande was earmarked as the operational hub as soon as it became obvious that, with or without air-to-air refuelling, the Super Étendards would need to operate as close to the Falkland Islands and the British Task Force as possible. The defence of Rio Grande then became the highest priority on Argentina's Atlantic coasts, and there was one officer more suitable than any to take on this responsibility. That man was Miguel Carlos Augusto Pita.

A Capitán de Navío de Infantería de Marina (senior naval captain – like brigadier in the UK's Royal Marines at that time, this was an appointment rather than a rank), Pita had joined the Argentine Marine Corps in 1947 at the age of seventeen and in 1952 graduated from the Escuela Naval Militar (Naval Academy) as an infantry officer, with the rank of midshipman. Subsequently he specialized in intelligence, and it was in this capacity, ten years after graduating, that Pita was selected for training at the UK's Secret Intelligence Service's establishment at Fort Monckton near Gosport in Hampshire (known colloquially as the 'school for spies'). Here for three months and in company with other students – mostly from European countries – he studied, and was trained in, clandestine operations.[8] In addition to discussing special forces operations with members of NATO, Pita examined modern tactics as practised by members of the Special Boat Squadron based at Poole. From these Royal Marines he learned, among other 'trade secrets', the techniques of night-time infiltration of beaches and rivers by rubber dinghy and canoe, and how to swim ashore from a submarine using self-contained underwater breathing apparatus.

In 1973 Pita added to his 'special forces' knowledge when he attended the United States Marine Corps' Amphibious Warfare School at Quantico, Virginia. Following this 'staff college', he remained in the US with 2nd Marine Division in Camp Lejeune, North Carolina. By now he was as experienced as possible not only in 'intelligence' but, importantly, in the covert and even clandestine use of that intelligence. Significantly, he understood, from close observation, how the British special forces operated and, vitally, how their minds worked when planning operations.

Capitán de Navío Pita was not alone in his understanding, indeed admiration, of the way the Royal Marines went about their business. He prefers, understandably, not to be described as an Anglophile, yet there is no doubt of his appreciation of many things British (his granddaughter is married to an Englishman). Speaking in June 2012 in Argentina, as part of the 30-year commemoration of the War, Miguel Pita honoured the Welsh Guards who fell in the attack on *Sir Galahad* at Fitzroy. In doing so, he mentioned his country's debt to the Welsh immigrants to Patagonia who had defended Argentine sovereignty against Chile. At the same time, Pita reminded those present that there is a long-established community of Welsh immigrants along the Chubut River and from the mouth of the river at Trelew west to the Chilean border.

Ever since the 1950s, when a team of Argentine Marine officers first studied amphibious doctrine and tactics in the United Kingdom, there had been an irregular exchange of information in both directions. One unplanned exchange occurred in July 1977 when Colonel Richard Sidwell, the Assistant Adjutant General on the staff of the Commandant General, Royal Marines, accompanied by Major Tim Downs, the Fleet Royal Marines officer, was en route to inspect Naval Party 8901. Colonel Sidwell described his brief stay in Buenos Aires for the Royal Marines Historical Society:

> We called on the Commanding General of the Argentine Marines, whom I had met in London a few months earlier. I asked if we could visit one of his units and he agreed immediately. The next day was spent with 3 Marine Infantry Battalion at La Plata. The Commanding Officer was Lieutenant Colonel Dover, who had recently been the Argentine Naval Attaché in London and who had visited several Royal Marines Units in the UK. He made Major Downs and me very welcome and showed us his men under training, mainly conscripts, and we had a close look at his tracked amphibious vehicles. We had a barbecue lunch with his officers, and after a few drinks I asked him which unit was going to invade the Falkland Islands. 'This battalion', was his reply! He seemed willing to talk as one marine to another, so I asked him how he was going to get his amphibians across the kelp on to the beaches. 'The initial attack will have to be by helicopter and then the amphibians can come round into Port Stanley,' he replied.

Colonel Sidwell had not then seen the Falklands kelp and so did not know that amphibians can pass across it; nor did he yet know that there is none offshore from Yorke Bay beach.

Inevitably, these exchanges were reciprocated. Later that year the British Naval Attaché in Buenos Aires, Captain Dan Leggatt, Royal Navy, told the officer then commanding Naval Party 8901 (the author) that he had just, 'Sent the head of the Argentine Marines to the British army exhibition in England and then on to spend a few days with the Royal Marines ... it all helps cement friendships and will undoubtedly strengthen the Argentine Marines' healthy respect for our Corps. No bad thing'.

No bad thing indeed!

In April 1982 Capitán de Navío Pita was the Brigade Commander of the Brigada 1de Infantería de Marina (the 1st Marine Brigade, consisting of five manoeuvre units split between the 1st and 2nd Marine Forces) stationed at Baterías Marine Base near Bahia Blanca and therefore close to Espora naval air base. Pita was also the Chief of Staff and Second in Command of Amphibious Task Group 40.1 ordered to conduct Operación Rosario under the overall command of Contraalmirante (Rear Admiral) Carlos Büsser.[9]

Under Miguel Pita's robust personal leadership, and with orders to cause no casualties 'if at all possible', 800 men from his brigade, formed from the 2nd Marine Infantry Battalion (BIM 2), a Comandos Anfibios team (the approximate equivalent of the UK's Special Boat Section or the US Navy's SEALs) drawn from BIM 1, plus a section of army snipers, spearheaded the assault on the Falkland Islands.

Using twenty ex-American LVTP-7s (landing vehicle, tracked, personnel) and five LARC Vs (lighter, amphibious tracked, cargo) from the 1st Amphibious Vehicles Battalion, BIM 2's D and E companies, with the Brigade Commander himself travelling in the second LVTP, launched from ARA *Cabo San Antonio*. This was the main infantry assault on to Yorke Bay beach (where there is no kelp) immediately to the north of Stanley airport. Earlier, the Executive Officer of BIM 2, Capitán de Corbeta Pedro Edgardo Giachino, himself a member of Comandos Anfibios, had, with his team, landed in rubber assault craft to the south at Mullet Creek from the destroyer ARA *Santísima Trinidad*. Giachino's orders were to capture Government House. This they eventually achieved after Rex Hunt,[10] the Governor, had ordered his own marines to lay down their arms. With the beach, the airport and the seat of government secured, follow-up army troops landed on Stanley's runway in Sea Kings and Hercules.

Giachino, described as 'hot-headed', was hit by small arms fire during the assault on Government House and died of his wounds, becoming the only 'notified' fatality of the day on either side. He could have saved himself if he had handed over the grenade that he was clutching, for had he done as asked by the British Royal Marines – his temporary captors – first aid would have staunched the fatal loss of blood. After the conflict the marine base at Bahia Blanca was to be named after him.

With Giachino that day had been Teniente de Navío Diego Garcia Quiroga (Buzo Tactico), who was badly wounded. Years later, at the Imperial War Museum in London, Quiroga was introduced to Lady Thatcher (as she had become). Much to the surprise of the British senior officers present, the two of them talked for about seven minutes, both enjoying a good laugh. When they parted, Lady Thatcher lent towards Quiroga, put her hand on his arm and said, 'Diego, I am so very, very glad we didn't kill you!'

When all was settled ashore, as far as the invading Argentine force was concerned, and the Governor of the Falkland Islands and his Royal Marines had been flown back to the United Kingdom, it was time for the new military governor to take stock. As has been explained earlier, the British were not expected to launch a counter-attack, so Brigadier Mario Menéndez was already planning to reduce the number of men under his command to around 500 to help him deal with the knotty problems of 'civil affairs ... and unwilling civilians'.

During times of tension (against Chile) 1st Marine Infantry Brigade's primary task (together with the 8th Mountain and 4th Airportable Brigades) was to act as the strategic reserve in the South Atlantic Theatre of Operations based at Rio Grande. One of the Brigade's manoeuvre units, 5th Marine Battalion (BIM 5) under the command of Capitán de Fragata Carlos Robacio, had been billeted there during Operación Rosario before it relieved elements of BIM 2 in the Falklands. BIM 5 was eventually to occupy Tumbledown Mountain, where it gave the Scots Guards a bloody battle on the night of the 13/14 June.

It was decided that the Argentine Marines, having achieved their objectives during Rosario, should return to the mainland to take up their wartime role as the reserve for those units now flooding into the Islands as the British response to the invasion became known. There now took place a form of musical chairs, with BIM 5 being transferred to the Falklands while the remainder of the Brigade that had taken no part in the action flew south from Espora naval air base to Rio Grande. Here they were to be joined by the elements of the brigade sailing from Stanley over three voyages in the hard-worked and only Tank Landing Ship in the Argentine Navy, ARA *Cabo San Antonio*.

Shortly after 3 April, and not believing (until the *Belgrano* was sunk) that the British would use force to recapture the islands, Capitán de Navío Pita was ordered by the Commandant of the Marines to return to the mainland to prepare his brigade for its wartime role. Leaving behind a company of heavy machine guns, a battery of 105mm field guns (manned by reservists) and a provost company, together with a handful of LVTP-7s to guard the 'naval base' in Stanley harbour, Pita gave instructions for all other brigade units to sail for Tierra del Fuego as soon as the Tank Landing Ship was available.

As the pace hotted up, an advance party of the Marine Brigade flew from Bahia Blanca into Rio Grande on 20 April with the Brigade's Second in Command plus a representative of each of the units that were to be deployed.

The day before, 19 April, ARA *Cabo San Antonio*, commanded by Capitán de Fragata Jose Luciano Luis Acuna, loaded twelve amphibious vehicles under the command of Teniente de Navío Mario Forbice, plus 600 marines, over the fore-shore in Stanley and sailed 'south about' to the deep-water jetty of Caleta La Misión, where she berthed on 23 April. The Tank Landing Ship returned immediately to Stanley to collect her second load, which she delivered back to Caleta La Misión. As before, no time was lost in sailing for a third load, which she landed on the mainland on 4 May. This was the last deep-water transit made by any ship of the Argentine Navy. Having transported all the Marine Brigade's heavy equipment and over 2,500 men, ARA *Cabo San Antonio* had earned her keep; following the loss of ARA *General Belgrano* on 2 May her shuttle service came to an abrupt halt.

The whole of the 1st Marine Brigade, less the 5th Batallon de Infanteria de Marina (BIM 5), now in the Falklands, was concentrated into the Rio Grande area, along with units from the Fuerza de Infanteria de Marina No 1. Capitán de Navío Pita's immediate command also included the 1st and 2nd Batallon de Infanteria de Campaña (BIMs 1 and 2) from his 2nd Marine Force. These infantry units were augmented by the Campañia de Exploración (a mobile recon-naissance company) with eight Panhard AML 245 armoured vehicles, each with a 90mm gun. The Batallon de Artilleria de Compaña of three 105mm howitzer batteries and one battery of 155mm howitzers, plus six LVTP-7 amphibious 'tractors', was supported by a logistics battalion. The 3rd Batallon de Infanteria de Marina (BIM 3) was also stationed in the area, with detachments ready to move west to patrol the border with Chile. In the region of 3,000 men were now under Pita's overall command for the defence of the Rio Grande naval air base.

Militarily, there is no doubt that Pita was the man for the job, but there was more to his obvious suitability than that: he knew Tierra del Fuego as well as anyone. One of his sons, Alejandro Pita, explains:

During the late 1970s my father was the Chief of Staff of the Fuerza 1 de Infantería de Marina in Rio Gallegos, and so we lived in Ushuaia for a few months. He still has first cousins who have been living in Rio Grande all their lives, as well as an uncle who is now deceased. He has known Tierra del Fuego inside and out, and has literally walked the border with Chile in Tierra del Fuego from north to south at least twice. He knows the area north from Lake Fagnano so well, like the backyard at his home. He doubts the SAS team had one chance in hell to make it even close to the airfield on foot, on that kind of terrain, at that time of the year.[11]

On his arrival in Rio Grande the Brigade Commander met the commander of La Fuerza for a briefing on the military situation and to allocate areas of respon-sibility to each formation. It was agreed that Fuerza de Infanteria de Marina No. 1 would be responsible for the area to the north of the Rio Grande, with the Marine Brigade responsible for the area to the south of the river. Notwithstand-ing this demarcation, from the outset the 1st Battalion's headquarters were based in the vicinity of the local branch of the Argentine oil company Yacimientos Petrolíferos Fiscales (YPF). This 'campsite' to the north of the Rio Chico,[12] close to La Misión Saleciana, provided better facilities and living conditions for the marines. A more military reason for billeting them here was that, with the unit at short notice for a move to Las Malvinas, they were close to the airhead along a hard-top road. This position also enabled the battalion to reinforce the air base quickly should that become necessary.

The Brigade's Field Artillery Battalion with its howitzers and 'amphibious tractors' was based in the national sewage works, locally known as the Running Water Plant or El Tropezon. South-west of the air base, this also straddled the Ruta Nacional 3, giving it access by metalled road to areas where it might have to deploy to provide fire support. All the exercises carried out by the artillery battalion, plus their reconnaissance for future gun positions, were conducted to the south-west.

Although clearly needed for 'local' defence, Pita's brigade's primary role was to act as 'the strategic reserve formation for the units serving in Las Malvinas'.[13] The fact that some of Argentina's finest men were available for the defence of, in effect, Tierra del Fuego, was neither luck nor coincidence: it was always the duty of the 1st Marine Brigade to move into 'this forward deployed area as the strategic reserve'. The same procedure had been undertaken prior to 1982 during periods of escalating tension with Chile.

With the bulk of his command now concentrated in the Rio Grande area, Capitán de Navío Pita, in conjunction with the 'Station Commander' (as he would be titled on a British RAF airfield), Capitán de Navío Alfredo Dardo Dabini, could make his plans and confirm his dispositions. Defending the area was perhaps the greatest challenge, but how to assimilate a mix of services, aircraft and their roles might well have been a greater test, given the rivalry and distrust between the Navy and the Air Force.

Prior to Operation Rosario, Rio Grande's airport had been used mainly by commercial aircraft, mostly operated by the Air Force-manned aircraft of Líneas Aéreas del Estado (known as LADE) that serviced the town and the widely spread, outlying *estancias*. This 'civilian use' continued throughout the conflict. Small military aircraft used the runway for flying practice, when transiting from Ushuaia in the far south to the northern coastal air bases of Rio Gallegos and Puerto Deseado. Aerial reconnaissance patrols of the border with Chile were conducted from here, while a squadron of eight Argentine Air Force Daggers under command of Commodoro Corino was stationed here. Corino also supervised an irregular number of chartered civilian aircraft moving troops and logistics from north to south and from south to north. Aircraft from the army, the *gendarmeria* and the local government used the base as well.

After 2 April the prime aviation task of Base Aeronaval Almirante Quijada was as an air operations centre. In addition to those mentioned above, the following were now also based at Rio Grande: the Primera Escuadrilla Aeronaval de Ataque (Aermacchi MB-326 and 339s); the Segunda and the Tercera Escuadrilla Aeronaval de Caza y Ataque (Super Étendards and A-4Q Skyhawks); the Primera and Segunda Escuadrilla Aeronaval de Sosté Logístico Móvil (Lockheed L-188 Electras and Fokker 28s); the Primera Brigada Aérea (Hercules and Boeing 707s); the Escuadrilla Aeronaval de Exploración (Lockheed SP-2H Neptunes); the Primera Escuadrilla Aeronaval de Helicópteros (Aerospatiale Alouette IIIs and Westland Lynx HAS Mk 23s); the Prefectura Naval Argentina (Shorts Skyvans, under the operational command of the Argentine Navy) and the Escuadrilla

Aeronaval de Propósitos Generales (Grumman S-2A Trackers, Pilotus PC-6 Turbo Porters and Beechcraft B80s).

As if these were not enough aircraft for Rio Grande to play host to, a variety of unarmed civilian aircraft belonging to the Escuadrón Fénix were also stationed there. This unit, answering directly to the Fuerza Aérea Sur, was manned by 110 civilian pilots and engineers, some of whom had retired from military service. Although their duties were confined mainly to transport flights over the mainland, their many aircraft still needed to be 'parked' at Rio Grande. Thus this already eclectic collection of aircraft was supplemented further by, among other 'types' within Escuadrón Fénix, aircraft such as Cessnas, Piper Aerostars, Aero Commanders, Gates Learjets (on detachment from the 2nd Argentine Air Force Brigade for duties that included radio relays, navigational guidance and diversion missions) and Douglas C-47s. A further mix of helicopters belonging to all three services, including Alouette IIIs and Sea Kings, also needed space, while adding to this overcrowding were Schreiner Air Taxis' own helicopters. Interestingly, Escuadrón Fénix was the only organization to include British civilians living in Argentina, two of whom were ex-RAF Second World War pilots.[14]

It is difficult to gauge how many aircraft were stationed at Almirante Quijada at any one time, but it is clear from the above, and from the few photographs that are available, that the presence of sometimes only two relatively small fighter-bombers among fifty tightly packed aircraft and helicopters of possibly twenty-three different types would have been easily missed. Each night the Super Étendards were dispersed around the taxiways and hard standings, mixed in among all the others, or occasionally secured within the airbase's one large hangar, hidden from view. They would not have been obvious to SAS troopers running around in the dark, almost certainly under fire, in the twelve minutes that was the planned time from the Hercules' landing to its taking off.[15] The only way that the men of Operation Mikado could possibly have known where individual aircraft were would have been via an observation post relaying last minute information, even as the C-130s approached 'on finals'. Studying reports and listening to those who were to have conducted this operation, it appears that there was a naïve belief that all four Super Étendards would be lined up in a neat row and easily identifiable in the dark. No account – from any known planning discussion – was made for the fact that they might have been just two small aeroplanes among very many others.

On 12 April, as Argentine operations in support of the occupation of the Falklands built up on the Islands, the overall mainland commander, Contraalmirante Carlos Garcia Bolli, ordered Capitán de Navío Hector Martini[16] to Rio Grande, to take charge of communications while also assuming responsibility for the coordination and support of all air operations across Tierra del Fuego and the Falkland Islands. Martini's official title was Commander of Naval Air Task Group 80.1; he also took under his wing Task Force 50, a search and rescue unit. A humane and professional officer, his was to be one of the most demanding tasks given to any man in the area. In his account of Argentine naval aviation during the conflict he was to confirm that, 'NAB Almirante Quijada was set up as the principal operational base for naval aviation.' To help him in these diverse duties his team included Capitán de Fragata Jorge Fiorentino as Chief of Staff and Capitán de Fragata Nestor Barrios as Operations Officer. Two Capitánes de Corbeta, Fernando Sola and Jose Guzman, were their assistants.

Martini established his air operations command centre in 'a fortified command post several metres below ground that had first been constructed in 1980 beside the main runway of the NAB.'[17] This 'allegedly bomb-proof' bunker was divided into two enormous rooms joined by a corridor to resemble a huge underground 'H'. The warren contained everything necessary to direct operations: a command centre with desks, maps and charts, a secure telephone system and radios, all centred round a large circular plotting table upon which the area of operations was depicted. Known locally as 'El Pozo' (The Hole), its two entrances were concealed at ground level and camouflaged as best they could be from the air. Access to the bunker was across the pampas grass and heather, while rain, sleet or light snow not only helped to camouflage the route but also made any approach impassable except by 4×4 or tracked vehicles. The ground was almost always 'completely frozen solid'.

As it was from this bunker that control of all air operations was undertaken, into it were fed meteorological data, up-to-date intelligence and all other necessary information for fighting an air war. The bunker had its own electrical, heating and fire-fighting systems, plus accommodation for a 20-man guard. Underground storage for logistics and especially ammunition was also dug down into other large bunkers close to the runway. Further logistic and accommodation hubs lay north of the runway among what Miguel Pita has described as the '*polverines*' area. These were magazines that now doubled as accommodation and offices. It was also from the main bunker that control of the airfield's anti-aircraft defences was exercised.

Four 'Triple A' anti-aircraft batteries of 20mm Rheinmetal (with a range of 5,250 feet or 1,600 metres) were controlled by an Elta Fire Control Radar, which, although 'belonging' to the Air Force, was under Pita's unified command. The Capitán de Navío also had six 40mm Bofors gun emplacements dug in along the north side of the runway. These naval guns, stripped from the scrapped Argentine cruiser ARA *Nueve de Julio*, were capable of firing at 'zero barrel elevation' – in other words, at point-blank range straight into the belly of a British C-130 Hercules idling on the runway. Pita also deployed four Army Hispano-Suiza 30mm guns.

Base Aeronaval Almirante Quijada was not protected by surface-to-air missiles, for the one available Roland system had been dispatched to the Falkland Islands. There were, though, standard infantry hand-held anti-tank missiles that could seriously harm an aircraft on the ground. Additionally, from mid-afternoon on 15 May, two destroyers from Task Group 79.3 under the Commander of the Southern Naval Area, Vicealmirante Horacio Zaratiegui, began patrolling off the coast, within the national 12-mile limit, from San Sebastian to Cape San Pablo. They were not only searching for any British submarine or surface activity but also acting as additional radar pickets.

Rio Grande air base's main electronic air defence was a transportable Westinghouse AN/TPS-43 area search radar, similar to the ones deployed at Stanley and Comodoro Rivadavia. This was operated by the Argentine Air Force and positioned neither at Cabo Domingo nor, as was also suspected, 5½ miles further south of the cape near La Misión Saleciana, but 660 metres south-east from Rio Grande's terminal building. The AN/TPS had a nominal range of 220 to 240 nautical miles, especially over the sea, and a rotation rate of six revolutions a minute. Inland it was subject to 'terrain masking', thus could not see quite so far and in some sectors not far at all; to the south-west this could have been as little as 10 miles.

Another defence that needed to be taken into account and that the British (with no other intelligence available) would fairly assume to be in position and operational, was a Precision Approach Radar. As has been described in the Laarbruch air-land operation, this radar 'saw' out to about 15 nautical miles from the threshold at each end of the runway and swept from between 10 and 15 degrees either side of the centre line.

In addition to the defence provided by the Fuerza de Infanteria de Marina No. 1, the base relied for its immediate protection on the men of the Marine Commando under Capitán de Fragata Garcia, together with the Guard and Security Company from Base Aeronaval Punta Indio commanded by Teniente de Navío Ruiz Lopez, with elements of army engineers attached. All these, too, came under Miguel Pita's command.

Surrounding the air base's 13,000-yard perimeter was a simple, low, sheep-proof fence, protected by numerous anti-personnel mines (one figure suggests 2,500), described as 'made from different components: M67 grenades, gelamon, black gunpowder and also stones. Of course these munitions relied upon explosive cord, fuses and detonators. The flares around the minefield were armed with fuel contained in bottles of sulphuric acid and potassium chlorate'[18] – the implication being that these 'mines' and 'flares' were home-made. (So unstable were they that after the campaign an Army engineer officer was killed when helping to lift these devices.) The perimeter was visited throughout every twenty-four-hour period by both foot and vehicle patrols, while across the inside of the base itself a company of the 2nd Battalion was on permanent patrol.

Conscious that his defences would be photographed by American satellites, Pita arranged for the gaps in the minefields to be marked. Heedful, too, that many of Rio Grande's 25,000 inhabitants were Chilean, possibly with 'contacts' further afield, notices were placed in the local newspaper and broadcast on the town's radio and television stations warning of the presence of these minefields.

One source has suggested that Pita ordered the airfield to be criss-crossed with shallow ditches to hinder any off-road vehicle movement, but Pita is adamant that these were never dug:

We never wasted man hours in digging trenches, least of all alongside the only available landing runway and taxiways. If the British had the *mad* [Pita's emphasis] idea of doing an Entebbe, then for sure he would use the taxiway for entering and leaving the aircraft dispersal ... There was a series of hutted buildings to the west of the control tower and it was here that the pilots had their accommodation that the Super Étendard pilots never used. Also here were the Base offices; the Commanding Officer's office; personnel accommodation; cabins for Base officials; their Club and dining room and also the house of the Commanding Officer and his family. Here were food stores, larders, refrigerated stores and everything needed to live away from the city. Some pilots may have stayed here but I have no idea how many of them did so as many left base and went to sleep elsewhere ... On most occasions there were only two Super Étendards because, owing to the continual movement of the missiles, they had to be made operationally fit for purpose since all movement affected the correct coordination of the radar in the nose of the missile with the radar of the aircraft. For that reason they used to fly to Base Aeronaval Espora where they were made effective in all respects.

From this and other comments by Miguel Pita it is clear that 'deep maintenance' of aircraft and missiles was not possible at Rio Grande, which was regarded by the Super Étendard pilots more as a forward operating base. Returning aircraft to their home base for in depth servicing is common in aviation, as this is where all the support equipment and skilled manpower required will be found.

One question that exercised the British C-130 pilots at the time and since was the matter of airfield lights – those on the ground to mark the runway and its approach and those fixed to aerials that could, for an intruder, have helped a pilot find the runway. Pita is quite clear about this:

Even the naval aviators cannot confirm that the red warning lights were always kept on or off. What they did say is that in the case of a situation of maximum alert everything would be switched off. Nevertheless [civil and military transport] aircraft used to arrive late in the day. They arrived at night and took off at night and did this many times. Those who did not comply [with the blackout] were the inhabitants of Rio Grande. So that is why we cut off the supply of electricity to the whole area. There were still those who were using other methods of lighting – diesel generators – and in general we had to crack the whip and make them toe the line.

Commenting in 2012, Harry Burgoyne finds this interesting:

It sounds like the red warning lights on the aerials located north and south of the runway were probably left on but, in the event of increased security, they were blacked out along with all of the airfield and the surrounding towns and villages. This is significant. It would appear that had the C-130s been detected any distance away from the airfield (by radar, patrol or picket ship) the whole place would have been blacked out. We now know that there would have been no moon, so night vision goggles would not have helped. Thus we would be doing something that I've never experienced, practised or heard of anyone doing in my entire aviation career: a two-ship, tactical air-land operation in total darkness, with only the naked eye and using small-scale, out-of-date maps. Finding the runway and landing on it in these conditions would have been virtually impossible. Perhaps the only help we may have had would have been from any anti-aircraft fire emanating from the target; as the old adage goes, tracer works both ways!

Although it has been suggested *ex post facto* that a number of the surrounding *estancias* had a permanent detachment of marines billeted on them in order to carry out local patrols, this was not the case other than one at the Estancia José Menendez, 5 miles to the south-south-west of the air base. Astride one of only two all-weather roads leading from Rio Grande to the Chilean border, this *estancia* is one mile west of the junction with the Ruta Nacional 3. There were other standing patrols, including one supplied by the 3rd Battalion along the border with Chile, a border unmarked except by the ubiquitous low sheep fence that delineated not so much the frontier as the boundaries of *estancias* on either side.

On 6 May the Brigade Commander issued the first Warning Order to his operational units, detailing his plans for the defence of the area. Overtaken by a worrying amount of new intelligence received from naval and military sources, this was immediately revoked, and a second directive was issued the next day before the first set of orders could be put into effect. Both addressed the dispersal of the Brigade's component units.

The 1st Battalion (as has been described in outline) was to provide a vehicle-borne reserve, with the addition of a Compania de Exploracion (reconnaissance company) plus a section from the anti-tank company equipped with Mamba missiles, against which any soft-skinned aircraft on the ground would be no match. This all-embracing unit was to be located on Ruta Nacional 3 in the area of the running water plant that serviced the air base. It was close by in order swiftly to counter the threat of a British helicopter assault.

The 2nd Battalion deployed a vehicle-borne infantry company at the strategic crossroads on the Ruta Nacional 3 where it crosses the town's main street, the Avenida San Martin, while the battalion's anti-tank company, augmented by a section of 105mm guns, secured the air base's perimeter. The remaining men of the battalion were held in reserve along Ruta Nacional 3 immediately to the north of Rio Grande, ready to deploy to the air base, or anywhere else that might be used as an enemy landing site. This battalion also provided a permanent section of snipers plus twenty-four-hour vehicle patrols within the perimeter wire.

Luis Bonanni (then Second in Command of the 4th Battalion) has confirmed that his responsibilities included the town of Rio Grande itself, plus everything along a line that ran from there to Estancia Jose Menendez, and thence to the border with Chile in the west and to the sea in the east. The 3rd Battalion was based in the area of Estancia Maria Bety and covered a line running from Estancia las Violetas[19] and Laguna de los Patos to the western border. Elements of the 4th Battalion covered the area from Rio Chico to Cabo Domingo. Not only did the second Warning Order give instructions for the patrolling of San Sebastián, Estancia San Julio, Estancia La Sara and Cullen y Cañadón Beta but, in some detail, allocated tasks for the wheeled troop transport and the various communications vehicles.

The following morning, 8 May, the remainder of the 1st Battalion's sub units, plus a variety of supporting arms attachments, was ordered to Pita's headquarters at Estancia Jose Menendez, from where they established a substantial patrolling schedule. At the same time all officers were invited to consider the measures necessary to protect not only themselves in their individual locations but, vitally, the air base itself against air attack.

Similarly, the enlarging and updating of existing maps of the area was undertaken, with 'new' material distributed across the Brigade. On 10 May 'some' men of the 4th Battalion relieved an equivalent number of men from la Fuerza in their work on defensive positions. This was to enable those who knew the area to safeguard the movement of the Super Étendards when they arrived.

This, too, was the day that the Field Artillery Battalion's Gun Position Officers began to reconnoitre positions for their 105mm howitzers. Once established, live firing was practised night and day.

Estancias such as la Sara, las Violetas and Miranda were used as temporary patrol bases on an 'as needed' basis with no permanent military presence. The only other permanent base outside the perimeter was the Frigoríco CAP or Slaughterhouse. This sprawling complex of large buildings dominated the access to the river from the south bank, allowing the marines not only to watch the river mouth but to keep an eye on the Atlantic beaches to the south. The Brigade Commander well knew the SBS's ability with canoes and as free swimmers. With Rio Grande's northern river banks closing to within 1¾ miles of the air base's control tower, he was taking no chances.

The moment he arrived at Rio Grande, Miguel Pita was convinced that any British threat would come either overland from Chile or by rubber boats or canoes from a submarine. He also considered the possibility of an attack by helicopter and the insertion of a small reconnaissance team of perhaps just two men to lay homing beacons in advance of such an assault. He did not consider an air-land operation by heavy aircraft on to the runway to be a likely option, not because he knew that it would fail and that the British would know that too, rather because he did not believe that the British would be so foolish. He deduced that they would know the Argentines considered Rio Grande to be a prime target and thus would defend it accordingly. Remembering his time at Poole, he knew, too, that the SBS prefer to operate by cunning – their motto is 'By strength and guile'. So sure was Pita of this that no arrangements were made to block the runway, even temporarily, by day or by night.

There was an added reason for not blocking the runway. Civilian airliners and freight aircraft, as well as C-130s and naval Electra aircraft, used it throughout every twenty-four hour period and, according to Captain Woodard, sometimes during 'silent' unplanned approaches to 'test the system'. A vehicle parked on the halfway point would not endear the Brigade Commander to an air force pilot on what has euphemistically been described as a 'speechless' approach.

The possibility that an assault might arrive by parachute direct into the air base was the one option the British did rule out, for lack of surprise and because, as a senior SBS officer has stated, 'That is not the way we should do things. It automatically implies a one-way journey.' For one of the very few Royal Marines operations ever conducted on a one-way basis it is necessary to go as far back as December 1942 and Operation Frankton, when Major 'Blondie' Hasler led a team of canoeists up the Gironde estuary in western France to attach limpet mines to German blockade runners moored at Bordeaux. The only way home was overland to Gibraltar, courtesy of the French Resistance. Parachuting small groups into a war zone for reconnaissance purposes (and hoping never to be discovered) may be one thing, but to parachute direct into a full-blooded fight with no way home was quite another; and Pita knew that too, for he had read of the lessons learned at Arnhem in 1944.

Mobile patrols by foot and vehicle to the north, west and south were conducted on a regular and frequent basis, but apart from the two static bases mentioned none stayed any length of time in the local *estancias*, although all were visited often. Particular attention was paid to the Ruta Nacional 3 as it ran close to the coast in the north before turning inland south of Rio Grande. The large number of small bridges and culverts that this main road crosses were regularly inspected as possible hideouts. At the beginning of the conflict the average number of people working at Rio Grande air base was about 300. As there was only ever permanent accommodation for 400, new arrivals were either billeted around the town in small groups or, if 'front-line troops' for the immediate defence of the base itself, then in hastily prepared underground bunkers and magazines scattered across the airfield. These were well-constructed affairs with wooden walls and floors, bunk beds and heated by kerosene stoves. With the arrival of Pita's marines the number of newcomers 'based' in the Rio Grande area as a whole was swiftly increased to over 3,000 and with them came an acute logistic and bed problem. To accommodate those marines not 'in the field', off-duty personnel and spare equipment were allocated an unoccupied school off the east end of the runway but outside the perimeter sheep-fence.

All this was to safeguard the air base in general, but in particular to protect the pilots, their Super Étendards and Exocets. The pilots were easier to hide than their aeroplanes; they were billeted in regularly changed places and except during the day were never together. As Miguel Pita explained, 'They did not sleep in the bachelor officers' quarters; they lived separately and moved around, never spending two nights in a row in the same place.'

The problem of protecting the Exocet-armed aircraft was not so easily solved, although a number of imaginative solutions were proposed, most of which were tried at some time throughout the conflict. A deciding criterion was the likelihood of an operation early on each morrow, at which time two aircraft had to be ready at 'dispersal', fully fuelled and armed by (and preferably before) first light, no matter where they might have been hidden overnight.

Three dispersal plans were drawn up, based on the time available, the threat assessment and the preparation required for the next sortie. Put simply, these three options were graded as 'close', 'medium' and 'far'. The 'close' option was within the area of the one hangar, or even inside it. The 'medium' involved dispersing the aircraft among the accommodation buildings, along the taxiways and 'shelters', mixing them in with the many other aircraft on the base. Up to three fighter aircraft (possibly two Super Étendards and one other) on 'quick alert readiness' through the twenty-four hours could hide in bunkers close to the north-eastern end of the runway.

The 'far' option, the most complicated one, was only put into practice once. During the afternoon of 7 May an L-188 Electra on routine offshore patrol spotted through the poor visibility beneath a low cloud base 'five ships with grey hulls heading towards Tierra del Fuego'. Ashore, it was believed, understandably, that this was the prelude to a night bombardment by British 'destroyers'. As naval gunfire was not likely to be directed at the town, it was decided that this was the perfect occasion to exercise the 'far' disposal option; and as a matter of urgency orders were issued for this to be executed immediately after sunset. The moment darkness enveloped Rio Grande two Super Étendards were towed by tractors out of the base's main gate and manoeuvred along the streets for 2 miles until 'parked' near what was described as a 'plaza in front of a refrigeration factory'. The two pilots slept in the same building, the only time that they did so.

This was an extraordinary operation, and not just from the security point of view. The road that leads out from the main gate is 20 feet wide, which was fine since the aircraft's 'footprint' is 11' 6". The wing span of 31' 6" was more of a problem, and even with the wing tips folded upwards this width reduces only to 25' 6". Where the road widened to 23 feet, telegraph poles had been erected along the verges, making it a tight squeeze, while the aircraft's height of 12' 8" had to be considered, because of sagging power and telephone lines. All this had been measured diligently in advance, yet this delicate operation – avoiding pot holes and pavement kerbs at a very slow speed – took time. A concern that must also have been taken into account was the high 'single wheel loading' factor of the Super Étendard's narrow tyres. To avoid the wheels sinking into the tarmac or the all-weather dirt surface, each aircraft needed to be emptied to its basic weight of about 14,000lb. To unload (and then reload in the morning) from an all-up weight of 27,000lb would have taken time. Arming and refuelling before dawn ensured that, in practice, the aircraft were not 'absent' for very long on this one occasion.

As it happened, this manoeuvre (witnessed and reported by a Mr Errecareborde)[20] had been a pointless exercise (although perhaps useful from the 'exercise' point of view), for at dawn on 8 May the Electra identified the 'five ships with grey hulls' as Polish trawlers.

Any move, even the option of hiding in the base itself, was fraught and came with a high chance of damage. The 'far' option was clearly the most trouble, for not only was it well nigh impossible to hide the presence of the moving aircraft from prying eyes, but the risk of damage to wing tips and undercarriages along narrow roads and around tight corners in the dark (sunset was about 1745 and sunrise at 0830 at that time of year) was high – probably the deciding factor that ensured this option was not undertaken again. The move of the fighters into town not only put the aircraft in danger of collateral damage; placing them among known Chilean sympathizers also required an inordinately large 'security bill'. They were also at greater risk of direct attack had a British special forces patrol, landed by submarine, been watching events.

When not flying or being hidden, the Super Étendards remained in, or in the close vicinity of, the one hangar when, during daylight hours, they were on full 'quick reaction alert'. As for the Exocets themselves, whenever a mission returned with unexpended missiles it was necessary for these to be checked. As flying at sea level over a boisterous South Atlantic produced a build-up of salt, one missile at a time was flown the 900 nautical miles north for maintenance by the men of Espora's Naval Air Arsenal Number Two.

According to Roberto Curilovic:

> About every ten days an F-28 flew to Comandante Espora with a missile. Here they were taken in hand by Missile Workshops for monitoring and inspection purposes, when the Exocet looked as if it was in intensive care with cables and glowing screens surrounding it while its vital components were monitored and checked. This inspection, which could last two hours, was compulsory after any mission when an aircraft had landed back with no missiles launched.

With the maintainers happy, the rejuvenated missile would be flown back to Rio Grande to be reconnected with its 'parent' ready for instant flight on the morrow, while another might then be sent north for maintenance. This regular turn-round guaranteed that there were always serviceable Exocets at Rio Grande.

At the beginning of hostilities Jorge Colombo's Squadron was designated as UT (Task Unit) 80.3.1, with its formal mission being, 'To destroy or neutralize enemy surface units in order to contribute to the defence of the Islands'. Once settled into their new home, training continued between 22 and 29 April, with simulated attacks against the 800 ton ARA *Alferez Sobral*, an ex-US Navy ocean-going tug. All they needed now was an enemy target.

Colombo's squadron was not the only Argentine unit itching to get into battle.[21] An Argentine Air Force Hercules pilot, Vicecomodoro Alberto Vianna, had, on 6 May, flown the first flight to Stanley after the Black Buck One raid and was to report:

> We saw the runway and went in to land even though we never heard from the [control] tower. We saw there was a crater to one side of the runway[22] so we landed down the other side ... Then the engineer told us that the leading tyre of the right main gear had blown. We could take off, but very carefully, because the rubber was dangerous if it began to shred.

Vianna, a pilot with Escuadrón 1 of 1 Brigada Aérea, believed that, following a modicum of engineering, the Hercules could be adapted to carry and launch the AM-39 Exocet. His proposal, discussed with the Chief of Staff of the Strategic Air Command, was to fly to the north of Argentina, then follow the Brazilian coast before turning eastwards to intercept the luxury liner turned troopship, *Queen Elizabeth 2*, as she sailed between the United Kingdom and Ascension Island. He would then return, via refuelling (he hoped he would be granted permission rather than internment) at the northern Brazilian airbase of Natal.

Vianna calculated that three Exocets could be carried under each wing of the Hercules, but when the crew discussed this possibility with the Super Étendard pilots they, hardly surprisingly, were having none of it! Colombo's men were adamant: 'The Exocet launcher can only accommodate a single missile while the Hercules's propellers will present a problem. There are just five AM-39s and they belong to the Navy!' However, the feasibility of similarly arming a Boeing 707 was also seriously considered, but the structural modifications needed were complicated and could not be completed in time.

Nevertheless, a principle had been established, and so Vianna's aircraft, TC-68, was fitted with bombs instead; although this came too late to attack the *QE2*, which by then was well on her way to South Georgia, it was a weapon load that found more favour with Air Force Command. In the end, and with four internal fuel tanks similar to those that would be fitted to the British Hercules (to compensate for the loss of the external wing tanks where there were now two multiple ejector racks, taken from a Skyhawk and each carrying three 551-pound Explosive Alaveses BR-250 iron bombs),TC-68 was reconfigured as a bomber with a calculated endurance of over twenty-four hours; and a nearly successful one at that, as the crews of the MV *British Wye* (attacked by TC-68 on 29 May) and the MV *Hercules* (attacked on 8 June) would eventually testify. A Pucara's gun sight and trigger had been fitted in front of the pilot; stories of the bombs being rolled off the ramp are unsubstantiated.

Meanwhile, little was known of conditions inside Rio Grande's perimeter wire until on 25 April Andrés Wolberg-Stock was able to write (uncensored, it is thought) in the English-language *Buenos Aires Herald*:

> Tierra del Fuego ... has gone nearly unnoticed amid the stream of reports of military activity pouring in from Comodoro Rivadavia ... The Rio Grande airport, a navy airbase, also used for commercial flights has changed considerably ... as recently as February it was only a commercial airport and an airstrip for small military aircraft.
>
> Camouflaged planes, their green and dirt-coloured fuselages blending in with the natural background ... some are covered in tarpaulins ... Ammunition for the planes sits in pyramids outside the civilian air station which has now been de-civilianised. Passengers on incoming commercial flights are advised a few minutes before landing that 'due to the special circumstances that the country is living in' the local authorities demand that window blinds be pulled down. 'Please refrain from taking any photographs,' the steward adds over the plane's speaker system as the aircraft begins its final approach.
>
> After the plane comes to a halt a bus drives right to the steps and the passengers are guided on to it by military police holding sub-machine guns. The windows on the bus are covered by curtains and the arriving travellers

can catch only a glimpse of the base before being driven to downtown Rio Grande where the Automobile Club Hotel has been converted into a customs, immigration and ticket office.

But a few hours later returning to the airport to board the connecting flight to Ushuaia, tourists, reporters and any eventual spies are allowed a far more comprehensive view of the facilities ... for the state-run LADE plane to Ushuaia has no window blinds and anyone on board can count the military planes sitting on the tarmac as the aircraft taxies its way through them ...

But the build-up in Rio Grande seems limited to the airbase. The town's streets are quiet under the pale sun and while fighter planes scream their way on to the nearby runway, garbage flies by at street level pushed by strong gusts of icy wind.

Despite being a prime target, with warnings of some of the defences even being placed in the local papers and on television, and with a substantial number of Chilean sympathizers 'in residence', the British knew very little indeed. If ever there was a Secret Intelligence Service mission waiting to be conducted, this had to be it, but ... 'nothing' – at least nothing that ever reached those who most needed to know.

Chapter 5

ARA *General Belgrano* and HMS *Sheffield*

HMS *Conqueror* sailed from the Faslane Naval Base, Gareloch, on 4 April. With swift and remarkable foresight the Officer Commanding the Special Boat Squadron, Major Jonathan Thomson[1] (not an SBS-trained officer), had sent 'at the rush' two teams of four men each to Faslane on 2 April. Led by Lieutenant David Heaver and Sergeant Terry Cooper, these members of 6 SBS were the first 'ground troops' to leave the United Kingdom.

Once clear of the European continental shelf, opposite the Bay of Biscay, the nuclear-powered (but not nuclear-armed) submarine's commanding officer, Commander Christopher Wreford-Brown,[2] noted in the Daily Comments section of his boat's log for 6 April, 'The depth of water is now such that I can go faster dived'.[3] On 16 April orders for Operation Paraquat, the retaking of South Georgia, were received on board while the submarine was in position 38° 23' S, 35° 23' W – over 1,000 nautical miles north of the island. Clearly these were preparatory orders, for Wreford-Brown noted that, 'The embarked Royal Marine officer is concerned about lack of frequencies and call signs.'

Nearing the various exclusion zones, the Rules of Engagement became even more important yet in some respects even less clear, for on 17 April *Conqueror* received an unequivocal order from Northwood: 'DON'T SHOOT. We await more diplomatic discussion.' Continuing to forge south, at depth and at speed, Wreford-Brown was well in sight of South Georgia by 19 April and able, with the SBS officer, to take several periscope photographs of Cumberland West Bay. At 1505 he wrote, 'Have looked into Cumberland East and West Bays, Jason Harbour and Moraine Fjord. No signs of any ships or activity. Intention is to head north-west to investigate Stromness and Leith Harbour.'

In the evening's summary *Conqueror*'s Commanding Officer then commented:

> The aim was initially to conduct sonar sweep among the coastline to check for contacts. When the visibility lifted I decided to close the coast to check out the two inhabited areas for shipping or other activity. Secondary aim was to give 6 SBS the opportunity to see the coastline and to check out the navigational aspects of a dived approach in case we have to land the SBS in the future.

There was to be yet another week of anti-ship and anti-submarine patrolling before the increasingly frustrated marines could consider 'joining the war'. During this time, as potential targets came and went, Wreford-Brown's crew shuffled the mix of modern Tigerfish Mark 24 and pre-Second World War Mark 8 torpedoes between the boat's six tubes.

Then at 2233 GMT (all times from here on are GMT unless stated otherwise) on 20 April the submarine received the order that Operation Dandelion had been initiated:

> The retaking of S. Georgia ... My instructions are to prevent Argentinian ships joining in ... Weapon load is now a mix of Mk 8 and Mk 24 which gives me flexibility ... Present Rules of Engagement and receipt of Initiation of Operation Dandelion means I am now (once I have dived!) in an aggressive Anti-Ship Posture. [But there were repairs to be made on the communications mast.] 0850 21 April. Replacing [the equipment] is taking longer than expected. Although it is after sunrise and I feel a little naked on the surface there are a lot of snow storms which make visual detection a very small possibility.

The submarine did not dive till 1315 that day and almost immediately obtained, at about 4,000 yards, 'a good strong echo, probably bottom however there is nothing aural ... and no biological'. The belief was that it could have been a dived conventional submarine, and as the ARA *San Luis* had, at that stage, not been located, Wreford-Brown prepared his boat for an attack ('Bow caps open').

False alarms were to continue throughout the day, with the uneven bottom and, inevitably, sea creatures being targeted, but never attacked.

Throughout 25 April *Conqueror*'s submariners and her 'embarked force' remained on anti-ship patrol, while South Georgia was captured – not by the SAS alone (as their own accounts wrongly suggest and as BBC's *Mastermind* in 2011 also erroneously informed the nation), but by a miscellany of men from 42 Commando's M Company, the SBS, the SAS and, crucially, with the intelligent use of traditional 'naval gunfire support' ordered to 'incur no casualties and cause no structural damage'. This was a masterpiece of old-fashioned projection of naval power ashore.

At 1412 on Monday 26 April the submarine was ordered to close with HMS *Antrim* off Cumberland Bay to disembark her marines at 1700, but at 2030 the wind, by then a Force 8, combined with fading light, prevented further helicopter transfers. Four Royal Marines and bundles of stores remained on board for another night.

On Monday 26 April at 2359 Commander Wreford-Brown wrote:

> The boat is about 14 nautical miles north of South Georgia ... Spent the first half of today waiting at periscope depth for further instructions ... [ordered to] transfer 6 SBS to Antrim, but by the time I started there was only enough light to achieve two thirds of the transfer. My major concern is the state of my communications mast. Am remaining surfaced overnight to attempt repairs and to complete the transfer of 6 SBS at first light tomorrow.

Sunrise on 27 April in position 54° 07' S, 36° 18' W was at 0930. A fresh wind of 35 knots continued to blow from the west-south-west, producing a 'sea state 5' beneath 20 per cent cloud cover. It was cold, with a marked wind chill across the spume-saturated casing. Transfer of the remainder of 6 SBS and their 'stores' began at 0940, but the conditions did not make the operation easy:

1130 Man overboard. Two men in the water, both recovered by helicopter, however the last load of stores was swept overboard.
1150 Transfer of SBS to HMS *Plymouth* complete.
1155 Transfer of two personnel from *Antrim* to me.

Early on 29 April, the boat's communications problems remained unsolved ('Spent one and three quarters of an hour at periscope depth to attempt to receive my 'traffic'. Unsuccessful ...'), but at 0545 Wreford-Brown was able to report that he had received Rules of Engagement 5/82 giving him clear instructions for Operation Corporate ('I now have these and an area so I can do a limited amount.') Some of these rules were as follows:

Rules of Engagement within 200 nautical miles of the Falkland Islands are:
• Maintain blockade
• All vessels positively identified as Argentine aircraft carrier, cruiser, destroyer, frigate, corvette or submarine may be attacked
• All non-nuclear submarines may be attacked
• After first attack withdraw and report. If one can't, after 12 hours continue
• Report at discretion on all Argentine 'units' and after all subsequent attacks

Without her SBS team *Conqueror* could now be dispatched westwards to carry out her duties in accordance with the latest issue of the Rules. She was to operate within a set quarter known as Falkland Green 'against Argentine surface group of the *General Belgrano* and her escorts'. This specific area straddled the United Kingdom's declared Total Exclusion Zone and an area to the south-west of it.

At Rio Grande the longed-for orders for the Super Étendard pilots came on 1 May and were greeted with considerable excitement. A signal had been received from Stanley's VYCA Grupo AN/TPS radar reporting three targets to the south and within range. Naval Aviation Command immediately ordered an attack. Leading from the front, the Squadron's Commanding Officer, Capitán de Corbeta Jorge Colombo, flying 3-A-204, with Teniente de Fragata Machetanz in 203 as his wingman, flew this first aggressive mission.

At 1605 (Rio Grande time, three hours behind GMT) the position of the intended target was updated to 52° 20′ S, 57° 50′ W, but take off was delayed due to a communications failure in Colombo's aircraft. With that resolved, the two aircraft took off from Runway 25 at 1638, thirty-five minutes late. The rendez-vous with the Air Force KC-130 went as planned, but Colombo's aircraft was still 'playing up'. This time it was a fuel leak that brought the refuelling operation, and thus the sortie, to an end. Obliged to turn quickly for home, a naval Puma helicopter guided them back, acting also as an emergency guard should the Commanding Officer have to ditch. Saving his fuel as best he could, while being escorted by his wingman, the two Super Étendards landed at Rio Grande at 1801.

A second pair of aircraft flown by Bedacarratz and Mayora had been stood-to, but with a lack of tanker support and the time already twenty minutes after sunset, never became airborne.

The next day the Argentine Navy ordered a combined strike against the British Task Force. Eight A-4Q Skyhawks of the 3rd Air Naval Fighter and Strike Squadron based on board the Argentine carrier ARA *Veinticinco de Mayo*, and two Super Étendards from the 2nd Squadron, planned to attack simultaneously on 2 May, but both arms of the attack experienced problems. The Skyhawks needed wind to help them take off from the carrier, yet unexpectedly, and very unusually, Aeolus (the Storm God) failed to oblige. The 2nd Squadron's opportunity to demonstrate the progress that had been made without French assistance was equally thwarted, for neither of the two Super Étendards, piloted again by Jorge Colombo and Carlos Machetanz, were able to receive fuel from the KC-130H Hercules tanker. Deeply frustrated, the pair were forced to return to Rio Grande. That afternoon ARA *General Belgrano* was torpedoed and sunk.

HMS *Conqueror*'s Commanding Officer wrote in his log on 29 April:

> Remain flexible!! ... Intentions are to continue transit west at 21 knots ... and slow down to penetrate the deep water between Falkland Islands and Burdwood Bank ... get to the western end [of the Bank] and then search west from there ... Given 'heads up' that *Belgrano* Group moving to South Georgia. Thinking about it, if they are off to S. Georgia a natural track to avoid [nuclear submarines] would be across Burdwood Bank. However I do not think that they will do this since it is inside the TEZ and why test the system.

The Burdwood Bank is a large shoal area (larger than the Falkland Islands), whose northern edge is 80 nautical miles south of the Falklands. The deep-water passage between them is about 50 nautical miles wide and up to 1,000 fathoms deep.

The Commander's hunch was right. On the evening of 1 May he began tracking the Exocet-armed Argentine Task Group 79.3, first as it steamed east then, at 0805 on 2 May, when it reversed its course towards the west. Through the periscope it was observed that during this change of direction one of the escorting destroyers had crossed from *Belgrano*'s port side to her starboard side. Permission to attack was sought and given:

> 1520 Closing to attack. Initially on the starboard side of *General Belgrano* but destroyer too close there, so crossed over to port side to obtain a good firing position.

At 1557 Wreford-Brown fired three pre-war 21-inch, Mark 8 torpedoes, each armed with 805lb of Torpex. Two hit the ancient cruiser, one forward and one aft. A United States Navy submarine (certainly the USS *Parche*, allegedly watching and listening in the area), on hearing three torpedoes running, immediately dived deep to make a speedy getaway from the scene. She is not believed to have returned. Numerous rumours about 'foreign' submarine operations still persist. One Argentine contact of the author's, Mariano Sciaroni, has reported:

Last year [2012] I was talking to an Argentine Air Force officer who told me that the Air Force interviewed an allegedly former Soviet sailor in a Spanish port. He claimed he was in a submarine trailing HMS *Conqueror* and 'witnessed' the engagement against ARA *General Belgrano*. He said that all inside his submarine wanted to attack *Conqueror*, but that that was against their orders ... Regarding the Soviet submarines, a friend of mine (a former submariner) was at the Odessa 2004 meeting of the International Submariners Association when some Russians (including Igor Kurdin, the author) approached him (with vodka, of course) and told him they were, in 1982, submerged near African waters, just waiting for 'the order'.[4]

ARA *General Belgrano*'s commanding officer, Capitán de Navío Hector Bonzo, ordered his ship to be abandoned at 1625. Despite much criticism from some members of the British public and parliament, among the Argentine military this attack has always been regarded as a perfectly legitimate act of war.

If they had not been off before, the gloves were certainly off now – on both sides – and the atmosphere at the Rio Grande air base was described as '*incandescente*'! That in the Task Force was subdued and accompanied by a sense of trepidation, while all waited for the 'revenge' attack by Exocet or a mass A4 Skyhawk assault. With conditions deteriorating in the area of the cruiser's foundering, on board HMS *Hermes* there was a marked concern for the survivors in the water, with little sense of triumphalism. As seen from Rio Grande, the time could not be riper to 'see if the Super Étendard/Exocet combination did indeed work'.

Two days later, 4 May, has been described as a memorable day in Argentine naval history; conversely, it is regarded as an equally black day by the British. It was the day when British hopes that Argentina had been unable, without French assistance, to marry the Super Étendard and the Exocet, were shattered. It has been suggested that the attack on HMS *Sheffield* – not the intended target – was in retaliation for the destruction of ARA *General Belgrano*. This, however, is not the way it was seen in Argentina, for, as has been described, an attack on chance targets was waiting to happen regardless of what action the British might or might not have taken in advance.

For Argentina's Comando de Aviación Naval the day began at 0507 (local). In the pre-dawn hours, and in advance of the dispatch of three Argentine Air Force C-130s for the Stanley resupply run, a surface search by one of the last two serviceable Lockheed SP-2H Neptune maritime patrol aircraft (0708/2-P-112 from the Reconnaissance Squadron) was ordered. Piloted by Capitán de Corbeta Ernesto Proni Leston (call-sign 'Mercurio'), the Neptune took off from Rio Grande to detect any British ships able to prevent the three C-130s landing at Stanley.

Two hours later a contact was detected at approximately 53° 04′ S, 58° 01′ W and identified as an 'early warning search radar' transmitting from a Type 42 destroyer. Having evaluated the information, and sensing that she was 'goal-keeping' for a major target, Comando de Aviación Naval authorized the launch of two Super Étendards. The Hercules supply flight was cancelled.

Proni Leston was instructed to remain in contact, which he did until gaining a further two contacts at 0843 and 0914 (local). Shortly afterwards, he was ordered to keep out of the area until at least 1000. Believing, correctly, that this was the prelude to an Exocet attack, the Neptune pilot headed for ARA *General Belgrano*'s 'datum point', pretending he was searching for survivors.

Itching to prove that his aircraft were ready for war, Jorge Colombo briefed Capitán de Corbeta Augusto Bedacarratz and the younger pilot, Teniente de Fragata Armando Raul Mayora, to take on the task. They would fly Super Étendards 3-A-202 and 3-A-203 respectively. Meanwhile, 'Mercurio' was back identifying surface contacts and at 0914 reported a single contact in position 52° 47′ S, 59° 37′ W. Half an hour later, another three contacts were registered at 52° 47′ S, 57° 40′ W. As its radar now became unserviceable, this was the last 'sighting report' from the Neptune for nearly an hour.

The wind, whipping in from across the pampas, ruffled the hair of the two pilots as, armed with the most up-to-date intelligence, Bedacarratz and Mayora – among the cream of Argentina's aviators – walked out to their aircraft. It was 0915 on 4 May. All around, the grasses of the airfield were flattened into endless Mexican waves of changing colour, while the sun struggled to find gaps in the low, scudding clouds. Some overnight ice had grudgingly melted into puddles as the temperature crept towards a maximum of 5°C, but the ground would be frozen all day and would remain so until the spring.

Bedacarratz, a neat, thin-faced man, was the second in command of 2da Escuadrilla Aeronaval de Caza y Ataque. Flying with him was Mayora, a stockier individual who also sported the almost obligatory bushy black moustache. He was the young officer who earlier in ARA *Hercules*' operations room, had seen how an Exocet attack might look from the perspective of a British Type 42 destroyer. As they leant against the wind the two men discussed the sighting of the British fleet, before parting to conduct their individual, pre-flight checks. The Super Étendards were parked on the apron, the coloured Comando de Aviación Naval Argentina insignia standing out against the steely-blue of their fuselages. Below the cockpit was the unit's personal badge, known as '*La Lora*' (the female parrot, though it more accurately resembled a belligerent sparrow hawk with a wooden club in its claw). Secured beneath the starboard wing of each fighter was an Exocet AM-39 that the pilots prayed would be launched at the British Battle Group's flagship HMS *Hermes*, or failing that, but nevertheless very satisfyingly, at the smaller and newer aircraft carrier HMS *Invincible*. As Bedacarratz climbed into 202 and Mayora into 203, they each knew that a good many 'eyes' would be focussed on their efforts that day. Although intending to conduct the sortie in radio silence if necessary, they would each use their allocated call-signs, 'Aries' and 'Liebre' respectively.

The two planes took off at 0944 along Runway 25. Once airborne, they swung back over the sea in a steady climb, heading a touch north of east. In radio silence they were aiming for 15,000 feet and a pre-arranged rendezvous with a KC-130 tanker at 1004. The 'pit stop' went without a hitch, so once fuelled the aircraft continued heading for the last known coordinates of the Task Force ships, now 260 miles away. At 1030 the Neptune's repaired radar spotted two contacts. Three minutes later three more were showing on the radar screen and quickly identified as 'two medium-sized ships and one large' at 52° 48′ S, 57° 31′ W. This position was passed to the fighter pilots at 1035 and noted but not acknowledged. Now it made sense for the Neptune to divert once again to search for survivors. It was important that to the British the aircraft was not seen to be involved in the build-up to an Exocet attack.

At 130 miles from their targets both Super Étendard dropped beneath the 300-foot cloud base. Conditions were perfect for the Argentine pilots, with visibility at sea level of about one mile. Climbing back to 520 feet, Bedacarratz and Mayora hoped to check that they were on course, but now not only were they faced with a blank horizon through the thinning clouds but their radar screens were blank of 'target paints' too. They dropped back to sea level for another 25 nautical miles. Climbing again through the low, scattered rain clouds, the targets now became visible on the fighter's radars and so, while they returned to 'ultra-low level', the coordinates were fed into the weapon systems.

The flight commander broke radio silence for the first time. 'I'll go for the larger target.' Bedacarratz announced. 'The one on the right.'

At an estimated 50 miles out, the two aircraft climbed, this time to 2,000 feet. As practised so often, each radar was switched on for three seconds. Long enough to pick up a target ... but there was nothing. They dropped to under 100 feet for another 20 miles. On reaching 2,000 feet again, the leader's radar showed one large contact to the right of a second, smaller and further away to the left. Mayora reported that his radar only showed the larger contact.

'We'll both go for that,' Bedacarratz ordered. 'Better chance of it being a carrier and of us both hitting it.'

Back at sea level they increased speed to 500 knots through the squalls until well within Exocet range but, as Mayora was to point out, still outside the range of British ship-launched missiles. With the necessary adjustments made and at an estimated 20 miles from the target, Bedacarratz gave the one-word command, 'Launch!' At the time he was hidden from his wingman by a rain cloud, but as soon as his Exocet was on its way he gave the second, similar command. Five seconds apart, at 1104 local time, both Exocets ran parallel towards HMS *Sheffield*.

Unable to visually track their missiles – even had they been minded to follow on towards the British Task Force and a certain 'wall of flak' – both pilots banked sharply to starboard and into a steady climb on the reciprocal course for home, where they landed at 1215. After taxiing to the hanger they were able to thank the Neptune crew.

The very successful 'eyes' of the Super Étendard were the Neptunes, but on 15 May, lacking spares and with growing obsolescence in the 'radar department', these aircraft were to be decommissioned. From then onwards the Argentine Navy was forced to rely on the three-dimensional radar AN/TPS-43F within the

Rio Grande air base and the surveillance radar AN/TPS-44 Alert IIA at Stanley airport.

The fighters had not needed to refuel from the waiting KC-130, while supporting the mission had been an Air Force Learjet 35 ready to act as a decoy and two Daggers as escorts for the tanker. It had been a professionally conducted operation all round, even if one Exocet eventually ran out of fuel to flop harmlessly into the sea way beyond *Sheffield*'s stern.

Argentine flight records show the missiles were released at 1104 local; the British Ministry of Defence recorded the time of impact as 1403 GMT. Even allowing for the different time zones, there is a slight discrepancy between the Argentine time of launch and the Ministry of Defence moment of impact. The destroyer's Commanding Officer, Captain Sam Salt,[5] ordered 'abandon ship' at 1750, and she was to sink shortly after 0700 on 10 May in approximately 1,000 fathoms at 52° 11' S, 53° 50' W.

The precise technical details of why HMS *Sheffield* allowed herself to be hit are irrelevant here. She had been mortally wounded, and as far as this Exocet saga is concerned that was that. However, whether or not she should have been hit is discussed in a number of painful accounts[6] and in the findings of the Royal Navy's Board of Inquiry, dated 22 July 1982. In brief, it would appear that of all the ships in the area she was the only one not aware that an Exocet was on its way until seconds before impact, when a visual sighting was all the warning a very few of her ship's company received.

Prior to the attack, HMS *Sheffield*, along with other Carrier Battle Group ships, had received 'piles' of highly classified intelligence that referred to Argentine capabilities and the operational state of the weapons believed to be available. One signal suggested that although the Argentine naval air arm was known to have 'some' air-launched Exocet missiles, it was not believed that they had been able to marry them up with the Super Étendard fighter. As Sheffield's Advanced Warfare officer at the time, Lieutenant Commander Nick Batho,[7] has written, 'The air threat against ships was stated to be iron bombs. The aiming system for these bombs was a visual sight and so for there to be a threat, the pilots had to be able to see their target.'

Ever since 0900 on 1 May, when she had crossed into the Total Exclusion Zone, within which the British had declared they would engage any Argentine ship or aircraft, HMS *Sheffield* had been at Air Raid Warning Yellow. The ship's company were in Defence Watches with about half at their action stations, the normal state if the ship 'might' be about to face danger. That day there had been sightings across the fleet, both by radar and visually, as attacks had closed in on HMSs *Glamorgan*, *Alacrity*, and *Arrow*, but no Argentine aircraft had been sighted.

Sub Lieutenant Steve Iacovou[8] was on duty, scanning the western horizon from the bridge through his binoculars. The sea was calmer that afternoon than it had been for the few previous days, with a long, gentle, six-foot swell rolling in from the west. He should have been bored gazing intently at the grey southern ocean, but the importance of the job forced him to track the horizon in slow movements, back and forth, back and forth. A request from the Operations Room for a report on the cloud cover and its ceiling had momentarily relieved the tedium. Iacovou's report had not been detailed enough, so the caller had come from below to see for himself the view from the bridge wings. The cloud cover could tell them much about the chances of seeing Argentine aircraft.

Shortly after 1410 something shone in the distance. At first Iacovou thought it was a torpedo, the shimmering light appearing to be reflected from the sea itself. 'Torpedo!' he shouted.

The Navigating Officer immediately turned and, with his own binoculars, squinted in the direction indicated. 'No. Exocet,' he said calmly but loud enough for all on the bridge to hear.

The missile was just seconds away; if it was already in sight then nobody needed to be told how long they had. The Officer of the Watch and the bridge crew ducked into cover. Iacovou and the Second Officer of the Watch stayed upright, transfixed by the approaching missile, even though they knew this was not the appropriate action to take. Iacovou watched the skimming missile almost to the point of impact, just before which he and the other officer dropped to the deck, bracing themselves for the inevitable explosion.

The Ministry of Defence report on this 'determined and very professional attack' records the moment of impact at 1403 at 2 Deck level on the starboard side between the galley, the forward auxiliary machinery room and the forward engine room. It tore a gash in the ship's side 15 feet by 4 feet. The report also concluded:

> Evidence suggests that the warhead did not detonate. There are few reports of shrapnel. Large fires broke out ... very rapid spread of acrid black smoke through the centre section of the ship and upwards as far as the bridge ... Missile propellant and burning diesel ... were the main sources of this smoke.[9]

When the Commander-in-Chief Fleet forwarded the Board of Inquiry to the Deputy Under Secretary of State (Navy) on 13 September 1982 he commented:

> [*Sheffield*] had been lulled into a false sense of security by the ineffectiveness of previous Argentine air attacks. Her loss was an expensive warning and a foretaste of the real Argentine capability.

The French, understandably, were not so sure about the lack of detonation and considerably more 'positive' about the effectiveness of 'their' missile. In their book *La Guerre des Malouines*[10] Charles Maisonneuve and Pierre Razoux wrote:

> *Sheffield* was hit by an Argentine Exocet twenty years after the first rumours that the missile did not work. Proponents of this theory point out that *Sheffield* was not ripped apart by the missile, unlike the target vessels used during practice. A difference that is explained by the modular method of construction of *Sheffield*. The first articles to be published indicated that the missile had detonated, but soon other columnists began questioning the

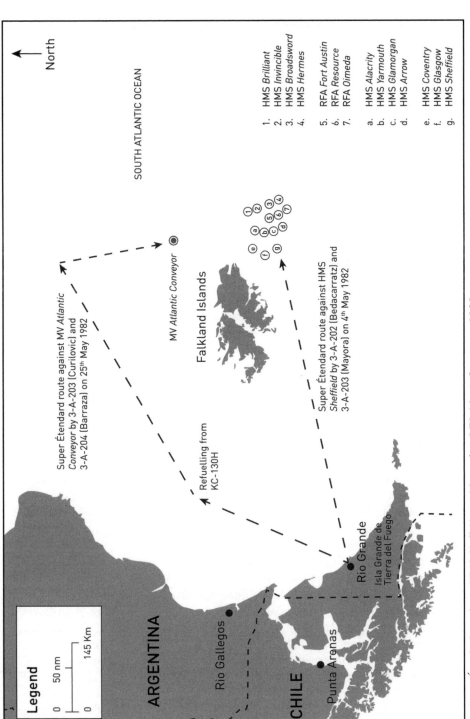

Legend

0	50 nm	
0		145 Km

North

SOUTH ATLANTIC OCEAN

Super Étendard route against MV *Atlantic Conveyor* by 3-A-203 [Curilovic] and 3-A-204 [Barraza] on 25th May 1982

MV *Atlantic Conveyor*

Falkland Islands

Refuelling from KC-130H

Super Étendard route against HMS *Sheffield* by 3-A-202 [Bedacarratz] and 3-A-203 [Mayora] on 4th May 1982

ARGENTINA

Rio Gallegos

Rio Grande

Isla Grande de Tierra del Fuego

CHILE

Punta Arenas

1. HMS *Brilliant*
2. HMS *Invincible*
3. HMS *Broadsword*
4. HMS *Hermes*

5. RFA *Fort Austin*
6. RFA *Resource*
7. RFA *Oimeda*

a. HMS *Alacrity*
b. HMS *Yarmouth*
c. HMS *Glamorgan*
d. HMS *Arrow*

e. HMS *Coventry*
f. HMS *Glasgow*
g. HMS *Sheffield*

The Super Étendard attacks on HMS *Sheffield* on 4 May and on MV *Atlantic Conveyor* on 25 May.

value of the Exocet. According to them, the fuel that had not been consumed in the body of the missile caused the fire which was fatal to *Sheffield*.

This thesis seems difficult to sustain, since the missile was launched at extreme range [we now know this to have been at just over half the missile's extreme range] and thus the residue of fuel would be very low. Even if specialists recognize that in exceptional circumstances the charge does not detonate several indications showed that the missile that hit the *Sheffield* functioned normally. The plates of the hull at the point of impact were torn apart to the outside, which proves that a blast had taken place inside. Moreover, if the missile did not explode, it would most probably have passed through the vessel from side to side, as did Argentine bombs on many occasions. This rumour, fuelled by industrial competitors for understandable reasons, was also fuelled by British naval officers, [yet] the Royal Navy remains an excellent customer of the Exocet!

The legend of the exploding Exocet did not last at Aérospatiale, which had manufactured the missile, for they would not argue against, for fear of being accused of 'advertising' with the corpses of British sailors.

One of *Sheffield*'s Leading Radio Operators described the impact as 'just like another big wave hitting the side of the ship, like a big dull thud', while another, presumably closer to the point of impact, remembers a more dramatic noise: 'I can only equate it to someone putting a galvanized iron bucket over your head and smacking it with a metal hammer – that came close to describing the sound.'

The attack on HMS *Sheffield* forced an already nervous command to consider even more seriously the danger the fleet, and especially the two aircraft carriers, now faced. Any complacent belief that the Argentines had not yet been able to marry up the weapon systems was history. The enemy had conducted a faultless attack.

According to Lawrence Freedman, Woodward's immediate assessment to the Task Force Commander in Northwood on 4 May was understandably 'sour'. Clearly 'writing for effect', the Battle Group commander signalled Northwood: 'Not a good day and a poor exchange for a clapped out cruiser ... and a job lot of spics flying around in ageing Canberras'.

In this signal Woodward made it clear that he was worried about more air-launched missile attacks and concerned that once the Argentine destroyers armed with surface-to-surface Exocets 'got among the islands ... they [too] would be difficult to handle'. Woodward's assessment contained his view that, 'A strike on Rio Grande will be essential for recovery of the Falklands'; and if that was not clear enough, the final words in his signal to the Commander-in-Chief settled the case as far as he was concerned: 'Some new initiative is going to be needed, maybe even a high risk raid right inshore to the mainland.' Was this, then, the genesis of the plan to attack the mainland? Not with Vulcans, as had been proved possible if not diplomatically acceptable, but perhaps by more covert methods, employing guile rather than the 'muscle' of iron bombs.

It is doubtful that the Admiral and his staff, apart from Colonel Richard Preston, his principal military and special forces adviser, had any idea what the options would be for a direct attack on the Super Étendards and their potent missiles. During this opening phase of maritime hostilities, most in the flagship were thinking only of naval options. ARA *General Belgrano* may have been ancient but she had been equipped with, among more modern systems, fifteen six-inch guns and was accompanied by two Exocet-armed destroyers. Ten years later, and with more measured reflection, the Admiral was to write that the *Belgrano* group had been part of a pincer movement and thus needed to be sunk: 'The speed and direction of an enemy ship can be irrelevant, because both can change quickly. What counts is his position, his capability and ... his intention.'[11]

Freedman's *Official History* considered that the Joint Intelligence committee's assessment of 5 May 'made for disturbing reading. The attack against *Sheffield* indicated that the Argentines may have managed to master in-flight refuelling ... and sort out the technical difficulties. If two missiles had been fired the Argentines probably still had three remaining.'

British naval superiority had been demonstrated by the sinking of ARA *General Belgrano*, but the lack of air superiority was emphasized by the loss of *Sheffield*. Action was clearly needed to protect the landing force from Skyhawks, Mirages, Daggers and Pucaras (respectively, single-seat attack fighter/bomber; single-seat, delta-wing interceptor; single-seat delta-wing multi-role fighter and twin-seat, twin turbo-prop ground attack aircraft mostly used for domestic counter-insurgency strikes) – while the Battle Group still needed defending against all of those plus the Super Étendard. The argument was that if one or both carriers were to be incapacitated or, worse, destroyed, there would be no amphibious landings anyway. As the Exocet was the only weapon likely to damage a carrier seriously (and many, even in Aérospatiale, doubted that one hit would cause the total loss of such a large vessel) it was in everyone's interest that these missiles be neutralized swiftly ... but how?

From the outset of hostilities a number of ambitious schemes for dealing with the Exocet threat had been dreamed up. Once a missile was in the air beneath a Super Étendard's starboard wing, with no airborne early warning there was little the British could do, for the Exocet's range exceeded that of any weapon carried in the British surface fleet. Unless detected as they took off from their base – confirmed by the CIA and Hervé Colin as being Rio Grande – there was no time for Sea Harriers to intercept before the missile was launched, by which time the Argentine fighters would be well on their way home. Defence would then, in all practical terms, depend on the judicious firing of chaff and sharp manoeuvring by the target warship.

Following Rear Admiral Woodward's signal of 4 May, and at the immediate suggestion of the Commander-in-Chief, the War Cabinet – with the hesitant approval of senior politicians and their legal advisers – was invited to study methods of neutralizing the Exocets at source, on the mainland. The most ambitious suggestion (as discussed by Freedman in his *Official History*) was to seize the whole of Tierra de Fuego; the second was a strategic bombing attack on Rio

Grande air base; and the third was the use of special forces against the air bases. Plans for this last were split further into sub-options.

These first two possibilities were aired merely to be dismissed. The first would almost certainly require an element of collusion with Chile, and while that country was happy to provide assistance it had to be behind the scenes and, inevitably, behind a smokescreen of apparent disapproval. To expect otherwise would be asking too much and would most surely have led to considerable military support for Argentina from other members of the Organization of American States. The second implied a direct, strategic attack on a country with which the United Kingdom was not at war in any legal sense. But no such niceties were considered when the third possibility was dissected. Admiral Fieldhouse was now requesting a small special forces 'reconnaissance or fighting' patrol, but decisions on such a delicate subject inevitably take time. Thus it was not until 13 May that the Chief of the Defence Staff, Admiral Sir Terence Lewin,[12] ordered the Director of the Special Air Service, Brigadier Peter de la Billière, to draw up plans for a two-stage operation – which he was already doing.

Knowing nothing at all about Rio Grande, and with no Secret Intelligence Service agent having been in the area for months if not years, Lewin's view was that the first phase should be a reconnaissance patrol inserted either by helicopter or submarine. Assuming that the intelligence produced by this 'initial look' was acceptable, and that the targets did indeed exist, then phase two would be an air-land operation using two Hercules C-130 aircraft flying from Ascension Island and carrying a squadron of SAS.

Even before planning began there were problems. For a helicopter insertion to have any chance of success it would need to be launched from within Chilean national waters, and that again was asking too much of an undeclared ally. The submarine proposal was a non-starter until the only conventional submarine capable of such operations was in the area. HMS *Onyx*, under the command of Lieutenant Commander Andrew Johnson,[13] had been sent south, almost as an afterthought, by the naval staff, and only then at the insistence of an SBS officer, Captain C, a member of the Special Operations Group. *Onyx* had sailed on 26 April and so was not due in the area until 31 May.

On 7 May the British extended the Total Exclusion Zone up to Argentina's 12-mile limit, forcing the Junta to believe that this heralded an imminent attack on not only their one aircraft carrier but, of more dangerous significance, their mainland air bases. Additionally, regardless of the Exclusion Zone's limits, it should have been a natural British assumption that defences at the base that housed the Super Étendard – Argentina's one serious trump card – would be well nigh impregnable.

Sadly, and nearly tragically, subsequent events show that this rather obvious deduction was not made.

Chapter 6

RAF Lyneham

Squadron Leader Arthur Roberts, known as 'Max', is a quietly spoken, placid man, who describes himself as 'a diffident and retiring type, always avoiding any form of limelight'. Maybe – but just fifteen days before Argentina invaded the Falkland Islands he was appointed Commanding Officer of the RAF's Special Forces Flight, not a job for the faint-hearted. Having flown Hercules in other squadrons for twelve years, Roberts had been with 47 Squadron since December 1980.

RAF Lyneham was home to, *inter alia*, four RAF squadrons: 24, 30, 47 and 70. All were strategic transport squadrons, while the latter two also flew tactical support missions. Within its Order of Battle 47 Squadron contained the Special Forces Flight made up of five Special Forces crews. Liaising with the SBS, SAS and various government departments for special missions, these crews had been used in operations worldwide. For instance, in Rhodesia between 1979 and 1980 they flew in support of the Commonwealth Monitoring Force during the country's transition to Zimbabwe, and during August 1980, following a local uprising, they operated in Vanuatu in support of British forces.

On first joining 47 Squadron Roberts' post was Flight Commander Operations and Training, until ordered to the Special Forces flight on 15 March 1982. This was a sudden move, for the officer originally posted was unavailable at 'very much the last moment'. Roberts was, in naval parlance, 'given a pier-head jump', unaware that within a fortnight he would be preparing his Flight for war – and way beyond its standard operating range.

Max Roberts' induction into the Special Forces flight had been fairly typical. When with the main squadron, a flight lieutenant had sidled up to him and asked, 'Would you like to join?'

'Yes,' he replied.

The officer slipped away, and Roberts heard no more for twelve months.

The personnel within 'the Flight' (as it was known at Lyneham) were regarded as an elite. In 'Top Gun' terminology they were 'the best of the best', with every man (there were no female members then) – captains, co-pilots, flight engineers, navigators and air loadmasters – specially selected. Extra training was vital for working with the SBS and SAS, work that involved 'high altitude, high opening' and 'high altitude, low opening' parachute drops; night-time, low-level flying; day and night strip-landings; 'sub sunk' operations; fighter evasion; and parachuting the SBS into water with their rigid inflatable boats. The crews were allocated their missions by the Flight Commander, and there were no requests for volunteers – they flew when ordered.

All aircrew were expected to undertake 'escape and evasion' and 'resistance to interrogation' courses, such as the RAF's own course at Mountbatten, Plymouth, or the NATO Long Range Reconnaissance Patrol course at Weingarten in Southern Germany. Training for night-time strip-landings took up much of their time and demanded the greatest of their flying and navigational skills. The technique for operations owed much to the experiences of the men and women of Britain's Special Operations Executive and America's Office of Strategic Services during the Second World War in occupied Europe. Here Lysander light aircraft and Dakotas had, respectively, landed and recovered agents or parachuted stores on to roughly prepared fields by moonlight. Then it would have been the French Resistance or Maquis that had prepared and lit the ground; now it was usually a special forces party that would have been parachuted in earlier, or made its way by some other covert method. The Special Forces Flight insignia was, therefore, symbolic: a fox – a night-time marauder – set against a quarter moon with three lights arranged in an inverted 'L' shape as used by the Lysander pilots. Indeed, the Flight regarded itself very much as the successor to its SOE forebears.

The strips the Flight used could be frozen lakes, all-weather vehicle tracks, grass fields, stony deserts or sandy beaches, with the 2,500-foot 'runway' marked by nine torches or Cyalume light-sticks. At the runway threshold, or downwind end, over which the aircraft must pass on its landing run, two lights 100 feet apart marked either side of the beginning of the strip. The left-hand one was known as the Alpha light and would flash a single Morse letter, usually Alpha (*dot dash*), as a final identification and assurance that the strip was 'secure'. Along the length of the left of the runway, the side of the aircraft where the pilot sits, a light was placed every 500 feet, with the sixth marking the end of the strip. On the right side, beyond the single threshold light, one more would mark the end of the first 1,000 feet; then nothing until the end light, 2,500 feet from the threshold and, again, offset by 100 feet from the final left marker. The right 1,000-foot light was vital. If the aircraft had not settled on the ground by this point, the landing was aborted, the pilot having to apply full power, carry out an overshoot and try again, or cancel the mission.

The lights would be lit for only two minutes before the landing was planned and remain on for two minutes afterwards. If the aircraft arrived outside this 240-second period there would be no operation. Occasionally, for operational reasons, timings were reduced to one minute before to one minute after the landing time (or 'L Hour'). For parachuting sorties, the timing was always plus or minus one minute either side of 'P Hour'. Thus the pressure on navigators to get it right – especially before satellite navigation systems became commonplace – was considerable.

The Special Forces Flight Commander had no aircraft specifically allocated for his use because the RAF hierarchy would countenance no such 'special' unit within their service. The result of this somewhat reactionary attitude was that when an operation was ordered in support of the SBS, SAS or the Foreign Office, the Hercules allocated was a 'bog-standard' aircraft from off the flight line. Having accepted their aircraft for the sortie, the crew would be given the normal authorization to proceed, even if it was for a night-time, strip-landing thousands of miles away. These rather naive-sounding arrangements, forced upon the operators by unsympathetic, fast-jet-orientated, senior officers, were demonstrably unsatisfactory and were to change once the South Atlantic campaign was over.

At Lyneham, as at other RAF stations, there was a well established chain of command which, in Max Roberts' case as a Flight Commander, was first to his Squadron Commander, thence to the Station Commander, then on to RAF 38 Group and finally to Strike Command itself. Nevertheless, from the very beginning of the Falklands campaign Roberts was placed in a most invidious position and one that, perhaps understandably, was to cause his station commander, Group Captain Clive Evans[1] (a fighter pilot turned transport pilot after injuring his back in an ejection) some concern. Because of the sensitivity of the tasks he was asked to undertake, Roberts was frequently ordered to bypass his Squadron and Station Commander and report direct to the senior officers at 38 Group. Initially, Roberts 'found this quite novel', for at Cranwell he had been taught that the chain of command should be strictly adhered to; he was soon to discover that, in war, such military niceties were sometimes ignored as they are not always for the best ...

Following his visit to Hereford on 3 April, Roberts ordered that training for opposed night-time air-land operations should start immediately, using the experience of and the lessons learned from his Flight's recent 'attacks' on RAF Laarbruch and RAF Kinloss. As a direct result of his involvement in the latter exercise, and following his discussions at Hereford (despite having no target) Roberts set in chain a series of exercises codenamed Purple Dragon. Incidentally, to avoid confusion, in the United States Air Force (and adopted by the RAF) the expression 'air-land' is used to differentiate from 'airdrop' operations.

When Operation Corporate began, Max Roberts, as a long experienced transport pilot, was happy as a risk manager. Now he and his colleagues were about to take part in the ultimate risk-taking operation. That the crews were willing to practise for the task knowing that it could, in all probability, end in disaster, was much to their credit. Nevertheless, there was scepticism coupled with hope that a tiny ray of common sense would prevail and that someone somewhere 'up the line' would exercise some wisdom and question what was being considered

It has been speculated that had the Laarbruch and Kinloss exercises not taken place it is quite probable that the idea for Operation Mikado, a 'two-ship' night assault landing on the Exocet's home base, Rio Grande, might not have been considered. Additionally, any suggestion that Entebbe was a forerunner from which ideas germinated should have been scotched, for the operational conditions were entirely different. Clearly, there were weaknesses inherent in all such air-land operations, weaknesses that the RAF liaison officers in Chelsea should have passed on to the SAS, thence to the Ministry of Defence politicians and the Special Operations Group, and then onwards to the War Cabinet. However, the Air Adviser to the Director, Special Air Service was Squadron Leader David Niven,[2] a helicopter pilot who was never seen by the two Hercules pilots during their Operation Mikado work-up exercises. Thus Niven never learned first-hand of the dangers inherent in conducting such an air-land operation against a defended air base; yet, in his defence, it is possible that the SAS's 'bubbles of security' were preventing even him from knowing the detailed plans. Niven later commanded two helicopter transport squadrons – 18 and 78 Squadrons – and served with the Royal Navy's 845 Squadron in Northern Ireland.

Burgoyne, who flew in both the Laarbruch and Kinloss exercises, would say later, not in hindsight but simply to add emphasis to his views at the time:

> I never saw Laarbruch or Kinloss as successes. I saw them as failures because I could not find a way to avoid being detected and, therefore, being shot down on the approach to the runway. The only phase I was interested in was how to get on to the airfield. I was pleased that we found the runways and lined up and I was pleased that we landed and that we stopped where we said we would, but the runways lights were on. It would only have worked for real against a third world opposition like at Entebbe. Argentina was not third world.

From now onwards the Flight's aircrew had to hone their night navigation expertise, their formation flying ability and their low-level and contour flying skills to perfection, while on each exercise the SAS practised their drills, despite these being well established. There had always been a close affinity between the Special Forces Flight and the SAS and SBS, with both the latter putting total trust in the RAF's Hercules aircrews. Equally, that trust was totally reciprocated. Petty inter-service sniping was out of place and unacceptable. Indeed, there are numerous examples of camaraderie and a deep understanding of each other's *modus operandi* (and thus philosophy), which in many other joint-service operations have not, alas, always existed. A story, happily not apocryphal, is told of a successful three-man SBS operation that had been recovered in awkward circumstances for both the Hercules crew and the exhausted marines. After a few hours of well-deserved sleep the C-130's 'passengers', commanded by Captain C with Derek Lynn and 'one other', were woken by the smell of frying steaks. Before them in the cargo hold the aircraft's Air Loadmaster had placed a table and set it with napkins, collapsible chairs, silverware and even candles. The Royal Marines were served a three-course meal with wine!

While Max Roberts was initiating the Purple Dragon air-land exercises, Harry Burgoyne was being briefed for a different task. These briefings also bypassed the normal chain of command, and in this case not even Roberts knew what was happening despite being the initial 'point of contact' with Hereford. Burgoyne's 'alternative war' began on 5 April when, with his co-pilot, Flight Lieutenant 'Bumper' Rowley and navigator, Flight Lieutenant Jim Cunningham, he was ordered to Lyneham's 'secure briefing facility' by the Station Commander, Group Captain Clive Evans. Before they entered the room, Rowley was instructed to wait outside as the briefing was 'highly classified', with only the pilot and navigator allowed access on the 'need to know' principle. Burgoyne, puzzled as to why his co-pilot did not 'need to know', kept his own counsel – for the moment.

The briefing was conducted by Squadron Leader Graham Young, Max Roberts' predecessor as Officer Commanding, Special Forces Flight and now the Special Forces Staff Officer in 38 Group's Headquarters. All talk of conducting a *coup de main* direct on to Stanley airport had been replaced by a more sensible and practical (but still verging on the 'unreal') proposal. Young explained that as the SAS felt there was an urgent need to get 'eyes' on the Falkland Islands as soon as possible, the outline plan was for a covert parachute insertion by men from Air Troop, G Squadron, into the hills, from where they could begin a programme of strategic reconnaissance.

Once landed, the patrol would monitor enemy activity and report back to the United Kingdom using a satellite link or a standard high-frequency radio. The position chosen for the drop zone, known as Bombilla Flats, was on East Falkland, about 15 miles north-north-east of San Carlos Water. North of Bombilla Hill itself is boggy ground dotted with ponds, so quite why this unsuitable site was chosen, against advice, remains a mystery. Lieutenant Colonel Mike Rose had been briefed by the author – an officer with local knowledge – that south of Bombilla Hill was one of only three areas in East Falkland that might be suitable for such a parachute insertion, with its gently sloping, reasonably dry ground.

At Lyneham's secure briefing facility Burgoyne waited patiently to hear how the plan would solve the conundrums of time, payload, distance ... and fuel. However, even the problems associated with the range of the Hercules had been addressed with a modicum of clarity and ingenuity. Simple – they would stage through Easter Island, deep in the Pacific Ocean, nearly 2,000 nautical miles to the west of Chile and one of the most remote places on the planet.

The United Kingdom had contracted to sell Sea Skua missiles to the Chilean air force, and Burgoyne would deliver them. The aircraft would fly to Easter Island with the SAS team and missiles on board – by what route had not yet been established – from where it would travel on to Punta Arenas carrying its own technical and engineering self-help stores, known as a 'Ranger Pack'. This was contained in several large boxes, which would be supplemented by other similar boxes in which eight SAS troopers would hide while the Hercules was on the ground. The turn-round time, during which the Sea Skuas would be unloaded and the aircraft refuelled, was planned to be between one and a half and two hours.

Empty of its cargo, the Hercules would then head back for Easter Island. Once clear of Chilean radar coverage, the aircraft would drop to low level and, in Burgoyne's words, 'Route back over the sea, well south of Cape Horn, to the Falklands, conduct the insertion and return to Punta Arenas to refuel before continuing back to Easter Island.' As a cover for this part of the operation the crew would continue sending the normal Air Traffic Control high-frequency radio position reports as though they were still heading for Easter Island. At the appropriate moment Burgoyne would then 'discover that we had forgotten to offload a box of fuses for the missiles'. As a result, the aircraft would be forced to turn back for Punta Arenas. The approximate flying time from Punta Arenas to the Falklands Dropping Zone and back to Punta was about eight hours, roughly the same as flying halfway from Punta to Easter Island, then returning to Punta. The radio call announcing the intention to return would be made at a time that would tie in with their reappearance 'from the west' on the Air Traffic Control radar.

The C-130 captain liked the idea and believed the outline navigational plan to be feasible, but there were other factors that needed dovetailing. Burgoyne had, two days earlier, attended an intelligence brief on expected Argentine capabilities and was struck by how good their reported high-frequency radio direction finding was. He immediately recognized a flaw in the plan. Worried that his air traffic control transmissions for the Punta–Falklands–Punta leg would be found to originate, as indeed they would do, from the South Atlantic and not from the South Pacific between Chile and Easter Island, his solution was to run a Special Forces 'two-ship' operation, with the second aircraft making all the normal air traffic control transmissions for both aircraft as it genuinely flew the Punta–Easter Island route, while he, Burgoyne, went on his circuitous way in silence.

Burgoyne's suggestion was accepted, although when he discovered (over twenty-five years later) that there were other RAF aircraft operating from Chile (in Chilean Air Force colours), he thought that these should have been tasked to make the spoof transmissions, thus saving a scarce C-130 and an overworked Special Forces Flight crew.

At the end of the briefing, the Station Commander instructed Burgoyne to begin planning then rehearsing immediately; an aircraft would be made available to the crew at any time, while the full resources of the base were at their disposal. It was made plain, though, that neither he nor Cunningham was to discuss the operation with anyone. Outside the room, the pilot and navigator decided that with such a complex and challenging task it would be impossible to train without the other members of the crew knowing what was going on; they had to take them into their confidence. After all, they were 'special forces aircrew' with no secrets between them and all 'security-vetted' to the same level. Immediately after the briefing Burgoyne let Rowley into the secret and the next day told his Flight Engineer, Flight Sergeant Steve Sloan and his Air Loadmaster, Flight Sergeant Mick Sephton. In reality, he could have done nothing else.

That afternoon, the captain, co-pilot and navigator started work. First, they had to look closely at the dropping zone and select a route into and out of it. Graham Young had brought clear-plastic map overlays, provided by the Royal Radar Establishment, for the Argentine radar coverage around Bombilla. Using these, areas likely to be shielded by the rocky Falklands terrain could be deduced. The AN/TPS 43 radar mounted on Sapper Hill overlooking Stanley was known to be effective, but from the overlays it was apparent that the crew would be able to fly in and out of the dropping zone undetected, provided they kept below 350 feet above ground level. In fact, the radar was not to stay there long, for it blew down in a gale around 10 April and was moved, three days later, to the south-west of the town. A dummy aerial was left in its place to confuse the British.

Now they had to look closely at the drop itself. The austral autumn in the Falklands can produce regular wind speeds of between 20 and 30 knots, with

40 to 50 knots 'not unusual'. In 1982 the existing low-level military static-line parachutes, the PX4 and the 22 foot Steerable Static Line or SSL, had, respectively, no or very little steering ability. The latter did, though, have a 'forward drive' speed of nine knots. Using either of these, the parachutists would be unable to counter the effect of wind drift, limiting their use to an absolute maximum wind speed at ground level of 18 knots. What was needed was a parachute that was both manoeuvrable and with good 'drive'; those that fitted the bill were the steerable, square-section 'chutes used for free-fall drops.

Several candidates were available that not only were steerable but, equally important, had a drive of 20 to 25 knots – ideal for reducing the speed over the ground on landing in, say, a 30-knot wind to a manageable speed. Unfortunately, all had low weight restrictions, and the SAS were thinking of dropping with Bergen rucksacks weighing 120lb (54kg), suggesting an all-up weight per parachute of 300lb (136kg). The aircrew needed advice, and that came from the RAF Parachute Jump Instructors attached to the SAS and the troopers of G Squadron themselves. They recommended using the GQ360, a parachute that was so new and of such an advanced design that it had hardly begun its Boscombe Down trials and so was many months away from being released for operations. But this was 'active service', and such restrictions have few places in combat.

The parachute came with an effective quick release that the parachutist could activate immediately on landing. The drop at Bombilla Flats would take place at night on to boggy and possibly stony ground, and if the trooper was unable to gauge the wind direction as he floated down, instead of heading at 20 knots into a 35-knot wind, thus giving him a 15-knot landing speed, he could be heading for a touch-down at 55 knots; with legs plunging into the peat, the likelihood of broken limbs, or worse, would be high. Without hesitation, and to everyone's admiration and respect, the troopers accepted this risk and agreed that they should use this untried parachute.

Initial jumps took place on to the SAS's Pontrilas Training Area near Hereford, using a Chinook helicopter. Then, with the troopers happy with the parachute itself, Burgoyne and his C-130 conducted four high-level night drops on Salisbury Plain. The worst accuracy recorded was 450 yards from the 'drop zone impact point', while the best was almost 'spot on'.

Concurrently with these trials, Burgoyne, Rowley and Cunningham were busy defining the route and tactics for the run in to Bombilla – and there was a problem to be overcome. The GQ360 could not be used at low level as it took time to develop fully after the ripcord was pulled, while the troopers needed time in the air to carry out their standard operating procedures before assessing landing direction and speed. The RAF's parachute instructors confirmed that, with the SAS's agreement, the minimum dispatch height could be reduced to 3,200 feet. Unfortunately, at that height, the aircraft would be exposed to the Argentine radar.

Under normal circumstances, during high-altitude free-fall parachuting, the aircraft would be steadied at the correct height and speed at least 5 miles out –

four minutes away – to avoid excessive manoeuvring that might cause the para-troopers to fall over. For the Bombilla operation that was unacceptable. The aircrew knew that the scan rate of the AN/TPS-43 radar was one sweep every ten seconds. They reasoned, therefore, that if they could keep the exposure time 'at altitude' down to about fifteen seconds they could only be illuminated twice at most and thus stood a good chance of being unnoticed by the operator, 'especially at 0200-ish in the morning'.

Unlike fast jets, the Hercules were not fitted with a radar warning receiver, so the crew had no means of knowing if a radar was looking at them; Burgoyne emphasized this to his Station Commander and Lyneham responded imme-diately. Following a request to the Royal Naval Air Station at Yeovilton, the Navy quickly provided an Omega hand-held receiver that the Fleet Air Arm pilots used in their helicopters. Because of its size and shape, this new apparatus was imme-diately christened 'the hair drier' by the C-130 aircrew.

Sadly, the information this instrument offered was extremely limited. It was possible to tell if the aircraft was being 'illuminated' by a radar in search mode, but any bearing information – acquired by moving the receiver around by hand and noting the direction of the strongest signal point – was so inaccurate that this function was disregarded. An audible alarm sounded if a fire-control radar 'locked on', but as the Hercules had no counter-measures to offer, there was very little the crew could do other than, in Bumper Rowley's words, 'Mutter "Oh dear", 'cos the next thing you'll know is that a missile the size of a telegraph pole will be coming through the front window at Mach 3!' Despite these short-comings, the crew were glad to have it and duly strapped it, facing forwards, to the instrument coaming in front of the co-pilot.

The drop procedure was refined further. It was decided that the aircraft would approach the dropping point at 240 knots and at low level, with the troopers prepared and standing in the rear of the cargo bay. At a pre-planned point the pilot would pull back on the control column to 'zoom' (Burgoyne used this word with caution, 'as Hercules do not zoom anywhere') the aircraft upwards with a 30°–40° 'nose-up' attitude. Approaching the drop height, the pilot would select the correct flap position, then order the rear door to be opened and the ramp to be lowered to the horizontal as he levelled off at 3,200 feet and the required 120 knots. Thereafter, the 'Red On', 'Green On', and 'GO!' calls would be made ... all in quick time. With the last man out, the Hercules would be put into a steep dive and return to low level.

Burgoyne's crew and the SAS conducted trial runs using dropping zones across South-West England. They experimented in varying wind conditions and with different speeds until a combination was established that worked by both day and night. To help their calculations Cunningham 'invented a wind table' by which the pull-up point in any winds likely to be encountered could be ascertained. In the rear of the aircraft, Mick Sephton, along with the SAS troopers, devised new procedures for donning equipment, checking kit, moving into position (without falling over) and maintaining balance during the sharp climb followed by the equally awkward moment of levelling off.

The pilots planned to enter enemy territory via the northern entrance to Falkland Sound and thence to San Carlos, before heading between the two 1,000-foot hills to the east and from there to the release point. Precise navigation relied on Doppler, occasional sweeps of the aircraft's weather radar and whatever co-pilot Rowley was able to see with the ITT night vision goggles. Having dropped their passengers, they would 'exfiltrate' to the north-west via a different route to mask the purpose of the flight.

At the end of the ten-day training period the average time spent at height and low speed had been reduced to between ten and twelve seconds. These impressive figures reflected positively on the coordinated team work of the Special Forces Flight, the Parachute Jump Instructors and the eight men of the Special Air Service, especially as Burgoyne's crew were at the same time involved in other training tasks and trials.

To extract the maximum value from these flights, the crew used them to polish their skills and develop the Standard Operating Procedures they would need for the Bombilla Flats insertion. Burgoyne explained:

While we were flying these long flights, testing the new fuel system, we also figured out how we could fly at 50 feet over the ocean at night, and on instruments, in case we encountered bad weather. We planned to be at that height for perhaps the last 200 miles towards the Falklands coast and even thought of taking a hint from the Dambusters' World War Two raid with their converging lights. However, we decided we could do it using just the radar altimeter but, for safety, we had a second radar altimeter – a repeater of the captain's – fitted to the side of the co-pilot's instrument panel. As both instruments were fed from the same source, it took us a bit of time to get used to trusting them at that level and at that speed over a featureless sea. It was bloody low – below a yacht's mast – so even quite small boats were a problem. Jim Cunningham planned to use two sweeps of his radar every 20 miles to keep us clear of shipping or any other hazards. As we were coming via Cape Horn, we knew that icebergs could also be a problem especially as they don't always show on the aircraft's radar. All that had to be factored in.

Having announced that they were ready to go should the call come, Burgoyne and Cunningham were summoned to 38 Group's Senior Air Staff Officer to brief the plan ... but Air Commodore Derek Bryant was unimpressed by the deliberations of the Hercules team. As an ex-ground attack Phantom pilot he could not see why the Hercules needed to take such a complex route to the dropping zone, then leave via a different route. He advocated flying in a straight line from the coast to the objective, before returning the same way. Burgoyne and his navigator tried to explain that there was nothing covert about that approach and that it was only acceptable if dropping bombs, in other words when 'waking the defenders was not a concern'. 'Delivering special forces,' the aircrew explained, 'different parameters apply. It is essential that the enemy know as little as possible about the flight and preferably that it has not taken place at all.'

Unconvinced, the Air Commodore ordered the team to come up with something less 'over the top', but the Flight Lieutenants continued to argue that to fly straight in and straight back again would give an alert enemy every clue he needed about the nature of the flight and the position at which its 'cargo' had been dropped. It would also mean overflying any enemy twice. Bryant continued to overrule, demanding that his plan be adopted. Then, following 'strong and vociferous protestations', the two officers were dismissed. Outside Bryant's office, and feeling no need for further discussion, the Hercules team agreed that the route they would take would be their own. Mindful of the retribution that could come from disobeying orders while on active service, Burgoyne surmised pragmatically that, 'Either a successful mission or being shot down by the enemy would save us from such censure.'

This planned insertion by parachute, whether it was to be via Easter Island or direct from Ascension, is relevant to the Exocet saga for a number of reasons. It was to help hasten the air-to-air refuelling programme, without which no mainland operation would be viable; it highlighted the shortcomings of the senior RAF decision makers as they failed to appreciate the realities of special forces flying; it sharpened minds to the vital business of flying under radar cover, overland at night in the pre-GPS and pre-night vision goggle days; and it emphasized the long hours that the Hercules crews would have to face on a daily basis. Although never to be put into practice at Bombilla, the trials were not wasted, as will be discussed.

With the war progressing and with air-to-air refuelling of the Hercules becoming a practical possibility, the new option was to mount any future operation out of Wideawake on Ascension. Consequently, the Easter Island alternative began to drift into the background, and with the Task Force creeping closer to the Falklands, helicopters of the Fleet Air Arm's 'junglie' squadrons would also soon be able to insert Special Forces patrols. This was just as well, for the Easter Island operation had not been cleared by (indeed it was unknown to) both the Special Operations Group and the Special Operations Coordinating Officer; yet it was precisely the type of 'privateering, maverick' operation that Whitehall and Northwood (in other words those responsible for 'running the war') were trying to prevent – or, at least, to control.

While Burgoyne and his crew were planning their 'Easter Island excursion' other events were unfolding. On 3 April Max Roberts had been briefed on the germ of an idea based on an Entebbe-style raid but with neither target nor date mentioned. From a gradual and hazy realization of what might be required of his flight, one thing was obvious: it would involve an SAS squadron operating against unspecified targets. Roberts' immediate action had been to instigate the Purple Dragon flights. These began on Sunday 4 April and were initially flown by a single Hercules at RAF Colerne, Wiltshire.

Instituting this training had been fast thinking by the Squadron Leader, but it was not all plain sailing. Colerne's north-south runway lies along the top of a hill, with the Fosse Way running almost parallel to it, 260 yards away. The main south-west runway's extension ends just 50 yards from the old Roman road. The public, not slow to draw conclusions at the beginning of a national emergency, soon gathered to watch a lone Hercules landing in very short distances, lowering its ramp, then raising it again to take off in under a minute from touch-down. This was too much for the 'rumourists'; soon the perimeter fence was lined with spectators having been summoned, no doubt, by a nationwide communications network similar to that enjoyed by fanatical birdwatchers.

The first 'two-ship attacks' were conducted at RAF Marham. On 10 April Burgoyne and Roberts loaded B Squadron, 22 SAS into their C-130s to conduct a '2,000-foot trail' formation flight to this Norfolk air field, where the troops practised in slow time the techniques that their colleagues had successfully used at Laarbruch just sixteen days earlier. As the day progressed, Standard Operating Procedures were invented and perfected in slow time until the routines for such an operation became clear. Eventually, several short flights were conducted, each culminating in a simultaneous, 2,000 feet-apart landing and offload at Marham. The following night (Easter Sunday), and with B Squadron Commander, Major John Moss, embarked, a second series of air-land assaults were practised, but with no aircraft lights other than rear-facing formation lights along the tops of the main wings.

There was, however, one artificial factor introduced into the exercise: the runway lights had to be kept on, as without night vision goggles the crew could not see enough to land. This had an unexpected impact. Burgoyne, in the number two position and 2,000 feet behind Roberts, found that on the final approach the lead aircraft's formation lights (which Burgoyne needed to see to maintain his relative position) disappeared among the runway lights.

Roberts and Burgoyne knew they were pushing the boundaries, but they were, after all, 47 Squadron's Special Forces Flight with an absolute duty to get it right for their 'ground users'. As Roberts explains:

> With the exception of the formation lights all other lights were off for the Marham landings despite that being illegal ... but we were bold, young and foolish. We knew that, for real, we would be unlit and it was best to practice under controlled conditions. This was a Special Forces Flight thing: other squadrons would never have been allowed to do that. But we regularly practised landing at Upavon and on Deptford Down's grass strip on Salisbury Plain with nothing more than nine torches on the ground and no anti-collision, landing or taxi lights on the aircraft.
>
> This latter landing zone is a 2,500 feet, natural terrain 'runway' and, by using Doppler, the approach was reasonably straightforward. But the Doppler, as has been explained, was not accurate without a good visual fix 20 miles out to make sure the system was up-to-date.
>
> On the approach the navigator would talk the pilot down the glide path – using distance to go and the calculated ideal height – aiming to have the aircraft at 900 feet above ground level at 3 miles from the threshold, then 600 feet at 2 miles, 300 feet at 1 mile, 150 feet at half a mile and so on until

touchdown. As a pilot, I just followed the navigator's instructions. Down you come, completely dark, looking out for the torches. Right we're on target. Strip in sight. Correct heading. Correct glide path angle. Correct speed. Aiming for 17 feet altitude. The moment the pre-set radar altimeter warning beeper goes off, close the throttle, pull back on the stick and wait for the bump. Then throw the propellers into reverse and stamp on the brakes! It was all perfectly safe.

Straightforward it may have been, but there was precious little margin for error. Members of the army's 47 Air Despatch Squadron were always on hand to provide the field ambulance and to lay out the strip's lights before watching the approaching aircraft from the edge of the 'runway'. But once, at Deptford Down, the dim outline of an approaching Hercules without landing lights was, the team thought, 'perhaps a little off the centre line'. At the very last moment they were obliged to run off the strip's left hand edge. Their concern was well founded, for when they walked back to their usual viewing spot they discovered that the main wheels had crushed their 'picnic boxes'.

On 13 April it was RAF Kinloss's second chance to prove that it was no easy target, and this time it was the Hercules that were nearly found wanting. Take-off from Lyneham was scheduled for 0320 on the Tuesday morning, with Max Roberts leading Harry Burgoyne. 'L' hour was planned for 0550. All at low level, the prearranged route took the two Hercules up the Welsh valleys, from where they would 'coast out' over the Irish Sea, fly past the Isle of Man, then along the North Channel before leaving the Mull of Kintyre to starboard. There they would turn for a transit of the Sound of Jura towards the Great Glen where it meets Loch Linnhe at Fort William. The plan, then, was to follow the Glen, before 'popping out' at Inverness and turning to starboard into Kinloss – still, it was hoped, in the correct running order to 'avoid confusing the troops' as they disembarked to dash towards their pre-planned targets.

But the well laid plans were interrupted shortly after they crossed the North Wales coast, when Roberts was obliged to order Burgoyne to take over the lead as the few aids to navigation he possessed had, in the idiom of the day, 'gone tits up'. In the dark, Burgoyne eased his aircraft ahead, knowing that at some stage before landing on the other side of Scotland it would be necessary to return to their correct positions. In the pitch blackness, at 250 feet above Loch Ness and well below the mountain tops on either side, the two aircraft thundered north-east until it was decided to reverse position, as Roberts by now had a limited number of navigation instruments back 'on line'.

Burgoyne remembers:

There were two of us inside the valley. It was dark and we were much lower than the hills. Max was coming past me, not showing a lot of lights and with only 300 to 500 feet between us. The moment he was ahead I looked away for some reason. When I looked back we were over lights on the ground but with no sign of Max. He had merged into the darkness with his few lights lost among those on the ground. I turned to my co-pilot, Rowley, and said,

'Bumper, I've lost him.' Luckily he was using a set of old night vision goggles and replied, 'Max is right in front of you. He flew out over the lights and I've got him again.' Once settled, I manoeuvred back into the 2,000-foot trail ready for the simultaneous landing.

But the drama was not over.

On our approach to Kinloss, Max's navigational kit became unserviceable again, or so it seemed to us in the number two position. Bumper Rowley reckoned that we were about half a mile off track for the final run in, with Max making no effort to get on to the runway's centre line. Bumper called him, 'Your target is 11 o'clock at a mile and half.' Roberts replied, 'Thanks very much', and suddenly banked and dived in the indicated direction. We followed him – diving sharply to the left – landed and offloaded. As sunrise was not until 0610 it was the first time we had attempted a nautical twilight approach with all runway lights off.

Wing Commander Barry Nunn, 47 Squadron's Commanding Officer, had been embarked in Burgoyne's aircraft, 'spending much of the flight sleeping on the bunk at the rear of the cockpit'. Safely on the ground at the 'hot wash-up', Nunn suggested that the landing could have taken place half an hour earlier when, he argued, there would have been enough light to land without aids – a view not shared by the aircrew. Flight Lieutenant Jim Norfolk, who had been travelling as an observer in Roberts' aircraft, expressed their collective opinions: 'We were probably beyond the limits of safety there, boss. Any earlier we would not have seen the runway. This is naked eye stuff looking for an unlit runway. Until someone takes us seriously and gives us modern night vision aids we will just have to keep on doing the best we can.'

Kinloss was properly prepared. This was not their 'tactical evaluation' but an exercise to benefit the Special Forces Flight. Indeed, so prepared was the airfield that the two aircraft had been spotted on radar the moment that they 'popped out of the top of the Great Glen', 25 miles away. With proper night vision aids, the pilots argued, they could have flown lower and reduced that distance considerably, but what that revised distance would have been, nobody knew.

Norfolk was right, for the Hercules' navigation aids had not progressed since the aircraft first entered operational RAF service with 47 Squadron in February 1968. The bubble sextant and Loran – the latter not available in the South Atlantic – were still in use on transoceanic flights, while Doppler remained the primary aid to low-level navigation. Max Roberts was not the first Commanding Officer of the Special Forces Flight to write papers requesting upgraded equipment, but the air marshals did not want to know. One example will explain: prior to 1982 a senior RAF officer, when asked for money to be released to armour vulnerable sections of the C-130s, had stated briefly, 'The Hercules will never be sent into a high threat environment.' This was an odd statement to make, for more C-130s had been targeted – and occasionally hit – by an 'enemy' than any RAF fast jet since the end of the Second World War ... except, perhaps, during the Korean war, when a handful of RAF pilots on exchange with the USAF had flown F-86 Sabres.

At Lyneham, Roberts called formally on Wing Commander Nunn and came to the point immediately: 'Sir, we have got to have proper navigational equipment as we can't go on like this. The Doppler kit is not up to scratch for this sort of work.'

'No, no, you're doing fine,' was the unhelpful reply.

Roberts knew that with all the serious money going to the fighters there was little point in pursuing the matter further, even if he thought he could convince their Station Commander, an ex-fighter pilot. That having been said, three Carousel IV Inertia Navigation Systems arrived from Farnborough shortly afterwards; support (not always in evidence) obviously existed up the command chain, but it seemed to be on a rather informal basis.

Further practice flights took place on to RAF St Mawgan's wide runway on the north Cornish coast and on to the slightly narrower runway at RAF Binbrook, Lincolnshire. A night landing at the latter airfield, conducted by Flight Lieutenants Jim Norfolk and Dane Crosby, very nearly saw the end of the experiments, for it was accurately described as having been on 'the ragged edge of safety' and only saved at the very last moment by Norfolk 'remembering a lump in the ground which he was able to avoid'. Just! Although the aircraft did get 'quite close' to the airfield before they were spotted, this was due solely to the fact that the Hercules were flown – as one member of the aircrew involved self-critically put it – 'stupidly and ridiculously low'; indeed, below the height of the airfield that sits atop a shallow hill. Everyone agreed that 'serious lessons were learned that night'. The ability to recognize when any activity had reached the limits of safety, plus the ability to be self-critical and accept advice from others, was a prior requirement for serving with the Special Forces Flight. Accepting mistakes and learning from them was drummed into the aircrew as part of their philosophy.

Other procedures were being introduced and practised, while some merely needed perfecting. Included in the first category was the use of night vision goggles, modern aids to navigation and air-to-air refuelling, while among the latter were terrain-masking, flying at 'ultra-low level' at night and fighter evasion techniques. The pilots could themselves address the latter, but the former needed money and commitment by those more senior.

Finally accepting that Operation Mikado would have to be conducted against unlit runways, the staff at 38 Group at last approved a trial of state-of-the-art, second-generation goggles known as Airman's Night Vision System Mark 2 or ANVIS; a number of sets soon arrived at the Flight's offices at Lyneham. Between 14 and 25 April several night sorties were flown using the ANVIS. Known as Operation Grey Mist, the training was conducted as a subset of Purple Dragon and produced promising results. The goggles worked as advertised, but one thing was soon obvious, they needed at least a quarter moon with a 30° elevation to be effective, this bare minimum level of ambient light being absolutely vital. If the moon went behind a cloud, or the crew encountered a rain shower, the ANVIS picture deteriorated instantly, and the pilot had to climb immediately to a safer altitude. While this non-tactical manoeuvre kept them clear of the ground it almost certainly ensured that the aircraft would be 'painted' on an enemy radar screen. However, progress was being made, and now the crews could contour fly safely at low-level and, at last, land on unlit, paved, full-length runways.

With everything else that was going on, the pilots only had time for a minimum of practice. Perhaps Burgoyne's training was even less than that:

I completed one flight of two hours and twenty-five minutes on 15 April, flying around the south-west of England; working down to 250 feet after about twenty minutes. We practised strip approaches at Merryfield airfield and then returned to Lyneham where we conducted four touch and go landings. Interestingly, 'touch and goes' are never attempted these days; they're considered far too dangerous! We then did a final, full-stop landing and that was it. I was considered qualified.

Roberts remembers flying some 'normal' training flights using St Mawgan's runway:

There were no manuals with these goggles so we had to work out for ourselves how to use them. What we did discover was that the flight instrument lights kept interfering and had to be filtered using special, blue plastic: in fact we switched most of them off. For those we really needed, we cut out suitably sized filters and simply 'sellotaped' them on. Especially the radar altimeter, which we did have to be able to read properly!

Other factors also needed to be considered. Early in April, Lyneham's Station Commander, Group Captain Clive Evans, had been called to his operations room's 'scrambler' telephone. On the line was 38 Group's Senior Air Staff Officer informing him that he was about to receive a number of auxiliary fuel tanks stripped from Andover aircraft and that they were to be fitted immediately to the appropriate Hercules under Evans' command. Although originally planned as a stop-gap measure to extend the C-130's range, once they were equipped for air-to-air refuelling they became a near permanent fixture.[3]

Hercules XV296 was the first aircraft fitted with the tanks, and the job of trialling the equipment was given to the Special Forces Flight. However, there were teething problems. Harry Burgoyne offers a tale that thankfully had a happy ending:

It was during a flight on the night of April 20th conducted at ultra-low-level, over the sea and just abeam Skye. The fuel collector box, situated in the middle of the freight bay floor, began to buckle inwards as soon as its internal pumps were switched on. Moments later, it imploded and ruptured. As it was connected directly to all four Andover tanks, they now flooded the freight bay with aviation fuel. The only 'fix' was to shut down the fuel system, isolate all the electrics, open the ramp at the rear then climb at a steep enough angle to let the fuel drain overboard. On our return, and thanks to prodigious work by the RAF Lyneham engineers, the collector box was quickly modified and a successful flight was conducted the following evening.

May Day 1982 was an auspicious one in the history of the Falklands campaign, for not only did an RAF Vulcan bomber attack Stanley airfield (incidentally causing a welcome and perhaps unusual diversion that allowed the Special Boat Squadron to conduct the first special forces landings on the islands), but it was also the day that the decision was made to extend the range of the Hercules by fitting them for air-to-air refuelling operations. Immediately, Squadron Leader John Brown, a Boscombe Down test pilot, began to work out the procedures for refuelling a Hercules in the air from a Victor 'tanker'.

At the same time, Marshall Aerospace of Cambridge, the designated Lockheed engineering authority, were awarded the contract to design, construct and fit the necessary equipment. This was not easy, for there was a shortage of refuelling probes but no time to manufacture the jigs to make new ones. Burgoyne delights in recalling a story that he is not sure is entirely mythical:

> Two RAF engineers were dispatched to the United States in Concorde. They caught a flight from New York to somewhere where an old Vulcan bomber was on display. They hacksawed the probe off and returned to the United Kingdom via the reverse route. In all, I think they were out of the United Kingdom for less than thirty-six hours.

Following a monumental effort by everyone involved, the first air-to-air refuelling-capable Hercules, XV200, emerged from Marshalls and was delivered to Lyneham on 5 May.

Roberts recalls:

> Close formation flying was not allowed in transport aircraft, although as pilots we had done it at the flying training schools but never with a Hercules. While formation flying was the daily fare of fast jets, Hercules pilots spent all their time in the air trying to avoid such close encounters. Knowing we were about to conduct air-to-air refuelling Harry and I started practising on 29 April so that we could begin writing the manual for flying Hercules in close formation.

On 5 May Roberts and Burgoyne, plus a composite crew from the Flight, assembled in a briefing room at the Aircraft and Armament Experimental Establishment, Boscombe Down, to prove the system and learn how to conduct refuelling operations at 20,000 feet. Using XV200, these trials progressed well despite four problems that needed addressing. Urgently.

In order to avoid obstructing the flight deck emergency escape hatch, the refuelling probe and its associated pipe work had had to be offset to the starboard side, directly above the co-pilot's seat. As the captain of the aircraft sat on the port side, this made lining up the probe with the delivery 'basket', resembling a giant shuttlecock, difficult; judging closure speed was similarly tricky. The solution was for the co-pilot to talk the captain into the 'basket' using distances in feet: 'Left two ... steady ... up one ... right a half ... steady ...' Closure rate guidance was just as simple: 'Good closure ... slowing down ... keep your speed up ... slightly fast ... steady ... steady.'

The second problem concerned the Hercules' tail fin. As the C-130 approached the Victor tanker its tail fin jutted up into the jet-wash of the Victor's engines, causing significant vibration on the rudder. Fortunately, when both aircraft were in the correct refuelling position, the vibration eased considerably. However, until that moment it was disconcerting and made minute corrections difficult.

The third problem was equally unexpected. During an early test flight it was found that the fuel going into the outer wing tanks stopped flowing before the tanks were full. The scientists scratched their heads. The test pilot hadn't a clue, but Roberts' Flight Engineer, Flight Sergeant Dick Ludford, offered a possible explanation. When on the ground, and thus with no lift, the Hercules' wings drooped, allowing fuel to flow freely into the tanks. When airborne, the wings flexed slightly upwards, causing the fuel float valve inside the tank to close before the tank was full. Ludford was right. The test pilot suggested that prior to connecting to the tanker, the Hercules pilots fly 'cross control' with one wing down, compensated by a degree of 'opposite' rudder, to 'fool' the valve into remaining open while fuel was transferred into the tank. Once that tank was full, the cross control procedure was reversed to fill the other wing. It worked ... and with both tanks full the Hercules could close with the Victor, refuel and continue its mission.

The fourth and most significant problem when refuelling a Hercules from a Victor was the disparity in speed between the receiving and giving aircraft. The Victor's refuelling hose was held out against a hydraulic spring by the 'basket' dragging through the airflow, an airflow that had to be at least 230 knots; any less and the spring would rewind the hose. At high all-up weights and typical air-to-air refuelling heights, the Hercules did not have sufficient power to maintain this speed and keep up with the more powerful jet. The ever-inventive John Brown's solution was to conduct the refuelling in a shallow descent, allowing gravity to compensate for the C-130's power deficiency. As he positioned behind the Victor, the Hercules pilot called 'Ready', and both tanker and receiver would begin their descent. Now with power to spare, he could manoeuvre freely and guide his probe into the Victor's trailing 'basket'. The procedure worked well and became known as 'tobogganing'.

The existing 'formation markings' painted on the underside of the Victor's fuselage aided the Hercules pilots in maintaining the correct approach, while a set of 'traffic lights' (red, amber, green) were used to help control the operation. With the receiving aircraft cleared to connect, the light was amber; once the probe was in the basket and fuel had started flowing, the light turned to green and was the signal for the Hercules pilot to stop pushing. A red light meant either 'do not connect' or 'disconnect immediately'. These traffic lights were used on their own during radio silence.

So intensive was the flying that the normally five-week air-to-air refuelling course (two weeks' ground school and three weeks' flying) was completed in as many days. An acceptance trial would conventionally have taken months. To have conducted both in so short a period was extraordinary; the Hercules had been cleared to refuel from a Victor tanker at weights above 155,000lb (the normal maximum take-off weight of the C-130) on four and three engines. Two-engine air-to-air refuelling had proved impossible at the extreme weights involved, but Burgoyne vividly recalls the excitement of flying for the first time in his ten years on the Hercules with two engines actually shut down.

Chapter 7

Deliberations: South Atlantic, Northwood and Hereford

If May Day was notable for the first British strike against Argentine targets on the Falkland Islands, then 4 May and the loss of HMS *Sheffield* marked the 'second beginning' of offensive operations, from which there would be no turning back.

Admiral Sir Henry Leach felt, 'The waves of emotion that spread through Whitehall were almost tangible',[1] although his personal belief, so eloquently echoed by Captain Kit Layman[2] of HMS *Argonaut* on the evening following the San Carlos landings, was that there was no point in having ships if one was not prepared to lose them. Layman was to write:

> Ships are there to be used and therefore risked ... The Royal Navy has never minded losing a few ships in the knowledge that warfare is a risk-taking business. Hitler, Mussolini and Anaya hated losing ships and withdrew them, in extreme cases scuttled them, rather than have them sunk.

The clear implication was that once they had sent us to war the politicians had better get used to the idea of losses at sea, on land and in the air.

Between 1976 and 1977 Rear Admiral 'Sandy' Woodward, then a captain, had commanded HMS *Sheffield*. Understandably upset at the foundering of his old ship and, probably of more significance, the fact that her loss had been – should have been – preventable, the Admiral took stock. The Exocet threat was suddenly real and no longer just a frightening supposition. Woodward's only surface command had been sunk with some apparent ease, and certainly with impunity, by the Argentine naval pilots.

According to his Staff Officer (Operations), Commander Jeremy Sanders:[3]

> Sandy was a great one for operational analysis. So we analysed the *Sheffield* incident forwards, backwards and inside out. Apart from tightening up our procedures when facing such a threat, one obvious option would be to remove the weapon system, the Super Étendard, at source.[4] Sandy spoke to Admiral Halifax about that on one of his secure voice phone calls back home. I certainly remember discussing the possibility at the time but I am not sure how seriously we took it as a real option. In Sandy's view, I expect, it was an SAS mission that he had in mind but I doubt that the delivery means had been seriously thought through at that time, by us at sea.[5]

It is interesting to note that Colonel Richard Preston wrote in his diary:

> 7 May. Realization seems to be dawning that we cannot achieve a landing until the mainland air threat has been removed and that the only way this can

be done is by attacking the mainland bases which may be unacceptable to the politicians. Spoke at length with the Admiral and with General Jeremy Moore at Northwood. The General was cagey but I believe plans are in hand to use Chile as a base for special forces operations against the southern air bases, principally Rio Gallegos and Rio Grande. It would be a high risk option but any losses would be small compared to another ship. Another option is to put a Type 42/22 mix west of the Falkland Islands to draw out the attack aircraft but this is a far higher risk option. [Preston noted later: 'Sadly it proved to be so'.]

In 2012 Preston amplified his thoughts thus:

I am sure that if Sandy had talked specifically about a mission to take out the [aircraft and missile] combination I would have noted it in the diary.

While the Argentines were known to have received five air-to-air Exocets, there had been considerable doubt over whether or not they had managed to match up the missiles with their aircraft. Now there was no question. This was clearly going to place the Carrier Battle Group's commander in some difficulty if he was to meet his orders to enforce a Total Exclusion Zone around the Falklands. Freedman puts it bluntly:

The eastern third could be controlled, the middle third terrorised, but the western third posed problems so long as [quoting Woodward direct] 'the Args can freely use their southern airfields'.

Because subsequent events swiftly overtook Woodward's signal, and because the Admiral's staff were not involved in the drafting of the message (and never saw it), it might be speculated that his thinking was of a night-time dash to bombard Rio Grande's one runway plus the associated hangars and aircraft parking areas with naval gunfire. His staff did not know – and were never made privy to – what method of destroying the Super Étendards was in his mind. As Preston puts it:

Sandy had the annoying habit of sending provocative signals in the middle watch when he was awake and bored. This led to major problems between Julian Thompson and me when they related to landing force matters. Julian naturally assumed that I had seen the signals before dispatch.[6]

The range of the Mark 8 4.5-inch guns of the four Type 42 destroyers (reduced from five with the loss of *Sheffield*) that might have been used was 12 nautical miles, the very edge of the Argentine territorial limit behind which its navy would now be hiding.[7] Not that the legalities of that would matter anyway, if the aim was to attack targets on the mainland. Rio Grande's aircraft hangars were another 2 nautical miles further inland from the high-water mark. For good measure, a Harrier attack, too, could have been launched, but all these would certainly have been extreme measures and certainly 'high-risk' – very high-risk indeed. Jeremy Sanders remembers that:

The riskiness and speed versus distance of making an attack with a Mark 8-fitted warship together with the very small chance of making a significant impact on air operations would have ruled this out had this option been put to the staff. Anyway, to have had any chance of success a spotter would be necessary to direct and correct fire. This alone would have resulted in this being a non-starter.

Colonel Preston was embarked in *Hermes* as the Admiral's 'land and special forces adviser', and yet his views were not sought on a projected raid by C-130s operating out of Ascension. Had they been, he would have offered an objective assessment of the likelihood of success, for Preston was well versed in the problems that attended such projects. Between 1976 and 1979 he had been part of a three-man team within the Ministry of Defence responsible for contingency planning for what was loosely termed 'the Rest of the World', and said:

> We had never been able to give the Officer Commanding Naval Party 8901,[8] when he visited us prior to deploying, any comfort over reinforcement in the event of Argentine aggression. We could only reinforce by sea with all the notice that that involved. C-130s could not, at that time fly direct from Ascension to Stanley.

Whatever might have been in Woodward's thoughts, a more effective method (at least, in principle) was now planted in the minds of those at Hereford and the Duke of York Barracks, Chelsea.

Meanwhile, the Prime Minister, confronted by the news of HMS *Sheffield*'s loss, drove to Fleet Headquarters at Northwood in Middlesex for a face-to-face briefing with the senior commanders. Robert Woodard recalls her presence in the Briefing Room, where she sat with Admiral Fieldhouse,[9] the Secretary of State for Defence, John Nott, and the Attorney General, Sir Michael Havers,[10] who was present to address Rules of Engagement.

Having listened intently to the report of the attack on *Sheffield*, Mrs Thatcher turned to Admiral Fieldhouse and asked, 'What is wrong with your destroyers that they are going to be hit by an Exocet for heaven's sake?'

Fieldhouse looked directly at the Prime Minister and, very carefully exercising his devastating, characteristic calm to the full, replied, 'Prime Minister you should not address that remark to me if I may say so. You really should turn to the gentleman on your left and ask him what happened to the letter from me that was on the top of his in-tray when he took over his job. In that letter I asked for the finances and backing for the new low-level capability to be fitted into the Sea Dart missile. That request was rejected. Had we had that extra capability this would not have happened.'

In the quiet that followed, the Commander-in-Chief continued, in case his audience was in any doubt, 'Sea Dart is an anti-aircraft missile that could have been equipped to take out an Exocet.'

The Prime Minister swung her penetrating gaze on to Mr Nott. 'Is this true?'
The Secretary of State muttered, 'I'll check, Prime Minister.'[11]

It was true.

Outside the briefing room, the Prime Minister and Admiral strode into Woodard's temporary office, which was 'so secret it was even beyond the Polaris Targeting Room!' Taking a leaf out of an illustrious predecessor's book, and mindful of a recent briefing by the Joint Intelligence Committee, Mrs Thatcher suggested, 'Surely the clue to all this is to destroy the Exocets before they can be fired off?'

'Quite so,' said Admiral Fieldhouse, then, turning to his Special Operations Coordinating Officer, he ordered, 'Devise a way! You may need to change your role. Start being more active.'

To Woodard, an ex-Buccaneer turned 'junglie' helicopter pilot, the solution should have been simple. Had the Buccaneer not been retired from naval service in 1978 with the demise of the 'old' *Ark Royal*, the Royal Navy would have had the almost perfect answer to such threats. Woodard's view remains unequivocal:

> If we had had a large, fixed-wing carrier we could have attacked anything that threatened us from the mainland. Anywhere in the world. But we didn't have a carrier with proper aeroplanes such as the Buccaneer that could do that. The Sea Harrier was not suitable as the carrier would have to come too close, into a dangerous position, to be able to achieve that. The range of a Buccaneer was four times the range of a Harrier. For instance, you could fly a Buccaneer 2,500 miles out and then back with refuelling, and we could have done that by using another Buccaneer as a tanker to meet them as they returned.
>
> So, attacking Rio Grande from the sea was a write-off. We could not have put our carriers in any form of risk for if we had lost air superiority in local spots we would have lost the war and that was always fully accepted.
>
> Those Buccaneers would have bombed the hell out of all the Argentine airfields and the Falklands war would have been over a damn sight earlier. They would have destroyed all the Exocets early on.

This all comes into the 'what if' category of sea-based air power, but it was a lesson that was being learned the hard way (and yet one that seems, once more, to have been forgotten, or simply ignored by the authors of the 2010 Strategic Defence and Security Review).

Captain Woodard may well have been ordered by the Commander-in-Chief to 'devise a way', but that way was already being devised, if still without a specific target. Now it was his task to coordinate the operation, especially ensuring that there would be no confliction with other operations being planned by those either in theatre or in the UK.

Ever since Squadron Leader Roberts had been invited to Hereford on 3 April the SAS had been 'desperate to get into the war'; an understandable desire but one that instantly led to a plethora of impractical schemes ranging from a full-scale air-land operation against Stanley airport to the parachuting of a small reconnaissance team into a remote plain (or flats) in East Falkland. While these ideas were being dreamed up by those with vivid imaginations and the need to 'perpetuate a myth',[12] it was equally clear that, hare-brained scheme or otherwise, the workhorses of the air transport world, the C-130 Hercules, would be involved. In the meantime, with no clear target, air-land operations continued to be practised and practised – and practised.

On 5 May the Joint Intelligence Committee began assessing the Exocet threat in greater detail than hitherto. Whether it liked it or not, the JIC came to the conclusion that, contrary to expectations and hopes, the Argentines had solved the technical complications of marrying up the missile to the aircraft without outside help. On one thing all were agreed: Rio Grande was the prime target, with, as Freedman has noted, various operational options being tossed around, most focussing on another Vulcan bombing raid, possibly mounted from the Chilean airport of San Felix. This depended on two major factors: Chilean approval and British legal endorsement. As neither could be guaranteed – for this was likely to stretch the loyalty of a 'privately friendly' country too far – thoughts therefore returned to a swift, clinical, special forces raid, the preferred choice of the charismatic Director of the Special Air Service, Brigadier Peter de la Billière.

Since 2 April de la Billière had been hammering away at those who would listen. Due not only to his appointment as Director but also to his personal reputation as a career-long, special forces officer with considerable front-line experience, everyone did listen – especially those at the highest levels. Thus it was no surprise that, following Mrs Thatcher's visit to his Headquarters, Admiral Fieldhouse ordered de la Billière to begin drawing up plans but to keep the Special Forces Coordinator very much 'in the picture'.

By 6 May an outline for what was to become Operation Mikado was already being discussed,[13] especially at a meeting held at Hereford the next day. Here, a collection of interested parties confirmed that there should be two reconnaissance patrols: one consisting of men from 6 Troop, B Squadron, 22 SAS against Rio Grande, and a second from 9 Troop to study Rio Gallegos. The intelligence feedback from these two exploratory expeditions would determine whether or not a full-scale assault was viable.

To look forward in time for a moment, it was not until 13 May that the Chief of the Defence Staff himself, Admiral Lewin, having received Cabinet approval, ordered detailed planning to go ahead. Taking advice from the senior SAS officers at the Duke of York Barracks, the Admiral directed that, as suggested, the operation be conducted in two stages, confirming what was, *de facto*, already being planned. The first phase, Plum Duff, was to be conducted by men based in the United Kingdom but using resources found from within the Task Force. The second phase, Mikado, would be launched *in toto* from the United Kingdom, staging through Ascension Island. The War Cabinet – unhappy about mainland operations but not wishing to stifle initiative – gave approval the next day for training to continue. The order to 'execute' either operation would be given, or not given, later.

Meanwhile, on 8 May another Mikado planning meeting was held at Hereford, again with representatives from the Special Operations Group; and, as so often with these meetings, outside factors kept breaking the surface to upset SAS plans.

The first was that, to most military planners, the ideal method – and one that was more in accord with the legal niceties than any other – of tackling a coastal air base was the use of Special Boat Squadron Royal Marines launched from a submarine close inshore on an 'in-and-out' raid. There were, though, two problems with this desirable option:[14] all the SBS were deployed and the only submarine suitable, HMS *Onyx*, a conventional diesel-electric boat, had yet to reach the South Atlantic. The fact that she had been dispatched at all was entirely due to the lobbying of Captain C, but she was not due to arrive in San Carlos until 31 May. Commodore Clapp and Brigadier Thompson both had asked for an 'O' boat to be sent south specifically for SBS insertions, but initially this had been refused by Northwood. She eventually sailed on 26 April. This late dispatch of a conventional submarine was an error not repeated in the Gulf War of 1991, when one 'O' class boat operated out of Diego Garcia with the SBS.

The second consideration was the use of a Task Force helicopter for Plum Duff. It was already assumed by the planners that any aircraft flown would not be able to return, thus denuding the overstretched troop-lift helicopter pool yet further with what might be described as a self-inflicted wound. Plans to launch the aircraft from Chilean waters in order that it could return would, again, have placed an unwarranted burden on relations with that country.

Nor was the Fleet Air Arm the SAS's favourite airline, because, without justification, Hereford, blamed the Royal Navy's pilots for 'bad airmanship' when attempting to rescue an SAS reconnaissance party from the Fortuna Glacier in South Georgia on 22 April 1982: two crashes were caused, 'apparently', by pilot error. This was insulting nonsense and ignored the emergency conditions under which the pilots had been required to salvage an avoidable incident. It was also a view not shared by the SAS in theatre, including those at South Georgia and, eventually, at Pebble Island, who came not only to rely wholly on the 'junglie' pilots but also to admire them for their navigational skills as well as their flying ability and courage.

Sir John Nott told the author that, 'When Operation Plum Duff was aborted the SAS command told me that they were furious, once again, with the Fleet Air Arm pilots for getting lost and thus causing the operation to fail.'[15] Sir John agreed that on the first occasion (Fortuna Glacier) the SAS had failed to see beyond their own decision-making and on the second (Operation Plum Duff) they were too quick to criticize others before learning the facts.

To begin with, de la Billière was not happy with the use of a helicopter (he had heard the erroneous rumours), believing that the word 'ditch' meant, literally, landing in the water and thus requiring his heavily laden men to swim ashore. In fact, to 'ditch' is aviator slang for landing or crashing on the water. This had never been in the plan; the word had been used in the wrong context.

At Hereford, as at Lyneham, there was no time to lose, for each day brought the renewed possibility of a second Exocet strike against the Task Force. An added fear was that replacement Exocets would be, even as the planners deliberated, finding their way to Argentina. Consequently, on 9 May Captain C and 22 SAS's Operations Officer, Major John Pearson, took part in a presentation on both operations at Hereford. Further meetings were held the next day, and by 11 May (two days before 'official' approval was received!) the full operational paper for Mikado was completed and presented at Hereford.

The RAF's Special Forces Flight, not kept fully 'in the picture' by Hereford and aware only of the possible need to conduct an air-land assault 'somewhere', were working flat out. By 11 May the air-to-air refuelling training was complete, and on the 14th Marshalls delivered the second 'converted' aircraft, XV179 (later to be tragically shot down over Iraq in January 2005 with the loss of all on board).

Already an experienced Qualified Flying Instructor and now with all of four flights and five hours experience under his belt, Roberts was nominated the first Hercules air-to-air refuelling instructor. Immediately he began teaching the art to other pilots within his Flight while forming what would become RAF Lyneham's Tanker Training Flight.

Another crucial figure now enters the saga. Prior to 1979, Squadron Leader Charlie Cartwright,[16] an RAF intelligence officer, was stationed at the Joint Air Reconnaissance Intelligence Centre within the National Imagery Exploitation Centre. This was part of the Joint Forces Intelligence Group inside the Department of Defence Intelligence and based at RAF Brampton in Cambridgeshire.[17] In November of that year he was posted to Headquarters 38 Group RAF at Upavon in Wiltshire as the Group Intelligence Officer (GIO) to the Air Officer Commanding the Group, Air Vice-Marshal Don Hall[18], and more specifically as the principal intelligence adviser to the Special Forces aircrew of 47 Squadron. In that position, Cartwright was witness to a number of pre-emptive (and prescient) command decisions: the extension of the hours allowed to be flown by the C-130 crews; additional pilots on the flight decks for extended sorties; and, as events hotted up, pressure on Marshalls to provide the air-to-air refuelling solutions. Cartwright was to be Operation Mikado's only source of real-time intelligence for the Flight, yet he was to become frustrated because no hard details on targets were ever available. No tactical detailed intelligence on Rio Grande was produced for either operation.

Part of Cartwright's task was to follow closely every Situation Report that was received from Rear Admiral Woodward and every Intelligence Report and Summary issued by Northwood. But as he said, 'After *Sheffield* was lost we felt rather helpless at Group Headquarters.' Needing to be 'on top of his game' and able to deal swiftly with the latest signals from the Communications Centre, Cartwright moved a safari bed into his office. That way he could guarantee that Air Vice-Marshal Hall received the most up-to-date information possible and in the most timely manner.

On 10 May, surprisingly unknown to Cartwright, further Operation Mikado discussions were under way at Hereford. While these (without RAF involvement) were deliberating the latest amendments to the plans, 38 Group's Intelligence Officer was warned by his Senior Air Staff Officer that he should expect a visit from a member of 22 SAS Regiment. Shortly afterwards, an RAF squadron leader presented himself in Cartwright's office to enquire what beach and landing ground information might be lurking in 38 Group's archives. To their joint surprise there was rather more on file than either was expecting and, as the RAF visitor left, 'a happy man', Cartwright prepared to walk to the officers' mess for lunch.

Then the telephone rang: 'It's the Air Officer Commanding's Personal Staff Officer here. He wants to see you immediately.'

In the 'boss's' office, where Cartwright's earlier visitor was also now sitting, his orders were unambivalent: 'Charlie, I want you to go south with these guys.'

Thrown into the campaign with little notice, Cartwright's next few days were 'chaotic'. On 13 May he flew by Chinook from Upavon to Lyneham. There he met, for the first time, Squadron Leader Max Roberts along with his navigator, Flight Lieutenant Dave Musgrave and Flight Lieutenant Nigel Watson, the co-pilot. A swift but necessarily broad-brush briefing by Roberts followed. They were, Cartwright was told, 'required to report to Task Force Headquarters for yet more briefings on a special forces mission to a destination somewhere in Argentina', and he had been assigned to help. More would be revealed at Northwood, to where they now flew. Preliminary discussions en route – as far as the noise inside the Chinook's cabin allowed – brought Cartwright up to date.

For Max Roberts and his crew events had gathered pace. Following several recent meetings about Mikado both at Hereford and Northwood, they had finally had their target confirmed as Rio Grande and had been given a satellite photograph of the airfield. From this small and indistinct image they could determine very little other than that, judging by the skid marks on the eastern threshold of the runway, most landings were conducted towards the west. From their exercises they knew that an overland approach to Rio Grande's runway would offer the best chance of avoiding radar detection; but doing so, they now knew, would almost certainly involve landing with a tailwind. However, on balance, that was probably the least risky option. Following the revelation of their target, the C-130 aircrew had already come up with a basic plan, which included, of necessity, an air-to-air refuelling, and had been ordered to report to Northwood to brief their intentions.

On arrival at Task Force Headquarters the officers were ushered directly in to the Air Commander's office. Air Marshal Sir John Curtiss, a Second World War veteran, needed personally to approve the plan that would take Roberts's aircraft to, in Curtiss' words, 'Ascension Island and beyond'. The airmen were told that a reconnaissance (no name was mentioned) would take place, following which, depending on the outcome, a decision on what he was calling Operation Mikado would be made. If the reconnaissance went well then Mikado would be executed as soon as the second Hercules, XV179, piloted by Max Roberts, arrived at Ascension Island on 19 May. No mention was made of any alternative plan, should the reconnaissance patrol encounter problems.

The Hercules aircrew were then invited to outline their ideas to the Air Marshal: two aircraft, XV179 with Roberts as the flight leader, and Burgoyne as his number two in XV200, would depart, when ordered, from Ascension Island and head for the east of the Falklands. Each aircraft would have its four internal Andover tanks removed and would conduct one formation air-to-air refuelling operation at a time and position to be decided. In place of the fuel tanks, two Pink Panthers and two Triumph motorcycles would be carried, plus about thirty men in each aircraft. The precise numbers would be confirmed with the SAS Squadron Commander at the time.

Because of the uncertainty of the navigational system, an electronic fix from a submarine would be needed at about the spot south-east of the islands that the aircraft would be turning towards a landfall in the region of Cabo San Diego. The last 200 or so nautical miles to the coast would be flown in darkness at 50 feet. Having coasted in, the two aircraft would maintain a 2,000-foot trail and route via the west end of Lago Fagnano, where the formation, using contour flying and radar masking, would turn north then east, ready to line up on Rio Grande's Runway 07.

Still in the 2,000-foot trail, the lead aircraft would touch down well into the 6,561-foot runway and stop 4,000 feet along it. Simultaneously, the second aircraft would land on the threshold and stop 2,000 feet behind the leader. The ramps would be lowered as at Laarbruch and Kinloss, and the SAS given twelve minutes to complete their task, a figure given by a member of the Special Operations Group Committee following his presence at Hullavington in September 1981 and subsequent discussions with the SAS.

With all back on board, less the vehicles, and burning the last of their fuel, the aircraft would take off to the east before turning for Punta Arenas in 'neutral' Chile. An alternative was to fly direct on to Runway 25 from over the sea, but that was denied to them because of the enemy's radar coverage. The reconnaissance patrol, it was assumed, would be briefed to study that possibility as well as many other vital aviation-related aspects.

That was the outline plan; but detailed planning would throw up a great many concerns.

Roberts, Musgrave, Watson and Cartwright were then joined by the Victor tanker flight commanders, and after some discussion this team felt ready to present their refuelling plan to the Air Commander.

The Air Marshal was not happy.

Although Roberts and Burgoyne were qualified in both day and night air-to-air refuelling, they had never done so in formation – their first time would be during the operation. Consequently, for safety reasons, Air Marshal Curtiss was insisting that the refuel must be in daylight. 'Take it away,' he demanded, 'and bring me another plan with that limitation firmly embedded within it.'

Shortly afterwards, they presented their new plan; the Air Marshal was happy.

Before returning to Lyneham and Upavon the team were, in Roberts's words, 'wheeled in to a very senior Royal Navy officer to discuss our request for a submarine to put up an aerial'. With their revised plan now accepted, and having had lunch, the officers expected to fly back to their respective homes. Instead, they were called to a meeting with ten members of 22 SAS. Security, always tight at Northwood, was even tighter, with access to the conference room guarded by an armed RAF policeman. As this area was 'above ground' and not 'down the hole', they were spared a search by armed Royal Marines.

When the four airmen entered the room they were surprised – astounded, even – to find themselves staring down at a large model of Rio Grande air base laid out across the floor; that is, the model showed what purported to be the air base's buildings, but – and this rendered it useless from their point of view – neither the runway nor its juxtaposition with the control tower were represented. Major John Moss, Officer Commanding B Squadron, was preparing to deliver an outline brief for what he, too, was calling Operation Mikado. Although the reconnaissance party for this operation was already on its way, no mention was made of Operation Plum Duff nor the fact that it was a fighting patrol also aimed at destroying the Super Étendards and their Exocets at Rio Grande 'if the opportunity presents itself'. This was extraordinary, for the Mikado aircrew would have wanted to ask vital questions of 6 Troop, concerning other air movements, state of the runway, airfield defences, wind strengths and directions, lights and so on.

Equally astonishing was the fact that had they not already been at Northwood to discuss air-to-air refuelling with the Air Commander they would not have been invited to the SAS briefing. With no prior discussion with the officers who would actually make the operation work, the SAS had planned a two-aircraft assault with the unofficial aim, as Moss explained, of 'wreaking mayhem, destroying as many Super Étendard aircraft and their Exocets as possible. Also seeking to kill as many pilots as possible who are believed to be located in the officers' mess.' The Israeli raid on Entebbe in 1976 was cited as a successful example of this type of operation, added to which the recent assaults on Laarbruch and Kinloss had, as far as the SAS were concerned, confirmed the possibility of success. Yet little or nothing had been sought from the experts for whom this was the first sight of their target. Entebbe (and Laarbruch and Kinloss) had indeed been successful, but ... the RAF contingent knew the differences, while the SAS seemed oblivious to them or were intent on overlooking them for fear that the operation would be cancelled. Clearly, all the RAF had to do was simply fly the troops to the airbase, and the SAS would then carry out the difficult bits; whereas in reality it would be the RAF that would face the lion's share of the risks and difficulties.

Towards the end of this briefing, the Director of the Special Air Service quietly joined the team (having driven from a Plum Duff meeting at Hereford) and sat at the back. When Moss had finished, the Brigadier stood and asked him if he was happy with the plan. 'Yes, sir, I am,' was the major's firm reply.

But the Royal Air Force officers were far from happy – not that they were invited to express an opinion. Charlie Cartwright was to comment, 'There were far too many questions screaming for answers but I was a guest and this was not my party.' He was suspicious about the accuracy of the model, while other inconsistencies preyed on his mind as well as those of his colleagues. There was a lack of 'tactical target intelligence' covering the ground and air defences, plus a complete absence of information on the land forces defending the air base. With the RAF unaware of Plum Duff, other vital factors which the SAS were apparently ignoring were the radar coverage protecting the surrounding air space and the likely weather conditions in the approaching austral winter. Of the utmost importance, no maps of any significance were produced.

'For such an audacious plan to have any chance of success far, far, too much intelligence was missing,' was, and remains, Cartwright's forthright view. Determined to offer as much as he could to his new colleagues, he then spent three days in London searching for relevant documents in the Ministry of Defence's Map Store, where 'there were some but of questionable value'. The Directorate of Military Survey had also been tasked with a similar search by the SAS. Cartwright drove, too, to the Joint Air Reconnaissance Intelligence Centre at RAF Brampton to collect a selection of enlarged satellite photographs of the target area. Unfortunately, these 30-square-inch, enlarged photographs taken by the United States Air Force's KH-9 satellites[19] of the possible target area were of such poor quality – and already out of date – that they had little tactical intelligence value. Nevertheless, as they were all that were available, the Squadron Leader took copies. Cartwright explains, 'We did use them to discuss an alternative attack option while we were at Ascension Island but trees and telegraph poles precluded such a possibility.[20] Other than that they served no useful purpose.'[21]

At that time there was considerable sensitivity surrounding the sharing of intelligence, particularly satellite imagery, between the United States and United Kingdom. In the US difficult political hurdles needed to be overcome by influential Anglophiles in Washington and the Pentagon in order to help as best they could. The relationship between Prime Minister Thatcher and President Reagan was a key motivator.

There were also physical difficulties in recovering film from the KH-8 and KH-9 satellites, with the associated delays in the processing, analysis and production of hard-copy prints and, where necessary, enlargements for the user. Additionally, the percentage daily cloud cover over Tierra del Fuego was high. United States KH-11 satellites had by now joined the constellation of imagery reconnaissance assets but, according to Cartwright:

> The data processing systems to convert their digital images to photographic hard copy still had a long way to go. To acquire images of the Falkland Islands and southern Argentina required changing the orbits of these satellites; orbits that, during the Cold War, were designed to collect images within the middle latitudes and thus of the Soviet Union, Eastern Europe and the Middle East. Our requirement was, in global terms, for a very minor scrap.

Certainly, any American cooperation, even with an old ally, needed careful consideration, for it could have had serious implications for that country's Cold War intelligence collection effort. As it happened, many of the pictures were of little value due to the delay in recovery, even before it was discovered that heavy cloud cover, poor scale and orbital constraints had usually taken their toll. Had any imagery of value been received there was also no electronic means of getting it to the user within a sensible timescale.

Squadron Leader Cartwright remains in no doubt that had good quality, up-to-date imagery reached the Commander-in-Chief at Northwood, the Admiral would have had no option but to cancel Operation Mikado before serious planning began. He explains:

> For instance, the earthworks visible on the 2005 commercial satellite imagery give testimony to the 1982 defences and categorically define the essential need for reliable and timely intelligence to support an operation like Mikado. That intelligence could only, effectively, have been obtained from an inserted reconnaissance team able to observe at close quarters and in real time, the defences, the movement of the aircraft, their missiles and the weather.

Cartwright's professional view was at the time, and remains, that he was offered hopelessly inadequate intelligence, even in the most basic of requirements such as mapping and imagery, with which to brief his crews. However, he was to state later:

> With hindsight it's easy to be critical but we were all caught up in the fever of war and were driven by the needs of the moment. No one ever had the full picture. It would be easy to criticize the military machine [for taking little or no interest in the South Atlantic] but frankly it was Her Majesty's Government and the Foreign Office ... with their South Atlantic policies and strategies – or lack of them – in the years before that were to blame.

Squadron Leader Roberts, whose two Hercules would be landing B Squadron at Rio Grande, remembers well the loose, almost naïve, planning that had accompanied the briefings:

> At the planning conferences much was made of this Entebbe thing, and forgive me for saying this, but sometimes our 'ground users' had a bent idea of our capability and how that transposed into what we could do compared with what they wanted us to do. Entebbe was not an airbase within a country at war. It was a civilian airport with a well-lit 10,000-foot runway and was approached by assaulting aircraft flying in as innocent a posture as possible, as though they were civilian aircraft following standard air traffic procedures until the last minutes. Nor was there any need to worry about surface-to-air missiles, enemy fighters, air-to-air refuelling over 4,000 miles or the certainty of air-defence radar based on land and at sea.

On 13 May the British Secret Intelligence Service received from mainland Argentina confirmation that the enemy now had just three Exocets left.[22] This tied in with the knowledge that Aérospatiale had only supplied five missiles before the start of the campaign; so with two expended against *Sheffield*, the subtraction sum was easy. According to Freedman, the technical advice was that the sea-launched version could not be converted to be air-launched. What was not expected was that it could be converted to be fired from the back of a lorry.

Over the night of the 14/15 May a successful SAS attack against the airfield on Pebble Island – launched from the sea by Fleet Air Arm helicopters with naval gunfire in support – gave the military and civilian planners in Hereford, Chelsea and Whitehall the confidence that a raid against mainland-based Exocets might be feasible. This vital destruction of so many counter-insurgency Pucara aircraft stationed just 22 nautical miles from the entrance to San Carlos Water so nearly did not take place. It only did so because Admiral Woodward, frustrated by delays with the 'advance party', ordered the attack to go ahead on the last possible night, despite the SAS's misgivings. The postponement that so aggravated the admiral was due to the reconnaissance party being landed, at their insistence, in the wrong place.[23] This is relevant because the poor standard of conventional military reconnaissance by the SAS, as formally noted by Major General Moore, was to be a recurring feature.

On the morning of 16 May three important players in the forthcoming operation landed at Northwood in a RAF Chinook. It had flown from RAF Upavon with Squadron Leader Cartwright embarked and had then collected Roberts and Musgrave from Lyneham. All were required to report to Task Force Headquarters for 'yet more briefings on Mikado', during which Roberts had been promised – but did not receive – more information. On 18 May a Chinook once again flew Cartwright from Upavon to Lyneham to collect Roberts and Musgrave; yet at Hereford there was still no mention of Operation Plum Duff. The 'bubbles of security' were being drawn too tight, with no one appreciating that the outcome of that operation was fundamental to RAF plans for the second phase. Nor was there any of the promised intelligence other than a vague suggestion that it would be forthcoming at Ascension Island.

Unannounced to the Special Forces Flight personnel, the SAS were hoping that 6 Troop's incursion towards Rio Grande, which had begun shortly after midnight (local time in Patagonia) that morning, was about to bear fruit. No one had briefed the most important intelligence officer of them all that this was underway; had they done so, Cartwright would have tasked the patrol commander with answering some very specific questions to help him advise the C-130 aircrews on the conditions at Rio Grande: geographical, military, climatic and, vitally, defensive. Had Cartwright been within the SAS's security bubble, as he should have been, he might have known that on that same day, 18 May, the Plum Duff patrol had not been landed close to Rio Grande in Argentina but some 75 miles to the west on the shore of Bahí Inútil.

One day later, on 19 May 1982, Cartwright flew to Ascension Island in Hercules XV179 piloted by Max Roberts.

* * *

The day before, Reuters had reported (repeated by, among others, the *Daily Express*) that seven British men had been captured at Rio Gallegos. This was followed by a similar report in a Buenos Aires morning newspaper, only for all reports to be then denied by the Argentine V Corps (causing the suspicious *Daily Express* to conjecture that the Junta had something to hide). It was also the day that the War Cabinet gave approval for the landings at San Carlos and the evening when a Sea King ditched in the South Atlantic with the loss of twenty-two personnel, mostly from D and G Squadrons, 22 SAS.

In Chile, after lying up all that same day, the Plum Duff patrol commander sent out a recce party to establish his position before deciding to continue eastwards towards the border with Argentina. At Headquarters SAS in Chelsea the belief was that the patrol had been captured.

In Rio Grande a blackout was imposed from 19 May onwards, with all civilian vehicles required to show only sidelights or, as infrequently as possible, dipped headlights.

Chapter 8

Ascension Island

On the otherwise sleepy Ascension Island things were also beginning to stir. Slowly at first, perhaps ...

From the British point of view, the campaign to regain the Falkland Islands would not have been possible without this convenient halfway halt, logistic hub and forward mounting base for operations in the South Atlantic. South of the Equator by 476 miles, at 7° 56′ S, 14° 22′ W, the island is marginally closer to the Falkland Islands than to Great Britain and is the tip of a seamount that rises from the ocean floor, about 14,000 feet below, to 2,818 feet above sea level. Barren and rocky, with little vegetation, it lies close to the divide between the doldrums and the south-east trades. The highest peak, Green Mountain, is aptly named, for it is only on its upper slopes that vegetation is found in any profusion. This elongated cone is the extinct remains of a comparatively young volcano; there are traces of at least another forty, possibly more, smaller eruptions. The island covers 35 square miles and has no indigenous population. In 2010, its five settlements contained 880 people, of whom 696 were from St Helena, about 700 nautical miles to the south-east. The island is richer in fauna than flora, at least at the lower levels, with a number of animals having been introduced over the years for obvious reasons: rabbits, wild goats and partridges formed a staple diet in earlier days. Green turtles land between December and May to lay their eggs, while the island is a breeding ground for sooty terns, known locally as 'wideawake birds' for their raucous dawn chorus.

Ascension's 'tropical maritime climate' is kept to a reasonably comfortable 68° to 88° Fahrenheit (20° to 31° Celsius) at sea level by the wind, predominantly south-easterly, that often blows at a good Force 5 for prolonged periods. Showers, sometimes violent, with near-zero visibility and unpleasantly mixed with volcanic dust, occur throughout the year, although they are heaviest between January and April.

The Portuguese were the first to sight the uninhabited island in 1501, but the second formally recorded sighting by another Portuguese sailor, Alfonso d'Albuquerque, on Ascension Day in 1503 gave it its name. It was not until 1815 that a British garrison was established, to guard against any French attempt to spring Napoleon from his confinement on St Helena. In October of that year the island was officially claimed in the name of his Britannic Majesty King George III, from which time it grew in usefulness as a 'victualling station' (what might today be called a forward logistics base) for His Majesty's ships of the West African Squadron employed against the slavers sailing between West Africa and the West Indies. Throughout this time a detachment of Royal Marines was based on the

Island as many graves in Georgetown's Garrison Church still testify. As the verses well known to all Royal Marines have it:

> Spent empties flung aside upon the dust heaps of the World,
> Who strew the tracks wherever Britain's flag has been unfurled,
> Lone stragglers from the colours who have long stepped out of time ...[1]

On the advent of the Second World War a radio station was established on the island, and once America had joined the war, an airstrip was constructed to support flights between the US, North Africa and southern Europe. The runway was named, imaginatively, Wideawake, after the sooty tern. After 1945 this runway fell into disrepair until the Americans reopened it in 1957, before widening and lengthening it in the mid-1960s to a smidgen over 10,000 feet, with a very large dispersal area. The US Air Force and then the National Aeronautics and Space Administration established a missile tracking base at Wideawake, with the latter organization also prepared to use it as an emergency landing site for the space shuttle.

The British use of Ascension Island in 1982 was not to be without many difficulties, and as far as this tale is concerned they were to centre round accommodation, food and water for both the C-130 crews and the SAS's B Squadron. These will be described in due course, but the additional problem of aviation fuel was an interesting one and went back many years.

All bulk aviation fuel was, at the beginning of Operation Corporate, stored in a 'fuel farm' outside the island's capital of Georgetown, some 5 miles from Wideawake. This depot was supplied by United States Sealift Command tankers pumping aviation fuel ashore through a floating pipeline.

On 9 April 1979 Lieutenant Colonel Richard Preston,[2] with Group Captain Mike Lee of 38 Group RAF and Lieutenant Colonel Nigel Winter of the 11th Hussars[3] from the UK Commander-in-Chief's Committee, had visited Ascension Island. Their mission was to draw up plans for the extraction of 130,000 British 'belongers' (as the Foreign Office called them) from Rhodesia if the then insurgency in that country deteriorated into a breakdown of law and order. The team found that there would need to be an increase in aviation fuel storage, while the capacity of the pipeline that carried the fuel from the anchorage to the airfield would also need to be enhanced. A second consideration was an expansion of aircrew accommodation. Both were addressed by the Americans, who, when Preston later visited the Pentagon and State Department, offered to supply extra Hercules and even C5 Galaxies should the worst occur.

In 1982 Group Captain Ron Dick[4] was the British Air Attaché in Washington and thus the direct 'air' link with many of the US forces that could, should they so wish, offer help. At the very beginning of the British operations Dick was ushered into the office of the American admiral responsible for logistics. He, Dick, explained that the Task Force would need to use Ascension Island as the primary mounting base for operations against the Falkland Islands. While Wideawake was a United States airfield on lease from the United Kingdom, the Group Captain felt that the US would not object to any increase in British use.[5] The conversation eventually turned to fuel, and while there was enough for most 'normal contingencies' including, it was hoped by the British, the earlier requirement for the evacuation of 'ex-pats' from Rhodesia, there was clearly not going to be enough with which to go to war.[6]

The Group Captain was asked how much he thought his colleagues would need. His answer was, 'An eight-million gallon oil tanker full of jet fuel off the Georgetown settlement within the next seven days, please!'

The admiral asked if they would need to supply any more.

'We will need a similar tanker seven days after the first and then another in seven more days and so on.'

'You can't use that much fuel!'

'We are going to try,' answered the Group Captain.

In due course, a 'can do' response from the United States allowed materiel such as AIM-9L Sidewinders to be delivered to the Task Force. Almost as important – at least to those who would be stationed at or were passing through Ascension Island – collapsible 'Concertina City' accommodation modules complete with kitchens also found their way to Wideawake.

But there remained near-insuperable problems that simply had to be overcome if the number of military personnel required to be based on the island were to survive. The first major concern was fresh water. With no natural water source apart from a few streams, and with the two distillation plants having a finite production capacity unable to satisfy the swiftly growing number of service men and women while maintaining a ten-week store in reserve, water rationing was imposed very early on and strictly monitored. Eventually, the situation was partially relieved by the arrival, by air, of reverse osmosis plants.

While the initial limited water supply could sustain 2,800 souls, there was only 'roofed accommodation' for 700. This was increased to 1500 by overcrowding, using all available buildings and, inevitably, erecting tents. At Two Boats Village, halfway up the western slopes of Green Mountain, and about to become the primary base for the RAF and SAS personnel involved in Operations Plum Duff and Mikado, a British army field kitchen eventually eased the pressure on food supply. There was little that could be done to increase the sewage capacity.

Two Boats Village is named after two ship's boats that were placed upright in the ground in the nineteenth century to provide shade for members of the Royal Marines garrison when they collected water. The camp on the western slopes of Green Mountain is about 3½ miles from the airfield as the wideawake bird flies, but considerably further by road. It was to be a popular 'dormitory village', for not only was it away from the incessant noise of aircraft movements but, at 700 to 800 feet above sea level, it enjoyed a near-constant five to ten knots of cooling breeze. Much appreciated as these advantages were, sleep at night without air conditioning was often difficult because of the prevalent temperature at that altitude, between 70° and 80° Fahrenheit (21° to 27° Celsius), coupled with high humidity.

This, then, was the island from which two British special forces attempts to destroy the Exocet, the sea-skimming missile which posed the greatest threat to the Task Force at sea, would – or would not – be launched.

In 1982 the island was a pressure cooker: a mix of urgent operational readiness with round-the-clock aircraft movements and an equally urgent 24-hour juggling of logistics – receipt, sorting, dispatch and storage for future use. With over 150,000 signals (three quarters of which should have been, but were not, 'routine') received by the understaffed logisticians, there was not often much room for humour. One example survives, however, to show that all was not lost. Early on, a priority call was received from an unnamed Special Forces unit for twelve knives. For one irate supply officer this simple request was one too many. He demanded to know why such a small order for such an everyday item deserved his 'immediate' attention. The reply was equally swift and apologetic, for the SBS unit concerned was sailing that night for the south: 'Reference request for 12 knives. These are knives, stabbing, not knives, eating!' The request was met with alacrity.

On Ascension Island the opening phases of the two operations to snuff out the Exocet threat began on 12 May with the arrival at Wideawake airfield in a VC 10 of the Hercules aircrew who would transport the Plum Duff reconnaissance patrol the 3,400 nautical miles of the first phase of their 'approach to battle'.

Harry Burgoyne's Hercules XV200 was delivered to the island by a regular, non-Special Forces Flight, C-130 crew. The procedure for the Ascension Island 'slip pattern' was for a crew to fly an aircraft from Lyneham to Dakar in Senegal, from where a fresh crew would fly to Ascension Island and return without refuelling at Wideawake. A third crew would fly the Hercules back to Lyneham. This allowed the aircraft to travel from Lyneham to Ascension and back in about thirty hours, but the crews could take up to a week to complete the journey. As Burgoyne's team were needed at Ascension Island as soon as possible, they were left out of the slip pattern, flying direct to Ascension Island. The crew that flew XV200 to Ascension returned in the back of the next Hercules to Dakar, where, in Burgoyne's words, 'more sun, sailing and beer awaited them'.

The crew of XV200 were themselves not short of sun and beer, but the closest they came to sailing was the name of the place in which they were now billeted: Two Boats Village. Better than a tent at sea level alongside Wideawake's noisy runway, the crews' accommodation was a 'Twynham hut' at the top of the settlement. Next to the football pitch, this single building they would call home for the next weeks was divided into a sitting room, a kitchen with 'rudimentary cooking arrangements' and a fridge, two non-air-conditioned bedrooms, one lavatory and one bathroom (with a shower but no bath). When Burgoyne arrived on 12 May two Special Forces Flight crews, Norfolk's and Crosby's, were already *in situ*: so now there were fifteen men 'living in'. In time, the permanent total would rise to seventeen.

Harry Burgoyne remembers it well:

It was terribly cramped, with only four single beds, two in each tiny bedroom, for up to a possible maximum of twenty-two temporary personnel. Priority allocation of the beds was in a strict order of need. First call was for crews resting prior to flying. The next priority was for crews returning from flying and the third priority was for anyone if there was an opportunity. Most people slept on the floor in the main lounge, out in the garden or in the garage. It wasn't too bad compared with the noisy airhead or the American domestic site.

After his arrival Charlie Cartwright would confirm Burgoyne's recollections:

Spot on, but I slept, and preferred it, outside near the back door under a plastic corrugated roof on a safari camp bed. Quite comfortable. My 'office' was up the hill past the soccer pitch at the Cable & Wireless satellite communications 'facility'. This was about 700 yards from our bungalow with B Squadron's communications centre also within this secure area.

There is no doubt now, and there was even less doubt at the time, that the RAF's accommodation was far from satisfactory for crews involved 'watch and watch about' in such long-distance and stressful flights. It is also a truism that the other services have often envied the RAF's ability to make themselves comfortable (sometimes, it is claimed, far more than is necessary) wherever they are in the world, but in this instance there was no such luxury. 'But then,' as Burgoyne recounts, 'most of the time we were flying. I sometimes felt that I probably slept better on the aeroplane than I did at Two Boats.'

Early on the morning of 15 May, his third day at Ascension, Harry Burgoyne had queued for the only bathroom. Refreshed, he joined his crew as they cooked a light breakfast in the rudimentary kitchen. Sunbathing and 'bluey-writing'[7] followed, while they waited for their first task. At 1100 someone switched on the bungalow's wireless for the daily 'briefing' by the BBC.

As the opening bars of the World Service's 'Lilliburlero' were playing, Burgoyne's robust sense of humour took a knock when Flight Lieutenant Pat Fitzgerald,[8] one of two officers in 38 Group's Air Transport Detachment, arrived at Two Boats clutching a Top Secret signal, headed 'For the eyes of Flight Lieutenant Burgoyne only'. This was the officer's first surprise, for he had never seen anything so secret in his career, but before that astonishment wore off he received another shock as the opening words stared at him: 'You are to conduct a one-way mission…'

Burgoyne's immediate reaction was that Mikado was 'on' and that whoever had sent the signal did not expect his crew to survive. However, further reading revealed that this was, in fact, a 'warning order' for the Bombilla insertion and that it would be mounted from Ascension Island. There was no date for the operation, nor was the final destination after the drop detailed, but it was noticeable that it would not be Wideawake. The originator of this signal is now unknown, but its author was clearly unaware of other operations being planned from Ascension Island and, equally clearly, was not working through the Commander-in-Chief's Special Operations Coordinator at Northwood, Captain Robert Woodard.

Later that day, at 1400, the telephone rang in the RAF's 'sitting room'. Burgoyne's crew were to report to the airhead operations tent, where Squadron Leader Nick Hudson, the Air Transport Detachment commander on the island, was waiting to brief them. Twenty minutes later, the captain and his crew were informed that they were definitely on a task but it was not to be a one-way mission. Burgoyne's orders, relayed from Joint Headquarters, Northwood via Hudson, were to prepare XV200 for a parachute drop of eight SAS troopers from 6 Troop, due to arrive after tea that evening, plus two containers, into the sea 60 nautical miles north of Stanley. The drop would be alongside the 23,000-ton Royal Fleet Auxiliary supply ship *Fort Austin* and was scheduled for mid-afternoon the following day. As the estimated flight time to the Drop Zone would be almost thirteen hours, take-off would have to be in about twelve hours. Time was suddenly very short indeed. Preparations began immediately.

XV200 was the first C-130 to be fitted for air-to-air refuelling. Now she needed yet more love, care and attention, but at Wideawake the RAF's over-stretched ground crew of just six Hercules engineers, aided by a small team from the RAF's Mobile Air Movements Squadron, were working every hour unloading and refuelling a steady stream of transiting aircraft and could not be spared for other tasks; it was up to the Special Forces Flight aircrew to prepare their own aircraft.

The aircraft's six internal wing tanks, plus the two external fuel tanks beneath each wing, had to be filled to their brims, while the four cylindrical fuel tanks cannibalized from the Andover fleet and now fitted into the cargo bay also needed filling to their maximum of 28,000lb of fuel. As the Andover tanks could not be refuelled in the air they would be used purely for the return journey. The air-craft's own tanks would be refilled just once, air-to-air, on the outward leg of the mission. Flying a Hercules almost 6,800 nautical miles to and from the Falkland Islands had never been attempted before and was now about to be conducted, for the first time, during an actual operation.

When they were delivered to the aircraft, 6 Troop's two 500-pound boxes would be rigged for parachuting and, as the Andover tanks took up most of the cargo space, positioned on the ramp itself. The 'knock-on' effect was that the primitive Elsan chemical loo – without which Burgoyne's Commanding Officer would not fly – had been shifted from its normal position on the port side of the ramp to the centre of the freight bay between the forward and aft pairs of tanks. Unfortunately, the privacy screens that surrounded this very public convenience could not be moved.

While XV200 was being 'made ready for action' the flight deck crew were busy with their broad-brush sums and calculations. Detailed planning would not be completed until two hours before take-off. By 1730 all preparations were complete, with the exception of the essential air-to-air refuelling plan. Most of the Victors were airborne, supporting a lone Nimrod returning from a Maritime Radar Reconnaissance flight of over nineteen hours, so there was no way of knowing how many tankers would be available for the Hercules task. Navigator Jim Cunningham remained in the 'air-to-air cell', ready to complete his calculations once the tankers were back on the ground. Satisfied that in all other respects XV200 was ready for flight, the rest of the crew returned to Two Boats for a few hours' rest.

Seven hours later, back at the airfield, Burgoyne and his team rushed through an intelligence brief before entering the flight-planning tent, where they rejoined Cunningham, who had completed his sums just forty minutes earlier.

Lockheed, the aircraft's manufacturers, gave an 'absolute maximum certificated safe take-off weight' for the C-130 of 175,000lb; beyond that, 'they would offer no guarantee that the wings would stay on'. This evening, the weight would be 181,000lb, over 2½ tons heavier than the maximum allowed and well off the graphs in the C-130 Performance Manual. Flight Lieutenant Jim Norfolk, flying with Burgoyne as an augmentee pilot, had already flown several long-distance, non-air-to-air refuelling sorties to the Task Force. Used to operating the Hercules at such heavy weights, his experience enabled Burgoyne to interpret the figures and estimate the take-off speeds. At 10,000 feet, Wideawake's runway length was not a factor, but if an engine failed immediately after take-off it was clear that, at that weight, a crash landing was inevitable and that there would be nothing Burgoyne could do about it. In his words, 'The remaining three engines would simply be taking us to the scene of the accident!'

Chapter 9

Operation Plum Duff – Phase One: Hereford and the Mid-Atlantic

At 0500 GMT on 15 May thick grey cloud masked the sky over Hereford. Despite its being the middle of May and shortly before sunrise, there was a chill in the air. 'Good, let's get acclimatised early', thought Captain Andy L as the other seven members of 6 Troop, B Squadron, 22 SAS Regiment began loading their equipment into the back of a 4-ton military lorry. 'It'll be a bloody sight colder where we're going ...'

The usual black-humour teasing between such hardened men – well used to early morning starts before an operation – was missing. The mood among the troopers was uncharacteristically bleak, reflecting, perhaps, the uncertainties that were enveloping their latest mission – and they had not even left Bradbury Lines. Had he been asked, Captain L would have admitted that for the first time in his brief military career he had misgivings.

The SAS Captain, who up to now had operated mostly under the wing of his Squadron Commander in the dust and heat of Oman, the salty, sticky breezes of the Musandam Peninsula and the jungle humidity of Belize, was being tasked not only to carry out a preliminary reconnaissance of Rio Grande airfield but, if the opportunity arose, to execute an attack itself. By any stretch of the imagination it was a tall order, and made taller by the lack of military intelligence, coherent maps and proper briefings. Preparations had been scant, hindered by 'the command' having no knowledge of how the troop would be inserted on to the mainland. Confusingly, Captain L's Brigadier had revealed the possibility of three very different choices: a submarine, a fast patrol boat or a helicopter. All would be revealed, the senior officer had stated, at Ascension Island.

Yet it was clear, even to the young Captain, that the SAS's 'in-house' advisers had not given the task the depth of study it deserved, for even he could guess that there were no conventional submarines yet in theatre, nor would there ever be helicopters to spare. The Royal Navy had not possessed fast patrol craft since the 1960s, and anyway the distances and the almost certainly prevailing sea state would have made their use implausible if not downright impossible. The only certainty to the venture was that Argentina had entered the conflict with five air-launched Exocets, each one of which was more than capable of seriously wounding, if not sinking, a capital ship. Ten days earlier the Argentines had demonstrated that potency by launching two and sinking HMS *Sheffield*, admittedly a comparatively small Type 42 destroyer. That left three Exocets ...

B Squadron's Sergeant Major, John F, was also standing by the 4-tonner. He was a highly regarded and very experienced man with a good sense of humour, who, when the going was awkward, would always raise the men's spirits. His repartee might have been welcome that morning, but John F's abnormally gloomy features, clearly in empathy with those of his men to whom he was bidding fare-well, were ominous.

'Listen, boss,' he quietly reassured his young Troop Commander, 'This is going to be a bit sticky. Take it steady, move slowly at first and have a good look around before you do anything. You will have to gather your own intelligence as you go.'

Captain L knew well that 'intelligence' for his mission did not exist, and this had been his foremost worry since 4 April when his Squadron Commander, Major John Moss, had first mooted the vague idea of the whole of B Squadron playing a part, somewhere near the coast in the deep south of Patagonia. Captain Andy L had been called into his Squadron Commander's office on that day along with the other officers. It had been a Sunday morning, and while all in 22 SAS were aware that the Falkland Islands had been invaded, few knew quite where, or even how, the SAS could fit in to any response. The islands were a long way away, and the news filtering out of the Ministry of Defence suggested that there was not much the Army or RAF could, or would, do.

Andy L's squadron had been heading for Canada on the morrow, and so the Major's summons was most probably to issue some last minute travel amend-ments ... but hanging on the Squadron Commander's wall was not a 'land map' of the vast Suffield live-firing training area in Alberta favoured by the British army, but an aeronautical 'chart' of the very furthest extremity of South America: Tierra del Fuego.

Moss was characteristically direct: 22 SAS Regiment would be involved. D Squadron under the command of Cedric Delves[1] and G with Euan Houston[2] were preparing to move – although Headquarters, Commando Forces had only asked for G Squadron.Unknown to Headquarters Commando Forces, Royal Marines, until too late, Delves had been ordered by his own commanding officer to take his squadron to Portsmouth and then on to any ship heading south. Full marks for initiative, but ...

A squadron would remain in the United Kingdom as the counter-terrorist unit. That left B Squadron, who, the major explained enigmatically, would play its part by remaining in readiness 'to address possible problems on the Argentine mainland'. Knowing only that they would not be caught up in the frantic packing that was taking place, B Squadron's officers feared the worst, expecting merely to be kept in reserve – talk of mainland operations being a soft-soap palliative to ease their disappointment.

Following Moss's briefing, B Squadron's collective heads were scratched vigor-ously. 'What, precisely, was meant by the mainland?' Allowing for the lack of knowledge at that stage in the campaign, it was easy to conjure up images of attacking airbases. It was what the regiment, which traced its origins back to the North African campaign of 1941, had been formed to do by its founder, David Stirling.[3] Even with a limited store of facts and a small-scale map, fertile minds were already considering the difficulties of approaching any Argentine military complex from the east, the sea. Thoughts turned to cross-border operations from the west, overland. By and large, Andy L felt relatively at ease with that idea, even though, at first glance, the distances to cover on foot in the austral autumn would be formidable.

Shortly, plans became clearer, in outline if not in detail. Captain L was taken aside and told that he would be leading one of two four-man patrols that would, by some unrevealed means, be landed to conduct reconnaissance operations against the two air bases from where Exocet-armed Super Étendard aircraft were believed to be operating: Rio Grande on the east coast of Tierra del Fuego and Rio Gallegos 142 nautical miles further north.

Depending on his and the other patrol commander's report, the dual reconnaissance missions would lead to direct action conducted later by the remainder of B Squadron. This assault would involve two 'or more' Hercules from the RAF's Special Forces Flight. So far so good, but for some unexplained reason the two patrols were kept in isolation from each other ... thus there were no opportunities to bounce ideas backwards and forwards.

Then the plan changed. Twice. On 4 May HMS *Sheffield* was struck by one of two Exocets launched by Super Étendards flying out of Rio Grande. With firm confirmation that the aircraft were not based at Rio Gallegos, the two reconnaissance patrols were merged into one eight-man fighting patrol to be led by Captain Andy L of 6 Troop against a single target: Rio Grande. Although reconnaissance was to remain the prime mission, Captain L was now to be prepared to carry out an assault if the opportunity arose. This second and most significant alteration was caused by the dawning realization in Hereford and Chelsea that any subsequent large-scale assault was unlikely to be sanctioned by the War Cabinet. As will be seen, this realization would not stop the SAS planning for Operation Mikado.

If the SAS wanted to 'make their own bang in the South Atlantic' it would have to be detonated by 6 Troop and not the whole of B Squadron. Captain L's men would be re-equipped accordingly. 'Good', he had thought, but that initial positive opinion dimmed the moment he saw the quality of the two maps with which he was expected to plan and operate. Those views were to darken further when he listened to the formal 'Orders', or 'O' Group, delivered by the Director of the Special Air Service himself just the day before departure.

The Squadron Sergeant Major decided to lighten the situation: 'You guys are really the lucky ones, think of the rest of us stuck inside a C-130 while the missiles are slamming into it!' Then, tellingly, he added, 'Believe me, you've got the better deal.'

Captain L grinned, but without conviction. Under normal circumstances he felt comfortable with his men no matter what was being placed in front of them, but the isolation of the 'task' that now faced him was fomenting a growing disquiet in his mind; and frankly, the Squadron Sergeant Major wasn't helping. He knew, too, that outwardly John F might have tried to appear sanguine about the main operation, Mikado, but deep inside he unquestionably shared the views of the other senior non-commissioned officers. From early on most of the

Regiment's SNCOs were openly suggesting, 'This is ridiculous. They are not even asking us if it is possible or not. Usually you get the old and bold being asked for their opinion. This time they are just telling us to do it.'

Similarly, Andy L believed that if the Squadron Sergeant Major had been placed 'on the rack' that day he might even have said something along the lines of, 'This is not a good option. Not a good option at all. When will they realize that this is not Entebbe.'

'The trouble was', Andy L explained later, 'one or two people, politicians and senior officers, thought that Entebbe was an appropriate model. If the Israelis can do it at Entebbe then the SAS can bloody well do it in Argentina.'

Over the preceding weeks 6 Troop had trained enthusiastically, but somehow the young Captain did not feel as energetic or as passionate for the task as he should have, and that added an uncomfortable guilt to his considerable unease. Neither he nor his men knew quite what they were training for. The standing joke among 'the boys' – every one of whom was older than he, although none was taller than his 6 feet 6 inches – was that not one of the team who had dreamed up Operations Plum Duff and Mikado at Hereford and the Duke of York Barracks, Chelsea, would be involved. In most Special Forces operations those taking part had a substantial say in the planning, in assessing the risks and options and in discussing the methods of recovery. Not this time.

The previous night, thanks to these thoughts eating away at his mind, Captain L had slept badly. Now, as he loaded his overweight bergen into the back of the 4-tonner, he felt weary. Yet he knew that it was time to go, time to stop fretting, time to say goodbye and time to get on with the job. 'Who dares . . .' and all that. He turned, shook hands with the Squadron Sergeant Major, muttered a brief farewell and climbed up to join the rest of his patrol, seven men similarly dressed in unobtrusive civilian clothes and soft-soled trainers.

Formal orders for the patrol had revealed little new to supplement the trickle of information with which they had been fed over the days. Up to that point Captain L had felt certain – or had at least hoped – that somewhere a degree of common sense would be gestating. He was to be disappointed.

There was a reason for Captain L's unease. The original intention had been for 6 Troop to conduct one of the two patrols in order to determine the location of enemy aircraft at, in his case, Rio Grande, and discover the strength of the forces protecting them, as a precursor to an air-land attack. Then it was decided that the intelligence gained by an augmented 6 Troop, only targeting Rio Grande, would be used by the rest of the Squadron to, in descending order of priority, kill the pilots, destroy the aircraft and their missiles and, if time permitted, kill the maintenance teams. While that 'final' plan remained extant it would only be carried out if the newly enlarged patrol itself was unable to attack. In anticipation that the chance would present itself, 6 Troop was now carrying explosives and timing devices, but at the expense of food and suitable clothing for Patagonia's autumn. As a result, the patrol was not equipped for a long term reconnaissance; with just four days of food, it was only fit for a swift, in-and-out, direct-action operation.

As he entered the briefing room, the Brigadier had looked around, intent on catching everyone's eye and gaining their attention. He stood up to the lectern. 'These are your orders. You are all no doubt aware of the fragility of the Task Force's position and what might happen should one of our aircraft carriers be lost.' Everyone nodded hesitantly. 'Your mission is to identify the location of the enemy aircraft and, if possible, destroy them.'

If there had been doubt before, there was none now. It was to be a 'seek and destroy' operation. 'You will leave here at 0500 hours tomorrow for RAF Brize Norton. From there you will fly to Ascension Island via Dakar where your VC 10 will be refuelled.'

Captain L tried to recall his geography. Dakar? West coast of Africa? That must be the one.

'Your equipment will be transported separately to Ascension Island, while you travel in civilian clothes. There you will change into uniform for the remainder of the mission. No badges of rank. No regimental insignia.'

Without appearing to pause for breath, the Brigadier outlined the next stage. 'From Ascension Island you will fly in a C-130, specially equipped with long range fuel tanks, to a Royal Fleet Auxiliary vessel off the Falklands. Approaching the Drop Zone the aircrew will determine whether conditions and enemy air activity are suitable for the drop. If not you will return to Ascension and try again another day.'

'Oh no we won't', thought the Captain.

'If you do parachute I'm advised you will need wet suits. The water is quite cold.'

Captain L sensed those around him trying to guess at the water temperature.

'You will be picked up and transferred to an aircraft carrier. Most likely HMS *Hermes*.'

The Brigadier hesitated, looking for a reaction; seeing none, he went on, 'There are a number of options to get you from *Hermes* to the mainland. The first is a Sea King, but there are several difficulties with this approach, not least of which is that its range means it will be a one-way trip.'

Captain L's immediate but unspoken query was, 'Will they really waste a helicopter and aircrew on an option with such a limited chance of success?' Accepting the scarcity of Sea Kings, and given the unarguable fact that helicopters 'make a fair bit of noise', he knew that there could be a danger of them all ending up in the wrong place having attracted masses of the wrong sort of attention.

'Moving on to the second and third possible methods,' continued the Brigadier. 'We transfer you to a submarine or a fast patrol boat, from where you will move into a position just off the coast and be taken to the mainland in inflatable craft.'

The Brigadier had mentioned 'a number of options', so what were the others? The eight members of 6 Troop waited. While Headquarters SAS may not have had other ideas, the patrol leader certainly did. 'The people doing the job,' he wanted to say, 'would all agree that, given the uncertainty, the better option would be to infiltrate across the border from the west.' It was clear to every

'Where exactly are the Falkland Islands?' The command team at Northwood, left to right: Vice Admiral Peter Herbert, Major General Jeremy Moore, Admiral Sir John Fieldhouse, Vice Admiral David Halifax, Air Marshal John Curtiss, Rear Admiral 'Spam' Hammersley. (*MOD*)

'Where exactly are Las Malvinas?' The command team at Rio Grande. (*Miguel Pita*)

Arming Super Étendard 204 with an Exocet. (*Santiago Rivas*)

Five Super Étendards at Espora air base prior to deploying south to Rio Grande. (*Santiago Rivas*)

uper Étendard 201 in the hold of ARA *Cabo de Hornos*. (*Roberto Curilovic*)

uper Étendard 202 refuelling en route for the Task Force on 30 May. Note the four Skyhawks ehind. (*Santiago Rivas*)

HMS *Sheffield*'s starboard side showing the Exocet's entry point. (*MOD*)

MV *Atlantic Conveyor*'s port quarter following a double Exocet strike. (*MOD*)

Hercules XV179 and XV200 at Wideawake airfield waiting for Operation Mikado. A re moment when they were on the ground together. (*Max Roberts*)

Co-pilot's view of air-to-air refuelling during Operation Plum Duff. (*Harry Burgoyne*)

Hercules XV200 fitted with four internal fuel tanks for Operation Plum Duff. (*Max Roberts*)

Hercules landing on USS *Forrestal* in 1963.
(*United States Navy*)

'Waterproofed' cardboard container similar to the ones used by 6 Troop on Operation Plum Duff. (*MOD*)

Sea King Victor Charlie flying over Royal Naval Air Station, Yeovilton before the conflict.
(*Alan Bennett*)

(*Top left*) Rio Grande's Runway 07 threshold and its defences. (*Top right*) North side of Rio Grande airbase showing the weapons storage site and the extra accommodation area known as *polverines*. (*Bottom left*) South side of Rio Grande airbase. 1, 2 and 3 are modern hangars plus three light aircraft. 4 is the power plant. The two entrances to the command bunker are still visible. (*Bottom right*) Rio Grande airbase showing Runway 25's threshold and its defences. (*Digital Global Imagery, annotated by Charlie Cartwright*)

A contemporary photograph of Colonel Richard Preston. (*Richard Preston*)

Captain Andy 'L' in Oman before the conflict. (*Andy 'L'*)

Lieutenant Commander Andrew Johnson at HMS *Onyx*'s periscope. (*Andrew Johnson*)

Miguel Pita at Stanley airport on 2 April 1982 folding up the Union Flag. (*Miguel Pita*)

Squadron Leader
Max Roberts after
the conflict.
(*Max Roberts*)

Squadron Leader
Charlie Cartwright.
(*Charlie Cartwright*)

Capitán de Corbeta
Roberto Curilovic
second from left with
Teniente de Navio Julio
Barraza. (*Santiago Rivas*)

Capitán de Corbeta
Alejandro Francisco
returning from the
'ttack' on HMS *Invincible*.
(*Santiago Rivas*)

ARA *Hipolito Bouchard.*
(*Washington Barcena*)

ARA *General Belgrano* at ancho
in the Beagle Channel. (*Armada
Argentina*)

HMS *Onyx* arriving at
HMS *Dolphin*, Portsmouth,
from the South Atlantic. Note
the Jolly Roger with a
'commando dagger' indicating
a special forces operation.
(*Andrew Johnson*)

Operation Mikado XV200 aircrew with the 38 Group Detachment staff. Left to right: Jim Cunningham, Nick Hudson, Harry Burgoyne, Pat Fitzgerald, Roy Lewis (XV196's Air Loadmaster), Bob Rowley, Steve Sloan. (*Pat Fitzgerald*)

47 Squadron's Special Forces Flight's crest. (*Max Roberts*)

Super Étendard 202 showing Two Squadron's crest and marking the sinking of HMS *Sheffield* and a 'strike' against HMS *Invincible*. (*Roberto Curilovic*)

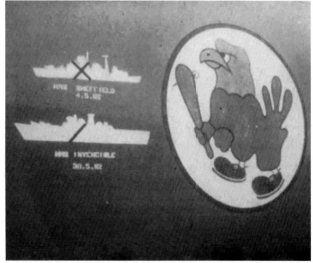

Victor Charlie landed 6 Troop on the flat, grassy headland in the middle distance, near to Estancia Cameron. (*Google Earth*)

One of the two entrances to the command bunker at Rio Grande airbase. (*Miguel Pita*)

The command bunker at Rio Grande. (*Miguel Pita*)

cluttered corner of Rio Grande airbase. *(Santiago Rivas)*

M 3 on the Chile/Argentina border. Note how flat and featureless the ground is. *(Miguel Pita)*

Series II A 'pink panther' Land Rover similar to that used by R Squadron, SAS, at Laarbruch and those planned to be used by B Squadron on Operation Mikado at Rio Grande. (*Simon Cars, via the Internet*)

HMS *Onyx* in dry dock in Portsmouth, showing the underwater damage before the damaged torpedo was removed. (*Andrew Johnson*)

One section of B Squadron, SAS, arriving in the South Atlantic on 14 June, with the tug *Irishman* in the background. Picture taken from HMS *Glamorgan*. (*Ian Inskip*)

A land-launched Exocet on its launching trailer. (*Pablo Vignolles*)

An unexpended, ground-launched Exocet lying in a ditch outside Stanley after the conflict. (*Ewen Southby-Tailyour*)

Nine of the Super Étendard pilots with their aircraft at Espora naval airbase, left to right: Juan Jose Rodriguez Mariana, Julio Hector Barraza, Luis Antonio Colavino, Jorge Luis Colombo, Augusto Bedacarratz, Roberto Curilovic, Alejandro Amadeo Francisco, (either Carlos Rodolfo Machetanz or Roberto Agotegaray), Armando Raul Mayora. (*Roberto Curilovic*)

Victor Charlie's crew thirty years after the conflict, left to right: Richard Hutchings, Peter Imrie, Alan Bennett. (*Alan Bennett*)

member of the patrol that, at its most basic, they were being tasked 'to conduct a full frontal assault into the unknown. Eight thousand miles to get wet and bloody cold. Then we get dumped on some godforsaken beach by an unknown process and left to get on with it.'

The Brigadier brought everyone back to reality with a hint of further vagueness in the planning processes: 'You will receive further orders in Ascension Island, by when some of the details and timings may have changed.'

There had been some good news. Although late in the day, it was announced that the patrol's signaller would be issued with a satellite communications system. Gone were the one-time encryption pads, Morse code and burst transmissions; Captain L would be able talk to the SAS Directorate throughout the mission. While he might have welcomed the reassurance that this facility would bring, he was aware of the obvious disadvantage that came with such advanced technology: it would offer plenty of opportunities for meddling from half a hemisphere away. Captain L – a genuine self-confessed cynic – regarded this as a very mixed blessing. A touch of cynicism was healthy, but …

The success or otherwise of the mission depended upon the patrol remaining undetected, yet the Brigadier now included in his closing remarks, almost as an afterthought, this comment: 'You may wish to consider carefully your options in the event of being found by civilians.' They all knew what was meant but they also believed that no directive could, or should, cover such an eventuality; it had to be left to those on the ground to judge the gravity of the situation at the time – and it was better to keep it that way.

An alternative circumstance, never mentioned but of far greater importance, and one that certainly did warrant guidance and advice, was the patrol's status if captured. 'Suppose,' every member of the patrol thought, 'we are not found by civilians but by the army. We will not be wearing the uniform of any recognizable force. We will not be wearing any badges of rank or any identifying insignia to prove that we are part of a formal military unit. Saboteurs perhaps, even "spies", for whom the penalty used to be death. Our fireproof dog tags give only name, religion and blood group. Hung around our necks in such a way that one disc can be cut off and sent home while the other remains with our body, for ever. Great!' There was a burning need to know whether they would be treated as combatants and whether or not the Government, when questioned in an international forum, would deny the operation or confirm it – but no one chose to speak.

The Brigadier called for questions, and while there were many that remained unanswered – most of which had been fermenting for days – no hands were raised. It would be easier to ask outside the formality of an 'O' Group. They might even be answered truthfully. The patrol had listened carefully to the Brigadier's briefing but, despite the gravity of the situation, some had found it hard to concentrate ('It all seemed slightly bizarre. Unreal. The world of fantasy.')

Usually at Hereford, following an 'Orders' Group, there would be 'more opinions than men in the room', but then this 'O' Group had not followed the standard format. The maps were a worry but so too was the lack of an intelligence brief that would normally, among other useful sections, have been included in the well-tested sequence of military orders. Where, for instance, was the 'Enemy Forces' paragraph? Absent. And the 'Ground' paragraph? Missing. And what about the 'Friendly Forces' section that should have tabulated those who might help, if not in Argentina then in neighbouring Chile, towards which 6 Troop was expected to 'escape and evade'? The Brigadier had made no mention of this phase other than, 'You will escape back over the border as best you can.' Obviously they would have to make their way westwards, but what then? Whom should they contact? Where? How?

Captain Andy L's thoughts were, understandably, not charitable: 'Fine, boss. Tell me about Argentine forces. Tell me what the target looks like and roughly where it is. Show me a model perhaps.' But there was nothing. 'The lack of any form of intelligence,' he was to say later, 'was scary.'

At the heart of the concern, not just for the patrol commander but for every one of his seven men, were the two maps with which they had only just been issued. Handed to Captain L at the beginning of the 'Orders' Group, one was a flimsy sheet measuring 16 inches by 12 inches (40 × 30cm) but spanning 150 by 140 nautical miles; it appeared to have been removed from a large school atlas of 1930s vintage, after which someone had carefully trimmed its edges in a crude attempt to camouflage its provenance. This document covered – in pale greenish tints – much of Tierra del Fuego, from the Straits of Magellan in the north to Lago Fagnano in the south and from the South Atlantic in the east to just beyond Punta Arenas in the west.

The second map had been printed by the Carta Topográfica de la República Argentina in 1942. To a scale of 1:100,000, it was 13 inches wide by 14 inches high and covered 28 miles north to south and 22 miles west to east, with Rio Grande roughly in the middle; contours and soundings were marked in metres. The original surveys had been conducted in 1931, with corrections made up to 1937. The one that Andy L now held was the 1943 edition and had been rubber stamped 'Cambridge University Library 1967'.

These two sheets were the best 'the system' could come up with. Neither showed the position of Rio Grande air base or many salient features other than the coasts, rivers and lakes, plus what Captain L guessed might be roads, tracks or streams. He would not know until he arrived on the ground and could compare these scraps of paper with reality. As the coloured map was far too small-scale for operational use – although it did mark and name some *estancias* (ranches) – Captain L immediately designated it the 'escape map' and thus a document that had to be kept safe. He assumed that proper maps would meet them as they travelled south.

The air base's exact position was to remain a mystery – which, Captain L reflected wryly, might be why they were being sent! Even so it would have been helpful to know of the presence or absence of such obstacles as perimeter fences and whether or not they were mined or covered by fire. Were there armed foot or vehicle patrols and dogs and security lights? 'Surely,' he pondered, 'someone in the SIS must know; surely there must be, somewhere, unclassified information on the airbase from before the war. Someone from the Royal Navy or the RAF must

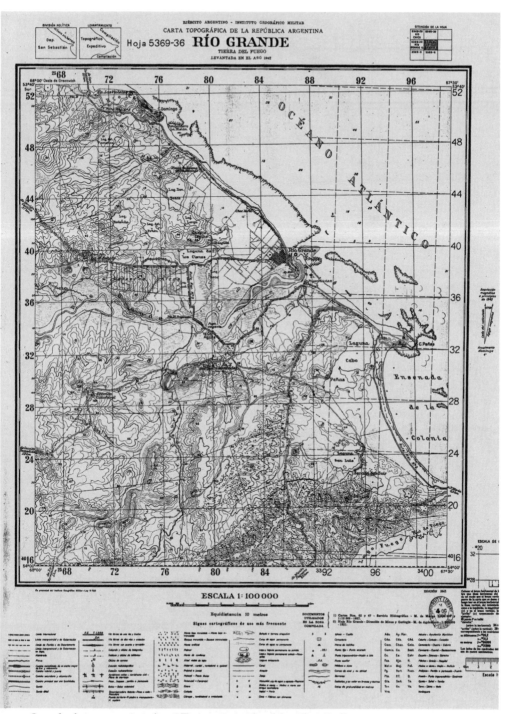

One of only two maps issued to 6 Troop prior to Operation Plum Duff.

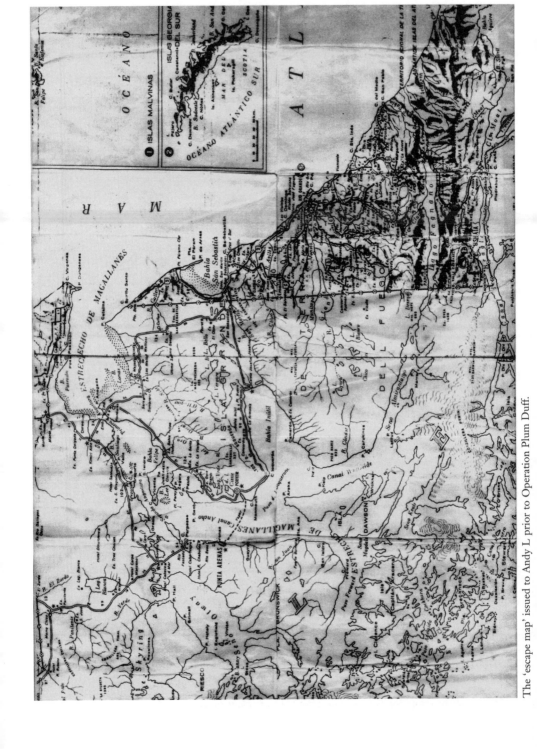

The 'escape map' issued to Andy L prior to Operation Plum Duff.

have visited; after all, had we not sold ships to Argentina and helped train some of their special forces? We hadn't always been enemies.' Thanks to cuts in the SIS budget, Mark Heathcote, the one SIS officer once 'responsible' for the whole area, had never found time to visit. There had been a British Consul at Rio Grande, but that post, too, had long gone.

Captain L was keen to know, too, how the border between Argentine and Chile was marked. Indeed, was it marked or was it merely an imaginary line that stretched north to south for mile after unmarked mile across the rough pampas grass and bogs of Tierra del Fuego? Bearing in mind local international relations, he would also have liked to know, for the escape phase, if the border was guarded and mined. Appreciating that the enemy had been on a war footing for six weeks or so, it was reasonable to expect that some level of air and surface defences was in place, but of what calibre and to what level of training and sophistication was a matter of guesswork. Any insertion would need to take that into account.

'Come to think of it', Captain L considered, 'none of that matters yet' – for he still had no idea how he was to get to the mainland. The Brigadier had offered three possibilities, but none of them seemed feasible to the Captain. From Ascension Island onwards life was an unpredictable blank, and in the Patrol Commander's profession unpredictable blanks were not a 'good thing', and certainly an 'unusual thing'.

'So that is it then,' he mused later, 'Common sense has not prevailed and here I am with seven others in the back of an army lorry on our way to Brize Norton. Somehow it still does not quite add up.' But there was anything but defeatism in the Captain's mind. Following weeks of waiting, everything seemed now to be moving at pace. There was clearly a rush to destroy Exocets before they caused more damage – or was this merely a case of demonstrating political will? 'Maybe best to leave that to the politicians,' he thought. 'In the meantime this is now and we need to give it our best shot.'

Before the 'Orders Group', and unaware of how his patrol would be inserted, the only sensible conclusion Captain L had drawn was that moving slowly across the border overland from Chile in the west, with enough food, would have been the least risky route. It would have given his patrol the opportunity to fill in some of the intelligence gaps while they probed slowly eastwards towards the target. Also, moving in such a way, in such a large number, would minimise the risks of compromise; thus in the longer term they would stand a better chance of success. Yet when he expressed his disquiet over the lack of information and the overlarge size of the patrol, coupled with his pragmatic suggestion that a lengthy approach from the west would generate its own intelligence plot, Captain L knew that he was making himself unpopular. The view from higher up the rank structure was that an approach from Chile would require a level of political co-operation that was not in place; such an operation would take time to execute, and time was fast running out.

The option favoured by 22 SAS's Regimental Headquarters was entry from seawards, for this would reduce the distance to the target. By coming from that direction the chances of being spotted would, it was surmised, be lessened; and if an approach from the sea was the answer, then surely there were specialists better trained in the art? Submarines were far stealthier than noisy, radar-visual helicopters. The Special Boat Squadron was trained for precisely the task with which 6 Troop was now confronted. The Captain knew, too, that by their very nature submarine operations tended to be two-way (in and out) affairs and not the one-way operation for which his troopers were planning. As things stood, and assuming they survived the reconnaissance or even the assault, they were staring at a lengthy, risky escape and evasion across 30 miles of featureless, cover-free, pampas grass to the western border. The relative, but as yet unconfirmed, status of Chile as a sanctuary remained an unknown factor at 6 Troop's level.

Realizing he had no idea what, if any, submarines were available, Captain L knew it was pointless to argue further. He wanted to 'do the job', his men wanted to 'do the job' and he risked 'getting chopped from the job' if he continued to express doubts.

In a summary of events so far it might be instructive to reflect (on behalf of the patrol commander) that a military 'Orders Group' is meaningless if there is no intelligence to support its contents. Even an intelligence-gathering reconnaissance needs to start with a modicum of information.

The young officer on whom the success or failure of the Exocet 'war' was about to depend had joined the army (Direct Entry Course Number 9) on attaining an MA in applied mathematics at Reading University in 1976. With his eyes set on the Parachute Regiment, Captain L's University Liaison Officer, in a pub near Reading and 'after we had put away about four pints', persuaded him that a far more suitable choice was his own county regiment, the Royal Hampshires. So, on satisfactorily completing Sandhurst, he was commissioned as a second lieutenant into that regiment at Ballykelly, Northern Ireland in March 1977, with seniority backdated because of university time.

Always in the back of Captain L's mind was the thought of eventually joining the SAS, for which the Parachute Regiment would have been a natural stepping stone. So, as soon as was tactful after joining the Royal Hampshires, he volunteered – a decision that his commanding officer, Lieutenant Colonel Bob Long,[4] believed to have been 'mad', but one that he agreed to forward later.

Andy L passed the Special Air Service selection board in the summer of 1978, but as his parent regiment was due back to Londonderry it was agreed that he would not be released until after that tour. As it happened, his appointment as the Close Observation and Reconnaissance Platoon Commander was excellent training for the SAS. Then impending marriage injected a further delay into his 'special forces' plans, and so it was not until 1980, two years later than hoped, that he was ready to begin training, following a second dose of the dreaded 'selection course'.

Successfully completing the main courses, Captain L became a 'badged' member of 22 Special Air Service Regiment and was appointed to B Squadron under the command of Major Hector Gullen[5] before that officer was relieved by John Moss. In January 1981 the squadron, with Andy L commanding 6 Troop, deployed to Oman, where he served on 'hearts and minds operations' in the Dhofar mountains in the south and in the Musandam peninsula to the far north.

That, then, was the officer now climbing into a lorry at 0500 on 15 May. In the back it was quiet, as the Captain chatted softly to Staff Sergeant D, known more familiarly as 'the Rat'. Unusually, his background had been with the Royal Army Medical Corps, so by now, the Captain reckoned, he was probably about 34 years old. Slightly built but tall, he was regarded as 'intelligent and deep' with a 'quirky sense of humour'. During ten years in the SAS no one was ever quite sure what he was thinking. With both men recognizing that there was not much to say, they avoided talking about the mission. Captain L knew Staff Sergeant D well, for the latter had been his instructor during one of his two 'selection courses'. He respected the Staff Sergeant's judgement and knew that he liked to operate through measured, calculated decision making. The Rat, the ultimate professional SAS soldier, would do everything reasonable to get the job done, but he would always ensure that the team got home. Captain L had asked him to come as his second-in-command.

Following the merger of the patrols, the Captain gained two experienced members of 9 Troop. The 37-year-old, droopy-moustached Sergeant N was known to all in the regiment as 'Nasty'. An ex-Royal Marine – he had been awarded the Military Medal in Aden with 45 Commando – he did not suffer fools at all and certainly never gladly. He was believed by some to regard, unjustly, all 'Ruperts' (the SAS troopers' nickname for officers) as only wanting one thing – medals – and if that meant leading the men into avoidable ambushes to win them, then so be it.

Then there was the interesting Trooper T or 'Taff'. He was also from 9 Troop, and Captain L guessed that he, too, was 37 years old. Having been awarded the Distinguished Conduct Medal as a Lance Corporal during Oman's Dhofar War, Taff then returned to his parent unit, the Royal Signals, where he reached the highest non-commissioned rank of all, Regimental Sergeant Major. From that illustrious pinnacle this tough and determined man, 'who enjoyed fighting more than most', re-joined the SAS as a trooper. He balanced his belligerence with a fine sense of humour.

Clearly these 'newcomers' were good men to have in a crisis, yet Captain L harboured a slight reservation: he could not help wondering whether they had volunteered for the right reasons. Unfairly, perhaps, he worried that they were just a little too bullish. Having seen action in many theatres, these experienced special forces men had every reason to view their current leader with the suspicion often felt about new officers ('Another one here for just three years. Wants to win fame but is highly likely to drop us in the shit and get us killed in the process.') Often voiced, maybe, but equally often proved wrong. Indeed, an opposing view was and is held by many observers: the SAS's senior non-commissioned officers were often unimaginative, blinkered even, and, unable to see the wider picture, thus needing good, perceptive, thoughtful officers for stimulation and, perhaps, guidance.

Captain L liked to think that over the previous two years he had worked hard to 'fit in' by showing good judgement and, whenever the situation had permitted, listening carefully to advice from the regiment's more knowledgeable members. By his own admission, leadership did not come naturally to him; he did not consider himself to be the 'born to lead' type nor had he expected or asked for any privileges from his officer status. This was his first independent operation, and he knew he would be judged fairly but critically.

Glancing around the back of the 4-tonner, Captain L was able to study in turn the remaining four members of his team. The youthful-looking Corporal P from 9 Troop was a tall, slightly built 'ex-Para' and a candidate for promotion. Lance Corporal G, also an ex-Para from 9 Troop, hailed from farming stock. The Troop Commander and he would have something in common, but otherwise Lance Corporal G would keep in the background.

Lance Corporal M, 6 Troop's 30-year-old signaller, had joined the SAS from the Gordon Highlanders five years earlier. A quiet man who enjoyed chess – unusual traits in both regiments – his spontaneous dry humour was welcome.

Another Dhofar War veteran, Lance Corporal S, had begun his special forces career in the Territorial SAS but joined the regular regiment in 1980. A slightly built 30-year-old, the junior non-commissioned officer was rumoured to have a degree but the subject was unknown. He never talked about his previous life, preferring to be 'just one of the lads'.

While their backgrounds and characters were different, there was at least one emotion that they all shared, although to varying degrees. Behind any false or true bravado Captain L knew that every member of his patrol harboured mixed feelings about this latest enterprise and, given the option, would rather have been deployed within the Task Force. No one had openly discussed these thoughts, but they were firmly present.

The lorry followed the familiar route to Brize Norton: through Ross-on-Wye, then via the bypass round Birdlip near Gloucester, before reaching Cirencester, where, this morning, the troopers had no time for their customary visit to Greasy Joe's Café in the town's main lorry park. On entering the RAF station they were met at the Guard Room by a Flight Lieutenant ready to escort them to a secure waiting area.

'Your flight will be at 1000 hours,' he announced. 'Have some breakfast here if you want, and we will call you forward at 0930.'

Although few of them had had much of an appetite in previous days, the eight members of the newly formed 6 Troop devoured all the bacon sandwiches and mugs of RAF regulation strong sweet tea that were placed in front of them. No doubt each man recalled the adage drummed into all recruits and officer cadets: 'A good soldier will eat every meal as though it is his last.' Captain L remembered that his instructors at Sandhurst also offered the same maxim on how to 'treat the ladies'.

Each clutching a white cardboard lunchbox containing one hardboiled egg, one wafer-thin, white-bread, spam sandwich and an apple, the eight troopers were called forwards on time and escorted to their waiting VC 10.

Well after 'tea time' on 15 May, following a sleep-filled flight in the nearly empty aircraft, the men of 6 Troop were introduced to the humidity and heat of Ascension Island's Wideawake airfield by Staff Sergeant L. This newly resident SAS liaison officer then reunited the team with their 'heavy luggage' before distributing the wet suits.

As government-issue wet suits then only came in three sizes there was plenty of scope for uncomfortable disappointment. Nor had Captain L's team been told at Hereford that while the body and the rubber-soled feet of the suit were a Ministry of Defence matter, the supply of gloves and hoods was a personal affair. Without them they would now be obliged to jump, barely protected, into 4° Celsius of South Atlantic water. In practice, gloves were a hindrance when dealing with the harness release gear, but hoods not only protected the head and face from frostnip in a choppy sea (exacerbated by a 'minus' wind-chill factor) but they also protected the ears from being ripped off by the webbing when the canopy deployed. Had the SBS been consulted, dry suits would have been recommended and made available. The same might have been said of the inadequate waterproofing of 6 Troop's bergens and weapons. Again, the correct 'containers' existed at the SBS headquarters at Poole and they, too, would have been issued, thus saving equipment and personal gear from becoming immersed in salt water – a problem that would, in due course, help to delay the launch of Operation Plum Duff by one vital day.

At an early stage the Royal Marines had offered two SBS-trained marines to augment the Plum Duff numbers, but this was turned down by the Director of the SAS with the odd excuse that their Standard Operating Procedures were different.[6] Had they been accepted, there is no doubt that the water jump would have been conducted with the correct equipment, after which who could tell how differently the rest of the operation might have panned out? Nevertheless, there has always been a sense of relief among Royal Marines that the SBS were not, in the end, involved.

As 6 Troop were changing into their wet suits, and unknown to Captain L and 'his boys', their immediate future was the subject of a less than positive discussion in Whitehall's Cabinet Office Briefing Room, where the Secretary of State for Defence was listening intently to an SAS officer. Originally, the Defence Secretary had, on guidance from representatives of all three armed forces, agreed enthusiastically to the principle of landing in strength on the Argentine mainland to destroy the Exocet missiles. He had, though, and on the recommendation of the Chief of the Naval Staff, insisted on the proviso that it was preceded by a reconnaissance that could, if the circumstances permitted, actually 'do the business'. Now he was becoming a touch hesitant. The legal advice he was receiving suggested that while a clandestine recce-cum-fighting patrol might be acceptable under the current 'rules of engagement', a full scale assault using two large aircraft would, arguably, be less so. If the first went wrong then ... so be it. Tough. It's what they do.

But the second, follow-up operation, had it been necessary and even if it proved successful, was likely to meet considerable international condemnation, exacerbated by an exceptional loss of men, experience, aircraft and materiel. The Secretary of State knew all this; he also knew, because he asked very carefully, that the chances of success for the reconnaissance, let alone any subsequent 'main event', were assessed as being 'slim'.

The original request to destroy the Exocets in their lair before they took off had, unsurprisingly, come from the Royal Navy and not the SAS. Looking for a role in an otherwise conventional conflict, the regiment had taken up the idea with, it has to be accepted, almost too much alacrity. Constraint was needed in the planning to account for the vast distances involved, absence of suitable equipment – including maps – lack of knowledge of the terrain, the target's geographical position and the austral weather; but, as senior politicians knew well, time for prevarication and considered thought was dwindling fast. The Task Force had already lost one Type 42 destroyer; now there was a burning necessity to try anything. Quickly.

There were other considerations that the Secretary of State needed to take into account. The Royal Navy, whose ships were the intended targets of the Exocets, might have queried the proposed loss of an invaluable troop-carrying helicopter in an operation with such a low expectation of success, but this view had to be balanced against the possible loss of an aircraft carrier and thus the entire campaign. Was, therefore, the loss of one helicopter not worth the risk? The RAF, too, might have queried the use of the only two air-to-air refuelling-capable C-130s, had 6 Troop's reconnaissance revealed exploitable weakness in the air base's defences while not being able to conduct the attack themselves.

A remarkable success, or the growing inevitability of a glorious failure, hardly seemed to matter to the SAS's hierarchy, providing the operation was conducted in (as expressed by one SAS officer) a 'blaze of glory'. This was not, though, how many of those whose duty it would be to face that blaze of glory regarded their future. It was true that the Royal Navy had much to lose if just one of the three remaining missiles found its target; yet the risk of attacking the Exocets versus the risk of not attacking them needed to be finely judged. The RAF, while their Hercules would not be targeted directly by Exocets, also stood to lose much should the operation fail; so did, in consequence, the Task Force itself.

In the Cabinet Office Briefing Room the SAS officer, looking closely at the politician sitting in front of him, concluded with his view that, providing ministerial permission was forthcoming, all was 'on track' for insertion into the mainland the following night. He would like, he announced, to have ministerial approval for the mission to proceed. The Secretary of State looked around the room gauging the general nods of agreement.[7] 'Very well,' he declared, then turned back to the uniformed officer. 'Please go ahead. We will reconvene here at the same time tomorrow. Good night, gentlemen.'

Darkness falls quickly 476 nautical miles south of the Equator, but the temperature does not. For 6 Troop's young commander it was a first visit to the southern hemisphere, and while some of his men slept in the open alongside a hut that stood off the western end of Wideawake's parking apron, he lay back and studied the unfamiliar stars. The still air was warm and sticky, and even though the sun was below the western horizon, sweat glistened on his forehead.

There was time to reflect on the last hours: the dramatic pre-departure briefs that consisted of little more than, in the words of a member of the patrol, 'Find Rio Grande air base, if you can clobber the Exocets good but if not carry out a recce and report back and by the way these are the only two maps you have and we don't know how you are going to get to Argentina and certainly we do not know how you are going to get home'. Then there had been the nine-hour flight, uneventful apart from the excitement of opening the white lunchboxes, the contents of which were washed down with endless paper cups of lukewarm orange juice; meeting up with their equipment; unpacking the army sleeping bags (otherwise known as 'green maggots') and now the chance to sprawl back, stare at the Milky Way and reflect. Much of the journey had passed in silence, each man having retreated into his private thoughts.

Once they had been told of the 'direct action' slant to their mission, one of Captain L's decisions before leaving the United Kingdom – and it was too late to change it now – had been to select the correct kit. They had to dress for an unknown time in the tropics, plus 'God knows how long' in the Patagonian autumn. They had to dress for a reconnaissance mission and they had to dress for an attack that, with everything still on their backs, would involve fighting and the need for great dexterity. The chances of stashing their heavy equipment before entering the air base was a nice idea but impracticable. They had to dress for a swift escape and a lengthy exfiltration towards Chile. Involvement with the equatorial climate would probably be transitory, so cold and wet weather gear held the overriding priority. Now, with their equipment unloaded alongside the hut, it was time to assess whether the decision on what to include or reject had been correct.

Before sunset each man had laid out then checked and considered his load. Priority for the weapons and explosives was unarguable. Only after they had been repacked into individual bergens was it possible to gauge the remaining space and weight available for clothes, food and survival paraphernalia. Of course they had done this at Hereford, but somehow, 4,000 miles away, it needed to be checked again.

With no dispensation for rank, everyone carried 4lb (just under 2kg) of C4 explosive and four timing devices. C4 is an off-white plastic substance possessing similar explosive characteristics to the more familiar PE 4: totally stable, it can only be set off by a detonator. Each man carried the standard issue M-15 Armalite with 100 rounds of 5.56mm, and, as a personal weapon, seven carried a Browning 9mm pistol and thirty rounds. The eighth man, Sergeant N, the ex-Royal Marine, packed a Welrod silenced pistol known by him proudly as 'the assassin's weapon'. Although its range was short and every 9mm round had to be loaded via a bolt action from a magazine of five, it was possibly the quietest pistol ever manufactured. Sergeant N was an acknowledged expert in its use and had requested that he bring his own Welrod as a 'weapon of choice'. Captain L was delighted to oblige him. Incredibly, no one carried any night vision equipment, despite the regiment having been issued with it.

Those were the weapons considered suitable for the mission. The personal gear had been chosen with equal understanding of the expected conditions. Each man would wear around his waist a belt kit of pouches that contained mostly ammunition and chocolate. Packed in each bergen was an individual camouflage net and a 'green maggot' sleeping bag, although some chose a 'useless' hollow-fill civilian version. Although they are the same, the SAS 'green maggots' are known to the Royal Marines as 'green slugs'. Each packed a one-man tent. Carried without their poles, these would be used as a form of outer waterproof skin for the sleeping bags. Four days of rations were broken down into their component parts and stuffed into the corners. Victualling with more days of food had been considered, but the latest change of role decreed that food had to be sacrificed. A knife, Silva compass and binoculars were standard issue, while the satellite communication system (and its batteries) was shared around the patrol. There was no room for luxuries or spare clothes, and although each bergen's all-up weight was 80lb (36kg) – less than was carried on training – note had to be taken of the likely distances involved, the possibility of hand-to-hand fighting and the eventual need for fast overland travel.

In anticipation of a southern hemisphere winter each trooper had taken cold weather gear that included a Gortex anorak purchased locally – along with the pole-less tents – from Cotswold Camping in Hereford. Captain L toyed with idea of not taking his, for it consumed valuable space. In the event he strapped it, as did the others, to the outside of his Bergen, but intended dumping it if it became an unnecessary burden. They were to be no burden, and probably saved lives.

Each satisfied that there was nothing more he could do – there was a limit to how many times a bergen can be packed and repacked – the eight men of Operation Plum Duff lay across the darkened scrub and waited.

A shadowy figure approached. 'Where's the boss?' it called. 'Is he awake?'

'Yes.'

'I've got HQ on the line,' said Staff Sergeant L, for it was he.

In the hut the satellite communications were secure, and Captain L could speak freely.

'Bravo Six, this is Control.' The Captain recognized his Brigadier's voice. 'Your mission is confirmed. You will take off at 0230. Assuming favourable "met" conditions we think it will take approximately thirteen hours to reach the Drop Zone. In accordance with your previous orders you will parachute into the sea and be picked up by a Royal Fleet Auxiliary vessel then transfer to *Hermes*. The Captain is expecting you. You will probably be flown in a Sea King to the mainland. Roger so far?'

'Roger so far,' answered Captain L, although his thoughts were far from being so straightforward. This was the first firm hint that there would be no submarine and no fast patrol boat but a lumbering, noisy Sea King with a one-way ticket. Up to this point everyone had harboured a modicum of hope that both Plum Duff and Mikado would be cancelled and that they would be ordered to rejoin G and D Squadrons with the Task Force.

'Any questions?'

'What happens to the helicopter after it has dropped us off? If it is seen or found it might increase our chances of compromise.'

'Not your concern. Local assets will dispose of the evidence.'

'Pointless going on,' the Captain thought. 'Not your concern,' he had been told. He could tell that the Brigadier was becoming exasperated. 'Just shut up and do as you are told. It's not their arses on the line,' he thought. It was time to bite his tongue and terminate the briefing before he said something he regretted.

Years later Captain L was to admit, 'I suppose the other part of it was that I felt that if we approached the mission the right way then maybe we could have achieved something. But if we approached it in the way he wanted us to do it I wasn't quite sure how effective it would be. I suppose that was a bit presumptuous of me as I was only a captain and he was the SAS brigadier.'

The Brigadier 'signed off': 'All that remains is for me to wish you luck and we look forward to seeing you when you get back to London. Out.'

'Fat chance,' thought the Captain, but, suppressing any outward emotion, he passed the headset and microphone back to Staff Sergeant L. 'Looks like we leave in four hours. Let me know when we need to load our kit into the Herc. I'll brief the team.'

At 0130, as instructed, 6 Troop, dressed in their wet suits – some men not fitting any of the three standard sizes as perfectly as they would have like – waited by the hut. Through the evening the temperature had only dipped to 86°F (30°C), and it was still sticky and uncomfortable. The eight bergens, weapons and explosives had earlier been packed into nothing more sophisticated than two large cardboard boxes. These were now 'waterproofed' with gaffer tape, polythene sheeting and black plastic bags; each package weighed about 500lb (just over 227kg).The SBS, used to such operations, had custom-made, 100 per cent waterproof containers. These had been offered to the SAS but rejected. At the last moment a number of sealed packages of mail had been hurried across from the RAF air head and stuffed inside, before the two containers were collected by 38 Group's Liaison officer's vehicle.

As they prepared for their uncertain future the troopers' banter and laughter pursued its predictable downward trend towards outright vulgarity, until two Land Rovers inched towards them through the near darkness. With them came the reality of the immediate future, closing in on them irreversibly. In silence everyone shook hands with the Staff Sergeant, then heaved themselves into the back of an open 'Rover. The moving air was deliciously cool and refreshing, a short-lived relief that ended as the vehicles braked alongside a waiting C-130. Painted in pale blue and light green disruptive patterns for camouflage at low level, and with a refuelling probe jutting forward above the starboard side of the cockpit, their Hercules brooded in the shadows, ready to conduct the longest flight yet undertaken by any aircraft during the Falklands conflict.

Standing by the ramp in flying overalls, Flight Lieutenant Harry Burgoyne turned to greet the approaching vehicles before watching Captain L vault on to the tarmac, stretching out his right hand. With the final stage of planning complete, the aircrew had earlier made their way to XV200, where Burgoyne and Captain L met for the first time. They shook hands as the pilot, with just forty minutes to take-off, outlined the plan: 'We'll be refuelling seven hours into the trip. It will be a fairly critical time and our only refuelling "stop". If all goes well we should be at the planned Drop Zone in about thirteen hours so you should be on board *Fort Austin* in time for tea.' Captain L nodded as his pilot resumed the impromptu brief: 'In the unlikely event we cannot refuel or we meet bad weather, my orders are to return and try again at the earliest opportunity.'

'Fine by me,' replied Captain L, desperately hoping that once they had taken off they would not see Ascension Island again.

Burgoyne continued, 'To complete the round trip we have made a few modifications inside. As you can see,' he turned and pointed, 'most of the cargo bay is filled with four large fuel tanks, but the Air Loadmaster has rigged up stretchers.'

To Captain L, well used to the inside of a Hercules cargo bay, there seemed no room even for stretchers, let alone his seven men, the Air Loadmaster, two RAF Parachute Jump Instructors and the two Army personnel of 47 Air Despatch Squadron who would be handling the cargo.

'In case I forget,' the pilot finished, 'we'll be dropping you guys first, then your stores. I know that is arse about face.' In normal circumstances the men would never be dropped first, for on the second drop were their boats, and if there was to be a malfunction either in the aircraft or with the parachutes ...

'Unfortunately, there isn't much we can do about the smell of fuel, otherwise we will do our best to make you as comfortable as possible. Unless you have any other questions then Mick Sephton, my "loadie", will supervise you getting on board. I'll see you once we get airborne but right now I need to get ready for take-off. Have you any burning questions that can't wait?'

'No thanks,' said the patrol leader, looking at his troopers staring into the cargo bay with undisguised incredulity. They twisted round briefly to shake their heads silently at their troop commander and pilot, before turning back, wondering, 'Where the hell are we going to sit, let alone sleep'. The C-130 was no longer a cargo plane but simply one huge flying fuel tank that existed purely to refuel itself.

'One last thing,' Burgoyne said. 'You are welcome to come up front, no more than two at a time, to check our position and watch the refuel. I'll tell Mick when it's a good moment.'

With this swiftest of 'troop briefs' complete, the aircrew, parachute jump instructors and air dispatchers concluded with their own, mandatory, parachute briefing before Burgoyne made his way to the flight deck.

In the cockpit the familiar, pre-start checks helped concentrate minds on the task in hand rather than what could or might go wrong over the next twenty-four hours in the air. Either way, the aircraft captain knew that his co-pilot, Flight Lieutenant 'Bumper' Rowley, was exactly the sort of chap he needed in their current situation – not only for professional support but especially when approaching a Royal Navy Task Force engaged in a 'live-firing' operation. Rowley's expertise was wide. His career as a fighter pilot included a tour with the Fleet Air Arm, flying F4 Phantoms off the 'old' HMS *Ark Royal*'s angled flight deck. 'Do not assume you can just approach our Navy trusting that they will recognize you. They won't!' was a familiar cry of his, but a comment that was never offered critically. From first-hand experience he knew how vulnerable ships were to air attack and he knew that the Navy knew that only too well. He had, though, damaged his back and was no longer cleared to fly aircraft with ejector seats. Determined to continue as an aviator, he willingly undertook conversion to the transport fleet, where his expertise was spotted by the Special Forces Flight. Now his knowledge of naval procedures was to be fully exploited.

Rowley's wealth of experience covered not just the Royal Navy but also fighters and air-to-air refuelling. He knew what he was talking about and had already introduced his fellow crew members to such delights as PIMs[8] and the Navy's identification procedures, about which Burgoyne and the others knew little. Rowley's view of 'how to get a lone aircraft into the fleet without being shot down' was invaluable, suggesting from personal knowledge that if all official procedures failed, a radio call of 'Do you want your effing mail or not?' would invariably persuade a jittery warship that the approaching Hercules was friendly!

Methodically, the crew nursed the sleeping Hercules into life, then eased their overloaded aircraft away from its parking slot to begin taxiing towards Runway 14. With all checks complete and a final 'Good luck' from the Air Traffic Controller, XV200 was cleared for take-off. Lined up facing east-south-east, and mentally ready, Burgoyne pushed the throttles forward and released the brakes. He glanced momentarily at the aircraft clock – 0245 hours GMT, 16 May – and while the aircraft gathered speed, worries of never seeing Runway 14 again receded.

The first 3,000 feet of the take-off roll were notoriously 'uphill' and, as anticipated, took longer than usual. However, with just over 10,000 feet to play with, all was well, and at the appropriate moment a 'tentative pull back on the control column' had the Hercules rising, almost hesitantly, into the thin, warm, night air. Choosing to build up plenty of speed before attempting any manoeuvring, Burgoyne kept accelerating along a straight course until he felt confident of easing the aircraft into an ascending turn to starboard. As XV200 settled on to its initial great circle heading, the Southern Cross appeared 'just port of the nose'[9] sharp against the blue-black sky. All was well; the only noticeable difference was that the aircraft felt a little sluggish.

Once the post-take-off safety inspections were complete, Sephton scrambled his way past the internal fuel tanks and up towards the tiny galley at the rear of the flight deck. Within two hours all twenty 'souls on board' had devoured fried egg and bacon 'sarnies', followed by hot sweet coffee, that did much to restore energy levels – especially for the air crew – in preparation for the refuelling operation. Around six o'clock, as the 'passengers' lay back on their stretchers strung above the internal fuel tanks, engrossed in their very private thoughts, the sun rose behind the pilot's left shoulder. It brought detail to the outside view, revealing a clear sky above a few cumulonimbus clouds far below. 'Thankfully,' thought Harry Burgoyne, 'they will not be a factor.'

From an initial height of 16,000 feet the aircraft had 'cruise-climbed', gently drifting higher to 22,000 feet as 33,000lb of fuel were steadily burned off. The tedium of those hours was partially alleviated by regular fuel calculations and routine checks of systems and instruments. 'On cue', just before 0900, Harry Burgoyne was roused by the harsh but more than welcome intrusion of a radio call from the approaching Victor. Thinking that his senior passenger would like to witness this unusual evolution, he called the Air Loadmaster in the cargo bay to pass on the invitation. Soon afterwards, Andy L appeared behind the Flight Engineer.

Having taken off from Ascension some time after the Hercules, the much faster tanker had gradually closed the gap and was now only 5 miles behind. Co-pilot Rowley acknowledged the call, and after confirmation that all was ready the delicate airborne ballet could begin.

Burgoyne adjusted his seat and restraining harness, rehearsing in his mind the procedure that he was about to undertake for only the sixth time. His palms were moist as he slipped on his flying gloves, and his mouth was dry. Then the elegant shape of the Victor, captained by Squadron Leader Martin Todd, steadily overtook the ungainly – but never ugly, in the eyes of its crews – Hercules from above. It slid into view through the cockpit's right upper windows and stabilized forward of the Hercules' starboard wing.

Keeping his control inputs to a minimum, Burgoyne carefully manoeuvred into a line-astern position about 20 feet behind the Victor's trailing refuelling hose. Under Rowley's calm directions and with the Flight Engineer monitoring the engines, the two giants slowly closed until the Hercules' probe and the Victor's 'basket' were 10 feet apart. On Rowley's call of 'Ready' both aircraft began a gradual descent of 500 feet per minute.

Air-to-air refuelling has been rudely but accurately described as 'trying to copulate with a rolling doughnut while standing up in a hammock', and this occasion was certainly no exception. Twice Burgoyne edged his aircraft forward but each time he failed to push the probe into the two-foot wide basket 'dancing' in the airflow. While he found the inability to connect frustrating, he forced his irritation aside. He was, though, aware that valuable fuel was being consumed as the formation dropped steadily towards the Atlantic. Passing down through 17,000 feet, and with the pilot's self-induced pressure almost unbearable, a successful contact was made. The Victor's 'traffic lights' turned to green and fuel began to flow. To transfer 37,000lb took a further thirty minutes, by which time the duo had descended to 2,500 feet where it became necessary to dodge between the cumulonimbus clouds that the Hercules pilot had, at 22,000 feet, assessed as 'not being a problem'.

Maintaining contact in the turbulent, low-level air proved difficult, and Burgoyne had to concentrate hard to maintain position. Within the Hercules' cockpit the crew knew that if there was an accidental disconnection Burgoyne would not have the power to climb and reconnect. Luckily, Todd in the Victor skilfully led the two aircraft around the worst of the larger clouds and showers, until Flight Engineer Steve Sloan was able to announce that the refuel was complete. With relief –'enormous relief', he said – Burgoyne eased back on the power, and with a soft 'clunk' and a slight spray of fuel from the 'basket', a clean disconnect was achieved.

The captain passed control to his co-pilot, wiped the sweat from his face and eyes, drank three cups of water, hauled himself from his perspiration-sodden seat and retreated to the crew bunk, conscious that a mild level of euphoria had spread around the flight deck.

The crew watched as the Victor completed a sweeping turn away from the Hercules, northwards to Ascension, while Rowley steadied his aircraft towards the Falklands' Total Exclusion Zone while climbing back to altitude. As XV200 was now well south of Ascension Island the colder air allowed the engines to produce more power and the wings more lift in the thicker atmosphere; twenty minutes later the co-pilot levelled off at 18,000 feet.

It was over three hours before Burgoyne returned to his seat. In the meantime, the rest of the crew had swapped around to gain what rest they could, but now, with one hour to the exclusion zone, each man resumed his station, appearing in a survival suit and life jacket and wearing his parachute.

To ensure that the Hercules stayed beneath the beam of the Argentine AN/TPS-43 radar at Stanley airport, the descent to the drop height of 1,200 feet began 250 nautical miles north of the Falkland Islands. As the captain reduced power, Rowley called the Task Force to inform it that they were inbound – and friendly. His call was answered immediately, and following a few authentication details the Hercules was cleared to 'continue inbound and descend without restriction'.

With forty minutes to run, Sephton gave Captain L a prod and shouted in his ear, 'Time to put on your 'chutes and life jackets. The news from the dropping zone is that the weather is suitable. Bit of a breeze from the west but nothing to worry about.'

The patrol commander shouted his thanks, although he was less than happy with the reply ('The bad news is that the water temperature is 4° Celsius!'). He then scrambled aft to the ramp, where their '22-foot Steerable Static Line' parachutes were stowed, along with the two containers that each held the outer clothing, bergens, weapons, ammunition … and the mail. At Ascension Island they had done their best to ensure all was watertight, but Captain L doubted, for the umpteenth time, that they had been able to do enough, unsure that the black rubbish sacks and strips of gaffer tape were up to the job.

On board XV200 the recently written Forward Edge of Battle Area Entry Checks were called for and completed. Descending past 5,000 feet, with the cabin depressurized and all 'emitters' switched off, XV200 was, in the words of its captain, 'set up to be in its best fighting configuration'. The two Air Dispatchers took up their positions as lookouts in the open 'para doors' and checked in on the intercom.

As the eight SAS troopers prepared themselves physically and mentally for the water jump there were, unsurprisingly, eight smiles of relief. These had nothing to do with their jumping from the aircraft after thirteen hours of enforced and not always comfortable inactivity, but rather more to do with leaving the increased turbulence at this lower altitude and the noisome smell of jet fuel, and with getting on with the job. Main parachutes and reserves were clipped on, followed by the standard checks on each other. It was Captain L's first operational jump and probably, as far as he knew, the first for the others too.

The flight deck crew peered into the gloom of a 'fairly typical' South Atlantic autumn day. The main cloud base was between 3,000 and 4,000 feet, with smaller, 'scuddy' clouds at half that height, mixing in with a few isolated cumulus around which Burgoyne knew he would have to fly to reach *Fort Austin*. It was not all bad. The pilots planned to use the main cloud base to their advantage by flying about 500 feet below it. This would allow the aircraft to climb smartly into the murk should a loitering Argentine fighter be spotted. As Rowley, the ex-fighter pilot, said, 'Neither their Shafrir nor their Matra IR missiles can lock on to us in the cloud, and there is not a fighter pilot in the world that can shoot us with his gun if he can't see us!'

In fact, Burgoyne was one of a few Hercules pilots experienced at outwitting fighters. If targeted, he planned to slow down, set the aircraft's flaps to 50 per cent, bank sharply towards the threat and watch the enemy fail to obtain a 'firing solution'. It always worked, and had particularly frustrated the pilots of the United States Air Force's Aggressor Squadron[10] on Red Flag exercises above the vast desert ranges of Southern Nevada; the Top Guns said that, 'They had never seen C-130s being flown in such an aggressive manner.'

Back aft, taking his cue from the cockpit and just able to make himself heard, Sephton bawled, 'Ten minutes!' and held up his fingers. There was no need for further instructions as the eight SAS troopers knew the well rehearsed Standard Operating Procedures. They stood, fastened their static line hooks on to the anchor cable running above them along the entire port side of the aircraft, and each checked the man in front.

In the cockpit the captain scanned the ocean, seeking a grey ship steaming slowly beneath a grey sky through a grey sea. The pilot was unsurprised that Royal Fleet Auxiliary *Fort Austin*, under command of the redoubtable Second World War veteran, Commodore Sam Dunlop,[11] was not in her reported position, for that had been given over fifteen hours earlier at the intelligence brief. A short call over the radio was answered with the assurance that the RFA had the Hercules on her radar. Then, within seconds of receiving a vector, the pilots spotted the 23,000-ton stores ship 5 miles off, heading slowly westwards. His 'target' now 'visual', Burgoyne manoeuvred to run in against the wind, approaching from the vessel's stern and 150 feet off her starboard beam. In his port cockpit seat, the captain, with the best view of the target, called for the Final Dropping Checks.

As the checklist was 'actioned', the upper door of the C130 slowly opened into the aircraft's roof to reveal to Captain L and his team an unquestionably uninviting South Atlantic below, officially classified, they had been informed, as 'sea state two to three'. It certainly looked choppy, with short, steep seas running at an angle across a long, low, south-westerly swell. Standing with their parachute static lines fastened, the troopers watched the ramp lower to the horizontal.

Jim Cunningham announced, 'Final dropping checks complete.' The cockpit crew were now concentrating solely on the run-in, with the navigator standing behind his pilot and poised to flick the parachute jump light switch below the left window.

With XV200's height steady at 1,200 feet above sea level and her speed at 120 knots, Rowley called *Fort Austin*: 'Running in. Live drop.'

On board the RFA the duty radio operator passed the message to the bridge. A few moments later came the expected response: 'Cleared live drop.'

Cunningham, watching the aircraft's instruments and with an eye on the ship began guiding XV200 towards *Fort Austin*: 'Two minutes ... tracking nicely ... drift two degrees to port ... make your heading ... 242! Steady ... speed good ... right two ... steady. One minute ...' Then the penultimate command, 'Red On!'

'Red on,' came Sephton's reply from the ramp.

As the aircraft drew alongside the RFA, the irreversible command that would immediately send 6 Troop towards its ambiguous future was given: 'Green on!'

'Green on!' Sephton relayed the scene back to the cockpit: 'Troops moving. One, two, three ... seven, eight. All troops dispatched.'

As he stepped off the ramp, Captain L experienced the familiar feeling of 'nothingness' as for the briefest of moments he was literally in limbo. The odd sensation, thanks to the slipstream, of not actually falling, nor of gravity yet taking charge – before the explosive tug on the straps either side of his groin took the strain as the lift webs jerked past his exposed ears. He looked up. Good canopy. He looked around. Clear of all others. He looked down and thought, 'Christ, I hope it's not as cold as they said.'

His parachute checked, Plum Duff's patrol commander twisted in the webbing to count seven other 'good canopies'. Roger so far!

In the departing aircraft Cunningham was already calling, 'Red on. Lights off.'

The Hercules remained on course, allowing Sephton to confirm that all parachutes had deployed correctly. 'Eight good canopies,' he declared above the noise. Waiting for the final message, Burgoyne kept XV200 steady at 120 knots and on the same heading, as the news from astern was relayed: 'One down, two down ...,' reported the Air Loadmaster, '... seven down, eight down. All troops in the water.'

With no refuelling 'stops' on the journey home, the flight deck team were keen that the troopers were recovered from the water as quickly as possible. They had planned to drop the two containers together on a reciprocal downwind course, but with men still in the water the aircraft was forced to circle until the dropping zone was reported 'clear'.

It was forty minutes before the final parachutist was recovered from the water, and the fuel state was becoming critical. At last, with the dropping zone 'empty',

Burgoyne descended to 600 feet, lined up again and, following a similar procedure, dropped the two boxes. Once clear of the ramp, the containers parted company to float down beneath their individual parachutes.

Drop complete, Hercules XV200 turned immediately back for Ascension Island, climbing gently towards the north-east. As the aircraft headed into the thickening gloom a faint voice confirmed that all troopers and their stores were safe on board the Fort Class Fleet Replenishment Ship. A little later the wireless operator added a final message, one of thanks for the thoughtfulness in cramming in as much personal mail as possible for the Task Force.

At the top of the climb a new problem arose. Unforecast strong westerly winds had developed, and after applying drift to counter them the aircraft's ground-speed was 50 knots lower than planned. As fuel consumption was correspondingly increased, the crew knew that if these conditions continued they would not reach Ascension Island. A solution was required, and quickly.

Jim Cunningham suggested a technique used by sailing ships – tacking. 'Instead of applying drift', he argued, 'we should just let the aircraft be blown east by the wind and then turn hard into it until track is regained.'

Harry Burgoyne, not being a sailor, considered this idea, 'a bit strange', but understood what his navigator was suggesting. 'As the only alternative options, ditching in the Atlantic or diverting to the South American mainland, were not terribly inviting, I elected to give it a try,' he later said. It worked, and the procedure was repeated until the wind abated two hours later.

During the rest of the eleven-hour flight seats were swapped and meals eaten, more to combat encroaching fatigue and boredom than from hunger. Games were played, but the crew quickly discovered that there is a limit to 'I Spy' at 22,000 feet. Meanwhile, the BBC World Service provided hourly updates on the progress of the campaign to restore the Falkland Islands to British ownership.

An hour out from Ascension, at the point where it might have been expected that the hazardous portions of the flight had passed, the crew felt able to relax; the fuel was holding out and the reported weather was fine for landing. This premature calm was shattered when the navigator announced 'in a commanding voice' that he had a contact on the radar 'at 10 o'clock from our position and 5 miles distant'!

Pre-flight intelligence briefs had mentioned the remote possibility of encountering a patrolling Argentine Air Force Boeing 707 equipped with air-to-air missiles. Indeed, a rumour had circulated that this aircraft had already 'intercepted' a British reconnaissance flight, although nothing further had developed.

The moment Cunningham had completed his terse report Burgoyne sighted lights resembling an aircraft banking left towards them. Immediately he disengaged the autopilot, reduced the power and pulled the aircraft into a steep, 'high G' turn towards the threat. Norfolk shot to the captain's side. This was a timely intervention, for he swiftly identified the lights as a string of refuelling Victors climbing out of Ascension. What had appeared to Burgoyne's tired eyes as an aircraft in a turn was a mass formation of tankers setting out on another Black Buck mission.[12]

Shortly afterwards, Rowley contacted Air Traffic Control to request the runway in use. 'Runway 14 ... we only ever use Runway 14 ... it's been Runway 14 for fifteen years, sir,' came the unambiguous reply from the United States controller.

Twenty minutes later, and after twenty-four hours and five minutes in the air, XV200 touched down – on Runway 14.

As the crew of XV200 unwound (no doubt arguing over the four beds and the remaining tins of Tennent's Lager) Captain L and his team were about to enter the second most dangerous phase of their own operation.

* * *

While Harry Burgoyne had been landing his empty aircraft at 0250 on 17 May (Argentina Day), a VC 10 with B Squadron's troopers, now under the command of Major Ian Crooke, and two Hercules with their vehicles were flying from RAF Lyneham towards Ascension Island, where they would also take up residence at Two Boats Village.

The SAS quarters were 400 yards from that of the aircrew and in a large dormitory-type building, 50 feet by 20, left vacant by the Harrier aircrews when they had returned to their ships for the transit south. B Squadron also took over an adjacent, smaller, two-roomed structure as their operations and planning rooms. The Two Boats Club, a large 'entertainment' building with a mobile field kitchen, bar and lounge, lay between the SAS and RAF accommodation. It was to be a popular meeting place for the men of Operation Mikado.

Chapter 10

Operation Plum Duff – Phase Two: South Atlantic

Eight good canopies.

At sea level conditions were 'moderate'. Yet at 'swimmer's head height', even in those reasonably benign circumstances, there was no discernible horizon, only an unending march-past of occasionally breaking, low waves slapping into the exposed faces of 6 Troop. RFA *Fort Austin*'s boat – lowered before the drop – was slowly manoeuvred down the line of parachutists (Captain L remembers being a little surprised that it was propelled by oars, which it was, if only for the last few yards while in the immediate vicinity of a swimmer), until the last man, Lance Corporal M, was pulled from the water after about half an hour, or so it seemed. Cold to the core, he was swiftly wrapped in a jacket.

Captain L was to reflect on this phase:

> Maybe I should have insisted that we jumped in dry suits as my geography told me the water would be cold. But we put on whatever we were given when we got to Ascension as it had all been planned without my involvement and the suits were waiting for us. We had life jackets and everyone popped them once we were in the water because one minute you could see this vessel and the next you couldn't as the swell was so high. We had become well separated.

The patrol commander was the fourth to be pulled over the side of the boat to join Trooper T, Corporal P and Corporal G shivering on the thwarts. As the crew rowed down the line Sergeant D, Sergeant N and Lance Corporal S were hauled roughly over the gunnels. Finally Lance Corporal M, the signaller, was hauled from the South Atlantic, muttering angrily that if he spent any longer in the water he would be 'on the way out'.

Perhaps not using words that come easily to an SAS officer's lips, Captain L spoke for all his men when he described the pick-up as being, 'Quite scary!' At the time, one of the men voiced his concern differently: 'This is really cold, boss. Which bloody dipstick decided that we should wear wet suits?'

Through no fault of the RAF and the Royal Fleet Auxiliary, whose combined efforts to deliver and recover the eight SAS troopers had been exemplary, this opening phase of Operation Plum Duff had been nearly scuppered by the decision to parachute men wearing inappropriate equipment into the South Atlantic's autumn waters.

Once they were on board the RFA, events were supposed to move quickly, but the drop had not been as faultless as their two earlier practice water jumps into

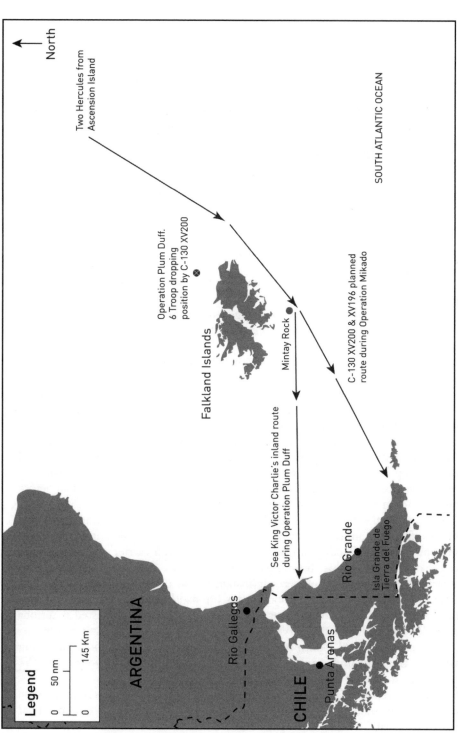

North

Two Hercules from
Ascension Island

Operation Plum Duff.
6 Troop dropping
position by C-130 XV200

Falkland Islands

Mintay Rock

C-130 XV200 & XV196 planned
route during Operation Mikado

SOUTH ATLANTIC OCEAN

Sea King Victor Charlie's inland route
during Operation Plum Duff

ARGENTINA

Rio Gallegos

Rio Grande

Isla Grande de
Tierra del Fuego

CHILE

Punta Arenas

Legend

0   50 nm

0   145 Km

Seaward approach route flown by Victor Charlie on Operation Plum Duff and the planned approach for the two Hercules on Operation Mikado.

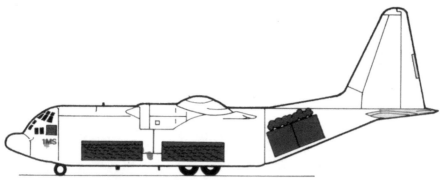

Diagram of a Hercules with four fuel tanks and its cargo on the rear ramp as configured for Operation Plum Duff.

Studland Bay on the Dorset coast. This time a number of Captain L's men were 'clinically' cold, and one of the containers, craned directly out of the ocean, had leaked.

With the arrival of *Fort Austin*'s chief purser came new orders and mugs of particularly delicious hot soup ('We don't waste anything!').

'You've got twenty minutes to change out of your wet suits into your wet clothes,' said the Purser, who had watched the containers being unpacked, 'and move all your gear up two ladders to the flight deck. From there a Sea King will whip you across to HMS *Hermes*. I'm sorry we can't do more for you here in the time we have.'

On the flight deck the men broke down their equipment into manageable piles – weapons, radios, bergens – ready for loading into the approaching Sea King. It was already clear to Lance Corporal M that while their arms and ammunition could survive a ducking, neither the fuses nor the radios came into that category. Checking and drying these delicate items had to be his first priority on board the flagship before any onward movement; there might not, he reasoned, be a second chance. No one, not even Captain L, knew just how long they had before embarking on the next leg of their lengthening journey.

As soon as the Sea King landed on *Hermes'* flight deck and Captain L had jumped from the aircraft's starboard door, a Royal Navy lieutenant was welcoming him on board. Taking in his first visit to an aircraft carrier, the SAS captain could only compare his dishevelled and damp state with the turnout of this smartly uniformed naval officer. He instantly, and oddly, felt that for the first time since this most recent episode in his life had begun, he was among level-headed people whose maintenance of personal standards suggested a serious attitude to front line active service.

'The captain would like to see you,' the Lieutenant shouted above the dying whine of the Sea King's engines. 'One of my men will look after your team. We have cleared a bit of space for you below.'

'Thanks,' replied Captain L. 'But I have one request that perhaps should not be delayed. Can someone help us to dry out our kit? Especially the comms. That would be great.'

The Lieutenant nodded and, indicating a Chief Petty Officer standing beside him, said, 'My Chief will do all he can. So, if that is everything, perhaps you would come with me please.'[1]

Captain L left his bergen and AR115 rifle with the patrol, yet for some reason he could neither explain then nor remember later he kept his 9mm Browning pistol tucked inside his SAS smock. The naval officer led the way into the 'island' then, via a stream of ladders, hatches and watertight doors (not designed for men of Andy L's height), through which they ducked and climbed, towards HMS *Hermes*' bridge.

As they hurried along the narrow passageways, the Lieutenant said over his shoulder, 'What you guys have planned seems hellish important, especially as the Captain has asked to see you. Normally this sort of stuff gets delegated well down the line.'

First impressions count, and especially so for Captain L, to whom warships in general, and an aircraft carrier at war in particular, was an unfamiliar, even alien, experience. He was reminded of the bridge on the Starship *Enterprise*, although sitting in a tall chair bolted to the deck and back from one of the many displays was not James Kirk but the rather more imposing figure of Captain Linley Middleton,[2] a South African and the only pilot within the Task Force with fixed-wing combat experience (at Suez in 1956).

'Good evening, sir,' said the SAS officer.

'Good evening.' The aircraft carrier's Captain came straight to the point: 'You chaps certainly seem to have appeared out of the blue. According to my most recent communication you are Captain L, with a team of special forces soldiers.'

'That is correct, sir,' Captain L replied.

'It seems that what you are being asked to do is so damned important that I am going to lose a Sea King helicopter and its crew.'[3] Without waiting for a reply, he continued, 'Naturally I am aware of the importance of the mission so I will be doing all I can to assist. What condition are you in after the drop?' The Captain swivelled fully round and looked the damp, cold soldier in the eye.

'The team are OK sir; the last ones out of the water are still pretty cold as the pickup took quite a while. The serious problem is our wet equipment, especially our satellite radio. We must get it dried out and working. Most of the other damage is fairly superficial, probably nothing that can't be fixed after a few hours in a warm environment.'

Captain Middleton nodded. 'We might not have that much time. Our instructions are to launch you tonight.' Middleton emphasized the word 'tonight'. 'I understand that you have already been briefed on this part.'

Andy L felt obliged to add some pragmatism. 'Actually, sir, I did not know that we were due to go tonight. Timings were never part of my brief ... and what is more' – he felt he had to seize the opportunity of preventing the whole thing going off at half-cock – 'I'm not sure that we are ready.'

The SAS officer was drained and knew the others in his team were in the same condition, but pulling himself together he said, 'Of course we can deploy tonight.' Then, knowing he had to grab at this one chance to 'get it right', added,

'To guarantee that we are operationally effective we would prefer to start with dry clothes, operational comms and dry explosives.'

Following his arrival in the Task Force Andy L had expected a short pause – a little recovery time – before embarking on the most delicate phase of the mission. He had vainly hoped that they might even have been able to catch up with their SAS colleagues and gain their perspective on the operation. That was all in the 'nice to have' category, but deep in the 'essential' category, or what would in the future become known as 'mission-critical', was the need to start the operation with working radios, explosives and detonators. The patrol commander also needed to establish a detailed plan with the aircrew, whom he had yet to meet.

Those were the practical imperatives. Now was as good a time as any to express his greatest worry of all, to someone who would listen, someone who had more sensible concerns than the maintenance of a myth. 'There is one other thing, sir.'

'Yes?'

'We need maps.'

Lin Middleton nodded again. Quite clearly it was time for a decision. 'Thank you for your assessment. I will be discussing the implications of a delay with those that need to know. In the meantime, I accept that your equipment must be fully dried out and serviceable. I also think that your men need a modicum of rest before such an arduous undertaking. Now get back to your lads, dry out your gear and ask for any help you might need. Then get some food and rest.'

Andy L, still hiding his emotions, wanted to say how grateful he was for such firm decision making, but tact and loyalty to his own service prevailed. 'Thank you, sir,' was all he managed.

'I wish you and your team well for the rest of your mission.' Then, addressing the Lieutenant, Middleton ordered, 'Make sure that Captain L and his men are taken care of as we have discussed.'

'Aye, aye, sir.'

'Thank you, sir' repeated Andy.

Captain L and his escort made their way back through the bulkhead doors and down steep ladders. Descending all the time, they rejoined the rest of the troop, who had been allocated a cross-passageway as a temporary base. The eight bergens had been emptied, and their damp, limp contents strung from the deck-head's pipework. Lance Corporal M was away with his communications equipment, while the remainder were anxious for news.

'What's the latest, boss?' Trooper T demanded.

'Right, gather round,' replied the Captain. 'We can brief M when he gets back. Believe it or not we are due to fly to the mainland tonight. But I said that we need time to sort out communications and dry our equipment.'

The six troopers guessed what had to be coming next, so each allowed himself the beginnings of a smile. 'The Captain has gone off to talk to those whose decision it is. But the basic plan remains the same. As of now we'll be taking a one-way Sea King flight on to the mainland tonight, so we have a few hours to meet the aircrew and finalise our plans with them.'

Andy L paused to look around his team. Spirits had lifted a little, for although keen to get going, all knew that they needed more time to ensure a good start. Now there was the inkling of a chance that they might get it.

As was his habit – and in accordance with SAS convention – the officer ate with his men in the Junior Rates Mess Room. While he was sure that he would have been welcomed in the officers' wardroom, Captain L remembered an earlier occasion when, during a period of diving training at Horsea Island, the troop had been billeted in HMS *Nelson*, Portsmouth's naval base barracks. With little time between breakfast starting and transport leaving, the SAS captain had entered the wardroom in a tracksuit ...

HMS *Hermes*' mess room was noisy and muggy; although they were hungry, few of the patrol were able to eat much. It was also crowded, forcing the troopers, once they had collected their tin trays of self-served food, to split up among the naval ratings. The impression, discussed after the meal, was that their 'shipmates' were cheerful and keen to make their guests welcome. The ship's company was well used to SAS personnel passing through,[4] so once Andy L's men had each stuck to the 'party line' that they were en route to join up with the rest of the Special Forces team in *Invincible*, the purpose of their visit was not questioned further. Fed, watered and warm, the eight SAS troopers returned to their cross-passage to rehearse, in their minds, the events they hoped would unfurl once they dropped on to the Argentine mainland.

What was unknown to Andy L and his team was that the same morning, as Hercules XV200 was approaching RFA *Fort Austin*, the Senior Pilot of 846 Naval Air Squadron, Lieutenant Commander Bill Pollock, had briefed those of his pilots trained in flying with night vision goggles, on the Plum Duff option. Concluding with the outline plan, he then called for volunteers. Those who took up the challenge were a Royal Marines lieutenant, a Royal Navy lieutenant and a naval leading aircrewman.

Bill Pollock explains how this delicate task was undertaken:[5]

When we were set the task, it was clear that it was extremely risky and would be a 'one-way mission' for the crew and aircraft involved. For this reason, I sought and gained permission to ask for volunteers rather than just allo-cating crews as for other operational sorties. I gathered all the night vision goggle trained pilots and aircrewmen in the Air Briefing Room and, in strict confidence, outlined the task and the rationale for it; they were to think about it overnight and let me know in the morning. Almost without excep-tion they volunteered; in fact Pete Imrie was so keen that he came to see me the same evening and very unselfishly pressed his case that 'being young and unmarried with no dependants he had less to lose than the old married guys'. Selection from among the volunteers was a delicate task: I had to pick the best crew for the mission but could not afford to strip out all the night vision goggle skills and experience from the remaining crews while we were still flying vital special forces missions every night. Both were excellent pilots, but I chose Wiggy particularly for his navigational skills, and Dick for his military and escape and evasion knowledge. Dick was made aircraft captain solely on grounds of seniority. They were happy with the choice of aircrewman, so Pete Imrie it was.

The directive for the Plum Duff mission came to me directly from Sandy Woodward himself, who quite rightly felt that he had to convince me personally of its importance if I was to successfully convince my crews. I don't suppose it occurred to Sandy to ask Commodore Mike Clapp's permission to task one of his Sea Kings as a long-range weapon, and it certainly didn't occur to me. Plum Duff may have been 'off the line of march' as far as the Commodore was concerned, but it certainly wasn't for Sandy!

When embarked in *Hermes*, we, the night vision-capable Sea Kings, were tasked by Sandy's staff; all our special forces insertion and exfiltration tasks were bided for by the Officer Commanding G Squadron, Major Euan Houston, with whom I planned the sorties.

Sandy knew that Plum Duff was a 'desperate venture' but he had obviously been persuaded that it had a reasonable chance of success and judged that the sacrifice of aircraft and probably the crew was justified if it helped neutralise the Super Étendard/Exocet threat. If he had been asked to conduct a second incursion[6] I don't think he would have seen it in the same way. I know I wouldn't! I certainly couldn't have spared another crew; as it was we were using replacements as co-pilots on operational sorties who were totally untrained on night vision goggles.

Lieutenant Alan Bennett, Royal Navy[7] remains certain that the reason why the three of them – despite being volunteers – were chosen was that they were, in the eyes of the Senior Pilot, 'expendable!' – and would probably have been chosen anyway had no volunteers come forward:

> Normally for an operation of such complexity the Senior Pilot would have selected one of 846 Naval Air Squadron's Flight Commanders, but Richard Hutchings[8] and I were both 'first tourers', albeit with two and a half years of front line experience under our belts. Whether we survived or not we were history as far as supporting Special Forces was concerned. Hence the desire not to use more experienced pilots. Pete Imrie, the Leading Aircrewman, just volunteered. It seemed, to me anyway, that we'd survive somehow ...

'Wiggy' Bennett's[9] pivotal role in this operation had begun on Saturday, 15 May, when the worried Senior Pilot cast a gloom over the lunchtime elation at the success of the previous night's raid at Pebble Island. It had been a coup not only for the SAS but perhaps even more so (this is often forgotten) for naval gunfire support and the Fleet Air Arm. In practice, it had been a triumph for 'joint warfare' at the scholarship level. Lieutenant Commander Bill Pollock had announced to his pilots that they 'would not credit the latest rumour! A one-way attack by a single helicopter against a mainland target'. He was right. His pilots, sapped after six hours of low-level flying within enemy dominated territory, and with the prospect of a similar night ahead, had only half listened before retiring for their well deserved rest. As Bennett noted at the time, 'We were too tired to be bothered, and turned in.'

The special forces operation for that next night, inserting, extracting, supplying and observing, was still on and would be conducted by crews already 'drained'. But active service can be relentless, and no more so than for the Sea King crews and maintainers during Operation Corporate. On the return of the last aircraft to HMS *Hermes* at about 0400 GMT on 16 May, Pollock summoned his team once more to the Aircrew Briefing Room and stood in front of an aeronautical chart that covered the area from Tierra del Fuego to the Falklands. The 'rumour' was true.

Bennett recalls:

I don't think I'll ever forget that briefing. Bill looked desperately worried, which no doubt he was ... The general reaction was one of incredulity – we were all pretty tired and had got used to operating in dangerous territory, but this was something new. To wander around the Falklands was one thing, but a one-way trip through Argentina was another. And yet it made sense. If we could succeed it really would save a lot of British lives. After thirty seconds' thought my reaction was – Yes!

Bill asked for volunteers to come to his cabin after 1200 that day but I couldn't wait, so as soon as he retired from the briefing I was close behind him. As I left his cabin, I hoped that I had convinced him that I was the man for the job ... my only proviso being that I wanted Nigel North to 'drive' and Corporal 'Doc' Love to be the aircrewman.

In both these latter respects Bennett was to be disappointed. However, before the decision was made he spoke to Love and, having outlined the broadest of plans, finished by saying, 'Come on. I want you as "crewie".' The Royal Marines corporal was not so sure, expressing concern for 'his people back at home'.

Bennett wrote in his diary later, 'Ironic really. If he had been selected he'd still be alive.'[10]

Later that day, just before lunch, Pollock 'with a half grin on his face' summoned Bennett from the wardroom. 'Right, Wiggy,' he said, 'You're on!'

'Great,' replied Bennett, before adding, 'Who else?'

'Dick Hutchings and Pete Imrie.'

'Who's boss?'

'Haven't decided yet.'

The decision was not long in coming. At 1240 the three of them met in the Senior Pilot's cabin for an initial discussion, during which Hutchings was nominated as the leader. After a short break for fresh air the Operation Plum Duff helicopter crew reconvened. The plan was taking shape ... but with an unexpected urgency. The insertion was due that night, and Bennett recorded: 'What this was going to need was a careful plan because we were off tonight! Could we do it in the time, considering that the SAS had not yet arrived? Possibly, but we were going to get very tired.'

What Bennett was less phlegmatic about was the 'cover story' allied to the 'plan' for their return to the United Kingdom ('They were both risible!'). Assuming all went well and the SAS were dropped, the aircraft would then land well within Chile at one of three of preselected sites. These had to be close to deep water to where it could be flown once Bennett and Imrie, plus their survival stores, had been removed. The aircraft could then be sunk without trace; the second best option was to burn it on the foreshore. Either way, the three crew then had an eight-day wait to allow the SAS party to carry out their reconnaissance (or their attack) before they made their own way to a neutral country. Chile may have been considered neutral, but rumours and information are commonly exchanged across South American borders, even at such times. After the prescribed period living in, and off, the Patagonian countryside, Bennett, Hutchings and Imrie would contact the British Air Attaché in Santiago. On the way they expected to be detained and questioned by the Chilean authorities, so it was for this inevitable eventuality that the cover plan had been devised. They had been, they would explain to any captor, on a surface search before developing engine trouble that forced them to ditch in what they hoped would be a 'friendly' country'. The delay of a week was so that they could indeed be sure of this last statement. Should the total destruction of the aircraft be unsuccessful, laughing off the fact that they were flying a 'junglie' aircraft and not an anti-submarine 'pinger' would not be so easy – depending, slightly, into whose hands they fell.

The phlegmatic Bennett recalls, 'My view was, "Anything for a run ashore!" Indeed, I called it Operation Run Ashore!'

Elsewhere, while his 'boys' were arranging their damp 'green maggots' across the deck, Andy L, had he been asked, would have confessed to weariness of both mind and body. Not only was the future uncertain, but a degree of unreality surrounded the whole affair. He also knew that he had to face this 'adventure' hour by hour, for events were so far out of his control that it was 'just not worth worrying about'. But that did not stop him worrying.

What did take Andy L's mind off the future was a request at 2000 that evening to follow the Lieutenant to an annex off the ship's wardroom that had been commandeered as the Special Forces operations, planning and briefing cell. The aircrew volunteers had been approved, and so with little time before the expected launch of Operation Plum Duff detailed planning was underway. In this room Andy L met for the first time the Sea King's pilot, Hutchings, and the co-pilot and navigator, Bennett, a jovial officer who, in typical Fleet Air Arm fashion, played hard, worked hard and was passionate about flying and his service. Leading Aircrewman Pete Imrie[11] was rather more taciturn. In fact, Hutchings and Andy L had met before, during a military course at Warminster; so once those memories had been revisited, it was on with the tasks in hand, the primary one of which involved choosing a dropping-off point from where the eight SAS troopers could conduct their clandestine approach towards Rio Grande naval air base.

Having mulled over an outline plan, the three aircrew repaired to their cabins to prepare their bergens and personal gear; then at 1600 they all met again in the carrier's Air Intelligence Room, 'to start drawing on the charts available'.[12] The only Admiralty chart to cover the area between the Falkland Islands and Tierra del Fuego was no 539.[13] This May 1976 edition, to a scale of 1:1,750,000, was engraved in 1965 and first published in January 1966. A second, and in some respects more useful, chart was no 554, covering the Straits of Magellan from the Atlantic to the Pacific.[14] According to its subtitle this British Admiralty chart was 'Taken from the Chilean and Argentine government charts to 1981'. The edition available to the airmen had been first published in London in August 1964 (their issue was printed in May 1977). Neither Admiralty chart showed any contours. All soundings were in fathoms, with heights in feet.

A third British Admiralty chart was also available – no 4200[15] – first printed from information supplied by Argentina, Chile and Uruguay. This was of too small a scale[16] to be of much value, especially as it did not extend to Punta Arenas, although offshore it included the Falkland Islands and thus the approaches to the coast. Soundings and heights on this 'modern format' chart were in metres. No contours were marked.

While these were all 'useful' it was important that Bennett planned his routes with the help of 'land maps' ('Which we were expecting the SAS to bring with them – little did we know!').

Maps or no maps, route-planning had to continue, with initial thoughts suggesting that the helicopter should 'coast in' well south of Rio Grande before approaching the SAS's choice of landing site 'from the back'. Additionally, the team studied their own possible 'crash sites' numbering them 1, 2 and 3 in descending order of preference.

The first choice, assuming the helicopter had not used as much fuel as might be predicted, was 30 nautical miles west of Punta Arenas and close to Pointe Entrada that guards the eastern entrance to the Fiordo Silva Palma; the second was 10 or so miles south of Punta Arenas and chosen from the chart, for deep water is marked close to the shoreline. The third, and certainly the least attractive, option was on the south-western shore of the Bahía Inútil. This last position would only be used if fuel was short, for it would give the potential escapees the problem of crossing the Magellan Straits (if they wished to reach Punta Arenas before contacting the Chilean authorities).

Alan Bennett's account takes up the story:

There was so much to do and so little time to do it. Gather our gear together, weigh ourselves and our bergens; weigh the eight SAS – who we had not yet even met; assess how we were to destroy the aircraft; plan for the final route in Argentina and decide the dropping point. The list was endless and time was running out ... At around 2000 we met Andy L and his team. It took an hour or so to discover what each of us wanted from the other. Then we retired to the Intelligence Room to start detailed planning.

Apart from our aeronautical charts our map coverage of the Argentine hinterland was virtually non-existent – all Andy had brought with him were two copies of his own black and white map that someone had stolen from

Cambridge University and his 'escape map' that was even more useless from our point of view. We had the nautical and aeronautical charts and one black and white map of about A4 page size and to a tiny scale that we called the '1947 map'. Gone were thoughts of pinpoint accuracy that we had become accustomed to. Because of this we decided to make our land track as short as possible. Hence we scrapped all plans to coast in south of Rio Grande and instead aimed for a point 60 nautical miles north up the coast.

It was now that Andy L produced the two maps with which he had been issued at Hereford, with a spare copy of the black and white map for the helicopter's crew, plus two satellite photographs of an unidentified section of the pampas. Bennett possessed the standard 1:1,000,000 aeronautical chart of the whole of Patagonia that stretched as far east as the Falklands themselves, and while this marked lakes and rivers and offered a number of spot heights in feet, it showed no contours.[17] It was, though, overprinted with the legend 'Maximum elevation figures are not believed to exceed 15,000 feet'.[!]

There was the one copy of a third land map issued to Wiggy Bennett. Known as the '1947 map', this black and white publication – to a tiny scale – did not reach as far westward as Punta Arenas, so Bennett was to use this scrap of paper for the initial land-leg of the operation before then handing it to Captain L when he and his team disembarked. Seemingly also torn from a school atlas, it, too, marked little of value other than the positions of a few Tierra del Fuego *estancias*. It no longer exists.[18]

Not one document, apart from the small-scale aeronautical chart, showed the position of Rio Grande's naval air base: the objective. With each 'team' expecting the other to have produced up-to-date cartographical information that they could pool, both were disappointed.

As the maps and photographs were central to the planning of Operation Plum Duff, this saga within a saga is best told in Captain Andy L's own words:[19]

There were two aerial photographs of a nondescript part of Patagonia. Marrying them up with the maps was next to meaningless for there was no way we could relate the photographs to maps of such a small scale and with so few details.

Hutchings had been briefed that he had to land us as close to the target as possible with no reference to us – the guys who were going to do the work. He also believed that he could translate the photograph into a position probably 4 or 5 kilometres short of the objective and so I was guessing that that was where he was going to drop us.

Even in peacetime all military air bases, worldwide, have at least one man with a rifle, which is all it takes – in theory – to hit an aircraft coming in low and slow to land. This made me think that it was more important to report that we had at least put some men on the objective – this is my personal view – irrespective of whether they achieved anything, because I think the people at Hereford wanted to be able to say just that to the politicians.

The one constant at this stage was the helicopter's launch position and time, chosen by the ship's Captain in concert with Rear Admiral Woodward. This crucial point was to be just south of Mintay Rock that itself lies 4 nautical miles south-west of Beauchêne Island, 33 miles south of mainland East Falkland. Take-off would be at approximately midnight local time (0300 GMT) during the night of 16/17 May. After that the approach route to a drop-off point acceptable to the SAS was up to Hutchings and, even more so, to Bennett. The outline plan had the aircraft being launched 325 nautical miles from the Argentine coast on to a course just a fraction north of west, 271° 'true'.

Once it had 'coasted in' the flight plan would take the Sea King roughly in a south-south-easterly direction, parallel to the coast, until it reached an area in the vicinity of one of only two named spots on the 1947 'scrap of paper': Seccion Miranda, and especially its associated Laguna (lagoon) Miranda that lies roughly 15 nautical miles north-west of Rio Grande. This position would, or should in fair visibility, offer a reasonable reference point not only from which Andy L could begin his approach but also where the helicopter could make its final departure for Chile. The only other named *estancia* in the immediate area, las Violetas, also with its own *laguna*, was identified as another possibility. Bennett preferred a corner of some easily identified natural feature, not only for his own ease of navigation but as a good, recognizable start-point to assist Andy L.

Like many military plans this was a compromise, representing the closest that Hutchings was prepared to fly towards Rio Grande because of Argentine radar coverage, and the furthest that Andy L was prepared to walk during the one-night approach. Thus interpretation of the tiny scale maps and charts, which the teams now possessed, made the north-east corner of Laguna Miranda, the favourite. Estancia las Violetas, which appeared from the sparse detail to be a 'featureless hill', was chosen as the secondary point.

Planning such an insertion was everyday day fare for 846 Naval Air Squadron's pilots, so once the destination had been agreed preparation continued much as normal. What was not going to be normal was the flight to the west after the SAS team had been dropped.

While the aircrew deliberated the finer aeronautical points of the insertion, Captain Andy returned to his men dossed down in their sleeping bags. Huddled in their passageway, 6 Troop, some lying, some propped against the bulkheads, were engaging in a free-for-all discussion centred around 'action on reaching the objective'. Just as important was the action to be taken should they be compromised at the primary landing point. If the latter occurred – and assuming the helicopter had not by then flown away – the routine was to fly to an agreed emergency drop-off point. Ideally, this position would be sufficiently removed from the first, compromised, location, in order for the patrol to have the maximum chance of continuing with the mission.

Opinions differed. Trooper T, the ex-Royal Signals RSM, and Sergeant N, the ex-Royal Marine, were both for being dropped even closer to the target, while the rest of the team, including their 'boss', preferred a more cautious approach. Captain L agreed that, given the level of risk, the collective decision for the emergency drop-off point should be close to the border, preferably on the Chilean side. The rationale was that if they were spotted when landing in Argentina the route to Rio Grande would be quickly 'swarming' with enemy ground and air patrols. The safest place to wait until all died down was in 'neutral' territory. Either way, the four days of food they would be carrying was always going to be a limiting factor, and while they might have been able to steal some from isolated settlements in Chile, to do so in Argentina would inevitably invite more patrols. There had been no briefing on Tierra del Fuego's edible flora and fauna.

Despite Trooper T and Sergeant N expressing a desire to get out of the noisy, obvious aircraft 'anywhere close and as soon as possible', the benefit of the 'Chilean approach' was that it gave time to observe any impact of an earlier compromise. Coming round to the majority view, Trooper T began thinking ahead ('we could steal a vehicle to get us back into range of the target').

At the time and subsequently, Andy L could not help reflect that the Argentine/Chilean border option had always been the preferred start position, the one for which he and the Squadron's senior non-commissioned officers had argued at Hereford ... The conversation in the *Hermes* cross-passage petered out as eyelids drooped. Ascension Island was a long way behind them.

The best way to dry out a government issue 'green maggot' is to sleep in it; but at about 2130 that evening of 16 May the team received a visit from their naval escort. He knelt beside Andy L's sleeping bag. 'Captain Middleton has told me to tell you that because of thick fog over the mainland and because your kit is not yet dry, your operation will be delayed by twenty-four hours. There is also more work to do on the aircraft.'

Andy smiled, both frustrated and glad.

'If the ship goes to Action Stations make your way to the assembly point down there,' the Lieutenant pointed, 'and wait. Is there anything else you need?'

'No thanks,' confirmed Andy. 'You have been very helpful. Please thank the Chief for his help too. It seems that our radio is now fine although we can't test it properly until tomorrow.'

While Captain L and his men caught up on sleep the Operation Plum Duff aircrew were also briefed on the delay, as Bennett recalled: 'At the time we were bitterly disappointed but in retrospect it was a very good thing. We were nowhere near ready and we had had very little sleep during the previous seventy-two hours. The whole operation could have become a tragic disaster.'

At 2330 the aircrew wrapped up the briefing. With a rare night of 'no flying' ahead of them, and too keyed up to sleep, an impromptu party to help them unwind was suggested. But there was a problem: the wardroom bar was shut. Bennett recollects:

Nigel North rang the Commander and explained the situation to the aircraft carrier's patient and understanding Executive Officer (John Locke) who was already turned in. The Commander phoned the Wardroom Mess Manager and instructed him to supply us with a crate ... and what a party it was ...

when you have been without booze for weeks just two cans were enough ...
but when those ran out there was another overriding priority: to get more.

Two absentees in Cabin 5S were Lieutenant Commander Bill Pollock and Lieutenant Richard Hutchings, which was a pity, for according to Bennett, 'Goodness knows how many bottles of bubbly appeared.' This unexpected resupply allowed the revellers to sit down to a champagne breakfast in the wardroom, where a 'standard meal' was served each midnight to cater for the many whose 'daily' routines were far from routine. Bennett and his colleagues eventually turned in at 0330, not to rise until 1130. The party had two functions: it was a safety valve after and before dangerous operations; while much-needed deep sleep was the other undoubtedly beneficial result of Moët et Chandon's best.

Further fine tuning of the insertion plans was achieved in Pollock's cabin after lunch, centring around the all-up weight of the aircraft, its fuel consumption and the expected wind strength and direction at take-off. The SAS kit was not weighed; all calculations were made on the assumption that each trooper and his kit, including weapons, 'came in at the standard 250lb'. As Bennett explained,[20] 'With a heaving deck the scales would not have been accurate, even if we had them!'

At this point, Sergeant Peter Ratcliffe, embarked in *Hermes* with the SAS, tried to persuade Hutchings and Bennett that he would be useful not only as a 'guide' for the escape and evasion phase of the operation, but also as a Spanish speaker. As Hutchings had attended various relevant courses it is hard to understand why the Sergeant's presence (and extra weight) should even have been considered. According to Bennett, it was eventually Ratcliffe's own Squadron Commander who decided that he was 'too precious a commodity' to be spared. However, had he flown on Operation Plum Duff, Ratcliffe might have been less critical of his SAS colleague Captain Andy L when he, Ratcliffe, wrote his book, *The Eye of the Storm*.[21]

All was now ready for the final briefing at which the plans that had evolved between the pilot, navigator and patrol commander were confirmed. These were based on the premise that the SAS needed to be dropped as close to their target as made operational sense, and with as much darkness left as possible in order that a lying-up position overlooking Rio Grande could be achieved before dawn on their first day. The need for the aircraft carrier to head eastwards to comparative safety by the same dawn was another factor. It was also announced that, as *Hermes* could not stay in the area for another night, the operation would be launched from the faster HMS *Invincible*. The cross-decking was scheduled for 1700 on 17 May.

Before that, Wiggy Bennett, Dick Hutchings and Pete Imrie met Lieutenant Commander Richard Harden, the Squadron Air Engineer Officer, in the hangar to be 'instructed on how to sink a Sea King'. The aircrew were shown where to apply an axe in order to reduce the watertight integrity of the boat-shaped hull while avoiding crucial fuel lines, electricity and hydraulic cabling needed for its short flight from beach to deep water. Bennett found discussing the deliberate destruction of their faithful aircraft a distinctly odd experience.

Although these were in short supply when compared to the number of anti-submarine helicopters, or 'pingers', in the fleet, the chosen aircraft was a 'junglie' Westland HC4. That decision having been made – much to the deep concern of the two 'amphibious' commanders, as discussed earlier – it was rather easier to choose the particular aircraft. It was to be Hutchings' 'own' ZA290, recognized by large white identification figures on either side of the fuselage as 'VC' or 'Victor Charlie'. The impending loss of ZA290 would reduce the Task Force's complement of commando-lift helicopters to twelve with which to support a Brigade of five 'battalions' plus the planned arrival in theatre of another three. The unarguably deciding factor had been that the 'pingers' were not night vision-compatible, whereas the 'junglie' aircraft were.

The remaining hours in HMS *Hermes* have been described as 'frantic' by Bennett, so the 1600 hours briefing for the 1700 launch to *Invincible* came as an almighty relief to all concerned with Operation Plum Duff. On time, the eight SAS men were escorted to the flight deck where they piled their kit beneath the island to watch Victor Charlie being fussed over by engineers. Close by, a 'quick reaction alert' Sea Harrier was tethered at the beginning of its take-off run facing the flight deck's 'ski-jump'.

A 'spare' Sea King with 6 Troop embarked took off first for the 5-mile 'hop' across to HMS *Invincible*. Victor Charlie with Hutchings, Bennett and Imrie (as passengers), plus their maintainers, followed shortly afterwards, waved off by a worryingly large number of the ship's company, a farewell that had Bennett concerned over the rather obvious lack of security.

Stepping on to *Invincible*'s flight deck, Captain L might have been excused a sense of *déjà vu*, for once again he was invited to follow a 'smartly-dressed-despite-being-in-a-war' Royal Navy lieutenant to the bridge to meet his 'new' captain. The same 'Startrek' scene struck him, as did an equally imposing Commanding Officer in his high swivel chair.

Captain Jeremy Black[22] turned. Following a brief greeting, he asked after the patrol's equipment. Andy L reassured him that it was dry enough and that he and his team were operationally ready.

Black explained that as the helicopter was being launched at extreme range it was, as he spoke, about to be stripped even further. It was not practical to carry extra fuel tanks internally. 'Nor is it feasible, as has been suggested,' he explained, 'to refuel from a surface ship or even a submarine on a return journey.' All non-essential kit, including flotation gear, the winch and associated equipment were being offloaded. Every seat was being removed, along with all the soundproofing panels.

'Taking off,' Black continued, 'might be a bit sticky, but to give the helicopter maximum lift I will bring the ship as close to her maximum speed as possible. Despite the light ambient wind that is forecast I hope to achieve more than 30 knots across the deck.'

Jeremy Black, *Invincible*'s avuncular and popular captain, 'whose easy going but professional manner that put his officers and men at ease', was concerned. Rumours had reached him that while the SAS's enthusiasm for the task was not in question, the standard of their initial briefing most certainly was. As with his colleague Middleton in *Hermes*, Black was worried about the loss to the Amphibious Task Force of a troop-lift helicopter and its crew even before the landings had begun. He knew, too, of the importance of the task; but it would be an even greater waste of invaluable men and aircraft if they did not succeed through avoidably poor briefings. After all, he and Middleton had better reasons than anyone for wanting the Exocets destroyed.

'What kind of information do you have about your target?' asked the Captain.

'Very limited, sir,'

'How do you mean?'

'The only planning materials we have so far are two old maps to a very tiny scale, and two aerial photographs of an unidentifiable piece of the pampas obtained from the Americans. We were hoping that the aircrew might have had something better.'

'I suspect they were hoping that it would be you that had better maps.'

But Captain L had not finished: 'Nor do we have any idea of the defences both in terms of weapon systems, numbers of men and physical barriers. I have no idea of any enemy patrols around and beyond the air base's perimeter and so on. I know that is part of our task to find out but ...' Here Captain L stopped. He knew he was 'whingeing' but he felt that his Headquarters, in concert with the Secret Intelligence Service and the United States' Central Intelligence Agency, could have come up with something better than the 'nothing' with which he was attempting to plan his approach to Rio Grande.

After a sincere 'Good luck' from Black, Andy L was escorted below.

While the eight SAS men might not have noticed any difference in the help and guidance offered by the two 'carriers', the aircrew were able to make significant comparisons, as Bennett has described:

If we had been frustrated in *Hermes* at the lack of facilities and support from the ship, the right move had been made for us. From the moment we landed on *Invincible*'s deck the whole operation was on oiled wheels – all 'domestics' were catered for while we were able to concentrate on our detailed planning. A briefing room was made available for our exclusive use, in contrast to *Hermes* where there had been nowhere secure despite the classified nature of the impending operation. It was in the Admiral's Operations Room that we finalized our plans with much supportive assistance from the captain and his team. Lieutenant Commander 'Des' O'Connor gathered items that had been 'unavailable' in *Hermes*, such as a roll of black masking tape (known ashore as gaffer tape), an axe, a Spanish phrase book and various other 'sundries'. After agreeing our timetable covering the remaining nine hours we retired to the wardroom.

For the eight members of 6 Troop there was now little to do but wait, as noted by Captain Andy L:

> During the late afternoon Action Stations were called for a possible air raid, but as far as we knew, battened down below, no bombs landed near *Invincible*. Drill was to move into an assigned area, putting on anti-flash masks and gloves for those that have them. All bulkhead doors tightly sealed. We sat there looking at each other wondering what next. I have a great respect for the sailors who didn't know what was going on above but knew that they must wait on one side of the door, hoping it wasn't the wrong side!
>
> Rested up during the evening, the men fairly quiet. Everyone does best to be cheerful, even Sergeant N tries a few jokes. We are given huge steaks cooked by sailors. Really nice idea, all very grateful and do best to eat, but underneath no one really seems that hungry.

After dinner, the aircrew and the SAS team met again in their dedicated briefing room, where the preferred drop-off points were once more discussed and agreed. Captain L describes the final decision making:

> We confirmed the primary landing site close to Estancia Miranda and the secondary one not too far away at Estancia las Violetas, as well as an emergency drop-off point on the border. The idea was to see what hue and cry was taking place because of any failed insertion or if the helicopter had obviously been spotted. From this third position we would be able to work out what could be done to retrieve the situation. It is not inconceivable that within a couple of days we could have been somewhere near the target.
>
> We were limited by the weight we could carry. As we had been turned into a large fighting patrol with extra explosives and extra ammunition we were now double the size of a recce patrol which makes concealment more of a problem. Originally we were supposed to be very light – just four people; able to keep as low a profile as possible.

With take-off confirmed at 0300 GMT (midnight local time), the SAS repaired to their allotted waiting area for a final rest and check of weapons and equipment. Meanwhile, the aircrew held their last briefing at 0100, and with that complete and the aircraft stripped and fuelled there was nothing to do while HMS *Invincible* continued her dash towards the closest point to the Argentine mainland that she could safely reach.

There was one last duty that Bennett needed to perform. While he knew that they would be flying into Patagonia regardless of any weather, it would still be useful to have a forecast. Their approach to the coast and subsequent exit to the west were going to be fraught enough, so it was as well to know just how much more difficult the weather was likely to make them. He went in search of HMS *Invincible*'s meteorological officer. There was a snag, as Bennett emphasized:[23] 'We got a forecast all right! The problem was that the mission was so "close-hold" that it was a problem to get the "Meto" to give me specific mainland details without telling him we were going there.'

Taking a slight risk, Bennett posed a hypothetical problem: 'Just suppose that an enemy aircraft was to be in the air at dusk, what are the chances of it recovering to the mainland?'

'Ah,' the Meteorological Officer replied, 'He might find it a touch tricky as he will meet fog. The winds will start off light from the west and then die to a gentle breeze if not an actual calm. But it will probably remain foggy for most of the night.'

It had been an academic exercise, for Bennett knew that they would be flying come what may.

While the 22,000-ton aircraft carrier steamed westwards through the sunset of 17 May, elsewhere across that troubled ocean other events were taking place.

Eleven days earlier, HMS *Conqueror*, shadowing the Argentine Navy's two 3,300-ton, Exocet-armed, Allen M. Sumner class destroyers, ARA *Hipolito Bouchard* and ARA *Piedra Buena*, had reported that both were now in the southern Argentine port of Ushuaia, 55 miles up the Beagle Channel. *Hipolito Bouchard* was there to repair 'storm damage', while her sister ship was suffering from condenser problems with her boilers. These two ships, with their Exocet missiles, 5-inch guns, radar and sonar, were a threat but only when in the vicinity of Rio Grande, sitting untouchable inside the internationally accepted 12-mile limit of coastal waters. The British Rules of Engagement specifically ruled out attacking any vessels within that zone, but on the night of the 17/18 May no one in HMS *Invincible* knew that the two destroyers had sailed north and were once more 'on station' off Rio Grande.[24]

Ashore in Rio Grande, the officer responsible for the overall defence of the area, Capitán de Navío Miguel Pita, knew that since HMS *Sheffield* had foundered Rio Grande would become a target for British attacks. Pita did not expect a British assault from the air – although he was concerned that Chile might seize that opportunity – but he did expect the SBS, using canoes or Gemini rubber craft, to land from a submarine. Hence his desire to keep the two destroyers on station for as long as possible.

Following successful repair of her unidentified storm damage, ARA *Hipolito Bouchard* had weighed anchor from Puerto Espanol, Ushuaia, at 0630 (local) on 14 May[25] to patrol the nearby waters in the form of a crew work-up. *Hipolito Bouchard*'s commanding officer, Capitán de Navio Washington Barcena, was concerned about the inexperience of his men, 40 per cent of whom had been drafted in for the 2 April landings. At 1930 the next day (described in the ship's log as a 'mild day') the destroyer again proceeded from Puerto Espanol but this time for Cabo San Pablo, 45 nautical miles to the south-east of Rio Grande, off which she patrolled until 0100 on 15 May, when she sailed for the Cabo Domingo area, 6½ nautical miles north-west of Rio Grande air base's control tower.

Here the destroyer anchored at 1040 on 15 May in position 53° 35' S, 67° 55' W with the Cape 7 nautical miles away on a bearing of 160° true. At anchor, the elderly destroyer made little underwater noise, while all her passive sensors were activated. The ship's log notes that the sea state was 'calm with small waves' under an 8/8th cloud cover and a north-westerly offshore wind between 15 and 25 knots. The sun was not seen all day, yet the visibility at sea level was 'good for the time of year'. The air temperature ranged between 36° and 43°F (2° to 6°C) and the sea temperature was recorded at 48° Fahrenheit (8.8°C). Interestingly, though perhaps not too much should be read into the statement concerning the crew's ability, 'The lookouts were grateful for the clement conditions in contrast to other [recent] days when the weather had made their task impossible.' She and her sister destroyer had been escorting the cruiser ARA *General Belgrano* and, once she had foundered, had spent time searching for survivors in poor weather.

During the latter part of that afternoon, ARA *Piedra Buena* under the command of Capitán de Fragata Raul Grassi anchored 3 miles to the south-east of ARA *Hipolito Bouchard*. Sunset was at 1749, and at eighty minutes before dusk sonar emissions every five to seven seconds were detected. Capitán de Navio Barcena's team originally believed these were stemming from their sister ship, but once it was established that they were not, both ships immediately went to Action Stations, with lookouts instructed to search not only for periscopes but also for aircraft in the increasing gloom. Between 2205 and 2210 a small, intermittent radar echo bearing 070° at 3,000 yards was detected in *Hipolito Bouchard*. Two minutes later this single 'blip' presented itself on the screen as three sharp echoes, swiftly assessed as 'being typical of *gomones* [inflatable boats] on a course of 340° and travelling at 18 knots'. During the next two minutes it was determined that these echoes were 'moving in a completely different way from any natural phenomenon or wildlife'.

The nearest point of approach of these 'targets' was plotted at 1,200 yards, before they began to move away. The atmosphere on the bridge and in the destroyer's operations room was described as 'tense', a state that was heightened further when 'hydrophonic echoes' were detected on a bearing of 070°, the same heading along which the original 'intermittent echoes' had been observed.

On board ARA *Hipolito Bouchard*, once the Mark 25 Fire Control Radar had also acquired the targets, permission was sought to engage with her 5-inch (127.2mm) guns. By now the operations room was only able to maintain contact with one clear echo, while the others became more intermittent although appearing to keep the same course and speed. Fearful of a submarine attack, Capitán de Navío Barcena ordered the anchor to be weighed, while the 5-inch gun was instructed to engage – which it did, but with no discernible results. The anchor was 'brought home' at 2255 and the search continued until forty minutes past midnight, when the destroyer returned to her original anchorage. It was now the morning of 17 May – Argentine Navy Day – with 'no further signs of an enemy incursion from the sea'.[26]

The source of these radar echoes continues to mystify both British and Argentines. If they had been rubber assault craft they could only have been launched by a submarine; yet all four British nuclear submarines (and one conventional boat) are accounted for over that night.[27] HMS *Onyx* was still on passage from the United Kingdom and at least ten days sailing away; HMS *Splendid* was patrolling far to the north keeping an eye out for ARA *Veinticinco de Mayo*; HMS *Conqueror* had moved, temporarily, to the north-east to repair her communications; HMS *Spartan* was patrolling off Comodoro Rivadavia; and HMS *Valiant* was to the north-west of the Falkland Islands.

A plausible cause of these echoes could have been inverted temperature or humidity layers (or both). These can create 'ducts' when the radar energy follows the curve of the earth as opposed to travelling in straight lines. To a ship's radar this can give extreme 'over-the-horizon' radar ranges. Such 'anaprop radar paints' travel quickly, and yet there is no clear explanation why this should be so. 'It is easy,' explains Wiggy Bennett, 'even for an experienced radar operator, to be initially confused by such ultimately false radar traces.' Richard Preston remembers that, 'These can, too, occur in warmer climates. Perhaps they were what we in HMS *Ashanti* in the Persian Gulf and Indian Ocean used to call 'Flying Dutchmen' [and what Harry Burgoyne calls 'radar ducting'] often travelling at 30-plus knots.'

There has been no satisfactory explanation for the hydrophonic echoes.

This 'major alert'[28] over the night of the 16/17 May led directly to a review of defences ashore to both the north and the south of Rio Grande. Subordinate commanders were ordered to immediately implement a new patrol regime. The 1st Battalion was now to investigate the south bank of the Rio Grande and to secure the bridge carrying Ruta Nacional 3 where it crosses the Rio Grande, 5 miles inland. The 2nd Battalion was ordered to secure the coast and the associated length of Ruta National 3 from the air base northwards as far as Estancia las Violetas and its lagoon. This required the establishment of checkpoints on the road itself and on the bridge where it traverses the Rio Chico, 10 miles further north. The Reconnaissance Company patrolled the coast road beyond the Rio Grande river as far south as the 'emergency road landing strip' at Punta Maria, 15 miles away, while the Logistic Battalion's new orders were to secure the refrigeration plant and slaughterhouse, plus the nearby Puente Neuve bridge over the river's estuary. While these new patrol areas were being consolidated and the field artillery battalion was conducting live-firing drills, representatives of all the Marine Brigade's units took part in the Navy Day celebrations in the local barracks.

On board HMS *Invincible* the penultimate crew briefing had taken place at 0100 (GMT) on 18 May, two hours before take-off, but there was no time to rest. With an hour to go, the aircrew held their own 'final, final briefing' to ensure that each man was clear in his own mind what he had to do. Andy L and his men listened in while all were heartened by the 'comforting and most welcome' presence of Captain Jeremy Black.

This would have been the last opportunity for 'the command' (had it known of any) to offer useful observations on other 'friendly forces' in the area. Operating out of Chile was a lone RAF Nimrod R.1 – presumably as part of the support to which President Pinochet was referring in a statement he was to make on 9 November 1998: 'When Argentine forces occupied the Falklands in 1982, I instructed my government to provide, within the context of our neutrality, whatever assistance we could to our friend and ally. I considered this a matter of Chile's national honour.'

Thus it was that Nimrod no XW664 from the RAF's 51 Squadron operated out of San Felix in an intelligence-gathering role. Despite being able to use Concepción as an alternative refuelling stop, it was backed up by a VC 10 tanker and earmarked to support, among a number of others also calling for real-time intelligence, both Operations Plum Duff and Mikado. Squadron Leader Charlie Cartwright explains:

Nimrod R1 operations in the South Atlantic are most interesting, particularly as the dates we know that it flew cover the precise period of the Plum Duff operation. Once Plum Duff had been blown, you can understand Chile's insistence that the Nimrod operations end immediately.

Cartwright is correct, for President Pinochet had only agreed to supporting British efforts providing that under no circumstances would Chilean territory be used by the British to mount any operation against Argentina.[29]

XW664 had flown two sorties between early and mid-May before, significantly, conducting what was to be its third and final reconnaissance on this same night, 17/18 May. Admiral Woodward had asked for further flights over the three days prior to the landings at San Carlos on 21 May, but with Plum Duff 'out in the open', Chile's demand that the Nimrod be withdrawn was understandable. XW664 returned to RAF Wyton on 22 May.

Years after the campaign, Commodore 'Wiggy' Bennett was to comment:

This is the first I've heard of any Nimrod support for our operation. We set off with absolutely no intelligence at all, and certainly no brief on supporting forces. Once we'd left *Invincible*'s deck, we were totally on our own – or certainly thought so. We were, though, asked to keep an eye out for the Argentine carrier, with instructions to break radio silence (high frequency of course) should we spot her. Other than that, we certainly had no dedicated frequency to monitor, and were totally unaware of a Nimrod in the area.

He was not to know, either, that it only operated within Chilean airspace.

At Hereford on 17 May, while the Operation Plum Duff team was preparing to fly from HMS *Invincible* to the mainland, yet another meeting was held between representatives of the Secret Intelligence Service, the SAS and the Special Operations Group. Assuming that the reconnaissance was about to reveal a possibility for direct action by a larger force, the subject was, once again, Operation Mikado. With plans, such as they were, in place, all that was needed was confirmation from the troops on the ground. With any luck that would come within the following twenty-four hours ... or would it?[30]

Chapter 11

Operation Plum Duff – Phase Three: Tierra del Fuego

I

Following their final briefings, both aircrew and 'passengers' moved to the flight deck, where Richard Hutchings began his visual pre-flight checks perhaps even more diligently than usual. Once airborne there was no way back, and with neither floatation gear nor life rafts a ditching due to some minor unnoticed snag would be fatal.

Wiggy Bennett recalls:

> Our small group of engineers were fantastic. Everything was absolutely ready down to the smallest detail. I will never forget one of the men shaking my hand and saying, 'Good luck, sir. Just like you to know that the boys think you're pretty cool!' Praise indeed, but at that time I felt as scared as a startled rabbit.

During that last hour Andy L and his seven troopers had heaved their laden bergens into the Sea King's empty cabin and begun to make themselves comfortable for the 320-nautical-mile flight to the coast and 'heavens knew what' that lay beyond.

Andy L's diary describes his thoughts:

> At the right time we are escorted to the flight deck in darkness and given immersion suits to pull over uniform. Patrol unenthusiastic as no one sees the point of the suit. Distances so great and water so cold that probably a waste of time. However we are sold on the idea by the Loadmaster [*sic*] Pete who says they will help us stay warm in the back. Next we are loaded into the Sea King. Inside completely bare, no seats at all and several buckets of what looks like pieces of silver paper. Realized this was chaff to be used as a counter measure should we be locked-on by enemy radar. Patrol sitting on floor leaning against the side of the fuselage. Kit set out down the middle opposite each man.

At 0314 on 18 May[1] Bennett informed 'Flyco'[2] that they were ready. In reply he received the ship's precise latitude and longitude, with which he updated his Tactical Air Navigation System – an elderly method even then, but in pre-GPS[3] days the one by which he would be navigating all the way to their final landing in, it was hoped, 'neutral' Chile. Before taking off, though, as the navigation system had a tendency to 'drift', it was vital that it was as up to date as possible.

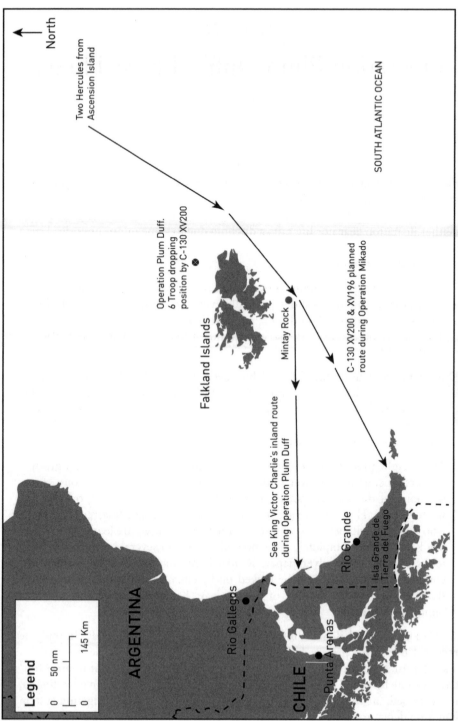

North

Two Hercules from
Ascension Island

Operation Plum Duff.
6 Troop dropping
position by C-130 XV200

Falkland Islands

Mintay Rock

C-130 XV200 & XV196 planned
route during Operation Mikado

SOUTH ATLANTIC OCEAN

Sea King Victor Charlie's inland route
during Operation Plum Duff

ARGENTINA

Rio Gallegos

Rio Grande

Isla Grande de
Tierra del Fuego

Punta Arenas

CHILE

Legend

0   50 nm

0   145 Km

Seaward approach route flown by Victor Charlie on Operation Plum Duff and the planned approach for the two Hercules on Operation Mikado.

Happy that he knew his exact 'departure point', Bennett indicated to his pilot that all was ready. The fuel tanks were being kept filled to the very brim while the engines and rotors were 'burning and turning' as the final take-off checks were conducted. With the eight laden troopers embarked and with all superfluous life-saving, 'domestic' and winching equipment removed, the Sea King weighed 22,255lb, or 855lb over the maximum permitted all-up weight. Guidance had been sought from the Aircraft and Armament Experimental Establishment at Boscombe Down in Wiltshire, whose prognosis was that the aircraft could fly at 1,100lb above what would normally be considered the maximum permitted weight. Their advice was straightforward, pragmatic and positive. Providing a maximum amount of wind was achieved across the flight deck, and providing the aircraft was not banked beyond 20 degrees and the air speed was kept below 75 knots until the weight had reduced to 'normal' maximum all-up weight – probably after the first two hours – Hutchings and Bennett were assured that all would be well.

Andy L again:

Time of take-off, just after midnight 18 May. Pretty tense moments in the back, probably in the front too! No one says anything; the noise is too great to speak anyway. Everyone knows that the stripped down Sea King will not float so we just sit there thinking of better times. Heart in mouth moment when helicopter seems to drop a bit towards the sea before stabilizing just above the waves.

Lack of wind is not normally a problem in the vicinity of the Falkland Islands, but at 0316 GMT on the morning of the 18 May it was marginally less than 'normal' and blowing at just 15 knots from the north-north-west. In order to increase the wind through the rotor disc by 20 knots, Hutchings decided to make a 'running take-off' to port to avoid the flight deck's bow 'ramp'. When added to the 28 knots that the ship herself was making[4], this meant that Victor Charlie rose into a 63-knot airstream – or the top end of a Force 10 – with little alteration of course required to bring her round to 271° true.

Allowing for crosswinds, the helicopter was heading for a coasting-in point 26 nautical miles south of Pointe Catalina at the entrance to the Magellan Straits, 50 miles from the SAS's primary drop point. For the first two hours, while the 'overload' of fuel was burned off, Victor Charlie flew at a comfortable 200 feet above sea level into a light wind that was beginning to veer towards the north-east.

Bennett later wrote:

Perfect for our mission, Argentinian radars based on the Falklands were no longer a problem but those of any enemy warship most definitely were, yet there had been no intelligence update on the position of any ship within the 12-mile limit. The Royal Air Force were aware of the presence of the two destroyers off the coast and had passed this information to the Task Force but it had not been passed on down the line to those who really did need to know.[5]

As navigator, Bennett would normally have been responsible for operating the Omega Radar Warning Receiver,[6] but on this occasion he handed the 'hairdryer lookalike' to Andy L, whose irregular sweeps detected nothing. Apart from slowly deteriorating visibility the first two and a quarter hours were without incident. The poor visibility that was to dog the whole operation from this point onwards was not, then, quite so evident 30 miles south of the Bahiá, for ARA *Hipolito Bouchard*'s log reports, 'Total cloud cover, falling barometric pressure, temperature less than 6°C, flat sea and a freshening north-north-east wind'. This was the same onshore wind that was beginning to help Victor Charlie.

Before take-off Bennett had assumed that the first 300 miles would be 'boring', but a glance at his contemporary diaries and navigator's notes suggests a different reaction:

I don't think I have ever been so busy. Navigation was taking up all of my time due to the rapidly changing magnetic variation as we flew west. The compass 'controller' was altered by ½° approximately every 40 miles. Then there was the continuous updating of the Tactical Air Navigation System to keep our Doppler input as accurate as possible as the wind changed. On top of that I still had to prepare parts of the overland route as we had been that short of time. Victor Charlie was flying steadily, and as we droned on towards the coast Andy made regular sweeps on the 'radar warner' but all was quiet. Our fuel consumption was doing nicely and despite our overloaded weight we were able to keep up an excellent ground speed of about 110 knots.

Our first concern occurred as we tried to use the radar altimeter when coming down to 50 feet. Normally it should have been able to cope but it seemed to become disorientated and started moving violently. This proved no problem over the sea as we raised our height to 80 feet as long as there was no radar illumination, but over the land it was going to prove a major difficulty.

The second anxiety occurred at 0530. Some 80 miles from the coast Hutchings reported seeing through his passive night goggles a 'mystery glow' dead ahead. Under Bennett's guidance the pilot swung his aircraft to starboard to head north for ten minutes, but as the 'apparent bearing' did not change he swung back to the south, again with no change. It was deduced – accurately – that the mystery object was a good distance off. It soon became clear that the light was an oil rig flare, the glare from which, reflecting off the low clouds, had first been sighted at 60 nautical miles. The visibility offshore – now that the flight deck crew actually had something to look at – was at that stage not as bad as has been reported. With the aircraft at 80 feet above the sea, the horizon was 11 miles away, and, supposing the gas flare was 100 feet above the surface, that gave it a 'dipping distance' of just over 23 miles. Thus the actual visibility, at least through the highly sensitive goggles, was of that order.

Not wishing to overfly anything that might report his presence, Hutchings turned north again until the low-lying land north of the Bahiá was sighted

10 nautical miles to port. Victor Charlie swung towards the south-west to intercept it at right angles. At 0615, and 3 miles north of the Estancia Cullen, the helicopter was turned south-east to parallel the beach towards Bahiá San Sabastian.
Victor Charlie had been in the air for almost three hours, clearly helped by the
same north-north-east wind that ARA *Hipolito Bouchard* was now experiencing.

Sitting in the back of the helicopter, Andy L and his men were alert; opportunities for rest were non-existent. The patrol leader – able to look forward past
the pilots' heads and sideways through the cabin windows – remarked later,[7] 'The
approach to the coast was interesting as the bright red lights on the horizon were
quite unexpected. I think they were oil rigs. Very, very bright.'

Bennett's plan had been deliberately to 'coast in' 50 nautical miles north of the
drop-off point to ensure that, allowing for wind-induced drift from the north and
the 'drift' so often associated with the Tactical Air Navigation System, he would
at least know which way he should turn on reaching this 'milestone'. He felt it was
in order to write later, 'Not bad after such a lengthy approach'.

Full identification came fifteen minutes later, when the coast – at the inland
end of the long spit of sand that runs just east of south, marking the northern
entrance to the Bahiá – suddenly turned to the north-west. This 'fix' at 0630
allowed the navigator to record later, '95 per cent confident that this is Punta de
Arenas. Final confirmation expected in five minutes'.

Bennett's confidence was well placed. ('Tactical Air Navigation System updated. Circa 10 nautical mile cumulative error after three and a half hours flight
over sea. Twenty-two nautical miles to run to drop off point. Flying at 70 feet
"mean safe distance". Would be lower if the radar altimeter was behaving.') Sure
enough of their position to update the navigation system again, he gave his pilot a
new course to steer of 'due south'. If Cabo San Sabastion turned up 'on the nose'
after exactly 10 miles then they were 'on time and in position'. It did, and they
were. 'Elation was high', as Bennett gave Hutchings the next 'waypoint'. Andy L
was informed that, with 15 miles to run, they would be 'on the ground shortly'.
The noted time was 0635 GMT, and the moment had come to struggle out of the
immersion suits and re-check personal equipment.

But the best laid plans … Three minutes later, Sea King ZA290 'hit fog and
lost all contact with the ground'. It was a sudden but not unexpected obstacle,
described by Bennett as 'a thick goldfish bowl' that had Hutchings 'instantly
initiating a rapid climb while turning to the north-east' towards the sea and
comparative safety.[8] This came as no surprise to Bennett, recalling that
HMS *Invincible*'s Meteorological Officer had told him, 'an enemy aircraft returning to the mainland might find it a touch tricky as he will meet fog'.

The new course should have been towards comparative safety, had it not been
for an alert radar operator on board ARA *Hipolito Bouchard*, whose log now takes
up part of the tale. In fact, the timings of Bennett's account and those of the
destroyer do not quite tally. As the two documents otherwise agree in most significant details, allowance has been made for the differing time zones operated by
each, plus the fact that the log may well have been written by what, in the Royal
Navy, would be termed the bosun's mate: probably a young conscript relying on

his own cheap wrist watch. It is not known which of the two Patagonian time zones the ship was keeping, but clearly it was not GMT.

At 0408 (ship's time) on board the anchored destroyer, the officer of the watch was informed that the SPS 10 surface-search radar operator had acquired a contact. In the words of the destroyer's Report of Proceedings:

> The radar operator moved to the Decca (Band 1) set on the bridge as this had better 'discrimination'. Both radars continued to emit. Informed ARA *Piedra Buena* of the contact bearing 340° at 9 miles in position 53° 26.7' S and 68° 00.2' W about 3 miles off the coast.
>
> Attempted to communicate with the aircraft on all frequencies without getting a reply. Asked the naval air base at Rio Grande if it was friendly. While this was happening the aircraft, with the flight profile of a helicopter, maintained its course towards the land.
>
> 180426: ARA *Bouchard* reported back to the 'officer in tactical command' (OTC) to announce that the contact had crossed the coastline and was continuing its incursion over the island [Tierra del Fuego]. OTC was reminded of the need to inform Rio Grande. D29 [*Piedra Buena*] confirmed that he intended to do so.
>
> 180442: D29 reported that he had been in communication with Rio Grande who confirmed that there were no friendly aircraft in the area. This gave the operations room team in *Hipolito Bouchard* a great incentive to maintain contact at all costs.

On board Sea King ZA290 the atmosphere was tense – maybe that is too mild a word – as the aircraft exited the fog climbing out towards the north-east. Piecing together all the available information from both Argentine and UK sources, and making educated calculations of time and speed with the help of 38 Group's Intelligence Officer and satellite image analyst, Charlie Cartwright, it is certain that the helicopter passed close to the north of the flare at the gas depot 4 miles north-north-east of Estancia la Sara ... it was at this point that Captain Andy saw a flare out of the starboard cabin window.

Once back over the Atlantic coast, Hutchings dropped his helicopter to sea level and turned on to a near-reciprocal course to regain the planned track. As they coasted in for the second time they hit the expected fog, between 2 and 3 miles inland. This new course took the Sea King to the south of the gas flare that was once more spotted through the fog by the SAS troopers in the rear of the aircraft. At the time they had no idea what had produced the light; certainly, a tall mast emitting flames was not uppermost in their minds. It has been confirmed by Capitán de Navío Miguel Pita that none of his patrols fired flares[9] that night, while it is common knowledge that the gas flare was lit.

A long five minutes later – at 0655 – speed was reduced to that of a 'hover taxi', 20 feet above the ground. As Bennett recalled,[10] 'It was so thick, almost impossible to make further progress.' Following a further four minutes of 'stumbling around, it was decided to land to discuss options before we crashed.' As the aircraft settled on to the tufted grassland both the navigator and the SAS in the rear cabin watched 'some ghostly lights visible through the "gloop".'

Because of many unfounded, and certainly ill-informed, rumours a false picture has been built up about the reasons for the failure of Operation Plum Duff. It is necessary to quote, verbatim, what Victor Charlie's navigator had to say soon afterwards, while dovetailing his words with those of Captain Andy L.[11]

Bennett wrote:

> It is difficult to describe in words the situation we found ourselves in. We had been airborne for some three and three quarter hours, and at least two hours of that had been in 'enemy airspace'. The fog gave an unreal look to everything that we could see and by looking around it seemed to us that this part of the coast was not as uninhabited as we had been led to believe. Despite operating from the '1947 map' and small-scale sea charts I knew where we were within an accuracy of ¾ of a mile. But our maps and charts showed no indication of any man-made objects bar a solitary road winding its way north-south and about a mile inland from the coast.[12] And yet there were eerie pools of light around us and possible evidence of buildings and inhabitants. Maybe it was the effect of the all-enveloping fog reflecting the light off the distant oil rig flares. Maybe it was my tiredness affecting my mind and imagination but the overall impression was that we were not alone. And we were sitting deep inside enemy territory in a machine that makes so much noise that you have to shout to be heard above the roar unless you speak on the intercom. We could not afford to remain there for long.

At this crucial point of the operation it was suggested by Bennett that they should head east again, then fly south just inshore, as the fog only seemed to form a few miles inland. The aircraft could then turn westward when opposite the drop-off point. As Bennett explained:

> We could perhaps have got to within 6 nautical miles of it rather than the present 14 miles. Dick's mind was running along the same lines for when I indicated my plans to Andy, the pilot nodded in confirmation. If there were destroyers just offshore, we would have seen them at 5 nautical miles, even if their 'darkened ship' routine was perfect. If it was not we would probably have picked them up at 10 miles.

Regardless of any visual sightings, had Victor Charlie been flown south its approach towards the airbase would have been reported to Rio Grande by the warships, already alert to the helicopter's presence on the ground at Estancia la Sara. There was little else these 'anti-submarine warfare ships' could have done other than engage with small arms, in the dark. Had Bennett been aware of their presence he might well have suggested an alternative route to the drop-off point – except that there wasn't one.

The moment the aircraft had landed among the pampas grasses of Tierra del Fuego Captain Andy moved to the cockpit to stand between the pilots' seats. He was not happy, and with very good reason. It was 0700 GMT on 18 May. It was dark, and the helicopter was effectively fog-bound in an enemy country. Twice the army captain and his troopers had seen flares, and now, on the ground, 'ghostly lights' had been spotted 'through the gloop' by them and their co-pilot. Unknown to all on board, not only were they close to Estancia la Sara, if not actually in the middle of it, but they were dangerously close to the main north-south road through Patagonia: the Pan American Highway or Ruta Nacional 3.

Andy L takes up the story from his perspective:

I informed Dick and Wiggy that in my judgement the drop-off is likely to have been compromised and we should go to our emergency drop-off point, on the Chilean border ... Dick clearly does not think the drop-off has been compromised. Not exactly dissent but I can tell that he is disappointed saying he has delivered us to the exact specified location. I think we should still get out of here. After a short debate Dick agrees that we will head off for the emergency drop off.[13]

Bennett was to record:

At this moment we were actually some 12 miles to the north of our intended drop off point; a site [that was itself] some 14 miles north of the Rio Grande airfield; thus we were dropping Andy 26 miles from his objective. [Bennett remains convinced that] while Dick was not forceful about where he thought we were I was 100 per cent certain to within an accuracy of three quarters of a nautical mile. The real issue was not, at that moment, how far Andy and his men had to walk but whether or not we had been 'compromised'. Andy certainly believed we had been. Of course if 6 Troop had got off there then our precise position would have been the prime focus of our discussion.

Nevertheless, the pilot was insisting – inaccurately – that they were only 7 miles from the drop-off point, and it was that figure which Andy L found impossible to accept; particularly since Bennett was pointing to their actual position, admittedly with a gloved finger on a tiny-scale map (the 1947 version) in very little light. Bennett's assessment ties in with the position of Estancia la Sara – neither marked nor named on his aeronautical chart, but named on Captain L's 'escape map'– while the entries in ARA *Hipolito Bouchard*'s Report of Proceedings and ship's log also agree:

180446: D26 [ARA *Hipolito Bouchard*] reported that the intruder had descended and had been lost in the proximity of the Estancia la Sara at 53° 26' S and 68° 11.5' W, a few metres from Ruta Nacional 3, about 26 miles from Base Aeronaval Rio Grande and only 15 miles from the border with Chile. A little later the aircraft was again detected. Contact was maintained for only ten minutes longer.

180502: D29 [*Piedra Buena*] reported that the aircraft was [heading west] crossing the Chilean border. Vigilance increased.

180804: Weighed and proceeded to Ushuaia where both destroyers secured alongside the refuelling jetty.

As a matter of record, Capitán de Navio Barcena has since stated:

> Between 19 and 21 May we were in Ushuaia replenishing and carrying out repairs and we went back out, always patrolling the Rio Grande sector. From 22 to 28 May we were on patrol in that area. From 28 to 30 May we were again at Ushuaia. From 31 May to 6 June we were on patrol in the Bay of San Sebastian and would anchor 2.5 miles off Cabo San Pablo and 3.3 miles off Cabo Domingo. On 6 June we were again at Ushuaia [the passage during which she was targeted by HMS *Valiant*]. On 25 and 26 May we were on patrol in the Bay of San Sebastian and later we were between Cabo Viamonte and Cabo Domingo between 3 and 5 miles off the coast. Our mission was one of prevention against submarine incursions although the ship and her equipment were old, with the exception of the Exocet Mk 38; we had a good detection radar but limited anti-submarine capability. In spite of that we picked up sonar emissions with our hydrophones and others with our depth sounder.
>
> The range of our air and surface coverage was 100 miles and our sub-surface detection was 2,000 yards. The hydrophone range was approximately 4,000 yards. We could pick up the noises of submarines but were unable to locate them.
>
> In respect of the detection radar at the base in Rio Grande, I believe they would have been able to identify aerial contacts coming from the east and west. We had permanent contact with them and with the base at Ushuaia.[14]

After the campaign and before any British accounts had been published, Contra-almirante Horacio Zaratiegui, commanding Argentine Naval Air South, wrote, 'Our radars observed that the helicopter flew from Chilean territory towards Argentina. It crossed the frontier, later it hovered for some minutes in the vicinity of the fuel depot 5 kilometres from Estancia la Sara, almost over the sea.'[15]

Zaratiegui, who had attended the British Naval Staff College, was convinced that the British helicopter was carrying a team of 'commandos', who were intent, among other tasks, on blowing up the fuel depot at Bahia de San Sebastian. The helicopter had reappeared on the destroyers' radar from the vicinity of the fuel plant five kilometres from Estancia la Sara, so to the admiral this made complete sense. When first seen, the helicopter had been heading due east towards the sea at 90 knots, a description that accords with Bennett's log entry, although he reported their heading as being to the 'north-east' or 045 degrees. According to a report published later in *Clarin*,[16] 'The fuel "depot" with the flare close to Estancia la Sara supplied the JP1 specialized naphtha used by the Super Étendard, the Dagger and the aging Neptune aircraft [the British did not know this] and thus could well have been a British target.' *Clarin* also reported that during daylight on 18 May six Argentine helicopters laden with 'marines' had 'travelled around the island [Tierra del Fuego] in search of their [the SAS's] tracks. They found nothing . . .' Nevertheless, the defences at Rio Grande air base were placed on the highest alert.

From the rear of the helicopter, just before they landed, Captain L had seen out of the port windows what the pilot in his forward starboard side seat could not see, namely what he was sure were the headlights of a vehicle followed by a 'flare disappearing upwards into the fog'. This confirmed in his mind that they had been spotted, and he was now unwilling to disembark into what he was certain had to be an enemy position. While the aircraft sat stationary, noisily, he feared that a hastily prepared ambush was at that moment about to be sprung.

This disagreement hinged upon a number of factors. The pilot had not seen the lights that the navigator and those in the rear of the aircraft had seen. Bennett was certain of their geographical position to within three quarters of a nautical mile, and that it was close to Estancia la Sara, an *estancia* that was marked on the '1947 map' but not the aeronautical chart. The patrol leader was less sanguine and certainly not convinced by Hutchings' estimate of their position. It did not take his Master's degree in applied mathematics to know that the aircraft, once it had coasted in for the second time, could not have covered that distance in such a short period at that slow 'hover-taxi' speed. He also knew from his own 'escape' map that the position indicated by the pilot was nowhere near a road; yet without doubt he had watched vehicle lights close by, immediately prior to landing.

The second-in-command of the 4th Marine Infantry Battalion, Luis Bonanni, states:[17]

> I'm quite sure that the defence was alerted by troops in position at the north of the defensive line: BIM3's position. All the defences were fully covered all that night and remained so until we received the information of the crash landing of the Sea King in Chile.

This would appear to be backed up the Super Étendard Squadron Commander himself, for Jorge Colombo wrote, 'You should ask Bonanni himself about the noise of the chopper reported by his troops and the flares which came immediately after.'[18]

As it was, the 'passenger' had the final say whether to get off or not with his seven men, for he had the most to lose. While the officers were 'discussing' this operational situation and their geographical position, Lance Corporal S had jumped out of the starboard door, where he waited to be handed the patrol's bergens. Pete Imrie put a hand up. 'Wait!' The Lance Corporal, wondering what on earth was going on when speed was vital, 'swore profusely', but as nothing could be heard above the aircraft's engines his words were wasted.

In two accounts of this critical moment a fictitious incident has been included. Allegedly, three troopers leapt from the Sea King on to Argentine soil; then, when told that they would be going instead to Chile, one replied with a vulgar misinterpretation of the word 'chilly'. The trite and 'old-as-the-hills' pun does not deserve to be repeated, for not only was it never used but, even if it had been, no one could have heard the words anyway. This fallacious vignette unnecessarily reduces a pivotal and tense few seconds to moments of near farce, which they most emphatically were not. No one was in the mood for flippancy, intentional or otherwise.[19]

In the cockpit at the time it was not known, certainly not by Bennett, that anyone had jumped out. Years later, when he heard that one man had been on the ground, the navigator commented that the trooper had been lucky, for Hutchings was ready to lift off at the slightest sign of any approaching enemy. Lance Corporal S would have been left behind, and 'we would not have found him again even if we had been able to return'.

With Victor Charlie burning precious fuel, thoughts raced through Captain L's brain. It struck him that they had been flying around their landing site 'for what seemed an age'. Although he knew that it could not have been as long as he feared, it had been long enough, in his view, to have destroyed any element of surprise. 'Hence the lights,' he thought. 'Hard to judge the distance through the fog, but maybe 200 to 300 metres away.' He knows – in retrospect – that all the SAS hierarchy expected him to do was to 'have shown willing' by getting out of the aircraft, even if it meant certain annihilation.

Later, Captain Andy L wrote:[20]

> This was a horrible situation, certainly a life-changing moment and in many different ways. There was such a huge weight of expectation for the mission to be successful, to be balanced against walking out of the helicopter into what may well have been an already compromised situation and perhaps even into an enemy position. Obviously there was little or no chance of success if that had been the case, and the consequences for everyone concerned would have been profound. It really felt like the posthumous Victoria Cross option versus living to fight another day. So in the end, for me at least, the logical part of my brain took over and the training kicked in. The decision for better or worse, in the event of a possible compromise, was to go to the emergency drop-off. This would give us more of a walk but seemed the best solution all round.

Bennett – at the time, and even more so after 30 years – is able to consider the events rationally. He recognizes the dilemma that faced Andy L and so his views remain relevant:

> In retrospect it is easy to criticise Andy's decision but one must try to understand his situation. Andy and his team had not worked with us before and therefore would not have had the confidence in our abilities that we had built up with his contemporaries in *Hermes* over the previous three weeks. He was in the back of a strange aircraft sitting on the ground deep inside enemy territory surrounded by thick fog with no recognizable features and being shown his position on a very shaky map by a team – us – unknown to him. Every second we spent there with the aircraft making its noise increased the chances of our being compromised.
>
> The next move was up to him. We were quite prepared to fly him further down the coast and insert him as close as possible, if not actually at the

briefed landing site. Or they could alight where we were, leaving them with about a 26-mile march to their objective of Rio Grande. During the debate with Andy, I used my gloved thumb and finger to transfer ranges and bearings to show where we were. Obviously, if they were to disembark there, I would have given Andy a direct read-out from the navigation system of our latitude and longitude with a range and bearing to his destination.[21]

Andy elected for neither of these; he demanded that we take off and fly across the border and into Chile from where he would return across the border back into Argentina. Dick and I expressed surprise at this and said so, but Andy was adamant. It was his decision. So with our hearts in our mouths we lifted off again.

Captain L's decision is easily supported. From the back of the aircraft it seemed more than probable that they had been spotted by Argentine troops. No one was to know for some time that they had also been spotted from the sea. The position from which the Plum Duff patrol nearly started its clandestine route towards the air base was among inhabited buildings. It was also close to the main road, along which reinforcement troops could easily and swiftly be deployed, and thus was very definitely not the 'back of beyond' that Andy L had hoped for. This starting point was also further than expected from his destination. His men only had four days of food and next to useless maps. Indeed, they were not even 'on' the only near-decent map – originally dated 1931 and courtesy of Cambridge University Library – and would not be 'on' that map until they had trudged at least 12 miles further south across wide open ground. The total distance from the helicopter to the objective was close to being the same distance as from the border to the objective, but across land that would not, it struck the SAS captain, be swamped all the way with enemy, on the ground and above it.

The attractions of an approach from the west were quickly and easily identified; hence the demand to be flown to the border. The operation could then start in 'neutral' territory, where, crucially, the approach distance would only be 5 or so miles further. Having alerted the Argentines in the Estancia la Sara area, it would be natural to suppose that the enemy's main effort, assuming he now believed that the aircraft had dropped off a sabotage party, would be concentrated along the route between that *estancia* and the air base and not in a line west from the base to the border. By chance the 'new' approach was precisely the one that Andy L and his erstwhile Squadron Commander, Major Moss, plus the majority of the men of B Squadron at Hereford, had preferred.

Whichever route was chosen, four days of food were not going to be enough.

Andy L's judgment had all the logic and military common sense needed to back it up, and yet over the years he has 'felt terrible for a number of reasons. I felt terrible because we hadn't got out of the aeroplane come what may but, personally, I did not feel like leading the guys into an ambush and I was certain that that was going to be the case.'

These, though, were not Hutchings' thoughts. Not believing that his helicopter had been compromised, he wanted the patrol to get out and get on with their job. Nevertheless, once Lance Corporal S had been summoned back in, the pilot, faced with no alternative, lifted his machine into the fog at 0700.

Once airborne, Captain L spoke positively to the pilot over the helicopter's intercom system: 'I'm not aborting the mission so if you can drop us just inside the Chile border ... that will be fine.' The nearest section of the border was 15 nautical miles due west.

Hutchings replied curtly, 'I'll do my best.'

Selecting 100 per cent power, Hutchings climbed through the fog using standard 'instrument meteorological conditions' take-off procedures while slowly turning towards the west. Still in the 'gloop', as they rose through 1,000 feet Victor Charlie was now 'seen' by a search radar that has since been identified as being on board ARA *Hipolito Bouchard*. Bennett's notes indicate that the aircraft was 'illuminated by radar at 0705' – a time that all but tallies with that recorded on ARA *Hipolito Bouchard*'s bridge – and with no intelligence on the two destroyers, the navigator believed they had been 'spotted' by the Rio Grande naval air base.[22] Unable to take avoiding action, the pilot brought his helicopter on to a new course, a fraction north of west. With no substantial high ground above 1,200 feet between them and the eastern shore of Bahía Inútil (despite Hutchings describing 'mountains ahead'), Bennett suggested that the aircraft be lowered back to 750 feet above ground level, as indicated on his radar altimeter.

By any stretch of an aviator's imagination the situation was serious, even desperate. Victor Charlie was now irreversibly involved in a 60-nautical-mile 'instrument meteorological conditions' transit at night, in cloud at best and fog at worst, below any sensible safety altitude, with no reliable map, and having been 'pinged' by an unknown type of search radar while over enemy territory. It is inconceivable that any flight throughout the Falklands' campaign was more hazardous.

Wiggy Bennett resumes his contemporary account:

> Our launch into the black fog from Estancia la Sara was probably one of the diciest moments in the whole trip. By the time we had become 20 feet airborne all contact with the ground was lost despite our passive night goggles. Dick held a full power climb on a steady course, initially, of west; from our outdated maps we had no indication at all of the terrain ahead of us. As we passed 1,000 feet a new aspect arose – we were illuminated by a strong signal of a search radar. The bearing indicated by our 'hair dryer' lookalike was consistent with Rio Grande – not a nice feeling.[23] We must have been illuminated for about five minutes, during which we had our hearts in our mouths waiting all the time for the continuous howl of a fire control radar. Which, thankfully, never occurred, as it is a noise you do not want to hear when over enemy territory!

Unknown to Bennett and Hutchings, the only fire control radar at Rio Grande was the Elta Radar controlling the four Triple A 20mm Rheinmetal anti-aircraft batteries. With its maximum range against aircraft being 5,250 feet (1,600 metres), Sea King Victor Charlie was 'safe'. The only other such radar that could have been brought to bear was the destroyers' Mark 25 fire control radars for their five-inch guns. Victor Charlie would still have been 'safe' from these.

Andy L's private narrative of the flight continues:

What seemed like a sensible decision now proved increasingly difficult, as the visibility was perhaps even worse and we were unsure of the terrain.

Maybe after ten minutes or so labouring forward we seemed to come very close to disaster. Suddenly a dark shape which I took to be the side of a hill loomed in front of us. In the nick of time Dick took evasive action and we banked right, missing whatever it was. I think that it was one of the moments I remember most, and I remember thinking it really was true that your life flashes before you. I think everyone was a bit shaken. I know I was.

There followed a discussion between Dick and Wiggy about whether we could continue to fly low-level given the dangers of poor visibility, or whether we should try and fly high-level. Flying high-level would mean we would be less likely to crash into the land but would also increase our chances of being detected by enemy radar.

The decision was taken to rise to 2,000 feet, above the bad weather, and head for the border. At this stage I did not realize that it would be difficult if not impossible to get us back down through the fog anywhere near the emergency drop-off point.

We reached the ceiling set by Wiggy where, almost immediately, he reported that we were being illuminated by enemy radar. This seemed to be the cause of some alarm as Wiggy had a fairly animated conversation with Dick, who ordered countermeasures to be taken. During a series of aero-nautical manoeuvres Pete deployed the chaff. The helicopter banked sharply while the buckets of silver paper were emptied through the door.

Those were tense moments. I wondered just how much you would actually know about being shot down by a ground to air missile. When it appeared that we were no longer being picked up on the enemy radar the atmosphere seemed a little less tense and even tinged with optimism. Maybe another ten minutes or so passed, hard to judge, before Dick informed us that we were crossing the border.

I had originally imagined that we would be able to land at the emergency drop-off but now came to realize that this was not possible as we needed to drop back into the poor visibility. In the end Dick flew over the water on the Chile side of the border where his team followed their drills and ditched their weapons.

The navigator's views are much the same. Half an hour after taking off from their first landing site, and still flying blind, Bennett was certain that they were at last over water. As a cross check between the radar altimeter and the barometer altitude confirmed this opinion, he advised Hutchings to begin their descent. At 400 feet an 'island' was sighted, but the relief was short-lived when this solid visual contact turned into a moon shadow beneath a patch of breaking cloud. Nevertheless, they could at least see the surface of Bahía Inútil and descended to

50 feet. 'After a few moments to work out what was going on', Bennett's tired brain 'reverted to basics'. He told Hutchings to head south for the 'real shore'.

Kneeling on the cabin floor behind the pilots, the SAS patrol commander was watching out of a port-side window. They were over a sizeable stretch of water, descending towards a low-cliffed coastline. In the dim, shallow rays of the moon's last quarter he watched white flecks of foam being driven ashore from what he assumed to be the west. 'So, this must be' – he tried hard to remember the sparsely-detailed escape map carefully folded in a thigh pocket – 'the south of Bahia Inutil'.

He was correct, and at 0755 Victor Charlie was crossing the beach, running almost parallel to the shore. Captain L was, however, surprised to notice that they were heading away from Argentina. The beach was on the port side, whereas he would rather have had it to starboard or, better still, disappearing astern, with the aircraft heading east. 'This is not quite what we need,' he mumbled to himself.

In the cockpit, the Tactical Air Navigation System showed their geographical position to be 53° 37′ S, 69° 40′ W.[24] Confident that this was correct to within 2 nautical miles, Bennett advised Hutchings to put down before they headed back into the fog. Victor Charlie's navigational system was suggesting that from here 6 Troop would be facing a 70-nautical-mile 'tab'[25] to their objective – just over 80 statute miles – but to return into the 'gloop' was not an option, no matter how much Andy L might have wished it.

Moments later, the eight 'passengers' felt the Sea King flare into a hover, while Leading Aircrewman Pete Imrie, the naval equivalent of the Hercules 'loadie', made signs that 'this was as far as they were going'. With the aircraft settling amid the boggy tufts, the troopers looked at their leader, waiting for the second time that night for the signal to disembark. This time there was no hesitation. Captain L raised a thumb and pointed to the starboard door that Imrie had slid open.

Wiggy Bennett continues:

> We had flown along a short stretch of the coast to check if it was deserted and then landed on a low grassy headland above the beach. Captain L and his team took about five minutes to unload. They seemed relieved to have their feet on dry land again and I can't blame them. Being flown in the back of a strange aircraft under such circumstances must have been no joke. Andy was so much happier about the overall situation. Despite a march of some 35 miles to the border and a further 30 miles on to their objective, he appeared confident that they could achieve what they had set out to do.

There was nothing more to say. Looking over his right shoulder from the co-pilot's seat, Bennett shouted his good wishes to the SAS officer while pointing with a gloved finger to their position on the '1947 map' before thrusting it into Captain L's hand. As the map went no further westward than their current position, Wiggy would now be relying on his 'even smaller scale' aeronautical chart.

Captain L took a good look at it in the glow of the cockpit's instruments. He could not see much other than that they were a long way – 'a bloody long way' – from the border with Argentina. In return for this scrap of paper he handed over two sticks of C4 plastic explosive that, although it would never explode without a detonator, might at least ensure that when her final moment came Victor Charlie would burn fiercely, if she had not already been sunk. 'With that,' according to Bennett, 'we wished them luck and lifted off again.'

Andy L concurs:

We wished each other well. Wiggy showed me our approximate location on his map. Not too much detail so the full magnitude of the implication of our position didn't really strike home. There was now a strong west wind blowing with some sleet.

Behind their Captain the SAS troopers were dragging their equipment on to the sodden Patagonian grass. It was dark, freezing cold (literally) and 0800 GMT or, now more significantly, 'five o'clock, local, in the bloody morning'.

The penultimate leg of 6 Troop's long approach to battle had ended. From here it was entirely up to 'the men on the ground'. And they were, literally, on the ground in all-round fire positions. 'Quite right.' Captain L thought, 'They have not been party to the communications and think we are still in Argentina.' As the Sea King's distinctive noise faded towards the west-north-west the Troop Commander allowed himself a few moments to reflect, take stock and frame his next words. 'Yes,' he thought, 'It's great to be off the helicopter. Some of the flight has been more than fraught and parts of it downright, bloody dangerous.' Yet there was a growing and rapidly sinking feeling in his stomach. 'We are a long way into Chile, not just over the border as planned. Maybe I've really messed this up.' he chided himself. 'Time to tell the boys the bad news.'

There were now eight SAS men on their own in Chilean Tierra del Fuego. Four would have been fine – two would have been better – for a fast, in-and-out, direct-action operation; but eight was too many, twice too many, for a long clandestine approach across 'bare-arse' countryside. Thanks to the extra ammunition and explosives they had been obliged to carry, the patrol was only catered for four days. Given the onset of the austral winter, the deteriorating weather, clothes and equipment still not fully dry after their immersion in salt water, and the 'quality' of the maps, Captain L could only grimace in desperation.

It was completely dark, a darkness that can only be experienced in remote areas. The waning moon was no longer visible and the fog had lifted, but to be replaced by sleet that was already bringing a dampness of its own and one just as capable of penetrating the most waterproof of clothing. Apart from the wind rustling eerily through the rough pampas grass there was no noise. There was nothing out of the ordinary other than the utter desolation, geographical and physical, of their position. The eight men lay still and prone. Uncomfortable after so long in the seatless Sea King, they longed to stretch and massage stiff, cold limbs; but not yet. After ten minutes Captain L struggled to his feet, flexing his thighs clear of cramp. It was time to explain the situation.

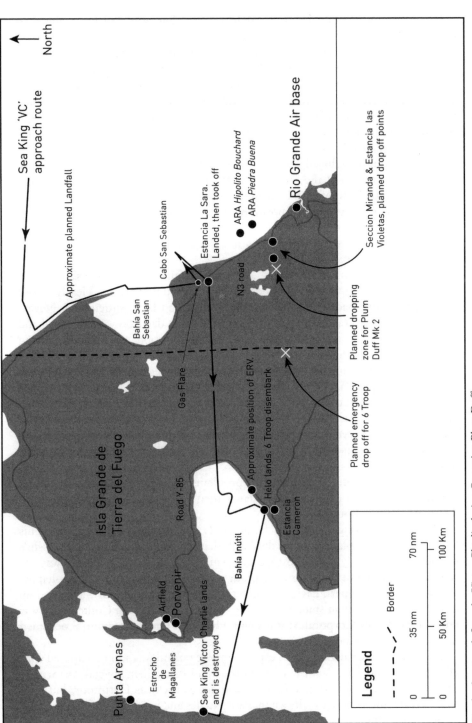

North

Sea King 'VC' approach route

Approximate planned Landfall

Cabo San Sebastian

Estancia La Sara. Landed, then took off

ARA *Hipolito Bouchard*

ARA *Piedra Buena*

Rio Grande Air base

Seccion Miranda & Estancia las Violetas, planned drop off points

N3 road

Bahía San Sebastian

Gas Flare

Planned dropping zone for Plum Duff Mk 2

Approximate position of ERV.

Helo lands. 6 Troop disembark

Planned emergency drop off for 6 Troop

Isla Grande de Tierra del Fuego

Road Y-85

Porvenir

Airfield de Porvenir

Punta Arenas

Estrecho de Magallanes

Bahía Inútil

Estancia Cameron

Sea King Victor Charlie lands and is destroyed

Legend

- - - / Border

| 0 | 35 nm | 70 nm |
| 0 | 50 Km | 100 Km |

Overland approach flown by Victor Charlie during Operation Plum Duff.

His view was unequivocal and would remain that way. He knew the men realized the gravity of the situation, more or less, yet it was necessary, now they could talk without having to shout above the roar of the engines and rotors, to offer a summary. The Troop Commander explained to the seven barely visible, blackened faces standing in a circle around him that the first landing site, some 26 miles from their target, had been compromised, and that once they had taken off the poor visibility had continued to present serious problems. Instead of being landed on or near the border with Argentina they had been forced to fly far further than planned.

Despite Bennett's gloved finger pressed to the map, Captain L was not sure how far along the coast the pilot had been able to reach; but with dawn – and with luck – some form of visual triangulation might offer a clue. The aircrew had explained their geographical position as best they could, so until sunrise Captain L was obliged to accept that they were where they were. In daylight he would do his best to be more precise, although given the absence of any 'relief' on the maps that was likely to be difficult.

The reaction among his men was, as expected, 'fairly stoic'. None showed any emotion – not that it would have been visible – although there was clearly a deep concern that they had far further to march than had been anticipated. Nevertheless, all accepted (as with all such SAS patrols, the decision was discussed and analysed among the team) that the best and only option was to start moving eastwards until first light.

While agreeing wholeheartedly (it had been his suggestion anyway), Captain L was far from happy. 'You really can't win as a "Rupert",' he thought, 'it's a sort of binary thing. Either you exhibit reckless behaviour, possibly getting good men killed by leading them into an ambush, or through your own incompetence and timidity you get everyone lost by not having the strength of your convictions ... A bit like now.' But then he muttered to himself, 'Shrug it off. It goes with the territory.'

Anyway, that was in the past, and the problems of the present were now calling for attention. They must march until dawn, then find a suitable lying-up position. There were three hours left.

The team adopting single file, Sergeant N was placed in the lead with his Welrod pistol. Captain L was doubtful that a man carrying 'the assassin's weapon' and possibly prepared to use it while still in 'friendly' Chile, was the right man to lead, but the veteran sergeant was most certainly not 'trigger-happy' and was anyway a superb navigator. Behind Sergeant N the patrol was closed up rather more tightly than standard spacing dictated. The Troop Commander was number six, Lance Corporal M was behind him and Lance Corporal S occupied the unenviable rear position.

They had no idea at all what to expect, but the terrain was soon compared with Wales' notorious Elan Valley, well known to all from their Special Air Service 'selection tests'. Where they now were was not as rocky as Dartmoor, but low-lying, gentle hills covered with vast marshy patches and hefty tufts of 'moon grass' made it difficult to place the feet, and it was awkward to move swiftly. Vast pools of surface water vied for space with patches of snow, and with each man carrying 80lb progress was slow.

After one hour the patrol stopped for five minutes. In a circle they lay, listening. The utter quiet merely emphasized – as if it needed emphasizing – just how remote a spot it was that the helicopter pilots had been forced to choose. That was fine, but the chances of being able to fix a position in the dawn light were clearly going to be just as remote.

An outline of hills was beginning to appear ahead, yet it was impossible to tell if they were low hills close to or higher hills further away. The weather was, if anything, markedly worse, with near-freezing rain blowing horizontally into their backs. By common agreement the 'speed of advance' was reckoned to be well less than 1½ miles an hour: a rate that it needed no 'applied mathematician' to calculate would mean taking two days and half their rations merely to reach the Argentine border.

For a further two hours, with another five-minute stop, the party struggled on, the going underfoot becoming more difficult and the rate of advance noticeably slowing. Progress was hard by any standards, and these were men certainly used to hard going. If it was rough in the pampas grass it was considerably rougher traversing the many rocky-sided ravines, where keeping to a strict compass course was well nigh impossible. Inside their windproof smocks they sweated copiously, while outside the sleet seeped into shoulders, backs and bergens. Beneath the thickest of cloud covers dawn was sure to be 'delayed', yet after a brief discussion a vote to halt was unanimous. Defensive positions were established, and two men sent to seek a better place to shelter. Tired legs and twisted ankles were grateful for the rest, but the cessation of exertion now allowed a real cold to set in towards each body's core. If no refuge was found, the risk of eight cases of exposure would be real. Few had been able to dry out their clothes as fully as they had hoped from the salt water immersion two days earlier, and now this uncomfortable fact was adding to each individual's 'exposure factor'.

Dispatched to seek a more sheltered lying-up position – while the rest waited in a circle, looking outwards, weapons cocked and ready, trying with little success to avoid teeth chattering and limbs shaking – Sergeant N and Corporal P returned after ten minutes. They bore news of a stream and a few gorse-like bushes 100 yards away.

Daylight on 18 May brought no relief from the weather or the uncertainty of their position. The hills whose outlines they had seen in the dark were on the far eastern horizon and, without discernible features, useless for position fixing. All around, on every bleak bearing, there was nothing but one sleet-blasted heath after another, cut and intersected by shallow ravines that in a warmer part of the world would be called *wadis*. Looking down the course they must take that next evening towards their goal, the countryside was clearly going to be as unforgiving. Yet it was not in the nature of any one of the eight men sheltering on the edge of their diddle-dee-lined gully[26] to 'give up' or to accept that the odds against them in the time available were simply too great. That is not the SAS way, yet all knew that it was only a matter of time before the officer, the youngest and most inexperienced man in the team, was forced to make a decision – a decision that, in the manner of the regiment, all could accept.

Before that watershed was reached a new obstacle began to manifest itself, one that had not been foreseen and one for which they had little remedy: sickness. Trooper T was not well. Shortly after the rudimentary camp had been established and each man not on watch had crawled into some form of camouflaged shelter, the 37-year-old ex-RSM announced that he had a sore throat. 'Tough', was the unsympathetic, yet expected, reply; but as he quickly and noticeably began to weaken, with a rising temperature, grudging, lukewarm sympathy began turning to real concern.

The Captain, faced with a new crossroads, briefly considered leaving three men to 'nurse', protect and guard the ailing man, while the remaining four continued. They would act purely as a reconnaissance patrol, leaving behind all heavy weapons, ammunition and explosives. With far less weight in their bergens they would be able to make better time. But consideration of this option was brief, for between them they only had two operational maps plus the 'escape map'. They only had one radio set, too. Captain L also believed, strongly, that as they had come together to do a job so they must stay together and attempt to complete that job. This was, as with the original decision to abort the first landing, a decision that was to haunt him through the years.

It was time to call Hereford. Not only was there a very narrow time window in each twenty-four-hour period when that was possible, but up to this moment the radio, thanks to its ducking in the Southern Ocean, had refused to cooperate with its operator, Lance Corporal M. Now, as if realizing the deteriorating situation, even the radio's electronics perked up.

With Trooper T 'dosed to the gills' yet showing no sign of improvement, the patrol's predicament was explained. Back home there was little appreciation of the reality of life in Tierra del Fuego, this transmission from Plum Duff being the first that anyone had heard of the operation since Victor Charlie had taken off from HMS *Invincible* and disappeared, literally, into the night. Those at home were made aware, forcibly, that the insertion on to the mainland had not gone as planned; that the first drop-off point had been compromised and the emergency drop-off point was not quite where the patrol leader had hoped it would be – by about 70 miles; and that the maps remained worse than useless.

It was also the first anyone at home knew of the appalling weather; but the lack of understanding by those 8,000 miles away was further underlined by a direct and unequivocal order that Captain L must continue with the mission. He argued back that as the man on the spot the decision was his, and his decision was that he would wait for twenty-four hours and then reassess Trooper T's medical condition. Nevertheless, he remained adamant that their situation was fast becoming unsustainable. What he longed to say, but was too tactful to do so, was that Hereford had been, in the collective opinion of his team, 'prepared to write us off from the very beginning'. He wanted to continue arguing, but did not. As no one in the United Kingdom had the slightest inkling of the position his patrol was in either geographically or militarily, or understood that it had no maps worthy of the task and even less intelligence with which to plan the approach towards a doubtlessly heavily guarded air base on a war footing, while wearing no formal uniform, any decision made would be his and his alone.

Throughout daylight on 19 and 20 May the men lay in their sleet-covered, poleless tents, eating a little of their precious food and conserving energy until after dusk each evening, when a two-man patrol was dispatched in an attempt to establish their position. Through the day various bleak landmarks had been spotted but nothing that would have been marked on a British, large-scale Ordinance Survey map, let alone in a school atlas. The marginally better news was that Trooper T was exhibiting some signs of improvement.

In each direction, through every one of the compass's 360 degrees, there was nothing but snow- or ice-covered, undulating plains of pampas grass, mottled with vast patches of the low, rough diddle-dee bushes. The shallow gullies criss-crossing the landscape might have offered daytime hides, but they made night-time manoeuvre and navigation a slow and inaccurate business.

Quite simply – as they had all begun to suspect from the first briefing onwards – Captain L and his troop had been dealt an impossible hand of cards, and now reality was closing in. Fast. Yet it was 'theirs not to reason why' but to get on with the job: head eastwards and after 50 or 60 miles hit the coast, then decide which way to turn for Rio Grande ...

With the sick trooper just about fit enough to attempt further progress, after dark on the 20 May the eight men restarted their increasingly pointless trek. The wind-driven sleet was as relentless as ever, and the latest message from Hereford had not been helpful. The perception now was that 6 Troop had, to a man, been captured; yet despite the troop's re-authenticating their transmission, the 'home team' remained unconvinced. This was a new worry to gnaw away at Captain L's decision-making processes as he and his men stumbled towards Argentina in weather as appalling as was possible in southern Tierra del Fuego during the onset of an austral winter. He knew, too, that with only two days rations left, they were at the very closest probably still 10 nautical miles from the border; and from there they had a further 30 miles, across enemy territory, to reach their target. In fact, he was being optimistic, for they were almost certainly over 20 nautical miles from the border. The single north-south road marked on one of their maps had yet to be crossed, and that was estimated to be at least 5 miles from Argentina.

As 6 Troop lay up throughout daylight on 21 May, eight men huddled together in the lee of a small gully alongside an ice-edged stream, it was decision time again. Some were enthusiastic for continuing east to the road, commandeering a passing vehicle, then driving to Rio Grande; but it was an idea born of desperation rather than rational thought. All knew that the game was over and that their patrol leader needed to make that firm, final and irrevocable decision.

Whatever he was about to decide, Captain L told Hereford that a resupply of food – by air-drop if necessary – was now imperative and had to happen before they re-entered Argentina. The response was swift and unexpected. The patrol was to head back to an Emergency Rendezvous, or ERV, that was to be chosen by 6 Troop and would be manned by Captain Pete Hogg of the SAS. Hogg had originally flown into Chile as part of Captain C's SBS team sent to debrief the Royal Marine detachment captured while defending South Georgia. When the freed prisoners returned to the United Kingdom with Captain C, Hogg, a Spanish speaker, remained in the country. Attached to the British embassy in Santiago, he was to support an SAS communications link that had nothing to do with Operation Mikado or Exocet missiles.

Despite asking many times, Captain L had never been made aware that such an emergency plan would or could be activated. Unknown to him, no proposals had been offered to extricate the patrol, since 'they were not expected to survive'. With Hogg now in Chile, it made sense for him to be co-opted into solving Plum Duff's dilemma.

At the Duke of York Barracks in Chelsea and at Hereford a revised operation to attack the Exocets was hastily being cooked up; no other word is suitable to describe this latest proposal. Despite the unlikelihood of the operation being given the go-ahead by the War Cabinet, Headquarters SAS, having been denied its moment of glory, decreed that Mikado would still take place but without the benefit of a reconnaissance. If there had been considerable disquiet within B Squadron over the original plan, then that disquiet about this most unmilitary of procedures was corkscrewing deeper. 'Time spent in reconnaissance is seldom wasted' is one of the most sensible if not inviolable of all military tenets, and yet Mikado – extremely risky even with a prior recce – was to go ahead regardless.

While Plum Duff's patrol shivered on the plains of Patagonia, plans for the execution of Mikado were being hardened in a mood not only of anger at the failure of their colleagues 'to deliver what might have been the most stunning special forces operation since the Second World War', but one of escalating tension.

Meanwhile, the problems besetting 6 Troop had not gone unnoticed in Argentina, for at 0330 GMT on 21 May Communiqué No. 67 was issued by the Argentine Joint General Staff:[27]

> The Joint General Staff reports that on 20 May the Chilean government informed us that a British Sea King helicopter number ZA-290 had been discovered, burnt and with no sign of its crew, in the vicinity of Caleta Agua Fresca 18 kilometres to the South of Punta Arenas. The Chilean authorities have ordered the necessary search and have made appropriate representation to the British Ambassador.

A note (the 'appropriate representation') was delivered by the Chilean Foreign Minister Rene Rojas Galdames to the British Ambassador John Moore Heath. A reply was subsequently given to Galdames by Heath in which, according to Muñoz in ¡Ataquen Rio Grande!, he explained that, 'The helicopter referred to in the note does belong to the British Task force and was carrying out a reconnaissance in Tierra del Fuego.'

That same day the British Ministry of Defence announced:

A Sea King carrying out a reconnaissance mission suffered problems in adverse weather and has come down on Chilean soil where its remains have been discovered by uniformed officers of that country.

The announcement went on to confirm that its crew had not yet been found.

If the Argentine defenders of Rio Grande had been in any doubt earlier, they now knew that the suspicious flights during the very early hours of 18 May had to be connected. Not having detected the Sea King until it was flying east over the coast, and as it was then tracked heading back towards Estancia La Sara before finally heading on westwards, it was clear that this insertion could only have been launched either from Chilean territory or from a British ship operating in Chilean waters. Suspicious Argentine fingers, understandably, pointed to the Royal Research Ship *Bransfield* that was known to have operated in the area during more peaceful times.

It is instructive to view the Argentine position as postulated by Muñoz in his book:

The Chilean authorities who released their statement at the same time attempted to maintain their position of neutrality in the evolving conflict. They informed our [Argentine] ambassador of what had occurred, they sent a note of protest to the British government and ordered a thorough investigation into the incident. Without detracting from it the Chilean government was obliged to make public statements distancing itself from any complicity.

In this context, eighteen years after the campaign a Chilean Brigadier-General, Fernando Matthei Aubel, stated,[28] 'We had to maintain Pinochet's position and to give long explanations assuring the Argentines that we knew nothing.' Later he denied, quite correctly, an Argentine account of the presence of the ship *Bransfield* acting in support of the Sea King, stating truthfully that, 'No British ship was operating in Chilean waters.'

None of this was known to Captain Andy L and his men, who still faced considerable and unavoidable dangers, as well as hunger and exposure, or worse. Although ordered to travel to a previously unknown emergency rendezvous, 6 Troop's immediate plight was far from solved. Over the air, on 'secure voice', Captain Andy suggested one of the coast road's many small bridges that cross streams along the southern edge of the Bahía Inútil and asked for two days. SAS HQ agreed the emergency rendezvous location but stated that it would only be 'open' for one hour after dark on the evening of 22 May – the next night. For unexplained reasons a delay was out of the question.[29]

Captain L's problem was simple: he had little idea of his geographical position. He was now pretty certain that he knew where they had been dropped and that they had, by compass, been slowly heading eastwards since; but with no recognizable topographical features their precise whereabouts was difficult to determine. He was not sure how far he and his men had to return but he knew that they had just twenty-four hours in which to do so.

The conversation with Hereford had not been satisfactory. Captain L had agreed a rendezvous chosen from a map with neither contours nor grid overlay, thus it was impossible to pinpoint a specific position. 'Without a grid reference I had to say to Hereford, "On the map that I've got I can see four bridges. Is it the western bridge? If not, which one?" Between us all we chose the bridge that Hereford, simultaneously talking to Pete Hogg in Chile, were agreeing.[30] Hogg would meet us the following night when the rendezvous would be open only for one hour after sunset.'

Following that conversation, the patrol's communications system died, finally and irreversibly.

Throughout the night of the 21/22 May and well into the abysmal visibility of 'daylight' 6 Troop slowly 'tabbed' westwards, covering, such was the difficulty underfoot, an estimated 9 statute miles. Although in theory they had by now consumed their four days' rations, each man had managed to conserve enough to give them – at the very most and on 'starvation measures' – a further day of food. By eking out this meagre amount Captain L calculated that they might, just, manage two more days of eating, providing they were static. There was no shortage of water.

Eventually, and with no clues to offer cast-iron confirmation, the consensus within the team was that they had, fortuitously, somehow ended up in a position overlooking the chosen bridge from a 'safe' distance of 500 yards. Wriggled down into the sodden undergrowth, the eight troopers waited for dusk. As soon as the light faded, Captain L 'sent a couple of guys forward. We waited for an hour. We waited for two hours. Nothing happened. They came back.'

The same routine was followed during the evenings of 23, 24 and 25 May. 'Each time the guys returned they did so with a "nil report". We had long run out of food and the weather was similar to that in the Shetland Islands. It rains, it freezes, it snows, it freezes, it rains …'

With no communications either with the SAS team in Chile or with their own Headquarters in England, the Captain once more faced a predicament that only he could resolve. There was a limit to how long his men could lie immobile by day in the undergrowth, with scant protection and nothing to eat. Action was called for. A bold, potentially perilous, move was needed.

Choosing his man carefully, Captain L decided to go forward with Lance Corporal M, the patrol's signaller and chess-playing ex-Gordon Highlander. They would hitch a lift in order to find some way of dialling the telephone number he had been given before leaving Hereford: the number of the British consul, who, he presumed, was across the Strait of Magellan in Punta Arenas. Captain L also recalled the vague, unwritten instructions issued at Hereford: 'When we started the mission we knew – we thought – we were going to get out through Chile, although we didn't actually know how. The Brigadier had said in his orders, "If you are successful you will exfiltrate to the west over the border and make your way to the Chilean authorities".'

It was time to do just that.

On the morning of 26 May Captain L and Lance Corporal M slipped their civilian 'Cotswold' camping coats over their SAS camouflaged jackets, handed their rifles to the remainder of the patrol, pocketed their 9mm Browning pistols and broke cover. Making sure that no one saw from whence they had come, the two men walked swiftly to the road before turning north. From this moment on there would be no communication between the patrol leader and his six troopers left behind.

Andy L knew from observation that traffic along this coastal, all-weather road (the Y 85) was 'light' but also that it was commercial and likely to have room for itinerant hitchhikers. The 'downside', he also reasoned, was that hitchhikers were unusual and would cause comment. But there was no alternative.

The duo walked a considerable distance before a truck laden with logs drew up from behind and stopped. 'The two guys in the lorry looked quite surprised but they were friendly. They didn't understand what was going on but we had just thumbed a lift and they made signs for us to get on the back.' The logging truck took them 70 miles along the dirt-track road till it neared the small town of Porvenir, where they were invited to get off. Dusty, unshaven, unkempt, smelly and hungry, the two men set off on foot again for ... they knew not what. What the officer was certain of, through his own deduction (and by staring across the water through his binoculars), rather than from any hard evidence passed on by Hereford, was that any SAS 'rescue team' must be based in Porvenir, or, for it was now four days after the rendezvous time, had been based in Porvenir; it was the only town for miles in any direction and 21 miles to the east across the Strait of Magellan from Punta Arenas. A further clue that it might be central to any hastily set up escape plan was that it boasted an air field 3 miles to the north-north-east and a ferry terminal 2½ miles to the west.

Porvenir was and remains a small, shanty-style town with, then, rundown shacks on the outskirts and smarter, wooden houses – some two-storey – towards the centre, all arranged in a symmetrical, grid of cement-paved roads around a 'square of formal gardens'. Captain L's and Lance Corporal M's second priority was to find a house that would take them in with few, preferably no, questions asked. Much as they needed warmth and food, the first priority was to make that telephone call to Punta's British consul.

Using no more than sign language, they were directed by an unsuspicious teenager towards a small wooden hut similar to dozens that surrounded it, where the single communal radio-telephone was operated by one man. He 'raised his eyebrows' when handed a slip of paper with the number scrawled upon it. 'It was a risk, but,' as Andy L was to comment later, 'the choices were if they helped they did and if they didn't they didn't!'

Once the Captain had parted with a few US dollars the 'operator' allowed him to make the call. The British consul in (he presumed but did not know for sure) Punta Arenas came on the line. 'I spoke to him and he was horrified as he hadn't been briefed. He was literally frightened, terrified actually. I said, "I've got all these guys in the field with no food and I need to do something about them", but all he could say was, "My advice is that you give yourselves up".' The lack of any offer of assistance, indeed the lack of any apparent understanding of his predicament from an official of the British Foreign Office, was a deep and unexpected disappointment. 'Maybe his hands were tied,' thought the SAS officer, 'but he offered nothing and sounded a very unhappy bunny!'

While it may well be argued that such an official should have known nothing of special forces operations, his was the telephone number given to Andy L by Headquarters SAS for just this purpose.

It had taken the best part of the day to reach Porvenir. Appearing inconspicuous in this town of equally scruffy working men was not difficult, yet they still needed to find someone who would accept two strangers in such an unprepossessing state. Striking it lucky early on, they happened upon a Chilean prepared to accept them – in exchange for cash. They possessed American and Argentine currency, but for reasons long forgotten had given all their Chilean money to the helicopter crew.

The chosen house was not a 'safe' house, but on receiving 20 American dollars, accompanied by a loud 'sssshhh', the owners eyes 'lit up' in a loose sign of understanding. Neither could speak the other's language, but US greenbacks have a patois of their own in such circumstances.

Returning to his 'parlour' with the SAS men in tow, the owner switched on a black and white television that, coincidentally, was showing shots of the Falkland Islands. He pointed to the screen then at the two troopers. "Yeeees," they nodded slowly, with fingers to lips. The Chilean kept quiet; he understood.

Once they had settled into their shared bedroom, the Lance Corporal elected to venture into town to buy a modicum of civilian clothes, soon returning with a couple of jumpers and two pairs of oversize jeans. Meanwhile, their new landlord had prepared a simple meal, and while that satisfied one need there was another that also needed assuaging. Captain Andy L, angry that the link given to them by the SAS had proved so useless, felt that a walk around the town might not only calm his frustration but also throw up a clue or a pointer to their next move. This was a shrewd, almost clairvoyant, decision. 'Believe it or not, in the dark, and as we walked past the open door of an eating house – restaurant would be too grand a word – we looked in and saw not only Pete Hogg but Brummie Stokes and Bronco Lane.[31] They could only have been there because of us.'

Captain L's search had ended almost as it began. He walked straight in. Hogg, equally surprised, quickly ushered him out again while pressing a set of car keys into his hand with the words, 'Go and sit in the pickup. We've been sent to find you and will be out in a moment.'

Bearing in mind the precise date set for the rendezvous, and believing that there could be no extension to it, Captain L's and Lance Corporal M's less than charitable but perfectly correct, assumption was that their rescuers had not been trying very hard, if at all, over the previous days ... but they did as they were told. For reasons that remain unclear it is obvious that this rescue party had made no attempt to make the emergency rendezvous at the bridge on the chosen night, nor on any subsequent night.

When Hogg's team had finished eating, all repaired to a two-room shed with a 'boardwalk veranda' along the front and a second, similar pickup truck parked close by. Over that night of 26/27 May, Stokes and Lane drove Captain L and Lance Corporal M to the emergency rendezvous bridge, where after recognition was established by shouting into the darkness, the six starving and drained men were reunited with their 'boss' and his signaller. Another 70 miles later, and after 'takeaways' of local steak and bacon sandwiches (planned as two meals – supper and breakfast – but all devoured within minutes), eleven sleeping places were allocated on the floor and veranda of the shack. As 6 Troop's exhausted patrol began to doss down, Hogg reappeared – clearly, in Andy L's view, in the area for other reasons – to announce a 'good night sleeping draught'. Hogg then dropped his bombshell: 'Once recovered, you will be ordered back across the border to complete the mission or, at the least, to undertake the reconnaissance phase. B Squadron's Operation Mikado is still "on".'

On Ascension Island, news that MV *Atlantic Conveyor* had been targeted by two Exocets the day before (25 May) was coupled with the realization that although the one missile the Argentines had left could still cause mayhem, yet the odds that that this last missile could bring about the end of the campaign in Argentina's favour were slim. As though to emphasize that fact, the only two air-to-air refuelling-capable C-130s were now deployed on almost permanent Task Force resupply flights: an undertaking that was, following the loss of the Cunard stores ship, not just vital but now critical.

Nevertheless, at the Duke of York Barracks the desire to destroy this one Exocet remained as urgent as ever, regardless of the practicalities of the hour. Operation Mikado was to continue, but without the benefit of a reconnaissance. Once more, though, confusion was injected into the process when a senior SAS staff officer announced to Captain C of the Special Operations Group that the 'failed' Plum Duff patrol into Terra del Fuego was now entirely 'an SAS affair' and thus would not be discussed further with any other agency, including Admiral Fieldhouse's Special Operations Coordinator. Any deconfliction of operations and overlapping of logistic needs would become yet more convoluted. The SAS Regiment was anxious to keep its 'failures' hidden at all costs.

Resting in Porvenir, Andy L and his men heard of the successful landings at San Carlos, but they also learned that a Sea King had ditched while conducting a routine night-time cross-decking of members of D and G Squadrons between ships of the Task Force. When combined with the news that they were about to be ordered, unilaterally and with no discussion outside the SAS, back over the border, this was a low moment. The decision came simultaneously with the news, relayed via Hogg, that as 'their' Sea King had been found and its discovery made internationally public, there were an estimated 2,000 Argentine troops scouring the area between their border with Chile and Rio Grande air base.

Throughout 27 and 28 May 6 Troop lay up in their shack, while Stokes and Lane purchased food as well as anoraks and an assortment of trousers to make them look more acceptable as civilians. During this time Hogg disappeared for long periods on unrelated tasks, although each time he returned he had a new or altered plan for 6 Troop. The latest was that they were still going back to Argentina but first had to fly to Santiago. No one in the troop saw the logic of this move to the Chilean capital, but all accepted that their destiny was no longer in their own hands.

Early on the morning of 30 May the eight SAS men were driven (virtually smuggled) the 3 miles to Capitan Fuentes Martinez airfield, where a light aircraft was waiting. The stated reason for the covert nature of this move was that there was now such a high level of activity and diplomatic interest across the region that their status was in danger of being compromised. Much to the patrol commander's surprise he was told that he and his team had still to regard themselves as being 'on operations'.

At the airfield, the troopers, dressed now in 'civilian' clothes, climbed into a single-engine aircraft for the 25-mile hop across the Straits to Punta Arenas. Here they were parked close to a larger two-engine aircraft which they immediately boarded, while their bergens were equally swiftly manhandled across. A Chilean Air Force officer name Hohe introduced himself as their pilot for the next two legs of the flight north. Once all were strapped in they took off for Puerto Montt, a flight that came close to a premature end as the pilot was forced to dive dramatically into warmer air when the aircraft's control surfaces began to ice up. For a few minutes they were in danger of plunging straight into the ground as Hohe struggled to force some movement into his ailerons and elevators. Thankfully, and only just in time, he was able to gain control and level out. At the intermediate refuelling point he announced to his passengers that he was as relieved as he ever had been on landing safely. Refuelled, they continued without further frights to Santiago. Here, away from stray camera lenses, they were met at the aircraft steps by a series of motor cars that whisked them to a 'safe house', under the careful eye of a minder.

Between 30 May and 8 June 6 Troop was billeted in a comfortable four-bedroom bungalow with a large secluded garden, beyond which they were not allowed to roam. Once more, regular takeaways were delivered by Stokes, although Lane sometimes took over this duty. Occasional visitors were the peripatetic Hogg and the newly appointed Commanding Officer of 22 SAS, Lieutenant Colonel Neville Howard, who had begun his involvement with the campaign as the SAS adviser to Captain Robert Woodard.

Yet another snippet of sad news filtered through to 6 Troop. Hohe, the Chilean pilot who had flown the team north from Punta Arenas, had 'disappeared without trace' while returning along the same leg of the outward journey during which he had been obliged to free his controls of ice. On his second emergency dive to warmer air, it was assumed, he had not been able to pull up in time.

Other news arrived in the bungalow. There were still plans for 6 Troop to re-insert into Argentina, but instead of doing so from Chile it would be, for the second time, from Ascension Island – from which it must be deduced that Headquarters, SAS, was continuing to work in isolation from other considerations, while also remaining heedless of the Task Force's paucity of troop-lift helicopters and the urgency of Hercules resupply flights. Those in the Duke of

York Barracks were unable to accept that, with the last of the Argentines' Exocets harmlessly expended on 30 May against HMS *Avenger*, there was no operational need for such an attack.

Then, on 8 June, Captain L and his team received the news that they were flying to the UK and not back to Argentina, and thus would be taking no further part in the campaign. This 'final' decision was met with relief, even among the most hardened men of the patrol. Andy L describes a common view:[32]

The Rat – my sergeant and second in command – when in Santiago and listening to all the hare-brained schemes coming out of Headquarters SAS, and via the various regimental representatives in Chile, said, 'Do you know what boss, I am actually looking forward to going home.' I could, we all could, see his point and agree.

II

Had there been good visibility along the border, and had Victor Charlie therefore been able to land where Andy L had always preferred, events might well have panned out differently. Assuming the patrol had established a covert observation post overlooking Rio Grande air base, then Operation Mikado would have been cancelled. Captain Andy L and his team would have reported the 'overkill' of ground defences in terms of men, materiel and weapons; they might have observed that the Super Étendard pilots did not sleep in the same place two nights running and then always away from the base, and they would have noted that the Super Étendard aircraft never spent two consecutive nights in the same spot, with each new position unpredictable in advance. They would have reported that there were never more than two missiles on the base at any time, and more often than not only two aircraft, which were 'hidden' among the many others scattered around the base. Furthermore, they would have reported that the wind blew constantly and strongly from the west; that the runway was permanently icy; that the surrounding countryside was snow-covered, with most identifying features masked; that the runway and aerial lights were sometimes lit at night while often, but unpredictably, the air base and surrounding town and countryside were in total blackout; that the incidence of fog was very high; that the runway was never blocked; and that civilian and military (mostly C-130s and F-28s) aircraft landed and took off through the dark hours.

Another fact (mentioned elsewhere but repeated here to add emphasis) has come to light that might have been relevant had the patrol been overlooking the air base. Some accounts have it that the one and only night that 'all four' Super Étendards were moved into the town of Rio Grande was the same night that Sea King Victor Charlie was attempting to insert the SAS team north of the town. In fact, the only night this tricky, delicate, operation took place had been ten days earlier, with just two aircraft. Nevertheless, it is interesting to speculate that had the 'reconnaissance' patrol managed to creep into position after the Super Étendards had left the base at dusk, Captain L and his troopers would have watched their slow return from the town at first light. To pursue this hypothesis, the SAS would then have had a near-perfect opportunity to engage them with small arms. The problem then would have been that the initial part of their escape towards the Chilean border, 35 miles to the west as the condor flies, would have begun at the break of day and the start of a major 'hue and cry'. A tricky decision for the patrol commander: an almost certain 'kill' versus an almost certain death ... while two other aircraft and any remaining Exocets would have remained unscathed.

Later, Rear Admiral Whetstone of the Special Operations Group was to write:

> The initial impression I gained [from the Sea King aircrew on their return] ... was that the SAS patrol commander believed that the helicopter had been detected before reaching the Argentine coast and that Plum Duff was doomed to failure ... In view of what we now know about the defences at Rio Grande it must be doubted if the SAS patrol had much chance of achieving its objective and the decision to abort was probably sensible, if taken for the wrong reason ... Had it taken place, Operation Mikado would have been impossible to disclaim plausibly if a diplomatic problem had arisen.[33]

The repercussions would have been more than diplomatic or military, for as early as 5 April 1982 articles had begun to appear in the English-language *Buenos Aires Herald*. A number of anonymous telephone calls were made to this journal over the subsequent weeks warning that, 'If Britain carries out any military strikes against continental Argentina, action will be taken against British property, personal and commercial, [and that these] operations against the British community in Argentina would be conducted under the codename Operation Thunderbolt.'

Whetstone concluded, 'The decision ... to use SAS troops from the United Kingdom on Plum Duff was ... not a matter discussed at the Special Operations Group.' That 'strategic special forces' from the United Kingdom were chosen in preference to 'tactical troops' already in theatre (of which, according to Major General Jeremy Moore, there were far too many anyway)[34] and who were used to operating with the Sea Kings of 846 Squadron, has always been questioned. Had HMS *Onyx* been on station in time, events might have turned out differently. This mistake, of dispatching such a submarine late, was not repeated in the Middle East ten years later.

III

Empty of 'passengers', Victor Charlie had lifted off from the beach at 0800 GMT. Hutchings, Bennett and Imrie then faced an interesting few days. These are briefly described below, having been taken from a narrative compiled by 'Wiggy' Bennett (times to 24 May are GMT).

18 May
0800: Victor Charlie has been airborne for almost five hours. Enough fuel left for a further hour and a quarter. Dropped SAS. Departed for Pte Santa Maria.
0835: Coast in, turn south ... buildings ... then north ... in search of a more desolate area.

0850: Land on beach 11 miles south of Punta Arenas. Hutchings remains at controls while Bennett and Imrie prepare the aircraft for sinking, plus a 200-foot line by which the pilot would be hauled back to shore.

0915: Take off. Pilot fails to persuade Victor Charlie to sink. Aircraft returns. Heavy landing on beach.

0935: Aircraft set alight.

1200: Daylight. 'Poncho' bivouac.

2000: Hutchings conducts local reconnaissance.

2100: Move, first west, inland, then north, eventually north-west. No water. No cover. Many hills. Very tired and weak.

19 May

0100: Camp among fallen logs.

1600: Iroquois helicopter searching the coast.

2030: Move to a source of water ('Bliss').

2130: Return to camp then move out.

2230: Rain.

20 May

0030: Cross river.

0130: Trio separate (in a 'mud climb').

0230: New camp position in woods.

1130: Improve camouflage.

1200: Approached by cattle herders but not spotted. Fine drying day.

2030: Short move to camp in scrub beneath a wood. Refill water containers ('foul').

21 May

1130: Renew camouflage.

1700: Horsemen close by.

1800: Decide to move.

2000: Overflown by light aircraft heading south then north. [Bennett was later told that it contained members of the SBS.]

2100: Move out.

2200: New camp. Search for water.

2330: Hutchings and Bennett retrace tracks for fresh water.

22 May

1200: Refresh camouflage.

2000: Hutchings and Bennett search for water.

2230: Risk fire for cooking.

23 May

1500: Bennett has a hair-wash.

1600: Continuous rain. No fire.

24 May

1600: Last river visit for water.

2100: Good fire. Burn rubbish.

25 May (Times now in GMT-4)

Daylight: Walk into Punta Arenas.

1200: Stopped by Captain Marco Torres of the Prefectura Carabineros de Chile

1445: Moved to safe house in Punta Arenas. Informed by an SAS officer that Mikado was cancelled.

2000: Depart Punta Arenas airport in Chile/RAF C-130.

26 May

0030: Arrive Santiago.

0130: Arrive home of the British consul.

0800: Photographed for passports.

1330: Press conference.

1415: Arrive Santiago airport.

1445: Take off in LAN Chile aircraft for Madrid.

1900 (Brazil time): Stop for one hour at Rio de Janeiro. Remain on aircraft.

27 May

1000: Arrive Madrid.

1330: Depart Madrid, British Airways.

1600: Arrive Gatwick. Only the Press meet the team.

1800: Taxi to Ministry of Defence.

2100: Team informed they would rejoin the Task Force.

2230: Whisky with the Chief of the Defence Staff.

2250: Leave MOD escorted by a Secret Intelligence Service officer and Captain C. Squadron Leader David Niven (then RAF's 'liaison' officer in Headquarters SAS) had formed part of the debriefing team.

28 May

0001: Escorted to a safe house 'in the country' by the SIS Officer and Captain C.

Bennett, Hutchings and Imrie did not return to the Task Force.[35]

Chapter 12

Operation Mikado – Outline Plan: Rio Grande

To those front-line men more intimately involved than the planners there was a worrying inevitability surrounding London's desire for swift action against the Exocet threat, an inevitability over which the proposed participants had no control whatsoever. Their worry was based on a growing certainty that, through a lack of a prior reconnaissance and thus intelligence, and poor if not non-existent orders, Operation Mikado was never likely to succeed. At Hereford a number of SAS personnel shared the view that a re-run of the Entebbe raid was not the correct way ahead against a well-armed and alert enemy. In addition to B Squadron's Sergeant Major John F (who had openly expressed his fears to Captain L as he climbed into the 4-tonner to take him to Brize Norton), there was Staff Sergeant Jake V. Realizing that, with 6 Troop's departure from Hereford on 15 May, the operation was clearly 'on', Staff Sergeant V knew that senior officers had not heeded their men's concerns.

If the air approach and ground assault were not worry enough, another ambiguity concerned the exfiltration. There were several options or combinations of options: one was based on the assumption that the aircraft would be destroyed on the ground, thus ensuring that a 30-mile escape and evade to the Chilean border faced the sixty men of B Squadron; another was that the aircraft survived and thus were able to fly direct to Punta Arenas with all on board – but leaving behind the Land Rovers and Triumph motorcycles; yet another assumption was that the aircraft would not survive but that the aircrew would – this would require sixty SAS men to 'escort' ten airmen to the border while being hunted down by Argentine ground and air forces across flat, featureless country with few natural hiding places. It was this last possibility that was the cause of much deliberation in Headquarters SAS, for it was, frankly, a nonsense. From the SAS's point of view it would be easier if they were not encumbered with 'passengers', who would slow down and possibly even prevent progress towards safety. The solution was to cut their losses early on and destroy their own Special Forces Flight Hercules with their aircrew as they sat on the tarmac. This 'option' was certainly considered in the UK ... and then rejected. Discussions such as these, abhorrent though they are, were necessary so that every aspect of the impending operation could be considered and then, in this case, dismissed. It has become clear, while researching this tale, that at Two Boats Village many 'time-passing measures' were introduced to do just that: complicated and unlikely courses of action to be mulled over constantly to while away the hours.

Similar indecision and ambiguities had boded very ill indeed for the commander of 6 Troop already conducting Operation Plum Duff; but, in due course, the situation would be even worse for the commander of B Squadron and the C-130 crews. The fact that the two Hercules might not make a safe landing at Rio Grande was not, in the early days of the planning, a factor that concerned the SAS; yet it was the RAF that faced the most daunting task of all.

Assuming – there were a great many assumptions – that the two Hercules did land safely, then the SAS's part was straightforward: a *coup de main* followed by an escape and evasion. Meat and drink to all troopers. However, as the rehearsals progressed, B Squadron began to appreciate the challenges facing the Hercules aircrew; yet this information did not progress up the SAS's chain of command. It had also been the duty of the RAF's liaison officers at Chelsea to reflect the RAF's capabilities and limitations, but this they failed to do – although, as explained elsewhere, there may have been good reasons for this. Additionally, apart from the presence of 47 Squadron's Commanding Officer on the Kinloss 'operation', no RAF officer attached to the SAS staff ever attended the Mikado rehearsals.

Staff Sergeant V of B Squadron's Boat Troop, a seasoned SAS member and veteran of many of the regiment's more recent adventures, had expressed sincere and professional doubts about the wisdom of the forthcoming operation, and his was a voice that should have been heeded by those further up the command chain. The Commanding Officer of B Squadron, Major John Moss, did heed it and tended to agree; he accepted the paramount need for the Exocets to be destroyed but decided there was a better way to achieve that than via the more than risky landing of two Hercules on a defended air base. Suspicions were growing that this method was being driven for 'image' reasons rather than by practical considerations. The 'maintenance of the myth' was casting its long shadow, and the senior officers, and those in government whom they advised, should have listened. However, that was not to be, and B Squadron, at a most critical point, lost two of its key personnel.

'Boss, this is bloody madness,' Staff Sergeant 'Jake' V had declared. 'None of the stupid bastards who are planning this will be in the back of the aeroplane.'

With a clear conscience, the Staff Sergeant offered his resignation to his Squadron Commander. Moss was obliged to inform their Commanding Officer, but because Mike Rose was in the South Atlantic he notified the only other person that he could, the Director of the SAS himself, Brigadier de la Billière.

When Moss told the Director of his Staff Sergeant's decision, while at the same time confirming his personal view that the attack would best be conducted overland, Brigadier de la Billière was:

Dismayed to find that the attitude of this unit seemed lukewarm … The trouble, I found, lay in the squadron commander, who himself did not believe in the proposed operation … I had to act myself. At midnight … I dismissed [John Moss] from his post, and in his place appointed Ian Crooke, a first class practical leader. By morning the attitude of the squadron had changed entirely and they were ready to go.[1]

Moss had been perfectly prepared to conduct the raid from the air, while at the same time believing that it was correct, as Squadron Commander, to put forward the view that the overland option had a greater chance of success. Nevertheless, his opinion was seen to be undermining his squadron's morale, so he paid the harshest penalty of all for an SAS officer.

B Squadron was indeed ready to go, but attitudes within its ranks were not quite as sanguine as some believed, then and now. By the morning of 16 May, Major Crooke,[2] 22 SAS's one-time operations officer and second in command, had only a few hours to stamp his own 'enthusiasm' for this unpopular adventure on to his men before they loaded themselves, their vehicles and their equipment into two Hercules and a VC 10. After the mandatory refuelling stop at Dakar, the Squadron arrived at Ascension Island late on 17 May, where the troopers were to remain equally ambivalent – if not publicly so – towards the 'proposed operation'. They were aware, too, that their new leader had not undertaken any training exercises with the RAF's Hercules for this specific operation and was thus – as were the RAF's advisers in Chelsea – unaware of the limitations.

On 19 May, Roberts, his crew and Charlie Cartwright flew XV179 direct to Ascension Island. At thirteen hours and ten minutes, the flight was a good test of the four newly-installed Andover fuel tanks 'bulking out' the C-130's cargo bay. After signing in his aircraft, Roberts was greeted by Squadron Leader Hudson, who handed him a 'very official-looking envelope'. Inside was a signal headed 'Top Secret, Personal for Squadron Leader Roberts only', and declaring in stark terms that, 'You are to lead a two-ship formation in an airfield assault operation on to Rio Grande airfield.' Roberts was not allowed to keep this scrap of paper, so having read its less than helpful contents he handed it back.

The signal, from Air Marshal Curtiss, contained no indication of who would be carrying out the assault, although clearly it was to be B Squadron. Nor did the signal indicate, as would be normal, timings, enemy strengths and dispositions, routes in and out of the objective (based on an intelligent assessment at a very high level) or what the action was to be on completion of the assault phase. If, as was assumed, they were to continue on to Chile – they would have no fuel to go further – what was expected of them there? Were they to surrender themselves to the Chilean authorities or try to fly on to, say, Easter Island, having refuelled in Punta Arenas. As an Operational Order it fell far short of military perfection. Apart from attending, almost by accident, the SAS Mikado briefing at Northwood, and offering his plan to the Air Commander, this was all Roberts knew.

Also unknown was from whom and when the final decision would come. Clearly, operational command of 47 Squadron's Special Forces flight was being exercised from Headquarters 38 Group at RAF Upavon, while B Squadron's operational command was vested in Headquarters 22 SAS at Hereford. Yet both of these Headquarters were far too 'junior' to sanction an operation of such strategic delicacy. If Roberts was not already suspicious of the unusual chain of authority for such an undertaking, he soon would be. The sooner he spoke to Major Ian Crooke the better.

Roberts and his crew were driven the four winding, dusty, uphill miles to Two Boats Village, where the Squadron Leader was confronted by a dark-haired man, a little under 6 feet tall, of medium build and carrying no 'extra' weight. Ian Crooke – or 'Crookie' as he was generally known – did not stand on ceremony. He presented a serious face where work was concerned, yet would throw caution to the wind on other occasions. He was regarded as a 'good chap' to have on your side, 'one who liked a few beers yet would be the first man on parade the next day'.

'I found Crookie,' explained Roberts of the SAS officer he would be taking into battle, 'to be an amusing and lovely soul but very "gung ho". Clearly a brave man but rather different from Moss, who was far more of a thinker.' Because of his sudden appointment, Crooke, unlike Moss, was unaware of the RAF's concerns; indeed, this may have been the cause of his apparently 'relaxed' attitude to Operation Mikado.

With the introductions over, Charlie Cartwright excused himself and made his way to Cable and Wireless's station on Donkey Plain, where a Government Communications Headquarters out-station was also located and where the SAS's and Cartwright's own communications hub would be sited. The Intelligence Officer, the interlocutor between the RAF's Special Forces Flight and B Squadron, was never to be privy to operational traffic. That was to come via encrypted voice communications from Headquarters 38 Group's Wing Commander Mike Watkins direct to Max Roberts. Instead, Cartwright's work was based around the receipt of Signal and Satellite Intelligence messages or, as he called them, 'raw Tactical Reports and Intelligence Summaries received via a satellite communications system'. This was his daily diet, and with hindsight was undoubtedly the 'best intelligence available ... but still not good enough for the task in hand'. He was to become increasingly frustrated.

Meanwhile, in the SAS's Operations Room Roberts and Crooke held their first operational discussion on Operation Mikado, which was, all were sure, about to be ordered for the next day, over the night of 20/21 May. It was now that Roberts was briefed – for the first time – on Operation Plum Duff's tribulations and the almost certain ramifications of its failure.

Roberts was shocked. Up to now he had been unaware that the reconnaissance patrol had already been dropped off. He explains:

At that stage, it wasn't clear whether there had been a serious cock-up with the reconnaissance or just a tedious hiccup. Either way, I was deeply disappointed that 6 Troop had been inserted without the aircrew being consulted for their input. Of more importance, it now looked as though we would have to execute Mikado without a team in position, and that deeply concerned me. For the aircrew, it was absolutely essential that there was an observation patrol overlooking the airfield.

Nevertheless, once he had outlined his preferred approach to Rio Grande and the action on landing, Roberts repaired to his flight's own accommodation ready to brief his two Hercules crews on the morrow's probable operation. Yet at midday on that morrow, 20 May, (luckily before the ground crew had begun to remove the Andover fuel tanks from XV179 and XV200), Roberts was ordered to conduct the first of his long-range logistic flights into the South Atlantic. This flight, codenamed Drop Julie, was to supply HMS *Alacrity* with vitally needed stores for further distribution through the fleet. Take-off was scheduled for 0140 GMT on 21 May. He would be in the air for twenty-three hours.

Roberts recalls:[3]

I also parachuted four SAS guys into the water as replacements for some of those killed in the Sea King cross-decking accident. There had obviously been a pressing need for those men, while Mikado clearly took second place. Then on 23 May Burgoyne was tasked to carry out another long range drop – Drop Katie. Again, Mikado took second place.

Whenever they returned from a sortie, and after the briefest of rests, both Roberts and Burgoyne would attend meetings with Crooke and his team but always as bystanders. As Roberts recalled, 'Often one hundred crazy ideas would be thrown up into the air and when the odd one came down it would be discussed in more detail with everyone's entire energy focussed on to that one proposal.'

This was a punishing routine for the Hercules crews and one not helped by the prospect, all the while, of dropping everything and setting off for Rio Grande. There is no doubt that these two challenges combined to sap morale if not professionalism. Sleep was another permanent and allied worry. The tension among those about to fly, the elation and exhaustion of those returning, and the ever present fear of being asked to conduct Mikado, meant that rest was hard to achieve at any stage of every twenty-four hour cycle.

Roberts and Burgoyne were never sure if B Squadron were fully aware that they had 'other tasks' to occupy their waking hours. Roberts explained:

So we never trained with B Squadron on the Wideawake runway, as we were either getting airborne for a twenty-four-hour flight or we had just landed after a twenty-four-hour flight. On occasions we both did several flights back to back. In one night and out the following night. We were constantly thinking, 'Is this a Temazepam[4] moment to help me sleep or have I got to stay awake?'

Burgoyne had his own views on the medication:

I didn't like Temazepam and tried to avoid using it. Although the RAF's aviation doctors said it didn't have an after-effect, I felt that it did. My brain would feel as though it was full of cotton wool so I did not feel as sharp as I would have preferred. But sometimes it was inevitable that I had to use them. How tired were we? Very. We were flying at a rate way above the peacetime safety limits of sixteen hours maximum duty time in any one go. We were normally restricted to no more than forty hours in any seventy-two-hour period with a maximum of 120 flying hours in thirty days and no more than 300 hours in ninety days. This time includes planning before a flight as well as flying. From 4 April prior to deploying to Ascension on 12 May I flew for approximately 130 hours. Then, from the Island I flew 160 hours in ten days at the beginning of the resupply sorties when it was just Max and me. And we continued like that throughout the rest of the conflict.

Chapter 13

MV *Atlantic Conveyor*

Meanwhile, across the wide South Atlantic, hostilities continued ...

On 25 May the Argentine AN/TPS-43 radar at Stanley identified a possible large target 95 nautical miles to the north-east. The coordinates were signalled to Rio Grande naval air base, where they were received at 0730 local time. Assuming, and certainly hoping, that this was one of the two British aircraft carriers, Capitán de Corbeta Jorge Luis Colombo, Commanding Officer of the 2da Escuadrilla Aeronaval de Caza y Ataque of the Comando de Aviación Naval Argentina, immediately ordered Roberto Curilovic (call sign 'Toro') to fly Super Étendard 3-A-203, with Julio Barraza (call sign 'Leo') as his wingman in 204; the duo were to be airborne at 0900. Then, unfortunately for pilots pent up after a spell with no suitable targets, the operation had to be delayed until the afternoon as there was no KC-130H available to refuel the aircraft. The Super Étendards eventually took off at 1428 and set a course for a point 120 nautical miles east of Puerto Deseado to take on fuel.

These aircraft were apparently spotted leaving Rio Grande by a British submarine (although the Reports of Proceedings from *Valiant*, *Splendid* and *Conqueror* make no mention of them), and the Task Force was alerted – only to be stood down when no attack materialized. What was unknown was that Curilovic and Barraza were obliged to take a long and circuitous route to the north for their fuel; hence the delay.

Full of fuel, the two pilots now headed east before turning south-east 'at altitude' towards their target, then 330 nautical miles away. They began their attack, in Curilovic's words:

> Flying very low, in electronic silence and with our Radar Warning Receivers detecting nothing ... At 1628 I made the first radar sweep confirming the presence of three targets exactly where the radars had predicted: 50° 38′ S, 56° 8′ W. This position was tapped into both weapon systems as the aircraft descended once more to sea level where we continued the penetration at 500 knots and at 100 feet preparing to launch. After a second radar sweep we selected the biggest target.

Barraza recalls: 'At 39 miles from the target Curilovic said, "I'm tracking it", and I replied, "I agree. Ahead 39".'[1]

Both Exocets were launched at 1632 from, according to Barraza, position 50° 38′ S, 56° 08′ W, and struck their objective at 1636 – although the time recorded by the British Board of Inquiry was 1942 GMT.

The aircrafts' Agave radars, transmitting during that 'brief scan', were picked up by HMSs *Exeter* and *Ambuscade*, who broadcast the standard warning for a potential Exocet attack with the word 'Handbrake'. *Ambuscade* immediately fired chaff from her 4.5-inch gun to cause general confusion among any incoming missiles, and then reverted to the 3-inch chaff launcher for her own immediate protection. This second decoy saved the Type 21 frigate ... but the Exocets now had a clear track towards MV *Atlantic Conveyor*, the last remaining echo within their computers, although it is believed that the missiles may have first turned towards RFA *Regent* and only later to the larger ship.

Which would have been the more significant loss is hard to determine, for *Regent* was carrying a substantial load of ammunition, without which the Task Force as a whole might have been hard pushed to continue; on the other hand, *Atlantic Conveyor*'s Chinooks, had they survived, would have brought the land campaign to a rather earlier conclusion. Being a Royal Fleet Auxiliary, however, *Regent*'s construction and her crew's training in 'damage control' might well have saved her cargo.

The Royal Navy Board of Inquiry states:[2]

At 1942 *Atlantic Conveyor* was hit in very quick succession by two air-launched Exocet missiles which penetrated her main cargo deck port side aft causing explosion and a fireball ... Dense, black, acrid smoke spread almost immediately through the after sections of the ship below the upper deck, soon spreading upward and forward. Uncontrollable fire spread quickly throughout the open-plan cargo decks giving no chance to her limited damage-control parties, who were driven back by smoke, heat and further explosions. The rapid spread of fire, the presence of hazardous cargo forward [kerosene and cluster bombs] and the onset of darkness prompted the timely decision to abandon ship.

The ship was abandoned in a calm and orderly manner. Twenty-two personnel were taken off by helicopter from the forward flight deck, four jumped overboard, the rest climbed down one of the three starboard jumping ladders aft. Being exhausted, wet and cold, many found entry into the twenty-five-man Royal Navy life rafts difficult. Three men died on board ... nine more failed to survive after entering the water.

Following a second rendezvous with their refuelling tanker, Curilovic and Barraza landed back at Rio Grande at 1838 (their time), having completed the longest mission of any Super Étendard attack.[3] The pilots had flown 1,406 miles in just under four hours, but instead of hitting a British aircraft carrier they had targeted, and in the end destroyed, an 18,000-ton cargo ship of the Cunard Steam Ship Company under the command of Captain Ian North, a Merchant Navy veteran of the Second World War, described by Michael Layard as, 'A man in a million – short, squat and with a snowy, bushy beard, he was the very archetype of the Merchant Navy skipper, exuding energy, confidence and "can do".'

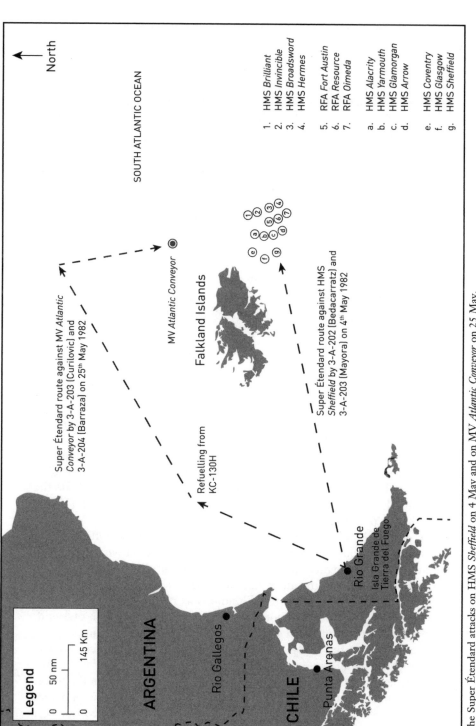

Legend

0   50 nm

0   145 Km

North

SOUTH ATLANTIC OCEAN

ARGENTINA

CHILE

Rio Gallegos

Punta Arenas

Rio Grande

Isla Grande de Tierra del Fuego

Falkland Islands

MV Atlantic Conveyor

Refuelling from KC-130H

Super Étendard route against MV Atlantic Conveyor by 3-A-203 (Curilovic) and 3-A-204 (Barraza) on 25th May 1982

Super Étendard route against HMS Sheffield by 3-A-202 (Bedacarratz) and 3-A-203 (Mayora) on 4th May 1982

1. HMS Brilliant
2. HMS Invincible
3. HMS Broadsword
4. HMS Hermes

5. RFA Fort Austin
6. RFA Resource
7. RFA Olmeda

a. HMS Alacrity
b. HMS Yarmouth
c. HMS Glamorgan
d. HMS Arrow

e. HMS Coventry
f. HMS Glasgow
g. HMS Sheffield

The Super Étendard attacks on HMS *Sheffield* on 4 May and on MV *Atlantic Conveyor* on 25 May.

Captain Layard[4] was the Senior Royal Naval Officer on board and in 2011 wrote:

> Air raid warning red. Emergency stations, emergency stations ... [arriving on the bridge] I found that *Atlantic Conveyor* was in a turn to port ... As the ship's head passed through east we felt and heard a loud explosion from aft ... Reports began to filter through that the missile (or two as it transpired) had come into the port quarter 8 to 10 feet above the waterline ... Captain North and I both reached the conclusion to abandon ship together. The decision was a dreadful one for a master to make but Ian's calm and good sense prevailed ... The climb down the ship's side had taken its toll on Ian for he was no chicken or greyhound. After he dropped into the sea beside me I held him up as he seemed to be floating rather lower in the water than was good for him, and I realized that our troubles had only just begun ... Ian and I rode a couple of duckings and buffetings but time was running out and it was high time we got to a raft. My last sight of that dear old friend was as I gave him a strong shove in the small of his back for the nearest life raft ... when I broke the surface again the scene was quite different. There was no sign of Ian North, merely an empty life raft and someone else floating face down beside me.[5]

John Brocklehurst,[6]*Atlantic Conveyor*'s Chief Officer in 1982 recalls his experiences in frightening detail:

> We had been attached to the Task Force for a week, having transferred our fourteen Harriers to the aircraft carriers on 18 May. During this time we had carried out a large number of helicopter cross decking of stores and bombs to vessels within the Task Force. Because of our valuable cargo of aircraft (we still had six Wessex and five Chinooks on board) we were stationed as close to the Seawolf-equipped goalkeepers of the two carriers as possible.
>
> On 25 May, the day before we were due to enter San Carlos (early on the morning of 26 May) the weather was overcast, good visibility, wind Force 4 with about a 6-foot swell running, if I recall correctly. During the late afternoon, post-1600, I went down from the bridge where I was Officer of the Watch to lower our stern ramp to permit the Chinook on our afterdeck to do a test run of its engines, prior to taking off. We already had one Chinook and one Wessex up in the air at this time. After lowering the ramp down below the level of its blades, the Chinook was run up and checks made. Something didn't satisfy the pilots or engineers because they didn't take off. The engines were shut down and I was advised to close the ramp.
>
> I went back to the bridge to continue my navigational watch. Shortly after reaching the bridge we received an 'Air Raid Warning Red' call with a threat direction. Our Action Stations plan was to turn away from the threat direction and present our stern towards it. The stern ramp was of a very strong construction, separate to the stern door, and represented our best defence against the known threat of Exocet, given that we had no passive

defence such as chaff. Our only offensive armament being a general purpose machine gun on each bridge wing.

Less than two minutes after receiving the air raid warning and while turning away from the threat we were struck by two Exocets in the port quarter. They acquired *Atlantic Conveyor* after being seduced away from their initial target by chaff from, I believe, HMS *Ambuscade*.

At the time of strike myself and a Royal Navy rating were on the port bridge wing, having carried a box of ammunition out to the machine gun and there I recall hearing sounds of chaff being launched from warships around us.

The missiles came into the hull, about 50 feet astern and 60 feet below the bridge wing. I remember two very loud bangs, the ship shook and almost instantaneously I watched black smoke billowing out of the port quarter. I think I also heard the noise of rocket engines, shortly after the missiles' strike, but memory is hazy on that. I do know that when back on the North Atlantic run on the *Atlantic Causeway*, when for the first time Concorde passed overhead with the characteristic double bang of supersonic flight, it made those of us who had been on the *Conveyor* duck!

Following the hit, the fires and smoke spread quickly through the open car and trailer decks and our attempts to tackle them proved to be fruitless, despite some brave attempts by the fire teams to get close to the seat of the fire. Attempts to inject CO_2 proved fruitless too, possibly due to piping from the CO_2 room at the aft end of the vessel being damaged by the missiles' detonation. Similarly our fixed sprinkler system, that we had put a lot of store in, could not be brought into action, though our engineers did their best. Merchant ships of the seventies were not battle-prepared like those during the Second World War.

Thick black smoke was coming out of fan room vents all along the upper deck ... We had the vents open because we had diesel engines running in the car decks at the time of the attack. Now there were occasional explosions from below as various flammable objects, such as drums of diesel fuel 'popped off'. Attempts to close the vent fans remotely also failed.

We had a large number of cluster bombs in the forward end of the Trailer Deck C, at stern door level, behind large sliding watertight doors and the fire was spreading forward towards these 'magazines'. There was a significant danger that if we could not put the fires out those bombs would cook off with devastating consequences.

I believe it was this consideration, along with approaching darkness, and our inability to have any significant effect on the fires that brought the two Captains to the decision to abandon the vessel. A very hard decision to have to make, and only those who have been in command of a ship can know the feelings such a decision can have. It was the only logical decision.

If we had stayed longer, while having little effect on controlling the fires, we would have likely lost our life rafts. Later, when I was going over the side I recall seeing a section of the hull glowing red hot. I returned to the bridge to give a situation report to the two captains when they made the decision to abandon the vessel. This was passed word of mouth due to our public address system being out of action. Our emergency plan had been to use life rafts for the majority of men and lifeboats for any injured as the high side of the ship made negotiating a ladder impossible for an injured man. I remember rigging the life raft ladders, the day after we sailed from Plymouth, with Mick Legge, the Royal Navy 'Buffer'.[7] He was an excellent man and represented all that was good in our military men.

I took a group of men down to the starboard lifeboat (the port side was untenable due to smoke and fire) to oversee the launching of that boat; on the way down I diverted by the casualty clearing station to pick up medical personnel and any injured. I recall smoke starting to enter the lower areas of accommodation at this time. As it was we had no injured personnel though twelve men were lost when survivors were eventually counted.

Rafts had been launched by men congregating by the ladders aft of the lifeboat ... no one needed instructions as the deck was getting hot underfoot ... We lowered the boat to the embarkation deck ready to launch, but I decided we could not launch immediately because several rafts had clustered at the end of their painters immediately under our boat. As we had no casualties I told the men with me to forget the boat and go for the safety of the rafts.

I ended up in the last raft to get clear of the *Atlantic Conveyor* ... we were towed away by a Zodiac from one of the warships. It was getting quite dark by this time and my last sight of *Atlantic Conveyor* was a view from off the starboard quarter, smoke and flames coming from her and the Red Ensign still flying from the stern jack.[8]

One aircraft that managed to escape in the nick of time was a Wessex HU5 of 845 Naval Air Squadron, with Royal Marines Corporal Ian Tyrrell embarked as the winchman. Thus far, Tyrrell had had an 'interesting campaign' accompanying two helicopters in an RAF Belfast via Gibraltar and Dakar to Ascension Island, where they were 'rebuilt'. Once they were airworthy he joined the Royal Fleet Auxiliary *Fort Austin* with 'his' Wessex until it was ordered across to MV *Atlantic Conveyor*.

Sometime during 25 May Tyrrell flew to 'a carrier', where he learned of the death of his colleague Corporal 'Doc' Love. Love was more than just a friend, for he was engaged to Tyrrell's wife's twin sister. Tyrrell takes up his tale:

That night I was on the way to evening 'scran'[9] having packed to leave the ship the next morning for San Carlos when one of the 'cabs' needed a check flight and I was allocated the job.

We took off (Lieutenant Kim Slowe, Royal Navy, was the pilot), completed the checks and as we were returning to the ship two Exocets overtook us to our starboard side and hit the ship. I photographed them and the damage but the photos were taken off me.

We received a message that a male had fallen through the entry hole but that his position had been marked by someone who cut loose a box and threw it after him. We found the 'casualty' and I lowered the winch. It was like fishing as he was so cold and hardly able do anything for himself. I managed to lift him into the 'cab' where I shoved him against the heaters. We shot over to *Hermes* to drop him off.

Tyrrell's Wessex then returned to *Atlantic Conveyor* to rescue a group of her crew from the bows. Despite only having space for eight, thirteen survivors were lifted off and also taken to *Hermes*. Slowe then faced a problem, for he could not land on any 'local' ship as none possessed the Wessex 5 'blade fold kit' and the aircraft would take up too much flight deck space. Tyrell continues:

So we had to wait for a Harrier strike to go off and come back before we landed on *Hermes*. They didn't want us fouling the deck if we had a problem folding. We sat in the hover for three hours.

During that time the 'souls on board' tally was collated by the ships. Someone remembered we were flying but only had the name of the pilot so I was posted as 'missing in action'.

That night I stayed in *Hermes* and the next day was shifted to MV *British Tay* and transported home but not before I had all my flying kit taken from me as spares, leaving me with a pair of boots, denims and a shirt, not even a jumper.

On 26 May my wife, her twin sister plus their family and mine, attended a memorial service for Doc Love after which she was approached by the vicar who gave her the report that I was missing presumed dead. Twenty-four hours later she received a telegram from the Ministry of Defence saying that my body had been recovered, then nothing else until, after another twenty-four hours, she was handed my telegram saying I was fine and coming home.

We arrived at Ascension where the civilians among us survivors were given a new set of clothes to fly home in. The RAF had their Number 1 uniforms flown out so they would look smart on arrival. The Navy chaps were issued with a new set of working rig (Number 8s I think) and us three Royal Marines were each given a corps pattern belt and a beret.

Three days after being hit and at 0350 GMT in position 50° 40' S, 54° 28' W, *Atlantic Conveyor* took with her to the bottom tents for 5,000 men,[10] six Wessex HU5s of 848 Naval Air Squadron, one Lynx HAS2 of 815 Naval Air Squadron and three Chinooks HC1s of 18 Squadron, RAF. Also lost were spare aircraft engines, a water distilling plant and aluminium planking for a makeshift Harrier 'runway'. Twelve men were recorded as dead or missing.

* * *

This was the defining moment of the 'Exocet war' and the event that most affected the logistic efforts of the British Task Force. It was also the moment that should have marked (but did not) the end of any pretensions to conducting Operation Mikado.

In retrospect, Max Roberts feels:

Immediately after *Atlantic Conveyor* went down on 25 May, I think was the time that someone very senior should have put all Mikado plans on hold while we dropped desperately needed supplies to the Task Force. If they did, they might have told us and B Squadron and thus saved us all at Two Boats Village a very great deal of unnecessary stress.

Chapter 14

Operation Mikado – Detailed Plan: Rio Grande

In sinking MV *Atlantic Conveyor* Argentina had expended two of its three remaining Exocets. Consequently, a clear headed military analyst in the corridors of Whitehall, Hereford or Chelsea might have considered that to jeopardize a squadron of SAS and the only two air-to-air refuelling-capable Hercules in a high-risk air-land assault (without a prior reconnaissance) against the one missile left would not be a 'cost-effective' operation. But that analyst would have been wrong; Operation Mikado was still 'on' and needed detailed planning.

Although Max Roberts and his navigator had, on 17 May, been able to offer those at Hereford a draft plan, their ideas would need to be fine tuned now that they were at Ascension Island and in direct contact with B Squadron. Roberts' and Musgrave's draft was based on a number of facts and assumptions, but there was much they had not been privy to, for the SAS's 'bubble of security' excluded the very men who would make any such raid possible.

For the RAF at Two Boats Village there were inevitably a number of problems to be solved, and with no idea when the 'execute' decision would be made, these had to be tackled immediately.

Navigating from Ascension Island across the South Atlantic was by the oldest method of all – celestial – through the diligent application of a bubble sextant and 'rapid sight reduction' tables. Instead of relying on a visual sea horizon at, say, 20,000 feet, this sextant used an internal 'bubble' to simulate a level parallel with the earth's surface immediately beneath the aircraft from which the sun's true altitude could then be determined.

This was not the precise art navigator Squadron Leader Dave Musgrave would have preferred for this particular mission; and this was why at Northwood he had asked if a Royal Navy nuclear submarine could make a brief transmission (compatible with the aircraft's Automatic Direction Finding equipment) to enable him to update his position prior to coasting in to Argentina. This had been agreed, although no submarine commanding officer was aware of the request. As the destruction of the Exocets was very much in the Royal Navy's interest, if the time came, so would the submarine.

To aid navigation further, XV200, Harry Burgoyne's aircraft, had a stand-alone Carousel IV inertial navigational system, while XV179 came out of Marshalls not only with the same apparatus but also with the 'new' Omega navigation equipment;[1] the latter system was good for area but not tactical navigation. As Operation Mikado would be the first time he would use it in earnest, Musgrave read the instruction manual during his flight to Ascension Island, although primary navigation during the low-level phase of the operation would still be by Doppler and map reading.

Covering the intelligence aspects, Squadron Leader Cartwright briefed the aircrew that two Argentine destroyers, ARA *Hipolito Bouchard* and ARA *Piedra Buena* of Task Group 79.3, had been stationed 15 miles north-west of Rio Grande and that, if still in position, these would present a significant threat to the Hercules.[2] If they picked up the aircraft on radar (as anti-submarine warfare vessels they had no anti-aircraft capability) they would alert Rio Grande immediately, destroying the element of the surprise that was essential if Mikado was to succeed.

What Cartwright could not advise on was the position of the oil rig that Sea King Victor Charlie had encountered. In retrospect, Harry Burgoyne has commented that, depending on the route chosen, they too would probably have encountered the same offshore oil rig as had Operation Plum Duff:

> Like the helicopter crew, our maps and intelligence were lacking anything about oil rigs so, when or if we came across them, we would probably have had to pick our way round them as best we could, just like Wiggy. How much of a diversion that would have involved with the subsequent impact on our time en route and fuel state is impossible to say now, other than that an already challenging mission would have become unexpectedly more so.

It was known, courtesy of a British submarine,[3] that Rio Grande had 'welcomed' what was termed at Northwood 'a speechless' night-time approach by an Argentine C-130 – in other words, a Hercules landing in the dark with no two-way radio chatter. This 'fact' spawned a number of rhetorical questions that did the rounds of 'The Hole' at Fleet Headquarters. The most plausible was, 'Could a British C-130 with a Spanish speaker embarked, able to converse in military patois, cause such doubt and confusion in the air base's control tower that the aircraft could land unmolested and remain unmolested long enough to allow the SAS to drive off the rear ramps?' This far from novel idea was quickly discounted as being unlikely to fool anyone. A straight-in approach from over the sea and over the Argentine destroyers was not an option. The C-130s would have to approach overland, from the west, and Roberts' crew now planned it.

The southern leg of the journey from Wideawake would follow the great circle route[4] but with a jink to pass 60 miles to the east of the Falkland Islands so that enemy ships and fighters lurking between the islands and the mainland could be avoided. Although the Argentine fighters did not fly at night, the Boeing 707 most certainly did and was believed to be armed with Sidewinder air-to-air missiles. The Omega hand-held radar warning receiver was still in XV200 and would be used to alert both aircraft if they were illuminated.

At 150 miles north-east of the Falklands both aircraft would descend to 50 feet for the final 380 miles to the chosen 'coasting in' point at Cabo San Diego on the southern tip of Tierra del Fuego. This course and height would also take the aircraft well clear of the AN/TPS-43 Search Radar at Stanley.

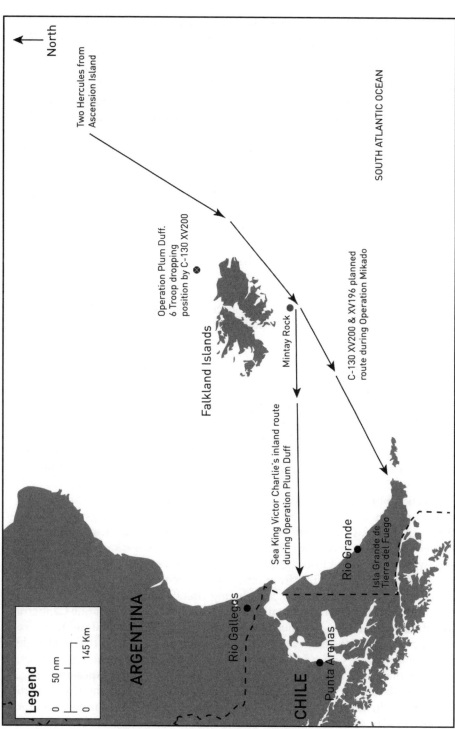

North

Legend

0 ——— 50 nm
0 ——— 145 Km

ARGENTINA

Rio Gallegos

CHILE

Punta Arenas

Rio Grande

Isla Grande de
Tierra del Fuego

Falkland Islands

Operation Plum Duff.
6 Troop dropping
position by C-130 XV200

Mintay Rock

Sea King Victor Charlie's inland route
during Operation Plum Duff

Two Hercules from
Ascension Island

C-130 XV200 & XV196 planned
route during Operation Mikado

SOUTH ATLANTIC OCEAN

Seaward approach route flown by Victor Charlie on Operation Plum Duff and the planned approach for the two Hercules on Operation Mikado.

The inland route after Cabo San Diego was selected by Roberts and Musgrave following careful study of the natural topography of the area surrounding Rio Grande taken from aeronautical chart ONC T-18.[5] To a scale of 1:1,000,000, this publication had been compiled in January 1965 then 'revised' in May 1976 and was the same issue that Lieutenant Alan 'Wiggy' Bennett had been obliged to use during Operation Plum Duff. Ominously, printed over the very area that Max Roberts intended leading his Mikado attack on their overland approach to Rio Grande, were the words 'Relief Data Unreliable'.

Luckily, the Hercules crew had by now acquired a few 1:500,000 aeronautical charts covering the area, and although they dated from 1937 the terrain detail was better than on other available publications; however, detail for roads and towns was believed to be inaccurate and would not be relied upon. As there were not enough originals for both aircraft, Burgoyne's crew would carry black and white photocopies.

Prior to 1 April few up-to-date editions of the 1:1,000,000 aeronautical chart had been available in the UK, but on that day an officer on Commander-in-Chief Fleet's staff telephoned the United States Defense Mapping Agency's Aerospace Center at St Louis, Missouri for assistance. This US department was swift to help.[6] Along with many other maps and charts, the ONCs were reprinted in quick time and dispatched immediately to Ascension Island. A USAF Warrant Officer was designated the Survey Adviser and given the task of overseeing the arrival from Missouri of all 'new' American-sourced maps and charts. He was then to ensure their immediate distribution to ships, squadrons and battalions as they staged through the island. To guarantee that the British had only the latest editions, he also withdrew all 'superseded' editions of US publications that might have been issued in the UK. Among these new charts were sufficient stocks of ONC T-18 with the latest corrections. On his arrival at Ascension this most vital of Americans received a frosty welcome at the overcrowded base ... thankfully, the reason for his presence was eventually understood, but he was nearly sent home, with his charts.

Selection of the most suitable overland route was helped not only by studying the natural topography on ONC T-18 (with its unhelpful warnings) but also by using radar overlays supplied by the Royal Signals and Radar Establishment at Malvern (as it was known in 1982)[7] ... and 'other intelligence sources'. Radar overlays were produced by using the precise geo-positioning of radars around the globe obtained, quite simply, from intercepts collected by ships and submarines as well as by electronic intelligence gathering aircraft (known as ELINT) such as the Nimrod R1. In 1982 anecdotal evidence suggested that at least one Canberra aircraft from the RAF's 360 Squadron operated from Chile in Chilean Air Force markings alongside the host nation's ELINT-equipped C-130s[8] fitted to provide useful information. Other intelligence was available from US satellite sources, although these images were not as helpful as might have been expected.

In 1982 the Royal Signals and Radar Establishment was working closely with GCHQ, Cheltenham, producing radar overlays showing the radar coverage for any given radar relevant to its surrounding land mass and terrain. Thus hilly or undulating country, even of moderate elevation, would create areas of radar shadow that could be exploited by low flying aircraft to avoid detection en route to a target. Such were the Royal Signals and Radar Establishment overlays for the approaches to Rio Grande provided to Dave Musgrave.

The propagation pattern for the AN/TPS-43 radar was already well documented, making it relatively easy to produce a rough radar overlay covering various ranges and heights from the source, in this case assessed to be at Rio Grande air base, out to the maximum radar range, which in theory was 243 nautical miles.[9] When this was laid over the 1:500,000 aeronautical charts Musgrave was able to deduce that within 25 nautical miles of the airfield the two aircraft would probably be spotted at any height above 200 feet.

Using these radar masking overlays, and their own experience, the Special Forces Flight planning team was able to plot a course that led from Cabo San Diego to the eastern end of the 55-nautical-mile-long Lago (lake) Fagnano, designated as Turning Point Number 2. Although the straight-line course to Turning Point Number 3 at the western end of the lake skirted its northern shore, Max Roberts would almost certainly have led his 'two-ship' flight down the middle of the lake. Not knowing the enemy dispositions, this had to be the safest option. He also knew that 6 miles short of the lake's end he would cross into Chilean airspace. That guaranteed nothing in the way of safety, indeed it might have produced a further complication: the Chileans would be guarding their air space against Argentine incursions by Hercules every bit as diligently as the Argentines would be guarding theirs against both Chilean and British aircraft.

The route then continued westwards until, at Turning Point 5, the formation would turn hard to starboard to head up the distinctive valley that leads from Seno Almirantazgo towards Lago Blanco and the western point of a prominent island in its middle. Here they would slowly begin turning towards the east via other waypoints, until at the final turning point, Number 9, they would be 1 nautical mile north of Estancia Maria Bety. From there, and now on a course of 89° true, it was 6 miles to the threshold of Rio Grande's Runway 07. It was hoped that the northern shore of the large Laguna de Los Cisnes that runs conveniently in an east-west direction would provide a final reference point and a near perfect line-up with the runway just half a mile further east.[10] It would be dark and the lagoon's icy surface would be covered with snow ... but there was just a chance that it might be recognizable. There was nothing else.

While on paper this was a workable route, there were a number of natural phenomena to be considered. Any wind – there was an expectation of at least 20 knots from the south-west – would be a major problem, particularly once the aircraft turned up the valley towards Lago Blanco. Here the hills on either side are in the range of 2,500 to 3,000 feet high, producing, in winds above 20 knots, turbulence and down-draughts that are hazardous to all aircraft but especially to the Hercules.[11]

From the island in Lago Blanco onwards the terrain becomes flat and featureless, and while turbulence would be less of a problem, with no discernible features from which the Doppler and inertial navigational systems could be updated,

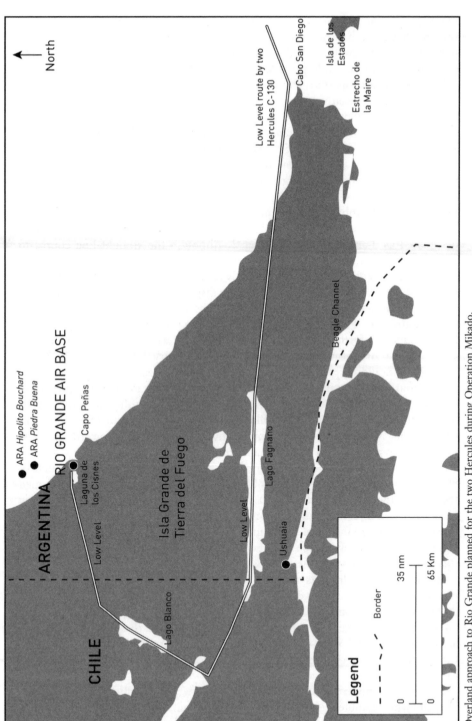

North

ARGENTINA

RIO GRANDE AIR BASE

● ARA *Hipolito Bouchard*
● ARA *Piedra Buena*

Capo Peñas

Laguna de
los Cisnes

Low Level

CHILE

Lago Blanco

Isla Grande de
Tierra del Fuego

Low Level

Lago Fagnano

● Ushuaia

Beagle Channel

Low Level route by two
Hercules C-130

Cabo San Diego

Isla de los
Estados

Estrecho de
la Maire

Legend

- - - Border

0   35 nm

0   65 Km

Overland approach to Rio Grande planned for the two Hercules during Operation Mikado.

course-plotting would be back to the old-fashioned 'heading and stop watch' routine. Large lakes could be used, but because of the lack of detail on the aeronautical charts it would be difficult to discern one from another, adding to the navigational dilemma. In RAF terminology, what was likely to be missing was a 'dog's bollocks fix': a visual sighting of a feature so distinctive from its surroundings that there can be no mistaking it for anything else. Ideally, had Roberts been asked to provide Plum Duff's commander with his requirements for a safe landing, he would have asked for an infra-red beacon to be placed on the centreline approach to Runway 07; but he was not invited to do so.

As the leader of the formation, the Squadron Leader had much more to think about, not least of which was the air-to-air refuelling. Having figured out the route, Roberts and his crew could now turn their attention to how much extra fuel they would need to complete the mission and at what time it should be received. There were a number of aspects to consider: the refuelling had to be conducted in daylight; it was possible that two tankers flying in loose formation would be involved, as one might not be able to supply the required amount; the Hercules had to be as light as possible for a landing which would almost certainly be downwind; and both aircraft had to have enough fuel for them to 'drop into Punta Arenas', another 120 nautical miles away.

At 31° S, 34° W, sunset in mid-May was (give or take a few minutes either side, for no one knew precisely on which day the operation would take place) about 1925 GMT. To allow a safety margin, the time of sunset (by which time the last drop of fuel had to be passed) was assumed to be 1900. So, allowing an hour for the entire operation, the rendezvous had to be at 1800. With that determined, the aircrew could now estimate both the take-off time from Wideawake and landing time at Rio Grande: 1300 and 0300 GMT respectively on the following days.

The Hercules planners now knew the aircraft weights for the entire flight. At take-off, with the internal tanks removed to make way for the Pink Panthers, the remaining fuel tanks would be filled to the brim (63,000lb), and each aircraft's all-up weight would be around 153,000lb, or 2,000lb below the normal maximum take-off weight. By the end of the refuelling they would be back to about 153,000lb. During the next eight hours' flying to Rio Grande the two aircraft would burn off 44,000lb of fuel each, giving them a landing weight of about 109,000lb. This was reasonable for an airfield assault, especially if there was the expected tailwind at touchdown.

In a perfect world the refuelling operation would be conducted in radio silence. Apart from any transmission being 'bad practice', there was always the danger of the Argentine Boeing 707 lurking in the general area. On this occasion, though, not only did the Victors have to be found but they and the Hercules had to be 'managed' into formation. Roberts considered that the chance of any radio transmissions being heard was unlikely; even if they were, the dangers inherent in that were far outweighed by the danger of not being able to communicate. Radio silence was not an option.

From the refuelling position onwards, the two Hercules would be on their own. The last friendly face, the last friendly voice, would have turned for home. If they wanted to follow suit, this would be their last chance. From then onwards there were only three possible destinations: Rio Grande in enemy Argentina, or the far from certainly neutral Chile or Brazil.

The plan was complete and could now be briefed to those who would ultimately authorize the execution of Operation Mikado.

Before Roberts' meeting with Ian Crooke the SAS's view had been simple: 'Just fly us to the airfield and we'll do the business. Then take us to a neutral country'. However, with everyone intimately involved now together (at least, when in between flights) at Two Boats Village, a new level of cooperation and mutual understanding was established between the RAF and the SAS.

In the UK, the SAS's security concerns had impacted severely on the RAF's planning for both Plum Duff and Mikado, despite the SAS having to rely totally on the RAF to 'get it right'. Bearing in mind the many joint exercises and operations that they had conducted together with a common aim, it seems odd that there was the very minimum of RAF participation in the planning not only of Mikado itself but, almost more significantly, of Plum Duff.

At a Royal Air Force Historical Society meeting held at the RAF Museum, Hendon, on 8 April 2003, the RAF's Air Adviser to Headquarters SAS at Duke of York Barracks in 1982, Squadron Leader (by then Air Vice Marshal) David Niven, commented on Air Vice Marshal Hayr[12] (at the time, Assistant Chief of the Air Staff, Operations) applying the 'need to know' principle too rigidly. Niven also confirmed that Brigadier de la Billière was doing the same and that this had created communication and coordination problems.

Other factors were also playing their part. In his book *Ghost Force*[13] Ken Connor states that some Special Forces staff officers were exaggerating the positives of Mikado, and downplaying or disregarding the negatives. If this was the case, it is utterly understandable that de la Billière was so optimistic about Mikado. In the beginning, even B Squadron were 'up for it', until they advanced further into their training exercises. Only then did they begin to realize what the problems would be and even acknowledged the RAF's limitations – which the aircrew had always aired in public.

If Niven and Connor are correct, then, as Burgoyne has since commented:

> That would certainly go some way to explaining why we, as aircrew, sometimes felt that we weren't being given the full story by the SAS during Mikado. I had already experienced tight security when I was ordered not to tell my crew about the Bombilla mission and I suspect that same, extreme, 'need to know' principle was being applied to Mikado, to the overall detriment of the mission. Security bubbles were being created all over the place.

Burgoyne again:

> As the evidence has mounted of the hostile reception awaiting us at Rio Grande, I've been thinking about what we might have done if we had known about all these things at the time and that (possibly) we weren't going to get airborne again. If we had known about the aerial farms north and south of

the runway would they have been lit as most aerial farms are – especially those close to an airfield? If they were lit, it would have made finding the runway at low level easier for us. If we had known about the high threats at the airfield, and the absolute requirement to avoid alerting them any earlier than necessary, would we have gone to all the trouble of routing in from the west and risking overflying outlying enemy positions? I suspect not as, even with night vision goggles, it would have been difficult to hide in the flat terrain. Therefore, the chances of detection would have been high if we had come in over land.

Roberts has stated:

By contrast, if we had flown straight in to Runway 25 over the sea from the east we would have probably been able to fly as low as 50 feet in reasonable safety even at night, in bad weather and, again, just aimed between the two aerials to try and locate the runway. This way, we may not have been detected until we were quite close in, say 10 to 15 miles. From the Kinloss and Marham experiences, perhaps closer. If we missed our landing, we could have just continued straight on over the border into Chile and Punta Arenas. Additionally, this approach from the east would have been about an hour and a half shorter and been even more attractive now we know that the two picket destroyers had actually gone to Ushuaia during that time!

Reaching the 'coasting-in' position was only part of the equation that needed to be solved and was merely the first of Operation Mikado's three very distinct phases. Unarguably – although it has been dismissed by some[14] as of less significance and even considered the lesser difficulty – the most vital phase was the approach and landing, and that was entirely the RAF's responsibility. The second phase – the attack by B Squadron – was, in some respects, a standard land force operation, the only questions being the location of the missiles, the aircraft and the pilots ...

Responsibility for the third phase would be back with the RAF, and in the wider context of the campaign this was the least important phase and the only one for which it was almost impossible to plan. The re-embarking into the aircraft, the take-off from Rio Grande and the landing in neutral territory – preferably at Punta Arenas – were of little tactical consequence. The vital damage to Argentina's Exocet 'war' had either been done or it hadn't. Either way, the Task Force would have lost the services of a whole SAS squadron and, of far more relevance, the only two air-to-air refuelling-capable Hercules and their crews. This posed a dilemma for the decision makers in the UK: 'Was this latter loss, when balanced against the destruction of one Exocet (or, as was looking increasingly likely to those who would conduct the operation, the destruction of no Exocets) worth the risk?'

One thing Roberts did know was that from whichever direction he approached Rio Grande he would have to fly the last 300 or even 400 miles as low as possible and in the dark.

'No Questions Asked'. Drawing by Hercules captain, Flight Lieutenant Adrian Obertelli RAF, of what B Squadron hoped to achieve at Rio Grande during Operation Mikado.

Six sets of ANVIS had been acquired from Farnborough but, as has been mentioned, these were only of value with a quarter moon or more and at an elevation greater than 30°. Cloud cover or precipitation (rain, snow or fog) would also severely degrade their use or even negate it altogether. If they encountered any of these conditions, Roberts's plan was simply to fly as low as he safely could.

With a planned transit speed between 210 and 230 knots, that final overland leg was not going to be easy. With everything else that had been happening prior to leaving the United Kingdom, he had only managed three nights of practice with the night vision goggles. Burgoyne had managed just one, and Operation Mikado would be his first experience of flying in formation. As it was, the 'new moon' (and they needed at least a quarter moon) was not due until 23 May. Regardless of whether there was a moon or not, one factor was almost certain: there would be thick cloud cover all the way inland.

Communications were another concern. During the normal Task Force re-supply flights, scheduled high frequency transmissions would be received from Ascension Island containing encrypted weather information, or perhaps a message telling the pilot to return. There would be a simple code word and authentication that required no reply. The same would have occurred had Operation Mikado been recalled.

Had there been a need for the aircrew or the SAS to abort the mission, a broken fuelling probe for instance, there was no fixed procedure. During the early part of the flight, the likely alternatives were to head back to Ascension Island or, as a very last resort, to turn for an airfield in Brazil. In the middle of Argentina and with no fuel to return to Wideawake, then a straightforward landing at Punta Arenas was probably all that they could hope to achieve.

Unlike on the resupply drops, the lead Hercules on this operation would have the advantage of the SAS's Satellite Communications system, allowing Crooke to talk direct to Hereford and, it had originally been hoped, to 6 Troop's now beleaguered patrol. This modern communications system – courtesy of a private arrangement between Hereford and the US Army's Fort Bragg – came in a small black briefcase. The cruciform antenna would be set up below the cockpit roof escape hatch's 'perspex' cupola, where the navigator would simply hold it in position for the duration of the call.

Initially, it was expected (although the RAF were not privy to any plan) that 6 Troop, on the ground, would be part of a communications network in order to pass last-minute updates of aircraft dispersal and hints of other aircraft movements, or even to report if there was a sudden blackout of those lights that might have been useful to an incoming Hercules pilot.

Thus a matrix of factors vied for priority: the date of the raid and the corresponding phase of the moon; the weather; the possibility of a friendly submarine offering navigational support; and the position of enemy ships. A crucial 'unknown' was the enemy's ground defences, and these would remain unidentified until well after the campaign.

One of the key factors in achieving a successful 'two-ship' airfield assault was maintaining the 2,000-feet separation. To preserve this precise juxtaposition both aircraft had to fly at the same ground speed, but any variation in wind direction and strength can play havoc with such precision flying. As a rough aid to station-keeping between the darkened aircraft, the lead Hercules would show only the formation lights located along the topside of the main wings.

On the approach, at about 5 miles out (or two and a half minutes before landing) and still ten seconds apart in the 2,000-feet trail, the pilots planned to slow to their tactical landing speed, expecting to see the runway from at least 2 miles away with their goggles. Although they knew there would be the minimum of ambient light – on 20/21 May the moon had yet to re-appear from its monthly 'absence' – they were hoping that the airfield and runway lights would be on. Had the RAF been asked, this would have constituted part of Captain L's reconnaissance. Oddly, there had been no suggestion that, despite being on a war footing, the airfield would be darkened – probably because, as had (apparently) been observed by one submarine, night-time 'speechless' landings by Argentine aircraft did take place. How awkward it would be if the British chose to land from the west at the same time that an Argentine aircraft was landing from the east ...

The most likely wind at Rio Grande would be from the south-west at around 20 knots, so given the runway's west-east alignment there would be a significant 'crossing tailwind' for the landing. Burgoyne recalls that, 'Landing in these conditions was going to be extremely challenging. The one small benefit from it was that, in the second aircraft, and positioned upwind of Max until the very last moment, I would at least be clear of his wake turbulence.'

The Hercules has, in peacetime, an absolute tailwind limit of ten knots and a crosswind landing limit of 35 knots; but these conditions are for a solo aircraft shining all its landing lights on to a 'standard' 90-feet-plus-wide, well lit runway, with no ice. Any variation in these factors affects the crosswind limit, which on an icy runway can be reduced to as little as ten knots. There were no published limits for a blacked-out, formation landing.

There was an added, unknown, component to the equation. Super Étendard pilot Roberto Curilovic[15] has confirmed that Runway 07 sloped down towards the sea by 20 feet: from 64 feet above sea level at the western end to 44 feet at the eastern. This 0.31 per cent downward gradient is perhaps not much of a slope over 6,561 feet, but it would have added to the difficulty of landing and stopping. However, it would have been a minor consideration when compared with the other factors that the pilots had to face. Ice, in particularly, could double the landing distance required. Had the opportunity been offered, Andy L would have been asked to check this latter aspect; it is doubtful whether he could have assessed the runway's slope.

Curilovic again:

> The approach to Runway 25 was over flat ground with no obstacles. At night we had no illuminated visual references so it was always an instrument approach. If we had to land using only visual references then it had to be from the west. However, from the west the approach to Runway 07 was over [undulating] ground crossed by small gullies. At the time in question it was all ice-covered land which made our orientation and 'visualization' of the runway totally difficult. We suffered several accidents and incidents due to these conditions, even during daylight.

This view was confirmed by Capitán de Navío Miguel Pita,[16] who has stated that throughout his time at Rio Grande the ground was frozen solid, while Capitán de Corbeta Jorge Luis Colombo confirms that there was an almost permanent 20-knot-plus crosswind. It is a matter of record that the prevailing wind in this area is between Force 3 and Force 5, with up to forty days a year affected by fog. Indeed, the average wind speed throughout the year is in the region of 16 knots, with the highest speeds recorded during the night and around midday. Gales, Force 8 and above, are recorded for 30 per cent of the time throughout the winter. Calm periods, when they do occur, tend to be at dawn and dusk.

Unfortunately, because of the almost total lack of intelligence on Rio Grande, none of this was known to the Hercules aircrew. Most of their planning for the landing was pure guesswork, supplemented by experience and one old satellite picture of the runway provided by the SAS before Cartwright joined the 'team'.

The two Hercules pilots needed to study their actual landing procedures very carefully, for although they were practised in solo downwind landings this one would be different for a number of reasons: it would be dark, with no lights either on the ground (it had to be assumed) or showing from the aircraft; there would be two aircraft in formation and the lead aircraft had to stop with at least 2,000 feet remaining ahead of it for take-off; the second aircraft had to avoid running into his leader ... whom he might not be able to see; when the aircraft reached 'finals' the tricky decision whether to abort or land would be firmly with the formation leader.

Once on the ground, if the leader did not have the required 2,000 feet ahead of him for take-off, then both aircraft would have to turn around on the 131-feet-wide runway and depart towards the west. If either aircraft was damaged and could not take off or turn, what then?

No matter what flight plan the pilots adopted, they knew that two un-announced C-130s approaching an airbase on a war footing while in a 2,000-feet trail at low level, at night and without lights, would arouse suspicion. Unlike a single aircraft, the duo had to be lined up with the runway at least 2 miles out to guarantee (as far as that was possible under these peculiar circumstances) that their landing was successful. Close to the ground and at slow speed, any evasive flying and manoeuvring would be severely limited.

Speaking in 2012, and aware of the enhanced defences at Rio Grande, Roberts' unequivocal view was:

> Our ability to confuse the enemy as to our approach path and intentions would have been zero. He would have figured out what we were up to very quickly and taken appropriate countermeasures. At Rio Grande this would have been to pour 2,000 rounds per minute from each of the four radar-guided Rheinmetal 20mm artillery pieces down the approach path as soon as we were within range: about one to 1½ miles out.
>
> The effect would be similar to being engaged by a Soviet ZSU23-2. We had numerous simulated engagements by its big brother, the ZSU23-4, during exercises in the United States most of which were analysed by the USAF and RAF experts. In virtually all cases, if we were in range – even man-oeuvring aggressively and using what limited electronic counter measures that we had and flying really low – the outcome was similar: terminal! We always considered the ZSUs, and similar AAA pieces, to be our greatest threat and went out of our way to avoid them at all costs.
>
> Approaching Rio Grande, I doubt that an engagement by the Rheinmetal would have been any different. Our only real chance of survival would have been to hope that the element of surprise in our unannounced arrival would have created confusion in the defenders and the 'clearance to engage' order would have been too late in coming. However, if the defenders were 'weapons free' then I think we'd have been toast before we got anywhere near the run-way. If by some miracle we had landed, once sitting on the runway we would have been at the mercy of the heavy and small arms fire from the ground troops.

Other factors demanded attention, too. Each aircraft came with a complement of five: the captain, a co-pilot, flight engineer, navigator – all on the flight deck – and the air loadmaster in the freight bay. On the long-range air drops there was always one extra pilot and navigator on board, plus either an additional flight engineer or air loadmaster. For Operation Mikado these 'supplementary aircrew' would come from Flight Lieutenant Jim Norfolk's crew, with his men split between XV179 and XV200. However, with the certainty of casualties, Roberts considered that it was more sensible to fly the mission with just the standard five-man crew in each Hercules. But as no decision would be made until the 'executive order' was received, all special forces aircrew at Two Boats remained on stand-by to fly until Mikado was formally cancelled.

Although the 4,000-mile approach and final 300 or so miles at low level were the most important flying aspects of the RAF's involvement in Operation Mikado, it was essential that at least an outline plan was developed to cover what might happen beyond the moment that the SAS sped off the stern ramps of the two Hercules. While it was assumed that, once ordered to 'go', the landing would take place, few really believed that there was much point, other than for purposes of morale, in planning for an orderly take-off followed by an uninterrupted flight to Punta Arenas. Without knowing in detail what defences were in place at Rio Grande, all in both the SAS and RAF camps (but particularly the RAF) were sceptical, dubious even, that there would be a third phase to Operation Mikado. A safe initial landing was almost beyond imagination, let alone a take-off by both aircraft with all eight engines intact, fully inflated tyres, no onboard fires or wounded pilots.

One alternative plan – had circumstances dictated and the SAS been prepared in advance – was for the aircraft to take off as soon as empty of vehicles and troops; in which case, trials had proved that this could be within ninety seconds of touch-down and about fifty seconds after stopping.

But ... Operation Mikado required the two Hercules to sit, undefended (for the SAS said they had no 'spare men' to guard the aircraft) on the runway with their engines 'burning and turning' while waiting for the troopers to return. Roberts recalls training at least one navigator, his own Dave Musgrave, to fire a 7.62mm general purpose machine gun from outside the crew entrance door, on the principle that with little more to do he was suddenly the most 'expendable' member of the crew. Early in the development of Mikado a general purpose machine gun firing from the port and starboard 'para doors' was considered, but concern for the aircraft's wings and external fuel tanks precluded that idea. Manufacturing a restrictive 'frame' – within which the machine gun's arc of fire would have been limited – was another idea that failed to meet approval.

Roberts continues:

> In practice, the 'ground plan' was always sketchy but we would have firmed it up with B Squadron once we had been ordered to go. I would have been happy with whatever was decided, but my personal feeling was that, if things went wrong, they would go so badly wrong that we would not survive anyway.

Many factors would affect the final take-off run. Both aircraft would have been lighter by two Land Rovers and two motor-cycles – and possibly by thirty troopers each (had they decided to 'leg it'). Using tactical take-off speeds, each Hercules could have been airborne in as little as 900 feet, although with a strong tailwind this might increase to 1,200 feet. If the pilots had stopped where they planned there would be enough room to take off, providing all four engines on each aircraft were working. Burgoyne would watch for Roberts' aircraft to start 'rolling', then they would both be accelerating down the runway 2,000 feet apart. Once airborne, Roberts would stay low to allow Burgoyne to get above his leader's wake at this vulnerable point.

As captain of the second aircraft, Burgoyne gave the take-off much thought:

> If Max was disabled could I still get away over the top of him? I figured out that if I was 2,000 feet away I reckoned I could have done it – just. But if I had any kind of engine failure then I would not clear him. A three-engine take-off in a Hercules is out of the question as you need about 7,000 feet of runway for that. Missing one engine makes all the difference because you are then too low on power on one side and have too much power on the other. To maintain control of the aircraft you can only accelerate slowly to allow the speed to build gradually until the rudder becomes effective. It's hazardous and only practised in simulators and with specially nominated instructors.

In other words, Burgoyne could have cleared XV179's 38′ 3″ fin and rudder, 2,000 feet ahead of him, but only if everything was working perfectly. In Roberts' case, while he would not have a stationary aircraft ahead, he still needed to get airborne before the end of the runway. As Roberts said, 'In the end, there were just too many "what ifs" so the planned departure from Rio Grande was tabulated, simply, as "to be decided".'

B Squadron's 'ground strategy' was equally sketchy. With no prior intelligence on enemy defences, let alone on the whereabouts of the Super Étendards, their missiles and their pilots, Ian Crooke could only plan in outline with the men he had: the balance of 6 (Boat) Troop, 7 (Air) Troop, 8 (Mobility) Troop and the balance of 9 (Mountain) Troop commanded by a small Headquarters element consisting of himself, the Squadron Sergeant Major and four troopers.

The control tower was to be the target of 8 Troop, while the aircraft and missiles were the responsibility of 7 and 9 Troops. As there was no information on the pilots' accommodation this was left vague, despite the certainty that since it would be impossible to distinguish fighter pilots from transport pilots when in their night clothes, many 'ordinary' aviators were about to be killed on the chance that some might be the target. Had Ian Crooke known that only two Super Étendards might be *in situ* anywhere across the base, 'hidden' among dozens of other aircraft, he would have appreciated the near impossibility of his task.

For the SAS, a ride to Chile in a Hercules would be a bonus, so their planning was conducted on the basis that they would be walking to the border. For the RAF the choice was equally stark but perhaps not as dire as the SAS might have feared. At Two Boats the RAF teams talked about escaping westwards with the SAS, despite not being trained for that eventuality. Only a few of the aircrew involved with Mikado had at that time attended the RAF's own survival and resistance to interrogation course at RAF Mountbatten, near Plymouth. Fortunately, Burgoyne and his navigator, Jim Cunningham, had attended the Long Range Recce Patrol School course in October of the previous year.

The general view among the airmen was that if they could stick with the SAS for the first 10 miles, then it would be back to basic aircrew survival skills as they made it alone from that point onwards. In 1982 there was no combat survival and rescue organization such as now exists. Burgoyne summarized the situation after the campaign:

> If you went down, nobody was coming to get you – you survived as best you could. The main thing I had learned from LRRPS was, whatever you do, don't give up until you positively, definitely have to 'cos it doesn't matter how unpleasant and how uncomfortable your life is while evading, it will get one hell of a lot worse in enemy hands! [He then corrected himself.] In fact, as it turned out, it probably would not have been. Look at Glover's[17] experience and indeed the Royal Marines who were captured on South Georgia ... and those who were captured in Stanley. All were treated extremely well.

Nevertheless, the enemy's conduct was a 'known unknown', and best kept unknown for as long as possible.

Burgoyne believed that, 'It was going to be a case pretty much of "suck it and see". In the event I didn't manage to pack a rucksack but I always ensured that I had some form of survival kit in the pockets of my flying suit.'

Max Roberts was slightly better off:

> Assuming we survived the landing we planned to cobble together some *ad hoc* stuff for our own personal bergens: just bits and pieces we could lay our hands on at Two Boats. The officers would carry Browning 9mm pistols and the non-commissioned officers Stirling sub machine guns. Legging it westwards would have been interesting for the aircrew as all we had was our standard RAF flying gear and I don't suppose our SAS mates would have hung around for us.

Roberts was almost certainly correct in his last statement which leaves open the perennial question: 'What would the SAS actually have done ... and did they really have any plans in advance?'

All the while there remained uncertainty over whether or not the operation was 'on'. With no news from the UK either way, those on the ground at Ascension Island (and in the air over the South Atlantic) lived on rumour. For each returning C-130 crew the first action on landing was to check if there were any Pink Panthers parked alongside the tarmac. If they were there – and they always were – the reaction was, 'Oh God. It's still on. Better check in with Crookie.'

One of the many fears that the Hercules pilots faced was the possibility of being targeted by a radar-guided missile. As stated earlier, the overland approach from the west had been dictated by the supposed presence of the two destroyers patrolling off the coast of Rio Grande. What was not known was that on 18 May both destroyers, believing that the British effort to attack Rio Grande or the petroleum plant close to Estancia la Sara that they had observed on their radars had now failed, felt able to retire. This they did down the 'safe' inshore route to Ushuaia, where they had secured alongside the refuelling jetty.[18] What then also went undetected was that, once fuelled, the destroyers were ordered north again.

On 15 May the Commanding Officer of the submarine HMS *Splendid*, Commander Roger Lane-Nott, had written in his boat's Daily Summary:

> The transit to the west has continued. Our original plan for going back to —[19] seems to have been cancelled, it looks as if we will cover the units at Ushuaia i.e. ARA *Hipolito Bouchard*, ARA *Piedra Buena* and the hospital ship *Bahia Paraiso*.

Neither of the destroyers appears again in his log for this period, although a description of the weather for the 20 May reads, 'The weather is a lot worse, particularly in the shoal waters.' This useful fact was not transmitted or, if it was, did not reach those then on standby at Two Boats.

ARA *Hipolito Bouchard* was next seen by HMS *Valiant* as the destroyer returned to Ushuaia through La Maire Straits on 6 June. The submarine had been dispatched back to the Straits (from an aborted reconnaissance of the Bay of Harbours in southern East Falkland) especially to monitor any breakout by the destroyers, who, intelligence reports received in the submarine had stated, were back at Ushuaia. This turned out to be incorrect, as the submarine's Commanding Officer, Commander Tim le Marchant, wrote:

> The destroyer was sighted in heavy rain ... and identified as a Sumner class DDG at a range of about 6,000 yards exiting the Estrecho de la Maire [to the south] and turning west towards the Beagle Channel. The submarine went to action stations and all tubes brought to Readiness State 1, but Rules of Engagement prevented an attack except in self-defence and the *H Bouchard* was frustratingly watched past an ideal firing position, regrettably only some 2½ miles off the coast, as she proceeded at 18 knots ... towards Ushuaia: this event clearly reduced the credibility of the intelligence and confirmed the belief on board that no DDG would pass *Valiant* while she was on patrol in the area without being detected.

Although by that date (6 June) Operation Mikado had, finally, been cancelled, it is symptomatic of the paucity of real-time intelligence that dogged much of the campaign. As it happened, this information reached neither Hereford nor the aircrew of 47 Squadron's Special Forces Flight, who by then were conducting long-range stores drops. The assessment therefore is that the Argentine destroyers had been on their picket stations between 18 May and 6 June and thus in a position to detect any approaching aircraft.

All the while, seventy men waited for the executive command ...

Chapter 15

Operation Plum Duff – Mark Two: Tierra del Fuego

Because much was happening simultaneously and 4,000 miles apart, it might be helpful to summarize the story so far with regard to the 'on/off' nature of Operation Mikado. The decision to execute or cancel had a 'chequered history'.

On 19 May Squadron Leader Roberts was ordered to 'Lead a two-ship formation in an airfield assault operation on Rio Grande airfield', but with no date given. This was the only 'instruction' received by the Hercules crews. The most suitable window (apart from the lack of a moon) during which the RAF and B Squadron could conduct the operation was between 20 May (the day after the second Hercules arrived in theatre) and 25 May (after which time Argentina had only one Exocet left) – but no orders were received.

On 20 May a discussion took place at Hereford that considered Operation Plum Duff's abortion; simultaneously, at Duke of York Barracks, the decision to continue with Operation Mikado without a prior reconnaissance was confirmed. On 21 May Mikado was put 'on hold'[1] at Ascension Island while Roberts flew a resupply flight to the Task Force. On this day Flight Lieutenant Burgoyne was shown a model of Rio Grande's accommodation by the SAS, after which a plan to land a Hercules on a road close to Rio Grande was first mooted. On 23 May Mikado was again 'on hold' while Burgoyne resupplied the Task Force. By the end of 25 May Argentina was reduced to one Exocet; this was also the day that the Sea King aircrew from Operation Plum Duff, now in Chile, were informed by an SAS officer that Operation Mikado had been cancelled. This news was not communicated to those at Two Boats Village. On 26 May B Squadron was still expecting to fly to Rio Grande, yet Mikado was 'on hold' once more while another resupply flight was flown.

On 27 May, worried that his colleagues' fears (and now those of B Squadron) were not being addressed adequately, Squadron Leader Cartwright felt it necessary to send the following signal to the Commander-in-Chief expressing his concern:

IMMEDIATE
XXXXZ 27 MAY 1982
FROM: 47SF DET ASCENSION
TO: CTF317 NORTHWOOD

TOP SECRET PD UK EYES A PD HVCCO PD
EXCLUSIVE FOR COMMANDER IN CHIEF PD

FROM 38 GP GIO PD SF CREWS HERE HAVE EXPRESSED DEEP
CONCERN OVER INTELLIGENCE TO SUPPORT
FORTHCOMING OP NOW RECENTLY POSTPONED PD
PROMISED TARGET RELATED INTELLIGENCE UPDATES
HAVE NOT MATERIALIZED PD CONSIDER PRESENT
INTELLIGENCE DATA INADEQUATE TO SUPPORT PROPOSED
OP PD PLEASE ACKNOWLEDGE AND ADVISE PD

As Cartwright received no acknowledgement it was assumed that Mikado was still
'on', yet on 1 June Max Roberts was ordered to the United Kingdom to train more
crews in air-to-air refuelling. It was now obvious, by default, that resupply of the
Task Force was the prime duty for the Special Forces Flight. Operation Mikado
was 'officially put on ice' in the UK on 2 June and the next day it was cancelled,
but at Two Boats Village this news was only received as 'hearsay' via the SAS.

Back in time ... on 20 May, during a meeting between the SAS and RAF at
Two Boats, Crooke had told Roberts that the Plum Duff team, of which the latter
knew nothing anyway, were in trouble. Few details were available – there were
rumours of two cases of exposure and possible pneumonia. Either way, it had to
be assumed that the patrol would be taking no further part in operations, for to all
intents and purposes it was so delayed that it was not likely to reveal timely intelligence. 'But,' B Squadron's Commander stated, 'the message from Headquarters
SAS is that Operation Mikado is still very much On'. Planning was to continue.

What also needs clarification, before the story moves forward, is that although
Mikado was 'on/off/on' over a lengthy period it was never 'on' to the point that
the aircrew and passengers manned the two Hercules at Wideawake. It is strange,
therefore, to read a report by a member of B Squadron who says that they did
just that – particularly since in most other respects his story's 'ring of truth' is
chillingly authentic.[2] In his book, *The Killing Zone*,[3] Harry McCallion states:

> The operation was on, only to be postponed for twelve, twenty-four or
> forty-eight hours. One moment we would be sitting in our vehicles ready to
> drive to the airfield, the next the job was cancelled yet again ... Major
> Crooke knew the effect these delays were having on the Squadron ...
>
> At 0600 [no date is given] those who could stomach it ate breakfast. We
> crowded on to the trucks once again, then drove to the airfield. We loaded
> the aircraft for the assault, then each of us went to his prearranged position.
> After all the false starts, I felt calm and at ease now that we were ready to go.
> I'd never been afraid of death. Sometimes I had even chased it. I wondered
> whether this was one of those times. On the faces of my comrades I saw a
> mixture of emotions: excitement on the faces of the younger ones, grim
> determination on the others.
>
> A Land Rover appeared with several RAF personnel. Crooky was called
> off the aircraft – I thought to be given last-minute instructions. Then the
> engines slowly died. The job was cancelled, permanently. The RAF had dis-
> covered that the Argentinians had deployed a new radar on a boat just off the

coast. The airfield we were attacking would have too great a warning of our approach. We unloaded and made our way back to our 'bashas'.

A lot has been said inside Special Forces circles about B Squadron and the operation that never was, and much of it has been derogatory. But, when the chips were down, when they told us to go, every man went, even those who thought we were doomed.

Contrary to the above narrative, there was no time when one, let alone both, Hercules were ready to conduct Operation Mikado. Consequently, the internal Andover tanks were never removed, and with them in place there would have been no room for B Squadron, the Land Rovers and motorcycles. It might, just, have been possible that 'for exercise purposes' Major Crooke managed to 'borrow' one standard Hercules as it 'rested' between flights to and from Lyneham and Dakar (although McCallion mentions 'turning engines'); but this did not happen, since the Hercules were only on the ground for a maximum of one and a half hours, during which time they were unloaded, serviced and reloaded. Flight Lieutenant Pat Fitzgerald, responsible for all air transport aircraft arrivals and departures at Wideawake, recalls no such 'exercise'. Nor did the VC 10 ever load any men either. It seems that *ex post facto* imaginations have been allowed too free a rein.

A reliable report comes from Corporal Robin Horsfall, also of B Squadron, in his own account of events:[4]

It turned out that the recce group had failed in the allotted task ... In brief we (now) lacked enough information about where the enemy aircraft were to mount the mission with any reasonable chance of success ...

After the first two false starts,

It was just a matter of getting on the Hercs and going and once more I steeled myself ... to attack the enemy on his home ground ... and yet again the mission was cancelled. It was bad enough preparing for a kamikaze mission but to then stand down yet again was almost mind-numbing.

Horsfall offers an interesting comment that backs up General Moore's views on the SAS's conventional skills:

We trained and worked as infantry sections for the first time since I joined the Regiment ... most of my sergeants didn't have a clue about infantry battle-drills ... They couldn't give section or platoon orders and would be dangerous to have around in a fire-fight. I for one wouldn't have followed some of my own sergeants ... War was bringing out the worst as well as the best in the SAS.

We continued to update our plan and offer new ideas to Hereford for approval (and) suggested a number of other ways we could knock out the aircraft. Every suggestion was met with a 'no'. (The Director SAS) insisted that (we) had to land on the airfield ... for he clearly wanted his Entebbe-style raid ... We were prepared to do it ... but we weren't too happy about wasting everything being shot out of the air and killed before we even landed on Argentinian soil.

Time dragged on Ascension Island. Every time we thought we were going in we were stood down ... Yet again Operation Mikado raised its battered head and we prepared once more to go into the breach. There was no change to the original plan. We unhappily surrendered to the inevitable and got back on with waiting. By now, though, the incursions of the Paras and Marines, who had succeeded in covering enormous distances on foot had forced the enemy to retreat ... There was no longer any good reason to attack the mainland.

In an e-mail to the author on 13 December 2013 Robin Horsfall elaborates further:

There was never a time when we sat with engines running ready to go but the mission was on and off several times. There was no separate (attack) directed towards the (Argentine) pilots; the (Super Étendard) were the only target. Killing the pilots could have been a war crime especially as, on the ground, they wouldn't have been armed. The Mikado mission was probably doomed to fail and I for one am pleased it never happened. It was a poor idea to sacrifice a squadron in the hope that we would get on the ground; that the enemy aircraft would be there; that we would achieve surprise and that we had sufficient numbers to carry out the mission. In my opinion (the Director SAS) would have lost us all for no return. Importantly and in spite of our feelings we were all ready to go. I did as I was told, happy or not, because I wore the cap badge of the SAS.

Another snippet was revealed in the *Daily Mail*[5] when a member of B Squadron at Ascension Island, 'Rusty' Firmin, was quoted as saying that, among others, he and John McAleese:

Were trained for a mission from which neither [of us] expected to return – flying in two C-130 Hercules aircraft into the heart of Argentina, landing at a military airbase and 'taking out' the enemy pilots who were bombing British forces. It was a death mission. Even if we'd survived, it would have been a question of escape and evading capture and getting out of Argentina across the mountains [*sic*].

Anxious to see action but frustrated that neither Hercules were available at any one time for training, Ian Crooke was hatching more plans. There was little else to keep his men occupied at Two Boats Village other than keeping fit and building newer models of their target. There was, though, one thing the Major could do: ask to be flown to Belize and launch the attack from there.

It says much for the 'clout' that the SAS commanded within 38 Group that, on 23 May, Flight Lieutenant Rob Robinson, a VC 10 captain was, 'enjoying a rest period by a hotel pool in Dakar when I was summoned to take a telephone call'.[6] The call was brief. Robinson was not returning to Brize Norton that evening but would be flying to Ascension Island in a C-130, within the hour. At Wideawake,

Robinson and his crew were met by Squadron Leader Hudson, who knew nothing, before being bussed to a bungalow at Two Boats Village, where they were kept separate from the other RAF crews. As no further information was forthcoming they spent an evening 'speculating'.

Early the next morning the VC 10's air loadmaster knocked on his captain's door and informed Robinson that, 'There is a gentleman who wishes to speak to you.' On the veranda Robinson inquired 'Who is there?' into the darkness, only to discover that it was Major Crooke 'lurking in the bushes'. Robinson, an ex-special forces pilot himself, and one who knew and had worked with Crooke, was unfazed; indeed, this invaluable background was vital to how he subsequently handled the tasking and his crew. A second short brief followed, best told in the Flight Lieutenant's words:

> We were to fly between eight and twelve men of B Squadron with their kit to Belize, from where they expected to be flown by a civilian aircraft to attack an Argentine fighter base. Their task was to locate and destroy the Exocet missiles held there. However, if the civilian aircraft was not available, and I suspected it would not be, then we would be expected to fly the mission. Take-off was planned for 1400 hours that day. Soon, I took a call from 38 Group who confirmed my tasking to Belize. To my great relief no mention was made of any further tasking to the South American mainland! We planned to stage through Nassau and pick up sufficient fuel to be able to divert back to Nassau if we weren't able to land at Belize. The forecast weather at Belize was one factor, the second was a suitable diversion airfield, considering our sensitive load! Prior to landing at Belize I would dump fuel to get down to a suitable landing weight for the length of runway available. I briefed the crew and we spent the rest of the morning planning the mission.

At 1230 that afternoon a VC 10 (a slip crew had flown a second prepared aircraft direct to Wideawake from the United Kingdom) was loaded with boxes of ammunition that were strapped to a cleared area of the floor at the forward end of the cabin. No men and certainly no vehicles were embarked. Then, at 1330, Robinson was told, over the radio, to 'stand down'. He and his crew immediately left the aircraft in the hands of the 'servicing crew' and in his words – and quite understandably – 'made themselves scarce'!

What is not in doubt about McCallion's story is the 'effect that these delays' (caused by the RAF's Hercules supplying the Task Force) were having on the SAS Squadron. The same can be said of the effect on the RAF crews, including, it is now known, the aircrew of the tanker fleet stood-by to conduct the air-to-air refuelling operation. The Victor crews were much exercised over their vulnerability to enemy aircraft (the armed Argentine Boeing was a particular worry) when on their lone refuelling sorties; for them, unlike the slower, propeller-driven Hercules, there were no 'fighter evasion' techniques.

Morale within the RAF's Mikado force was not improved by the knowledge that B Squadron was just as hesitant about its chances of survival; indeed, by now it had fully dawned on even the most aggressive troopers that simply arriving on the ground in one piece was unlikely. Max Roberts detected that, 'They now realized that they were likely to die in the aeroplane. They knew the problems we faced and they did not fancy them very much either.'

None of this was assisted in either the RAF or the SAS camp by the operation never being officially 'on'; it would, all guessed, just happen at no notice on an order from Northwood (although six hours per aircraft would be needed for reconfiguration, a delay that was unlikely to have been allowed for by those in either Whitehall or at Hereford).

It has been suggested elsewhere that popular names for Operation Mikado, among B Squadron and the Hercules crews at that time on Ascension Island, were Operation 'Certain Death' or Operation 'Suicide'. Unremarkable to those who know both organizations, no such defeatist descriptions were ever contemplated, let alone tolerated. Along with the fictitious description of the conversation purported to have been held outside the Sea King helicopter while on the ground close to Estancia La Sara, the Operation 'Certain Death' tag belongs in fiction. Both 'stories' are untrue. Certainly B Squadron's Robin Horsfall in his book *Fighting Scared* makes no mention of this fabricated 'nickname'.

On 28 May the teams at Two Boats Village were informed that Mikado had been 'finally, definitely, cancelled'. Unsurprisingly, this news was met with substantial relief; yet twelve hours later, it was on again. Bitter disappointment enveloped both camps. It was a difficult and dark period.

The Mikado teams were told on 30 May (the day the last known air-launched Exocet was expended) via the SAS's communications system that the assault was (for the second time) 'absolutely, definitely, finally cancelled'. This now proved to be the case, although in London (and thankfully unknown to those at Ascension Island) it was still only regarded as being 'on ice'. Roberts and his team, Crooke and his team, greeted this latest decision with immense relief ... and more scepticism. Two days later Roberts flew home, and with that 'hint', allied to the lack of any contradictory statements, B Squadron felt it safe to organize a celebratory football match between themselves and the Special Forces Flight on Two Boats' cinder pitch. It was a carefree, riotous event: every time a goal was scored the 'offending' player was required to down a beer ... until honour, accompanied by multiple asphalt burns, was finally satisfied on both sides. Afterwards, the teams drove to the far side of Green Mountain for a joint barbecue, a party well away from everyone else.

Burgoyne remembers the occasion:

A huge drinking exercise. A great day with morale fully restored, for the SAS were as pleased as we were. Their fear was, as was ours, that neither aircraft would actually reach the runway and all would have been in vain. All the aircrew had to do now was continue flying twenty-four-hour missions to the Task Force; avoid being shot down by Argentine Mirages (or the Royal Navy!); not lose an engine and end up ditching or diverting to the mainland; then land back at Ascension without falling asleep during the approach! A breeze, really, compared to Mikado. I was pleased that I wasn't going to die but I was more pleased that we were not going to make a futile gesture and waste this extraordinary asset that we had created in four weeks. We could now put that terrible memory aside and really sort out the resupply of the Task Force.

In reality, Operation Mikado was never called off, it simply withered away through a combination of a lack of targets and the imperative of resupplying the Task Force by Hercules. In Whitehall's corridors it had never been a 'goer' because of the legality of such a mission, but no one had had the courage to say so to the SAS or to those others most closely involved.

However, Mikado had not been the only preoccupation.

Back in time again ... With Operation Plum Duff aborted and with the likelihood of Mikado being ordered without a prior reconnaissance, it was clear to those whose lives were literally at stake that a more workable solution needed to be passed back to the UK: in effect, a scaled-down Mikado or a beefed-up Plum Duff. Once on the ground, the SAS's duty would be the same; the problem that now needed addressing was how to 'guarantee' getting those men on the ground alive and fit to fight.

What was never known as 'Operation Plum Duff Mark Two'[7] had its beginnings on 21 May at Two Boats Village. That day, with Mikado 'on hold' while Roberts conducted Drop Julie to HMS *Alacrity*, Harry Burgoyne, along with Jim Cunningham and Bumper Rowley, were invited to the SAS quarters to discuss matters with Ian Crooke and his Squadron Sergeant Major, John F. The latter knew Burgoyne and Cunningham and trusted them; they had spent a month on exercise in Kenya in February of that year. Crooke took the aircrew into his confidence by showing them his model of Rio Grande air base. As with the one seen by Roberts at Northwood, this did not show the runway and was fashioned using the same satellite photograph from which Burgoyne ('shocked that he had not seen the model before') knew the C-130 aircrew had deduced that all landings took place in a westerly direction.

The general discussion was along the lines of, 'What can we do to get this thing back on track that would be good for the project but that will also increase our chances of success and survival?' Immediately the conversation revolved around air-landing the troops on a road, from where they could 'scoot into town, do their work then leg it to Chile'. However, before that could happen it was still necessary to establish an observation party in the absence of Andy L's team.

With no conventional submarine yet available – and the SAS were unlikely to pass the baton to their SBS colleagues anyway[8] – the only way of landing a reconnaissance party on the mainland had to be by Hercules and in the manner of the original Bombilla Flats operation. Squadron Leader Cartwright had briefed the aircrew that two Argentine destroyers, ARA *Hipolito Bouchard* and ARA *Piedra Buena* of Task Group 79.3, had been stationed 14 miles north-west of Rio Grande and that, if still in position, these would present a significant threat to the Hercules. Any proposed plan would need to take into account not only the perceived capabilities of the Rio Grande radar but also those of the warships, whether their presence was confirmed or not.

Although he had never used the 'new' GQ360 parachute, John F was receptive to the idea of being parachuted into Argentina using the same techniques that had been practised for Bombilla. His mission would be twofold, much as the original Plum Duff had been. With four other troopers he would either attack Rio Grande himself or, if that was not feasible, his patrol would prepare a 'strip-landing zone' on a suitable piece of road and await the arrival of the rest of B Squadron. It was what they specialized in, and anyway nobody in his squadron wanted to arrive by aeroplane direct on to the Rio Grande runway.

The more detailed plan was for one Hercules to 'coast in' at low level over the spit of land on the northern edge of Bahia San Sebastian (much as Victor Charlie had done, although the RAF pilots did not know this – nor, as has been mentioned, did they know about the oil rigs which would need to be avoided) and from there fly direct to a dropping zone at 53°41' S, 68°06' W, behind a shallow ridge of hills roughly 16 miles north-west of Rio Grande. This area was chosen because it appeared to be in the radar shadow as viewed from the air base. The Andover tanks would not need to be removed for this preliminary flight of five men, so the Hercules would make the return journey from Wideawake with only one refuelling on the outward leg, as happened with Plum Duff.

Although planning to use the standard low-level parachutes (PX4 or 22 Foot SSL) if the wind was too strong, the option of switching to the GQ360 was now available; how the wind strengths would be assessed in advance was not discussed at this stage. Much would also depend on the perceived capability of the radar at Rio Grande and the whereabouts of the two Argentine destroyers. No one knew of the oil rig that had caused Sea King Victor Charlie to divert.

Burgoyne recalls further considerations at the time:

We hoped that, once on the ground, John F might be able to carry out the attack on Rio Grande himself so subsequent landings on the road would not be required. However, if they were, we planned to space them about fifteen minutes apart. Simultaneous landings were unnecessary and, frankly, stupid with so little known about the landing zone. Besides, it made more sense for the first aircraft, mine, to be in and out of the landing zone before the second arrived. That way, if we had problems (shot down, crashed on landing, bogged down – we considered this unlikely as the ground was probably frozen solid – burst tyres and so on) Max could abort the mission early and divert to Punta. Assuming the main assault party was needed, we would have had about six hours on the ground back at Ascension Island after John F's insertion before returning to the strip with Max Roberts and B Squadron. If it worked it would be exactly twenty-four hours after dropping John F in the middle of the night that we would return.

Burgoyne continues:

We were working with no intelligence and very old charts, circa 1937, so we were far from sure that the ground information would be accurate. We dis-counted the roads running close to the coast as they would be busy and we didn't want a repeat of Operation Eagle's Claw in Iran, when a bus-load of civvies pitched up on the road running through the landing zone that the Yanks had earmarked. In addition, we wanted to avoid roads running north/south for the crosswind on a narrow track would be a significant factor. Consequently we only considered the road running east/west about a mile west of John F's drop zone.[9] There was, though, likely to be a snag. It was assumed that for much of its length telegraph poles ran down one or other of the highway's verges, and as the wingspan of the Hercules is in the order of 132 feet, 53 feet either side of the road would need to be clear of obstructions. The aeronautical charts were too small-scale to show power lines, but as they were at least 45 years old we couldn't trust them anyway. It was vital that the advance party check for these and the road's width, flatness and load-bearing strength. The C-130's wheel track is just under 15 feet and it was hoped that a suitable long and straight section could be found. We even considered remotely detonating the telegraph poles with some kind of radio controlled trigger if John F and his team were elsewhere when we arrived. This sort of thing had been done before; the Americans switched on the Desert One airstrip landing lights by a radio signal during Eagle's Claw.

Unknown to the SAS and RAF aircrew at the time, the Argentine naval pilots had long practised using emergency landing strips for their fast jets on two sections of Ruta Nacional 3: 19 miles to the north of Rio Grande and 16 miles to the south, known respectively as the Rio Chico and Punta Maria Highway Strips. Super Étendards, with their 31-feet wingspan, had landed and taken off, but a Hercules had never done so, although after the campaign the Argentine pilots told the author that it would have been possible.[10]

While these were all feasible options, Ian Crooke was constantly throwing out other ideas. His was not an enviable position, for with the Hercules crews either away or sleeping there was no chance for his men to practise their drills and little time for him to have lengthy discussions with the two pilots together. As time moved on he saw the chance of a dramatic SAS demonstration of daring – come success or failure – slipping away, yet he continued tossing concepts to his RAF colleagues. One such was to load a Puma helicopter into each of the Hercules and fly them to Punta Arenas or Port Montt. There the Pumas would be re-assembled and the assault launched. As with other plans to launch an attack from Chile, this would have stretched the 'host nation's' support too far, probably beyond breaking point. It would also have played havoc with the timings, as a 'large team of engineers' needed at least three days to re-assemble the helicopters and have them proved airworthy.

Chapter 16

Operation Kettledrum –
Puerto Deseado

Elsewhere, a third implausible plan for a mainland operation had been maturing . . .

Lieutenant Commander Andrew Johnson, the Commanding Officer of the diesel-electric submarine HMS *Onyx*, brought his boat alongside HMS *Fearless* in San Carlos Water, as his log and additional supporting comments for 31 May show:

0530: Surfaced.
0830: Dived on aircraft sighting.
1200: Position 50° 35′ S, 59° 30′ W.
2100: Rendezvous with HMS *Avenger* for lead in to San Carlos Water.
0045: Berthed alongside HMS *Fearless* to collect SBS and associated equipment.

Dived at short notice when possible aircraft sighted. Bright light on steady bearing. In retrospect, consider it was a planet, but better safe than sorry! Spent day making slow transit to rendezvous, with brief periods of snorting[1] to keep battery high. Lead in to San Carlos went well, using periscope to follow, con and fix. Delayed while other movements took place, but arrived alongside HMS *Fearless* about midnight. Long chat with Jeremy Larken, the Commanding Officer and a fellow submariner[2] [and from whom he received, in Larken's words, 'much useful, avuncular advice'], then briefly with the Commodore Amphibious Warfare before full briefing sessions with the SBS.

Having expended the last of their Exocet missiles on 30 May – the day before *Onyx*'s arrival in San Carlos – the two Super Étendards had been flown back to Espora to join the others at their home base on 1 June, so Rio Grande was no longer a prime concern; but Espora could still have been. [Whether or not this move of the Super Étendards was known by the British remains unclear and makes the reasons for Operation Kettledrum even more puzzling.] Although the Secret Intelligence Service were adamant that no replacement Exocets had reached Argentina, a tiny doubt remained; and as long as that doubt was present, the Super Étendards constituted a target, wherever they were. Nevertheless, it was towards Puerto Deseado, and not Espora, that HMS *Onyx* was about to be ordered to sail on 2 June.

With HMS *Onyx*'s berthing alongside HMS *Fearless* had also come a 'rather scruffy cardboard tube' that Andrew Johnson was at last able to hand to its addressee, the Officer Commanding the Special Boat Squadron. When the 'seals' were broken, the SBS command team in the amphibious flag ship 'simply could not believe the contents', for they were the outline orders for an attack on Puerto Deseado. This was an air base that had not featured in any 'direct action' plans by the British, for two simple reasons: it was 400 nautical miles from Stanley, let alone Woodward's carrier battle group, and there had never been any indication that an attack – by Super Étendard, Mirage, Dagger or Skyhawk – had ever been launched from there. Yet ... an SBS team was now required to embark in the submarine, sail north, observe and attack if feasible any relevant aircraft that they might detect at an air base inside the borders of a country with which the UK was not, in any legal sense, at war. While there had been a brief advance warning of the possibility of a mainland operation, nothing else was known – especially not its target, although this had been assumed to be Rio Grande and the Exocets.

The collective view among the SBS officers was uncompromising:

> We think it was the timing that annoyed us most because Operation Kettle-
> drum, as it was called, had clearly been dreamt up some considerable time
> before but no one in England had thought to tell us in San Carlos. Had they
> done so we might have had a chance of doing some realistic planning and
> perhaps have been able to bring some up-to-date reality to the discussions.
> Instead we were reduced to having several DSSS conversations [Defence
> Secure Satellite Communications System, known simply as 'D triple S'] with
> people at home who kept on telling us that 'the birds were expected to come
> in there' [Puerto Deseado] and other such inanities.

SBS officers recall that these discussions were backed up by signals to which Jeremy Larken, as the Commanding Officer of *Fearless* and as Flag Captain to the Commodore Amphibious Warfare, was properly privy. As a result, he was able to offer practical advice tempered by the observation that in his experienced view the Royal Marines and HMS *Onyx* faced 'a bit of a problem'. Apart from Jonathan Thomson, Richard Preston (in whom Thomson had confided his concerns) and Jeremy Larken, the only other three officers 'in theatre' who knew anything at all about Operation Kettledrum, then and now, were Andrew Johnson of *Onyx*, Colin Howard, the SBS's Operations Officer and (once at sea in the submarine) Lieutenant David Boyd, the Royal Marine who would command the operation.

The one officer who should have been consulted at the very beginning, but was not, was Michael Clapp, the Commodore Amphibious Warfare, responsible to the land force commander for SBS operations. He had certainly welcomed Lieutenant Commander Andrew Johnson to his amphibious domain and had discussed in outline the use of the submarine operating with the SBS around the islands; but no more than that, as far as Operation Kettledrum was concerned. Without Clapp's prior knowledge, the submarine sent south to do his bidding was about to be removed almost before HMS *Onyx* had arrived. As with the earlier loss of one of the Commodore's 'junglie' helicopters to Operation Plum Duff, the normal amphibious chain of command, long established in order, *inter alia*, to safeguard and control invaluable assets, was once more being ignored by those far removed from San Carlos.

Captain Brian Woolvine, an SBS officer on Admiral Fieldhouse's staff, had handed the sealed cardboard tube to Johnson when the submarine called at Ascension Island on its way south in the middle of May. Apart from the orders, this 'scruffy' cylinder also contained one map, one chart and a handful of satellite-derived images. Richard Preston, now back with Jeremy Moore's headquarters in *Fearless*, recorded in his diary:

> HMS *Onyx* arrives tomorrow night to start training with the SBS for a possible mission against the Argentine mainland air bases. This kind of strategic task should be mounted from the UK. We have no need to know about it; neither are we able to provide adequate briefing.
>
> [Following the submarine's arrival Preston's diary continues] Jonathan is very worried at the way the operation is being set up. It is unbelievable that anyone should be expected to plan, let alone execute, a mission of this complexity without comprehensive intelligence and topographical information. We [Headquarters, Land Forces Falkland Islands] signalled Fleet expressing grave misgivings over the operation. It is a Boys Own Paper scheme which is likely at best to create only political embarrassment and at worst could lead to our whole team being killed, and I suspect it would achieve nothing.
>
> The only map Thomson has been given by Fleet Headquarters looks like a piece torn from an RAC road map. It has the outline of the coast and roads but little or no other information and certainly no indication of the target or any contours. I am horrified.

Marginally more detail was to be found on the 1:35,000 Argentine chart no. 23071 entitled 'Rada Puerto Deseado'. This 'second edition' was based on 'Surveys by the Argentine Naval Hydrographic Service to 1969' and published by the US Defense Mapping Agency Hydrographic Center on 20 November, 1976.

Preston continues:

> When the SBS officers sought my views I could not believe that anyone sane would have considered mounting a military operation on the basis of the information that they had been given, and said so. They appeared to agree, and that, I assumed, put an end to the madness, especially as their Officer Commanding, Jonathan Thomson, also consulted Jeremy Larken.
>
> [Preston added later] I have to say that I was surprised to learn subsequently that they had launched the operation.

The senior SBS officers 'down south' were not happy either, with one major (who wishes to remain anonymous) stating unequivocally:

> We were in a period when people in the UK were prepared to believe in the myths as much as the reality. However, we in the SBS were not prepared to believe in myths and said so. But once that discussion was over, we were ready to mount the operation against the Puerto Deseado air base despite

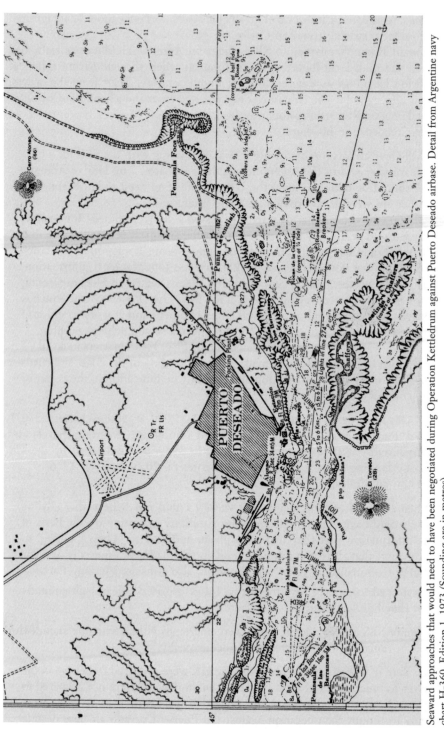

Seaward approaches that would need to have been negotiated during Operation Kettledrum against Puerto Deseado airbase. Detail from Argentine navy chart H-360, Edition 1, 1973 (Sounding are in metres).

thinking it politically unwise and probably militarily impossible. We felt we had a wider duty to say that myth and reality had more than parted company, but when overruled by Fleet Headquarters we had to get on and attempt to follow orders. If you don't do that, you get chaos.

The same member of the SBS command team 'in theatre' continued to elaborate their collective views:[3]

Argentina was a country against which we were not at war. Having men killed or captured on the Argentine mainland would have been counterproductive in the global media war in which the United Kingdom was then engaged.

This opinion certainly affected the SBS command in its discussions with Northwood and influenced the eventual decision made by Fleet Headquarters to abort the operation. No one in the SBS wanted to be associated with pointless failure or, as is now known, with an operation that was based on outdated intelligence and aimed at an Argentine base that had never been of any military significance. Further comments from the same source in Headquarters SBS have recently surfaced:

Now that we know that the airbase was of little tactical importance it just makes the whole thing more serious, for it implies that the special forces planning staff in the UK had lost grip of reality. We in the SBS had had enough of living that sort of dream by then and were trying to concentrate on the much less glamorous, but realistic and essential, mission of supporting the landing force.

Following discussions between the South Atlantic and Northwood on the 'D triple S', described at the time as being a series of 'remonstrations from San Carlos' (caused in part by conflicting orders on the target that were also flowing from the Ministry of Defence), the SBS planners in HMS *Fearless*, having made their point, complied with their orders.

The precise details of those orders – the Aim, or what is now termed the Mission – are lost, although the declared reason for this operation was that Puerto Deseado was believed to be a 'staging, refuelling and mounting base' with 'pilot accommodation', and the 'command needed to know how, precisely, it was being used, by whom and when'. This rather vague 'mission statement' was based on an unfounded worry that the Super Étendard pilots might have been using Puerto Deseado as a diversionary air base for rest and security immediately following a mission. The basis of this rather spurious deduction (given that only two aircraft and two pilots were involved in each sortie), offered to the SBS during their planning, was that Puerto Deseado had 'large accommodation facilities'.

It has to be remembered, too, that these orders were written in the UK three weeks earlier and then delivered, 'by hand of officer', to HMS *Onyx* at Ascension Island before she continued her voyage on 16 May. At that stage of the campaign there were three air-launched Exocets 'unaccounted for'; but in the meantime, and while the submarine 'swam south' for two more weeks, all were to be expended. By the time of the submarine's arrival in San Carlos there were no missiles left, and that much was known in the Task Force, if yet to be appreciated at home.

According to the SBS Operations Officer at the time:[4]

> As with Plum Duff and Mikado, no one in the United Kingdom had done their sums, for the landing itself at Puerto Deseado would have been equally as fraught as any attack or reconnaissance. The river is very narrow, very fast flowing and the submarine would not have been able to get close enough because of a ledge.

Indeed, the British Admiralty's *South America Pilot* Volume II talks of a complicated approach for surface vessels that also face tidal streams running up to six knots at 'springs', with just five minutes of 'slack water' at each change of tide; and the landing was planned for two days before the 6 June full moon.

Concerned that he was sending men on a mission that was unlikely to succeed, the Officer Commanding the SBS, Major Jonathan Thomson, decided to lead the attack himself. Although not trained as an SBS officer, Thomson felt strongly that he could not send his men on a 'raid' that all regarded as 'stupid, with a near certainty of death or capture', without accompanying them. On this occasion there would be no underwater work involved, only a straightforward landing by rubber Gemini assault craft followed by an overland approach to, and possible raid on, a well defined target, prior to a lengthy escape towards a 'neutral' country; on the face of it, normal fare for a Royal Marines major.

However, that was not Thomson's job. His task was to advise the Land Forces Commander (first Thompson and now Moore) and the Commodore Amphibious Warfare (Clapp) on maritime special forces operations, while also providing deconfliction advice on such operations in relation to conventional plans.

Additionally, according to Preston, who had been personally involved in the early stages after *Onyx*'s arrival, the operation also presented an interesting moral dilemma. When given a task that is clearly impossible and would at best end in failure and political embarrassment (with, inevitably, the commander becoming the scapegoat, as happened to Captain Andy L) and at worst lead to the capture or death of all involved, do you have an obligation to lead the mission yourself? And what of the position of a commanding officer who personally believes a task to be unachievable, yet is leading men who have placed their trust in him? 'In the end you just get on with it as part of your contract' – but it remains a dilemma.

If the pre-arranged timings contained in the orders were to be met, there was no time to prepare plans prior to departure; thus the main planning could only be conducted once HMS *Onyx* was on her way north. The Special Operations Group (with the War Cabinet's agreement, it has to be presumed) had originally ordered that the operation should involve fourteen men, but Thomson felt that this was twice as many as required for what was, after all, not an 'invasion' but a 'quick nip in and out', leaving the smallest of 'footprints'. Quite apart from that, there simply was not enough room in the submarine, while the allotted team was already well formed and self-contained.

Without yet knowing the reasons behind its failure, Thomson was also conscious that Operation Plum Duff had not succeeded; he also knew that his own men did not, as 6 Troop had, have a nearby international border to make for: the nearest point of Chile lies over 250 miles to the west of Puerto Deseado. To limit any damage when things went wrong, just six men would conduct the operation. Another reason for reducing the numbers was that this was expected to be, contrary to the way the SBS prefer to operate, a one-way journey. Any chance of successfully conducting a lengthy 'escape and evasion' would be greater with the fewest men possible.

HMS *Onyx* sailed from San Carlos at 0700 GMT on 1 June for a day of pre-Operation Kettledrum trials with her 'embarked force' of SBS led by Lieutenant David Boyd[5] and Sergeant 'Wally' (William) Lewis,[6] who with their four Royal Marines had been waiting in *Fearless*. Also on board was the SBS's Operations Officer, Captain Colin Howard,[7] who could now view the 'Northwood mission' for the first time in detail. Once at sea, Howard was able to produce a first draft of his Operation Order, as he explains:[8]

I then wrote the orders with Andrew Johnson and of course with David Boyd and his team 'conferring'. We did not really have much technical information to go on but the chart and the *South America Pilot* painted the picture! The assault team was not going to retrace its entry down the river either, as that would have been near impossible without the river taking charge.

The fact that Jonathan Thomson tasked me to go forward in the submarine meant that 'London' would get an SBS Operational Order for their approval, written with the team that would conduct the landing after we had all analysed the available information and balanced that with the team's capabilities. Boyd's team was 'good to go' and prepared to be ordered! However, for obvious good measure we required answers to a list of carefully thought out key points that needed clarification.

David Boyd was to write:[9]

Much of what happened I had long since forgotten and some I was never aware of as a young, relatively inexperienced officer just getting on with a job. This was because Jonathan Thomson was quite determined to do everything possible to protect Operational Security, to the point that none of my team, including me, were told of anything until HMS *Onyx* had departed San Carlos. We were to remain on board until the task commenced or, as it happened, was aborted and diverted elsewhere.

[Boyd's most enduring memory of the operation was the paucity of up to date intelligence.] The air photographs we were supplied, presumably through the United States, pre-dated the Argentine invasion of the Falkland Islands let alone the outbreak of conflict. I also recall that we had little in the way of stand-off munitions to deal with the target we were assigned; which meant we were back to the 'get up close and personal' with a target in a potentially heavily defended air base.

Although on a far smaller scale than Mikado, this mainland operation, too, was beginning to display all the makings of a backroom-driven disaster.

HMS *Onyx*'s log adds some detail to this bizarre affair:

1 June
0700 Slipped to clear San Carlos before daylight.
2130 Surfaced for lead in by HMS *Avenger*.
2350 Alongside HMS *Fearless* for SBS dry drills and briefings.

Day spent loitering off North Falkland Sound. Weather deteriorated through day, so no chance of SBS drills. Change of plan resulted in return to San Carlos for further briefings. Planning proceeding slowly but too many unanswered questions.

The 'too many unanswered questions' were posed on this day in a three-page signal sent by Howard and Johnson in *Onyx* via Thomson (still in the amphibious flag ship) to Northwood for discussion by the Special Forces Coordinator, and then onwards to the London-based Special Operations Group. Nevertheless, before receiving any answers the submarine slipped once again from alongside *Fearless* and proceeded northwards for the operation:

2 June
0245: Sailed for Operation Kettledrum. Landings on Argentine mainland.
1200: Position 50°37′ S, 59°57′ W.
2124: Action stations for wet drills. Rigged casing lines then dived to repair ballast pump defect.

Very quiet forenoon with snorts to keep battery up while crew recovered from two nights at diving stations. Still much info required which may arrive by signal – hopefully. Briefing/planning in afternoon. This was for operations against one of the airfields – not sure which at this stage. Sea calm with long swell, bright moon and some mist – not good for secrecy, but convenient for rehearsals.

The questions that needed addressing had centred in particular around one of many concerns: was the operation to be 'in-and-out' or one-way? Careful study of the chart suggested that for seabed profile and security reasons the Gemini would need to be launched as far as 20 miles offshore, where the water begins to shoal sharply from 230 to 100 feet. This would mean the use of noisy outboard motors that, if it was a one-way operation, would be jettisoned over the side before the men began their final approach using just paddles against a possible 6-knot current. An added fear, following the experience in South Georgia when all outboard motors had failed, was that they would behave likewise off Puerto Deseado – less than 500 nautical miles north of Cape Horn in the austral autumn – leaving the crews stranded at sea and almost certainly in an offshore wind. If an 'in-and-out' operation was planned, the craft – with their motors – would need to be hidden on the river bank, probably to the west of Puerto Deseado town; although an approach via the exposed Atlantic beach to the north-east of the airbase was a possibility, it would need unseasonably calm weather. If a one-way journey was what the planners had in mind, the craft would need to be sunk without trace on the river bank – not an easy task.

An 'in-and-out' operation, although preferred by the SBS, had its problems, as elaborated by Howard in his signal. The river journey past the docks and built up areas would need to be conducted twice beneath a moon two days short of full. On their return the team would have to rendezvous with the submarine way out at sea using standard SBS operating procedures through the use of a hand-cranked, underwater noise-making device called a 'trongle', towards which the submarine would 'home'; yet this distance offshore was simply too far if, as was likely, the weather was bad.

A one-way operation, with Chile over 250 miles away, produced other worries. Howard needed to know if there was an established 'pipeline' of safe houses and sympathizers that Boyd and his men could contact; he needed to know the status of his team *vis-à-vis* the Geneva convention if they were captured; and, a vital consideration, he needed to know what the precise action on the target was to be: reconnaissance or direct action.

Not one of these points, or other operational concerns, had been aired in the original 'orders'. Additionally, because all Exocets had by then been launched, Howard and Johnson pointed out there were far more valuable tasks that the submarine could be conducting around the shores of the Falkland Islands, rather than being dispatched on such an indistinct, mainland operation to the north.

Unlike the aborted Operation Plum Duff, but similar to the cancelled Operation Mikado, there was no half-plausible excuse for six heavily armed SBS men attempting to enter Puerto Deseado air base. The diplomatic fallout would have been impossible to 'laugh off', while the military embarrassment would be acute; and all for no readily discernible reason.

To assist in the planning of this contentious operation and, possibly, to lead it, the Officer Commanding the SBS flew by helicopter to join the submarine in North Falkland Sound shortly after she sailed. The major's transfer from HMS *Fearless* to HMS *Onyx* was described as 'hairy' by both Johnson and Thomson, not only because all such operations involving a conventional submarine under way in the dark and in typical Falklands weather are 'hairy', but also because the helicopter pilot with his night vision goggles was confused and blinded by the well-lit hospital ship SS *Uganda*.

The next day brought further changes:

3 June
0600: Action stations. Wet drills.
1200: Position 49 43S, 61 53W.
p.m.: Operation Kettledrum cancelled. Returning to Falklands.
2250: Action stations. Wet drills.

Surfaced at 0600 for SBS drill. Launch completed by 0715. Static dive very slow. Gemini engine failed, otherwise no snags. Further drills in afternoon, then more planning. Operation Kettledrum cancelled at about 1800, turning back to Falklands but still did full run through at 2300 to check out drills. Operations Officer SBS had embarked on 31st May and was still keen to utilise the submarine which seems sensible. Heading back to San Carlos for a decision.

Planning continued in between 'action stations' and 'wet drills', the latter being when two Gemini were brought on to the submarine's casing, inflated, launched (the submarine dived beneath the craft), recovered (the submarine surfaced beneath the craft), deflated and struck below (while the First Lieutenant monitored every move with a stop watch). Meanwhile, the 'direct action' team plus the Officer Commanding SBS and his Operations Officer, all in *Onyx*, waited ... Then, as the boat's log states, the signal to abort Operation Kettledrum came from the United kingdom at about 1800 on that day. The signal drafted by Preston on Moore's staff, and the three-page signal from Howard combined with Thomson's personal remonstrations on the 'D triple S', had all finally found their target in Northwood. Lieutenant Commander Johnson immediately ordered a reversal of his submarine's course.

While the ire of Northwood's staff may well have been risked during the earlier conversations over the 'D triple S', those in the South Atlantic had always known that Puerto Deseado was such an insignificant air base that it did not warrant a major military and diplomatic failure – and failure it would have been, as Santiago Rivas has stated:[10]

> I don't know what was the intention of attacking that place. There was an Argentine battalion located in the town, but it wasn't a strategic target and had no importance to the operational theatre. The most valuable targets were [always] Trelew, Comodoro Rivadavia, San Julián, Rio Gallegos and Rio Grande.

As with the aborting of Operation Plum Duff – although at the time for more clear-cut reasons – the cancellation of Kettledrum was the correct decision. Prompted from 'down south', it had also dawned on those in Northwood that, for instance, the unknown status of Weddell Island (to where *Onyx* was originally planned to head after her arrival) was of far more importance to the amphibious and special forces planners in San Carlos than what was almost certainly *not* happening in Puerto Deseado some 400 nautical miles away.

The 'Weddell' operation had been planned long before Kettledrum burst into HMS *Fearless*'s Special Forces Operations Room; indeed, it was Boyd's team that were earmarked to conduct it. The island was an enigma to Clapp's amphibious staff, who wanted to know if the Argentines had managed to place a team there with a guidance system for their aircraft approaching the archipelago; if so, it needed to be 'taken out'. Conversely, it would be helpful to have a 'home team' inserted, able to offer last minute advice to San Carlos on how many aircraft were inbound and in which direction they were heading.

Back on board the amphibious flagship, Thomson was obliged to wrestle with the thought that he might have been wrong to suggest to Northwood, and through that headquarters upwards to the War Cabinet via the Special Operations Group, that the operation was 'as near to madness as it was possible to get'. He was conscious that officers and men in the armed forces are taught to receive orders and then carry them out, based on the assumption that those up the command chain see a wider picture. In this case the reverse was true, which may explain why, on his return to the UK, no one was prepared to discuss Operation Kettle-drum with him.

There may have been another reason: very few at Northwood had known about the operation, while even fewer in the 'theatre chain of command' had known about it. This would certainly not have been the case had Thomson lacked the moral courage to try to prevent what would surely have become a diplomatic and military disaster – this time instigated by the naval rather than the military staff. In truth, and with hindsight, on the Task Force's return all at Northwood were delighted that both military and common sense had prevailed, and all felt that there was no point in further discussions so long after the 'non-event'.

Although the submarine was to conduct a number of Special Forces landings and extractions around the Falkland Islands, any chance that HMS *Onyx* would again be employed in an excursion to the mainland was destroyed on 5 June, as her log explains:

0410:   Slipped HMS *Fearless*. Proceeding south through Falkland Sound to attempt SBS insertion at Chatham Harbour.
1200:   Position 52° 16′ S, 60° 23′ W.
1314:   Struck rock pinnacle south of Cape Meredith. 5 and 6 tube bow doors and shutters damaged.
p.m.:   Weather unsuitable for landing at Chatham Harbour; moving on to carry out reconnaissance of Weddell Island. [This with Boyd's team still embarked.]

Dived at 0915 south of Falkland Sound, heading west at periscope depth initially, then down to 180 feet as water allows. Up to snort 1000–1230 then down to 180 feet again to sprint. Struck bottom off Cape Meredith at 150 feet – glancing blow only, luckily – 25 fathom patch among minimum sounding of 42 fathoms! All well except 6 Tube shutter. Bow cap sprung so unable to drain tube or move bow cap. Hopefully will be able to investigate in San Carlos at some stage and repair/remove shutter. Slowed down con-siderably to sort out trim, damage etc., so not arriving off Weddell until midnight.

In an aside to the author, Andrew Johnson later added:[11]

The SBS Operations Officer was sitting in the seat nearest the wardroom door when this happened – we were having lunch. He was trampled by the rest of the wardroom who literally ran over him to get into the control room. He arrived some minutes later wearing a lifejacket and enquiring politely if everything was all right!

With Howard's arrival in HMS *Onyx*'s control room came the inevitable request for him to don his diving gear and exit the submerged submarine to carry out an initial inspection. Howard's response was, perhaps, equally inevitable: 'As we could not "hover" but still appeared to be motoring well, at at least 1 knot, I gave a "polite" negative answer!'

Andrew Johnson's summing up is alarming:

We were much less concerned about the grounding at the time ... and were some weeks from discovering, once in dry dock in Portsmouth, that both bow tubes were damaged while the torpedo in one tube was cracked like an egg, with the safety range clock 'wound off' as the battery had partially energised!

In 2013 Johnson explained just how close his submarine had come to destruction, not only at the time of the 'grounding' but throughout the 8,000 mile journey home:[12]

The cracked torpedo was a Mark 24 Tigerfish. It has a battery which is salt-water activated, so with the torpedo casing damaged, the battery developed part of its charge – enough to turn the motor and propeller slowly which 'winds off' an interlock for releasing the safety device designed to make sure the torpedo doesn't turn 180° and attack its launching submarine. As I understand it, this device was released. However, the torpedo wasn't 'armed' in the true sense, as this only happens when it acquires a target.

Nevertheless, when we returned to Portsmouth, this situation was so rare that the experts in the armament depot had no idea how to dismantle the torpedo while it was still in the tube – and we couldn't move it forward or back. In the end, the dockyard staff cut away the area of the torpedo tube around the warhead, then an engineer from the dockyard, with myself and one of my 'fore-ends men' hacked the sonar head off the torpedo with drills and crowbars in the middle of the night. The area around the floating dock had to be evacuated and the cross-channel ferry terminal closed while we did so.

So I guess from that we can conclude that the torpedo was in quite a dangerous state. One expert assured us that it could certainly explode at any time – not that we knew that until we entered Portsmouth. Ignorance is bliss! I have the sonar head at home, presented to me by the Squadron Weapons Officer.

Chapter 17

HMS *Avenger*, HMS *Fearless*, HMS *Intrepid* and HMS *Glamorgan*

Following the successful two-missile attack against the *Atlantic Conveyor* the Argentine Navy had one Exocet left. The British aircraft carriers remained their prime targets.

Operation Mikado had yet to be cancelled in Whitehall, while at Two Boats Village imaginative ideas for what could have been 'Operation Plum Duff Mark Two' were still being dreamed up by the RAF's Special Force Flight in cahoots with B Squadron, 22 SAS.

Far further south, on 28 May HMS *Invincible*[1] was located by the Stanley AN/TPS search radar at 51° 38' S, 53° 38' W.[2] The Comando d'Aviación Naval Argentina (Argentine Naval Air Command) decided to launch an attack with their one remaining Exocet the following day. However, in a growing spirit of cooperation, the Fuerza Aérea Argentina (Argentine Air Force) suggested that it be a joint operation against such a vital target. The Navy agreed and accepted a day's delay to allow the Air Force aircraft to be relocated from their base at Rio Gallegos.

Four A-4C Skyhawk pilots from the Grupo 4 de Caza (4th Fighter Group) were dispatched to Rio Grande on 29 May to hatch ideas with their Navy colleagues. Two of the pilots, Teniente Ernesto Ureta and Teniente José Vázquez, had volunteered, and chose two others as their wingmen, Teniente de Navío Omar Castillo and Ensign Gerardo Isaac. The outline plan was for the Navy's Super Étendard to launch the remaining Exocet, then the Skyhawks to follow in the 'wake' of the missile with their 500lb (227kg) bombs. Hopefully, the latter would hit the target while it was still reeling from the shock – emotional and physical – of an Exocet strike.

On 30 May the Stanley search radar again identified a group of ships as a suitable target and sent the latitude and longitude to Rio Grande, where all were waiting for just this information. Two Super Étendards took off at 1230 local time, with 3-A-202, piloted by the leader, Tenienta de Navío Alejandro Francisco, using the call sign 'Ala' and carrying the Exocet. He was followed down the runway by his wingman Tenienta de Navío Luis Collavino, in 3-A-205. Five minutes later, the four A-4C Skyhawks (call sign 'Zonda') also screamed into the air from Runway 25 and, once airborne, turned back over the airfield towards the South Atlantic.

The six aircraft climbed quickly to 21,000 feet for a pre-arranged rendezvous with two KC-130Hs. After topping up with fuel, an operation that lasted for

162 nautical miles while heading in an easterly direction, the aerial flotilla turned to the north, a direction of approach they hoped the Task Force would not be expecting. The Super Étendards were separated, laterally, by a mile, with two Skyhawks behind each. At 190 miles from the target's last known position all six aircraft dived to sea level until, at 1432, Francisco, with Collavino as escort, ascended momentarily to 'have a look'. Reporting that he had locked his Exocet on to the largest of three radar echoes in the target area, Collavino confirmed the acquisition. Down once more at 100 feet, Francisco launched his missile. Immediately, both Super Étendards banked sharply away from any threat and towards the waiting tanker, then returned to Rio Grande with no complications. Upon their arrival at the air base the 2nd Fighter and Attack Squadron's part in the 'defence of their Malvinas' ended.

Not so the 4th Fighter Group's Skyhawks, who now, as agreed, would follow the missile until it either detonated or fell harmlessly into the ocean. Unidentified by the pilots, the ship for which the missile was racing at Mach 0.9 was the Type 21 frigate HMS *Avenger*, commanded by Captain Hugo White;[3] while, also unknown to the pilots, the Super Étendards' radar emissions had been detected at 1430 – two minutes before the Exocet was launched – by HMSs *Ambuscade*, *Glamorgan* and *Cardiff*. All three warships fired chaff as they turned to present the smallest target to the missile's radar.

Avenger also fired her chaff rockets, and it was this cloud of 'silver paper' that seduced the missile away – still close, but far enough to be harmless. Unable to keep up with the Exocet, pilots Ureta and Isaac (the only two Skyhawk survivors of this audacious raid) claimed to have seen a column of thick black smoke suddenly welling up from a British warship, which on return they optimistically claimed was the smaller of the two British aircraft carriers, HMS *Invincible*.[4]

On the four Skyhawks flew at very low level, but before any could release their bombs Vazquez's aircraft was hit by a Sea Dart fired by HMS *Exeter*. It remains a mystery what brought down Castillo's Skyhawk, although HMS *Avenger*'s crew are positive they were responsible. According to Professor Freedman in his *Official History*, it could have been, 'Either a hit by small arms fire from *Avenger* or debris from the explosion that had taken out Vazquez's A4.'

The surviving two pilots, Ureta and Isaac, dropped their bombs without success and headed back to the waiting tanker and thence to Rio Grande, where they arrived after an eventful sortie of three hours and forty-seven minutes.[5]

What happened to Argentina's last air-launched Exocet must remain an enigma, despite strong claims that the frigate hit it with her 4.5 inch gun.

HMS *Avenger*'s First Lieutenant, Lieutenant Commander Tony Bolingbroke,[6] commented:

> I really don't know if we hit the Exocet although I would like to believe we did. Thinking it over rationally afterwards it would have been a hell of a lucky shot if we had so I suspect we did not. There was a school of thought that suggested that the Exocet may have been blown downwards by a shell burst: sufficiently close to have forced it to hit the sea.

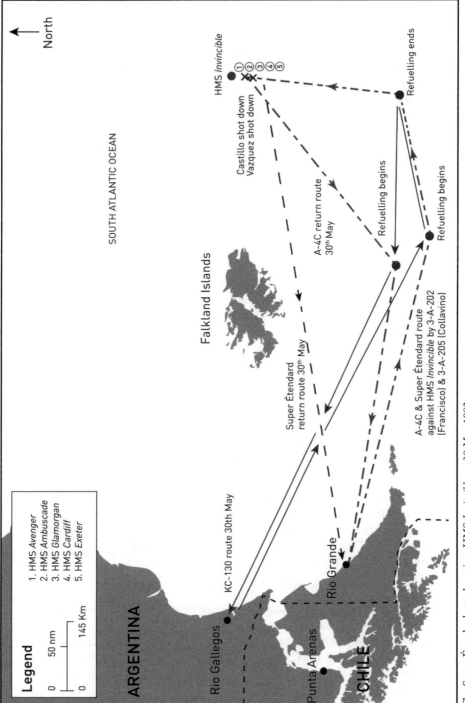

The Super Étendard attack against HMS *Invincible* on 30 May 1982.

Legend
50 nm
0
0   145 Km

1. HMS *Avenger*
2. HMS *Ambuscade*
3. HMS *Glamorgan*
4. HMS *Cardiff*
5. HMS *Exeter*

ARGENTINA

CHILE

Rio Gallegos

Punta Arenas

Rio Grande

Falkland Islands

SOUTH ATLANTIC OCEAN

North

HMS *Invincible*

Castillo shot down
Vazquez shot down

Refuelling ends

Refuelling begins

Refuelling begins

A-4C return route
30th May

Super Étendard
return route 30th May

KC-130 route 30th May

A-4C & Super Étendard route
against HMS *Invincible* by 3-A-202
[Franciscol] & 3-A-205 [Collavino]

The actual attack remains a blur of rapid information, sights and sounds, so it is really difficult to be certain about the outcome. Our team was, of course, 'positive' that we had downed an Exocet but if we did it was surely a fluke. We certainly shot down one of the four Skyhawks and later recovered bits of the aircraft and its pilot[7] (who we buried in a proper and dignified manner) but as *Exeter* shot down the other that was effectively fired over us, you can imagine that, with the explosions and noise – to say nothing of the adrenaline – we were all at full chat. The Skyhawks that flew in behind the missile flew directly at *Avenger* and were so low that standing on the bridge relaying a sort of commentary to the lads below decks I found myself almost looking down at them. So close did they pass that I could see their faces! So, with that sort of excitement it was really difficult to recall seeing an Exocet or even one getting hit. The Skyhawks had a smokier trail than the almost vapourless Exocet and this caught one's eye more than the missile's, plus the fact that they were bigger and slower and thus easier to see.[8]

The last of Argentina's five air-launched missiles had been expended, and the four Super Étendard fighter bombers that had (with every demonstrable reason) put the 'fear of God' into the British Task Force, flew home to Espora on 1 June, their task completed. But the 'Exocet war' was far from over.[9]

On 29 May French press agencies confirmed to the world (a little late, perhaps) that Argentina had only received five Exocet AM-39s but that the country still had further Exocet MM-38s (surface-to-surface missiles) that it was trying to adapt to be fired from the Super Étendard. This uncorroborated information was not entirely without credibility, especially as the Argentine naval commander in the Falkland Islands, Contraalmirante Edgardo Otero, suggested that some of these should be modified so that they could be launched from land.

Fear of the land-launched Exocet then became widespread throughout the Task Force, following rumours that a number had reached the Falkland Islands. As an example, it is interesting to note that as early as the night of the 2/3 June Captain Jeremy Larken wrote in HMS *Fearless*'s Night Order Book:

At sea off Pebble Island. Remote possibility of Exocet attack ... Defence is: launch chaff, turn away to put threat on starboard quarter using maximum revolutions to accelerate turn. Essential that the launch flash is observed therefore two Gun Direction Platform lookouts do nothing but watch on bearing of Pebble Island.

In 2012 Larken offered the following comment:

Fearless was escorting convoys outbound and then inbound over the night of 2/3 June and we were somewhat late returning with more light rounding the corner into Falkland Sound than I enjoyed.[10] The land-based Exocet threat over that period was (a) Cape Pembroke (correct) and (b) Pebble Island (wrong – but not definitively so assessed at the time; I did caveat my orders with 'Remote possibility ...'). Plainly the precautions I described in my Night Order Book were appropriate.

There was to be a marked difference in the warning time of such an attack. An air-launch was preceded by radar emissions from the Super Étendards' Agave radar that could be detected by an alert ship's operations room; with the land-launched version there was no such warning.

Four days later, the threat of a land-launched Exocet in the Stanley area (mistakenly reported at the time to be at Cape Pembroke) was to have a profound effect on naval tactics that, in turn, led to the loss of so many men on board the RFAs *Sir Galahad* and *Sir Tristram*.

On 6 June, at San Carlos, the 2nd Battalion, Scots Guards embarked in HMS *Intrepid* under the command of Captain Peter Dingemans[11] with orders from Commodore Mike Clapp for them to be launched towards Bluff Cove from 2 miles south of Elephant Island in the entrance to Choiseul Sound. From there the soldiers would have had a 15-mile journey of, all being well, about two hours in four landing craft. As part of 5 (Army) Brigade, the Battalion was needed for the assault on the Argentine defences surrounding Stanley. Meanwhile, two Royal Marines commandos and two Parachute Regiment battalions were 'waiting' for the Army brigade to catch up.

During his briefing of myself (then the Officer Commanding the Task Force Landing Craft Squadron, who would be leading this tiny flotilla of open boats) Dingemans announced that he would not be sailing *Intrepid* east of Lively Island. When I asked 'Why?' the captain's reply was interesting and relevant to this tale: '*Intrepid* is not politically [Dingemans's exact word] allowed further east than Lively Island. The risk to an LPD[12] from an Exocet is too great.' This would have been news to Clapp, who had given the original command.

In my diary[13] for that night I noted:

> In *Fearless* I had been shown by the Commodore's staff the likely arcs of a shore-based Exocet and they extend in a semi-circle south of Stanley with the western arc ending at an angle of about 215° from the most likely Exocet position. This leaves a clear passage up to 3 miles offshore from the eastern reefs off Lively Island at the approximate maximum range of Exocet. I pointed out to Dingemans that this was going to be tricky enough for us in the landing craft without a 12,000-ton ship failing to reduce our navigational problems by taking us closer. My pleas have fallen on decidedly stony ground. I suggested to the captain that the loss of 600 men of the Scots Guards was, perhaps, the greater risk at this stage of the campaign, with the loss of an LPD small beer in comparison.

Few believed that an Exocet striking an LPD, designed to take on nearly 5,000 tons of seawater in order to flood the stern dock, would lead to the loss of the ship anyway.

My sole concern at that time was having to navigate the landing craft across, now, 35 miles of open sea and, as it was to turn out, over a seven-hour passage in rapidly deteriorating weather. I had no charts of the area other than in my memory, the craft had no echo sounders or logs and only rudimentary radars that we were loath to use for fear of being 'seen' by the enemy.

The reluctance of *Intrepid*'s Commanding Officer to risk an Exocet strike was to have far greater consequences than my own navigational concerns. As a direct result of that night's decision by Dingemans, coupled with (indeed, causing) the appalling and unnecessary experiences of the Scots Guards, and knowing that a similar move of the Welsh Guards was planned for the next night, I hitched a lift in a helicopter back to the Amphibious Flag Ship, HMS *Fearless*. There I wanted to make my views known, in person, to the Commodore. At the time this made sense, for a revised and less timid plan for HMS *Fearless* was agreed. In hindsight, though, absenting myself from my landing craft, now anchored in Bluff Cove preparing to ferry the Welsh Guards ashore on their arrival in *Fearless*, may be seen as an error, for while I was away in San Carlos the landing craft were, in simple terms, hijacked by the 2nd Battalion Parachute Regiment to conduct a move from Bluff Cove back to Fitzroy. That this did not go according to plan (and was, anyway, against my orders to the coxswains' to 'stay put, come what may') is not relevant. What is significant is that when I returned there were no landing craft with which to unload the approaching HMS *Fearless*. Thus only half the Welsh Guards battalion was put ashore, the other half being returned to San Carlos and brought around to Fitzroy on 8 June in RFA *Sir Galahad*. The guardsmen were still on board *Sir Galahad* when, at 1710 three Argentine *Skyhawks* of the V Brigada Aérea, each carrying three 500-pound retard bombs, targeted RFA *Sir Tristram* and RFA *Sir Galahad*. Forty-eight men were killed in *Sir Galahad* and two in *Sir Tristram*.

Larken, in HMS *Fearless*, was bolder; but the damage had been done. When he arrived 2 miles south of Elephant Island, there were no landing craft ...[14]

Later, *Fearless*'s Commanding Officer was to write:

Overall, our luck held with Exocet. My potential tangle with it was during our non-meeting with the landing craft off Elephant Island. I reckoned we judged the Exocet risk envelope from the Cape Pembroke [sic] vicinity with some precision. Anyway, I hung around substantially longer than I should (in terms of a return to San Carlos in darkness), and whether or not the Exocet team knew we were there or not they didn't have a pop at us: in which regard it was *Fearless* ten, and *Intrepid* and poor *Glamorgan* lower scores. It was then a nasty scurry up Falkland Sound, however, ultimately in broad daylight. Fortune sometimes favours the foolish!

As Jeremy Larken says, HMS *Glamorgan* was not so fortunate.

According to Dr Alejandro Amendolara[15] in his paper titled 'Inventiveness under Pressure: the Exocet Coastal Launcher in the Malvinas/Falklands War',[16] on 1 May the Argentine navy, conscious that its arsenal of air-launched missiles was limited to just five, began evaluating the possibility of converting some of its surface-to-surface missiles for firing from land. The eventual catalyst for this unusual development was the shelling of Argentine positions by British warships from the 'gun-line' south of Stanley. If this could be prevented by the threat (real or imagined, but planted in the minds of the British naval commanders) of a land-launched Exocet, it might take the pressure off the defending Argentine troops.

It was at night, when Argentine Navy and Air Force fighter aircraft did not fly,[17] that the British ships would close the coast and come within range of a surface-to-surface missile; if 'spares' could be found, a firing mechanism could be devised and it could be transported to the islands.

As a number of Argentine Navy warships were fitted with MM 38 Exocets with a range of 22.5 nautical miles, these were not only available but in good supply. The problem was therefore not the missiles themselves but the availability of launchers and generators. Capitán de Fragata Julio Perez, a naval electronics engineer officer, was tasked together with two civilian engineers to provide a solution. This they achieved within ten days by designing and building what they termed the 'Do it Yourself Firing Installation' or, when in 'jocular mood', the 'Poor Quality Firing System' or even the 'Instalación de Tiro Berreta' (meaning 'cheapo' and not therefore a slight on the Italian Beretta firearms company, as has sometimes been assumed!). This consisted of a generator, supporting hardware and two ramps for the Exocets themselves. The device was more formally named the Lanzador Terrestre del Misil, or Terrestrial Missile Launcher.

Once the launchers were removed from two Argentine Navy ships (including the ex-United States Navy, Second World War vintage, 3,300-ton Allen M. Sumner class destroyer, ARA *Seguí*, a sister ship to ARA *Hipolito Bouchard* and ARA *Peidra Buena*), Perez and his engineers devised an ingenious firing system using four manually operated telephone switchboards. ('Each had to be thrown in a specific order and at such precise intervals that the timing was controlled by a stopwatch'.) Also involved were Pablo Vignolles, whose delicate task it was to transmit the correct information from the radar to the launching platform, and José Scaglia, an Argentine Marine driver of the towing truck, who was offered the privilege of pressing the firing button.

According to Dr Amendolara:

This land-based system was ready in mid-May but an attempt to fly it and Perez to Stanley on 24 May was thwarted by British air activity.

[In early June the system and its inventor managed to reach Stanley] but very, very wet weather had set in and since there was a danger of the firing installation trailer becoming bogged in mud a short stretch of the tarmac road between the town and the airport was selected as the firing point.

Each evening at 1800 local time the system was dragged from beneath camouflage netting and placed behind a 16-feet-high bunker. It had to be ready by 2030 which was when the British ships tended to begin their bombardment. The Argentine Air Force Westinghouse radars with the 2nd Air Surveillance and Control Group swept a 60° arc to the south of Stanley Common for long range search. The army provided fire control with its AN-TPS 43 system. Three Exocets were sent. The first one proved to be defective, the second was wasted when a connection to the transformer was incorrectly fitted and veered to the right as opposed to the left. The third was more successful.

Tony Bolingbroke believes that HMS *Avenger* might have been the first intended victim of this ingenious weapon system:

[On the night of 27/28 May] a large projectile hurtled across the flight deck while we were on the gun line south of Harriet Cove and out of range of conventional artillery. We thought we had been targeted by a badly fused Exocet – which failed to explode – fired from the shore-based launch site that eventually claimed *Glamorgan*. We were firing 100 plus shells at targets near Stanley when the Flight Deck team reported the 'whoosh' of a missile. Hugo White (the Commanding Officer) was a bit dismissive at the time for it was interrupting his 'fun with the gun' but the next day the SBS or SAS reported that an Exocet battery had been established in a position that could have tied in with such a shot. Hugo then agreed that it could well have been an Exocet.

Whether *Avenger*'s 'whoosh' was a missile or not (according to Dr Amendolara it could not have been), and whether or not special forces had identified a firing site, it was already suspected that Argentina might well have installed an Exocet system on the Falklands. To minimize the risk to his ships Admiral Woodward created a sanitized zone of 25 miles circumference from the suspected launch pad that they were not to enter.

Dr Amendolara elaborated in his paper:

Four more missiles arrived by C-130 during the night of 5 June but it was not until about 0235 [local time] on 12 June that a target presented itself. At 0215 HMS *Avenger* and the County class destroyer HMS *Glamorgan* had both completed the night's mission of providing naval gunfire support to 3rd Commando Brigade attacking Mount Longdon, Two Sisters and Mount Harriet and left to return to the Carrier Battle Group. Unfortunately for her commanding officer, Captain Mike Barrow, as his ship clipped the sanitised area her radar footprint was detected by the Exocet launch team and a missile was launched. Originally mistaken for a 155mm shell HMS *Avenger* recognized the radar configuration to be an Exocet, and the target was *Glamorgan*. Barrow held his fire, then when the missile was within a mile and a half he opened up with a Seacat but missed. The incoming missile, deflected sufficiently upward, missed the hull of the destroyer, slithered across the pitching deck into the hangar and exploded. Burning fuel from a wrecked helicopter spilled down a hole in the deck into the galley area causing a major fire with a fireball ripping into the gas turbine gear room. An officer, six air maintenance crew, four chefs, a steward and a marine engineer, totalling thirteen men, were killed, and fourteen injured. Very many of those ashore witnessed the glow of the missile and the tiny explosion on the horizon as the Exocet exploded. Although HMS *Glamorgan* had an eight-degree list from the weight of water needed to fight the fires, she maintained a steady 18 knots and remained fully operational in spite of the damage.

The following, unabridged, account is by Ian Inskip, HMS *Glamorgan*'s navigating officer at the time:[18]

I can confirm that the missile's delayed action fuse was initiated on hitting the spurnwater, which was bent over. That is how close we came to destruction. It exploded about one foot above the upper deck. If it had not exploded, there would not have been a big hole!

I recall vividly the radar echoes of incoming shells. These were smaller and faster moving than the Exocet. I did not spot the missile visually. On launch, the Sub Lieutenant on the bridge, Mark Garratt, said, 'Look at that ammunition dump going up!' I moved from the radar to have a look and was brought up sharply by my short-lead headset. (I had been requesting, unsuccessfully, a long-lead headset from the day we were diverted. Minor items can make all the difference in war.) I put my head back into the radar hood and some thirty seconds later I saw the faintest of blips on the bridge display bearing approximately 020° at 8½ miles. It was not there on the second sweep, but regained as a firm echo on the third sweep. It was there again on the fourth sweep and I alerted the Operations Room with the words, 'Have you got that fast moving contact at 020°, 8 miles?' Greg Gilchrist, the Principal Warfare Officer said, 'It is a helicopter'. I replied (my exact words), 'It is moving too bloody fast!' Greg replied, 'It is an aircraft!' I could not believe that an aircraft would have flown through all the tracer which was flying about on the battlefields, and in my heart I just knew it was an Exocet, even though it was some 15° off the threat bearing. I immediately ordered, 'Starboard 35!' (If it was an aircraft I should have turned the opposite way.) Although it says in my book[19] that the helmsman repeated, 'Port 35', I did not hear that but felt the 'kick' of the rudder which initially makes the ship heel into a turn before heeling out from the turn, and realized that opposite helm had been applied. (The OOW did not notice!) I repeated loudly, 'No! – STARBOARD 35!' Correct rudder was applied. Full rudder at 25 knots gave the ship a 14° heel, lowering the ship's side just enough. If I had only used 30° of rudder, as most people did in an emergency, the missile would have gone through the ship's side into the Seaslug magazine. The turn was a pre-planned manoeuvre. The Weapons Electrical Officer, Peter Galloway, had analysed the missile's seeker head, and in order of preference we should take a missile at a fine inclination on the port bow, starboard bow, port quarter, starboard quarter. Not having time to turn bow on, I elected to go for option three, port quarter, but with the rudder fiasco we did not complete the turn.

A few years ago I went to Argentina and met José Scaglia,[20] the marine who drove the Exocet truck and who pressed the 'Fire' button. I had also been in e-mail contact with the Perez family. At no stage was there any mention of another Exocet being fired that night. All the accounts I have heard are that *Avenger* saw the missile coming for us and tried to alert us.

When Admiral Woodward embarked on 4 April, he told us that he expected to lose ships (in the plural) and that escorts were expendable. Of the first group of six ships to be diverted south, every one of us was either sunk or seriously damaged. Captain Barrow always put the common good before his ship's safety, and that took great courage.

In amplification of Inskip's report, Mike Barrow has commented:[21]

On the night of 11/12 June 1982, HMS *Glamorgan*'s orders were to support 45 Commando's attack on Two Sisters mountain and be back on the carrier screen by dawn. *Glamorgan* detached from the main body at 1700 GMT and proceeded inshore at 26 knots, arriving on the gun line, on time, at midnight. To get back to the carrier screen by dawn would necessitate leaving the gun line by 0500.

It was not until 0115 on 12 June that 45 Commando required *Glamorgan*'s support, and they did not take their first objective (the Western Ridge) until 0520. A command decision was taken to continue supporting 45 Commando until the Two Sisters' eastern ridge was also taken. This was achieved at 0615.

Shortly before leaving the gun line, information was received that the Carrier Battle Group had moved overnight 50 miles further east, an additional two hours steaming away. *Glamorgan* was going to be very late back on screen.

An intelligence-assessed Exocet danger zone had been charted, based upon a 20-mile arc from Cape Pembroke Point. This was the only information *Glamorgan* had about the land-launched Exocet threat. *Glamorgan* had to cross part of this danger zone to get to and from the gun line. On release from the gun line at 0615, *Glamorgan* headed due south away from danger until Cape Pembroke Point was lost on radar (and thus a radar at Cape Pembroke Point would have lost *Glamorgan*). To minimize time late back on the screen, course was then altered to 150° to make good 50 per cent of our speed towards the carriers in exchange for a 13 per cent loss of speed away from danger. Unfortunately, the Exocet battery was not located at Cape Pembroke Point, but some miles further west close to Hookers Point. The Exocet battery held *Glamorgan* on their radar.

At 0636, very conscious that the ship was still within the Exocet danger zone, the bridge detected a fast closing radar contact some 15° off the threat bearing, seemingly coming from Eliza Cove, a few miles west of Hookers Point. It was not until after Ian Inskip's *Ordeal by Exocet* was published that it was discovered that the missile had been fired from a position close to Hookers Point.

Correctly assessing this contact as an Exocet missile, the bridge immediately executed a pre-planned manoeuvre to take the missile at a fine inclination in an attempt to 'bounce' it off the ship's side. The ship was still turning at speed, under full rudder, when the missile hit. Fortunately, heeling at 14° lowered the ship's side just enough to deflect the missile off the upper deck instead of the missile entering through the ship's side and exploding in the Seaslug main missile magazine.

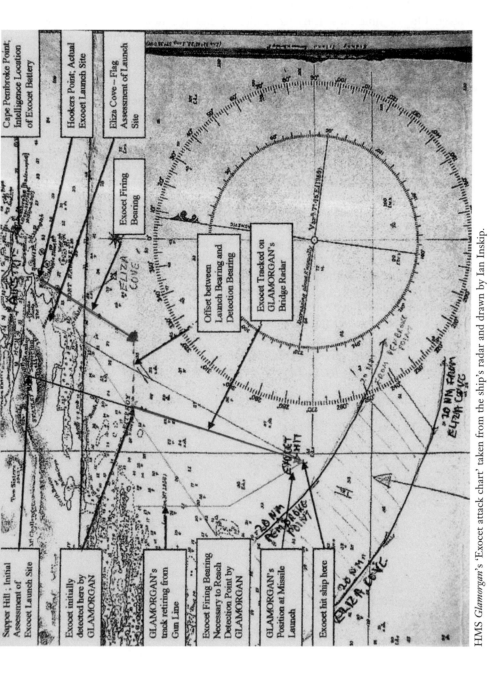

HMS *Glamorgan*'s 'Exocet attack chart' taken from the ship's radar and drawn by Ian Inskip.

For the next three and a half hours the crew fought floods and fires, and saved their ship; but they had lost thirteen of their shipmates, whom they buried at sunset. On 14 June Argentina surrendered, and the news of the destroyer's remarkable and supremely professional achievement in surviving an Exocet strike was buried under that good news.

*   *   *

Two days after HMS *Glamorgan* had been 'wounded' the conflict was over, and while the United Kingdom had decidedly won 'the campaign' there is equally no doubt that Argentina had dominated the Exocet 'battle' within that conflict. True, the British, through a noteworthy counter-intelligence operation, had managed to prevent any resupply of missiles reaching Rio Grande, but that must not deny Argentina the credit for using the few Exocets that it did have in the most effective way conceivable. Even when they did not hit, and sometimes when they were not even launched, the missiles had caused considerable 'Exocetitis'[22] within the Task Force – from the very beginning to the bitter end of hostilities.

It was only afterwards that the pilots of 2da Escuadrilla Aeronaval de Caza y Ataque, back at their Espora Naval Air Base, learned that prior to 1982 the French had only ever launched three air-to-air missiles and that two of those had failed.[23] Between them, the Argentine technicians and pilots, without outside help, achieved a 100 per cent success rate with their launches. That two out of five air-launched Exocets missed their targets was not the fault of the pilots, the missile or the system, but the result of successful decoys.

The land-launched missiles, cobbled together, may not have had quite the same success rate; but by their very existence they, too, had affected British tactics.

Epilogue

Across the South Atlantic between March and June 1982 Argentina made many mistakes at both tactical and strategic level (let alone the legal and diplomatic complications of the original 'invasion' of the Falkland Islands); but during the Exocet 'campaign within a campaign' the Argentine Navy got it right while sections of the British special forces (*pace* the Secret Intelligence Service) did not.

Lying at the heart of this extraordinary story is the Argentine determination to inflict, with its limited number of Exocets, so much damage on the approaching British Task Force that the Falkland Islands could not be repossessed. Countering that was the British desire to stop the missiles hitting their targets, in concert with an equal resolve to prevent replacements reaching Rio Grande.

The Argentine Navy nearly achieved its objective through ingenuity and cunning. The British, hampered by a lack of early-warning aircraft and suitable long-range, carrier-borne jets, had to fall back on imprecise, old fashioned, reactive methods of defence. These included 'last-second' decoys, speed of reaction by ships' companies and a reliance on reports from nuclear submarines inshore, who sometimes could report aircraft taking off but never their destinations. To a large extent, all of these measures failed, including Woodward's decision to move the carriers further east for their safety. This was demonstrated on 30 May, when six Argentine aircraft penetrated the radar and air-defence screen without being challenged in air-to-air combat, thus helping to confirm that the controversial move negated neither the Exocet nor the Skyhawk threats to the Carrier Battle Group. The only noticeable consequence of the move east (which was not reversed even after the last Exocet had been expended) was the additional reduction in air defence for the ground forces and their amphibious ships during the final, crucial days of the campaign: sometimes with catastrophic consequences.

On the face of it, what was needed was a 'direct action' operation, and in practical terms the British possessed two such options. Following the RAF's Black Buck operations against Stanley airport Britain had demonstrated that she could bomb targets in Argentina; but the risk to civilians and international relations (let alone the illegality of such action) precluded this course. That left an attack by special forces, and, with many in the War Cabinet understandably (but ill-advisedly under these 'conventional' circumstances) in awe of the SAS following the lifting of the Iranian Embassy siege on 5 May 1980, this was the preferred course of action. But was it the correct one, particularly as a third rather less dramatic option made more sense?

Bearing in mind that the utmost priority for the British was to destroy the Exocets before more ships were sunk, the answer had to be a qualified 'yes'. One qualification was that any mainland assault had to be swift and clinical; the less drama that attended it the more likely it would be acceptable to international opinion. An allied condition, amplified below by a member of the Special Operations Group, was that it had to be a viable plan based on good intelligence.

The Special Air Service was inevitably, bearing in mind de la Billière's influence in Whitehall, 'chosen' for the task, although a 'frequently asked question' remains: why was a noisy helicopter insertion, possibly followed by an even more obvious Hercules assault, preferable to the use of a submarine and the Special Boat Squadron? It is as well to address that question immediately, for the answers are telling and instructive. The SBS could not have accepted the task for many reasons, one of which was that the Squadron employed by the Commodore Amphibious Warfare was fully committed to its wartime role of pre-landing reconnaissance – ignoring, for the moment, Operation Kettledrum, which was ordered from London. A member of the Special Operations Group, with his wider perception of the campaign as a whole, considered the Rio Grande attack thus:

> It would have been unwise for anyone to accept the task as it stood for there was a lack of strategic thought being applied to the Mikado venture. The 'attack' philosophy was vestigial, there was no intelligence and, frankly, it was a daft plan anyway.

There were more practical considerations. To have met the timings, HMS *Onyx* would have had to have sailed from the United Kingdom long before the initial deployment, and that would have required remarkable foresight.

The SBS's Operations Officer at the time, Major Colin Howard, has since stated:[1]

> There were other difficulties such as infiltrating into the Rio Grande base from a submarine surfaced a long way offshore – as with Puerto Deseado, maybe as far as 20 nautical miles – thanks to the shallow, shelving coastline; nor were canoes very practical in this area.Once there, we had no idea where the Super Étendards were. A return to the submarine was considered too risky therefore an exfiltration was to be by foot/vehicle/air, *and we did not think it wise to publicise our presence.*[2] [My view was] the most useful thing my men could have done was to watch and report on Super Étendard movements and that we were on our way to do [using HMS *Onyx*].

For the War Cabinet an attack against a mainland target was acceptable provided it was small-scale. Operation Plum Duff might have met that description but, as has been pointed out, eight men were four too many, while it should also have been supported by deep 'strategic' thought, and a 'more than vestigial attack philosophy'. Additionally, even an intelligence-gathering patrol needs a modicum of intelligence to begin with, including maps. Recognizing the above, the wisdom of the SAS's command decision to continue with planning for Operation Mikado following Plum Duff's failure has to be questioned. But, and it is probably the most important 'but' of them of all, was there an alternative?

The answer is 'yes'. The Task Force lacked airborne early warning; had it possessed that capability it might reasonably be assumed that no mainland assault would have been contemplated.[3] So, to adhere to the 'legal position' it was necessary to establish an alternative means of achieving early warning. Eventually, the nuclear-powered submarines were tasked with this responsibility, but they had other duties for which they were more suited. Had the Secret Intelligence Service been asked (it was not), it could have placed in the local town two deniable agents (possibly a 'married' couple), not of British nationality and definitely not SIS officers. After all, Rio Grande was a cosmopolitan municipality of between 15,000 and 20,000 people with a significant number of Chilean sympathizers.

Airborne early warning, whether originating from an 'up-threat' aircraft or a land-based 'agent' (whose value can be as good or even better when he or she is living alongside a 'target'), does not, rather obviously, destroy aircraft, but it would have offered three priceless advantages: it would have given the Sea Harriers the extra time needed to intercept the Super Étendards; it would certainly have given the ships more than a few seconds to lay chaff and engage with their most suitable weapons while turning to present the smallest radar target to the incoming missile; and finally, it would have precluded any mainland assault.

This would have been a more subtle method of approach, in line with unconventional counter-insurgent operations rather than the 'two up and bags of smoke'[4] philosophy the SAS were proposing for Operation Mikado. The Exocets had to be stopped, but despite the desires of those at Hereford, Mikado would not have been authorized by the government, while Plum Duff was never realistically going to work either.

Now we know that the original twin Plum Duff reconnaissance patrols were, almost at the last moment, turned into one large fighting patrol (too large for the bare countryside and long distances across which it was to operate), it might fairly be conjectured that, with government unease over Mikado, this was the only attack that would ever be sanctioned. Yet the Mikado option was to be kept open until three days after the last air-launched Exocet had been expended. This was not a government-inspired delay, for as Admiral Whetstone says below, Mikado (as planned) was not going to happen anyway.

With Plum Duff's demise, it was only the SAS command that considered Mikado still to be feasible. As no evidence has been unearthed to suggest why, the reasons for those at Two Boats Village being kept on permanent tenterhooks can only be guessed. No signals from any source other than via B Squadron's 'private satellite communications system' were ever received (apart from the initial signal handed to Squadron Leader Roberts on 19 May), giving rise to an RAF fear that the SAS might have considered 'going it alone' without the necessary clearance[5] – such was the desire to 'do something that accorded with their reputation'.

In amplification of the above, and since they come from an officer with a seat as close to the centre of affairs in Whitehall as possible, Rear Admiral Whetstone's words[6] should be heeded:

Operation Plum Duff was the only operation considered worthy of serious discussion by the Special Operations Group. I have no recollection of it being approved as a reconnaissance for Mikado but as a one-off operation against Rio Grande ... I don't believe that Mikado would have had much chance of getting ministerial approval. My own view is that once the proposed operation was considered in more detail by the SAS and RAF it was not brought up for serious discussion by the SOG.

If it was not 'brought up for serious discussion by the SOG' then it would not receive ministerial approval ... and yet the threat of a suicidal landing at Rio Grande dragged on; and, for those intimately involved, it dragged on, inexplicably, even after the fifth and final Exocet had stalled harmlessly into the Southern Ocean.

Whetstone concludes:

I find it hard to believe that what amounted to a major attack on mainland Argentina, a country with which we were not formally at war, would not have caused serious misgiving.[7] Approval for Plum Duff was only given after considerable discussion and consideration of the diplomatic and political risks. There was a cover story for Plum Duff, however improbable, that the Sea King had a navigational error when on a routine flight. Mikado would have been almost impossible to disclaim plausibly if a diplomatic problem arose ...

And a problem most certainly would have arisen; while the same would have applied to Operation Kettledrum.

In other words it was Plum Duff or nothing; yet no one who mattered was told. A member of the Special Operations Group has commented further:[8]

This whole operation was the 'Hereford hooligans' demanding an operation to help 'maintain the myth'. I also know that we had a Deputy Chief of the Defence Staff (Commitments) who was in awe of de la Billière and the Hereford team. With more strength of character he would have axed both operations at birth, and advised the War Cabinet accordingly. Remember, there was a very strong planning team at Hereford who were dying to get some action for all the wrong reasons.

From the outset of the campaign the Plum Duff/Mikado saga threw up a number of anomalies and 'lessons to be learned'. Yet they were never likely to be learned because the SAS was (perhaps reasonably) intent on keeping its failures secret. Two events confirm this. When Plum Duff was cancelled the reasons could not be analysed by the Task Force Commander's staff at Northwood, for Headquarters SAS declared, suddenly and inexplicably, that this was, 'No longer a matter for the Commander-in-Chief [deliberately ignoring the fact that the SAS were also under the command of the Commander-in-Chief throughout this conventional campaign] and thus no further information will be forthcoming.'

The second event occurred at the end of the campaign, when the SAS's Report of Proceedings was, bizarrely, kept from both Admiral Fieldhouse and Major

General Moore. On hearing this, the Commander-in-Chief 'demanded that it be on his desk immediately'– where he personally redacted it with red-ink deletions and corrections in front of a hapless SAS brigadier, Tony Jeapes.[9]

Despite the SAS having been under his direct operational command and control, Moore never saw the report.[10] This might have been understandable had the SAS been involved in supporting counter-insurgency operations directed from London, but they were conducting conventional reconnaissance tasks in support of conventional forces in a conventional campaign, and as such were (or should have been) an assimilated part of the whole.

Major Roger Blundell,[11] the Fleet Royal Marines Officer, was, with Lieutenant Colonel Tim Donkin, closely involved in this sad little vignette:

> The SBS report by Jonathan Thomson was wholly honest and in absolute contrast to the SAS report. This mature approach served things well for the SBS, placing them squarely on the national map.
>
> Commenting on the SAS report, I made recommendations about command and control of special forces and how they should be under command of the Central Staff rather the Army's Assistant Chief of the General Staff. Once he had seen the report, John Fieldhouse instructed me to draft a letter for him to send to the Chief of the Defence Staff, who was by then General Bramall,[12] suggesting that this new command structure for special forces be adopted. Bramall could not have been more helpful and positive in his response and then put his words into action by creating the set-up that is in place today.[13]

The control of special forces operations is an area where there should have been a considerable number of 'lessons to be learned', as General Moore recommended. Committees such as the Special Operations Group and the Special Operations Coordinator's team were set up for a reason. Ignoring them (the precedent established between Combined Operations and the Special Operations Executive in 1942 has been mentioned earlier) can end in dangerous chaos. Bypassing the formal chain of command[14] through a 'private communications system' led to middle-ranking Army officers (unaware of the wider picture and certainly not understanding the imperatives and nuances of amphibious warfare) muddying the waters of naval command and decision making.[15]

A lesson identified (but, as tales from the Middle East were to demonstrate later, seldom applied) was that commanders at all levels must be aware of what special forces are planning; and these plans must complement the overall mission. It should make no difference whether this is in conventional or what is now called 'asymmetric' warfare. The commander should have control over the allocation of assets to the special forces units within his area of responsibility and thus the final say on whether or not a special forces operation is to be mounted in support of his strategy. The absence of such lines of command and control causes confusion and suspicion, ultimately jeopardizing the mission itself, as was firmly demonstrated on more than one occasion during 1982.

The 'bubbles of security' (not all generated by special forces) that surrounded Operations Plum Duff and Mikado are an allied topic. Colonel Richard Preston has commented:[16]

> The SAS were paranoid about security and failed to understand that in conventional operations it is vital for the commander and his staff to know what the special forces are up to. They are, after all, a subsidiary to the main (conventional) effort in defeating the enemy.

At the end of the campaign Major General Moore elaborated:

> SAS security consciousness has been developed to a degree that obscures the vital need in conventional operations to pass information to every unit or formation that might find it useful.

Thanks to these less than helpful 'bubbles', some decisions remain incomprehensible. It is convenient to list them in turn:

- Why was a 'conventional' submarine not ordered south the moment the 'on-the-spot' commanders asked for it?
- Why were the first two Plum Duff patrols kept in total isolation from each other? A simple answer could have been that if one patrol was captured the other would not run the risk of being compromised; although under the circumstances a cross-pollination of ideas would have been helpful, as each was anyway aware already of the other's existence and 'target'.
- Why was Squadron Leader Roberts not invited to set pertinent questions for 6 Troop to answer once it arrived in Argentina? Indeed, why was Roberts – on whom the success or otherwise of Mikado largely depended – not told of Operation Plum Duff even after it had been 'launched'?
- Bearing in mind Admiral Whetstone's views that Operation Mikado would never have been approved by the War Cabinet, who authorized B Squadron's deployment to Ascension Island? It was not – as it should have been had it been an acceptable operation – the War Cabinet itself or the Commander-in-Chief in Northwood.
- Why were Roberts and his team only invited to the initial briefing on Mikado (held in Northwood by Moss) once it was discovered, by accident, that they were in the same building?
- Why was the Bombilla Flats operation kept from both the Special Operations Group and the Special Operations Coordinator, against the Commander-in-Chief's orders? As has been demonstrated, this was one of many questionable decisions that were made outside the chain of command by 'special forces'. This was not the fault of the Admiral's staff (although a more reliable replacement should have been sought for Lieutenant Colonel Howard than the blinkered Massey), rather the ability of the Special Air Service covertly to by-pass 'the system' to suit its own aspirations.

- Why, as far as the Hercules pilots in Ascension Island were concerned, was Mikado 'cancelled' via the SAS 'rumour mill' and not by the Commander-in-Chief's staff. Was this because ministers in Whitehall and officers at Northwood (but no one at either Hereford or Chelsea) accepted that it was never 'on' in the first place (*pace* Max Roberts' ambiguously worded Top Secret signal on 19 May)?
- Why was Mikado not 'cancelled' earlier, thus removing a background of severely morale-sapping anxiety from both the Hercules crews in the air and the troopers of B Squadron sitting unemployed and more than anxiously kicking their heels at Two Boats Village?
- Why was the Director Special Air Service not aware of the Hercules crews' deep concerns over the practicalities of an air-land operation against a heavily defended airfield with no prior reconnaissance in place? Had he been made aware of the problems by his Air Adviser (and ignoring, for a moment, the War Cabinet's negative views on such an operation on to mainland Argentina), planning for Operation Mikado might not have reached the intensity that it did.[17] Clearly, Squadron Leader Niven was so unaware of Mikado's details that he did not realize he needed to consult his own RAF colleagues ... the SAS's 'bubbles of security' were working even within their own headquarters, as has already been explained by Niven.
- The Royal Air Force knew of the presence of the two Argentine destroyers acting as radar pickets off the Rio Grande coast during the early morning of 18 May and had given this information to their Air Commander. Why, then, was this most essential piece of intelligence not passed on to the Commanding Officer of HMS *Invincible* prior to the launching of Operation Plum Duff? Failure to keep all informed was not the sole prerogative of Special Forces.
- Why was the British Air Attaché in Santiago not aware of the proposal to land a Sea King on Chilean territory? The answer to this is convoluted, for President Pinochet had agreed to help the British providing no operation was mounted from Chile. As this was not planned to be 'an operation mounted from Chile' but rather a crashed aircraft that had 'suffered engine failure', it was felt that there was no need to announce the operation in advance ... despite the undeniable fact that this was taking a considerable liberty with Chile's offer of help. This incident, understandably from the Chileans' point of view, led directly to the withdrawal of the only Nimrod electronic intelligence aircraft after just three sorties.
- Despite not being asked to do so, why did the Secret Intelligence Service not seize the initiative and arrange for a 'married couple' to stay in Rio Grande?
- Flight Lieutenant Robinson's simple anecdote (flying B Squadron to Belize to wait for a civilian aircraft to conduct Operation Plum Duff) suggests a number of inconsistencies – which must be why his flight across the Atlantic was cancelled before it began. A 'civilian' aircraft (similar to

his VC 10?) would have found the distance to Rio Grande (including diversions to avoid 'unfriendly' airspace) a problem. Nevertheless, had it arrived intact on the enemy airfield (as slim a chance of that happening as for the C-130s) how would the SAS have unloaded, other than via inflatable emergency slides? It must be conjectured that 38 Group were hoodwinked by those in Chelsea (so taken in that they dispatched an empty VC 10 to Wideawake?) until Crooke's scheme was handed up the command chain to be dismissed by the War Cabinet. Had the 'civilian' aircraft taken the squadron as far as, say, Punta Arenas, it might be remembered that President Pinochet was adamant that no offensive operations against Argentina should be launched from Chile. As John Moss's experiences testify, the SAS command was determined that any such attack against Rio Grande would begin (but not necessarily end) in Argentina. So why was this waste of resources even contemplated?

- A fundamental question has been asked ever since Operation Plum Duff was first mooted. Why was it conducted by strategic troops flown from the United Kingdom, when according to Major General Moore there were far too many tactical SAS troops already in theatre looking for non-existent tasks? The answer is that the SAS command was determined to give a clear demonstration of the regiment's overall capability, regardless of any other considerations. On the other hand, it is also interesting to note that questions were raised in General Moore's Headquarters over why Operation Kettledrum was being conducted by SBS men from within the Task Force and not by those from the strategic reserve in the UK!

Thanks to these same 'bubbles' we may never know the 'whole' truth in answer to a number of these queries. Two other questions remain unanswered:

- Why, after all Exocets had been expended, was the Officer Commanding the SBS still ordered to mount a raid on Puerto Deseado contrary to his advice, experience and on-the-spot knowledge? This was a target that had never been directly involved in operations against the British. Captain C of the Special Operations Group has since stated,[18] 'Although it was approved by the SOG and mentioned to Colonel Garrod it should have been hit on the head early on by the Ministry of Defence.' This question is especially relevant when, as has been stated, the SBS did not consider a submarine-launched raid against the far more important target at Rio Grande to be feasible, allied to the fact that they had other pressing duties 'closer to home'.

- Of all the mainland operations that were planned, an assault against Puerto Deseado would not, even had it been unexpectedly successful,[19] have moved the campaign forward by one jot; and yet it would have taken the only diesel-electric submarine away from more important tasks involving direct support for the troops ashore on the Falkland Islands. For no tangible gain and at great risk to international opinion and relationships, the planners in Northwood and London were prepared to risk much in life and reputation. The reasons behind this ill considered adventure remain unfathomable, and as a member of the Special Operations Group has since said, 'Was there any regret that the operation was cancelled? It was not given a second thought!'[20]

- There is a final question that has not hitherto been asked but nevertheless deserves addressing: why was the SBS, using the fit-for-role, conventional submarine, HMS *Onyx*, not ordered to attack the known, shore-based Exocet battery close to Stanley? (A tailor-made operation, it might be argued.) The answer, we now know, is straightforward and explained by the Squadron's Operations Officer at the time:[21]

  It was one of many 'moving targets' [literally] that we were aware of. The lorry-mounted system did not stay still and lived within a strong military compound. Thus it was not a sensible 'immediate action' project. After *Glamorgan* was hit there was an obvious push to know more. We carried out a periscope reconnaissance of Pebble Island (after *Onyx* was 'dented') as we had a team there too, for it was a possible site for the Exocet.[22] All special forces were fully deployed looking at likely missile sites until the final stages but this was becoming 'clumsy' with too many people, with too many 'ideas', in too small a space. Deconfliction was a nightmare. While the two brigades were focussed totally on Stanley we (SBS and SAS) remained concerned elsewhere as the enemy outstations still had the potential to make life difficult.

There was no doubt that the Argentines still could have conducted air attacks from Pebble Island, while at the same time they were suspected of having a number of Forward Air Control teams well able to call in air strikes against British logistic rear areas and supply lines. It was essential that all these possibilities were kept fully 'covered'.

In fact, the 'mobile' Exocet launcher was targeted not by Special Forces but by the RAF, as an excerpt from No 1 (Fighter) Squadron's 'war diary' written by the Commanding Officer, Wing Commander Peter Squire,[23] confirms:

Combat Report. Another poor weather day ... and only one operational sortie flown looking for the land-launched Exocet which hit *Glamorgan* as she left the gun line a couple of days earlier. In fact the launcher is mobile but we attack known positions on Stanley Common at the same time as doing a photo-recce.

At the conclusion of the campaign, and on a nearly positive note, a number of the RAF's previously 'jet-centric' senior officers visited the Special Forces Flight, seemingly interested in what the Flight did and what it had achieved.[24] Unfortunately, these visits only generated surprise at the Flight's capabilities rather than stimulating a desire to consolidate or expand them. Among the Royal Air Force hierarchy (unlike the Special Forces Flight aircrew) lessons were there to be identified rather than learned – and thus ignored or implemented as required.

Following the Falklands campaign, and after many attempts by succeeding Commanding Officers, further development of Special Forces Flight operations was eventually authorized. This was begun in a somewhat piecemeal fashion in response to individual tasks during the First Gulf War, followed by the relief of Sarajevo and operations in Kosovo. Happily, by the time of the Second Gulf War the Flight's position was much improved, and it has made a valuable contribution to nearly all United Kingdom operations then and since.

One aspect of the 'Hercules war' in 1982 that does stand out clearly is the intensity of support, at 'ground level', for the aircrew (especially from Lyneham's Engineering Wing) that helped the aircraft achieve what was being asked of them, initially with ill-equipped airframes and only via a series of isolated operational orders. Where there is criticism, it is aimed at the higher echelons of the Royal Air Force who, through the lack of a 'chain of responsibility', denied or hindered a number of 'urgent operational requirements' for the Special Forces Flight; apart, notably, from the remarkable Hercules air-to-air refuelling development.

Before leaving the final words to Captain Andy L, it is useful to hear the summing up of the Hercules pilots. For both Roberts and Burgoyne the overriding question remains, 'Could we have done it ... Mikado or Plum Duff Mark Two?' They answer their own question thus:

> Looking purely at the physics of flying to Rio Grande via the long route together with a formation air-to-air refuelling operation, we think we could, just, have got away with it but it would have been far from ideal.
>
> However, [we were faced with] possible poor weather; no moonlight; lack of practice with night vision goggles and, in Burgoyne's case, no practice at all of formation flying using them; lack of decent aeronautical charts and land maps; little experience of using the new navigation kit; no intelligence on Rio Grande and the absence of a reconnaissance party to provide it, plus the massively augmented airfield defences – including radar-laid 'Triple A'. It would have been a miracle if it had worked. To expect any chance of success at all, a mission like Mikado needed much more time, intelligence support and rehearsal than we had.

Roberts continues:

> With 6 Troop in position we reckoned our chances of success would have been fifty/fifty but with no prior reconnaissance, then ... little or no chance. Of course, had 6 Troop been there it is more than likely that, with the strength of the defences, coupled with everything else, Mikado would have been cancelled anyway.
>
> I got the impression that, primarily, the operation was eventually called off because events overtook us. The crew and aircraft had a more pressing requirement and that was to conduct long-range resupply drops (especially indispensable to the Task Force after the loss of MV *Atlantic Conveyor*) while the priority for Mikado reduced as the number of Exocets diminished.

It is only in recent months that Roberts, Burgoyne and Andy L have become aware that Operation Mikado would never have been approved no matter what the reconnaissance had found – or had not found.

Finally, as Operation Plum Duff is central to the whole saga, it is right that Captain Andy L should have the last word:

In Hereford I had to endure a Board of Inquiry chaired by Lieutenant Colonel Massey, Officer Commanding A Squadron. He was fair but that did not prevent me reaching the point of not giving a damn as I felt I had been used. All of us in 6 Troop had wanted to go to the Falklands but we all felt cheated. All of us wanted to be involved, as one does as a soldier, but we considered, with good reason at the time and certainly in hindsight, that we had been sent to do something that was unlikely to succeed.

Nevertheless, we – or rather I – were held to account for it all going wrong ... and that was the end of my military career. As de la Billière was displeased that we did not get out of the helicopter I didn't want to be in the army if I could not be in the SAS ... so I quit.

There are risks associated with what we do and we accept that, but we always like to be sent off on something that we think is reasonably sane and with a reasonable chance of a positive result. We don't want to fail so everything we do is planned, meticulously, down to the very last and tiniest of details. Although the newspapers may see everything as a wonderful, trigger-happy piece of SAS work and not realize – not wanting to realize – what actually goes on behind the scenes. That is not how it is; but Plum Duff does seem to have been different.

I had always wanted to do something like this and felt almost 'hard done by' that it turned out that way. People might be entitled to say (and they did), 'Andy, you had a chance of glory and you didn't take it.'

On my return a friend came to see me at Hereford to tell me to calm down, to keep a low profile – to 'chill out'. However, he also relayed a popular opinion that it would have been better for me to have gone there and failed – mown down in a hail of bullets – to demonstrate political will if you like, rather than come back alive.

For Operation Mikado Max Roberts and Harry Burgoyne were going to do it but that did not stop them being scared for they knew their own risks better than the SAS. Their fear was the certainty that they would not reach the runway in one piece. As that was out of the SAS's control we never considered it as a risk to be dreaded. We had our own concerns and were happy to ignore those of the RAF. It was probably the same the other way round too. The RAF guys knew jolly well from the practices at Laarbruch and elsewhere that no matter which way they approached the runway they were at risk and that was even before they knew what actual defences were in place.

With Plum Duff we had only a minimal chance of success even if the airfield had been guarded solely by the peacetime defenders. The Argentines knew that the British knew that Rio Grande was used by the Exocets and so they had to be expecting us. Headquarters SAS should have realized that; the RAF certainly did.

Interestingly, among 6 Troop, we were all thinking about these things but we didn't talk. We were just going to go in there and make it happen. But . . . I don't think anyone believed that they could make it happen and maybe that's the difference. The guys were dead quiet. That's a giveaway because in the SAS if you have to do something everyone has a different opinion on how it should be done and is not frightened to air it! But with Plum Duff all the guys just sat there. No questions. Nothing.

Captain Andy L, now happily enjoying a successful 'second' career, sums up:

It is good to hear now that there is support for my decision but it is the sort of thing that will stay with me until the end. Others say that I didn't live up to the best traditions of the regiment, but at least I saw my children grow up which I would not have done and nor would a great many other people, had Operation Mikado been carried out. I suppose by cancelling Plum Duff we saved them too. After all, the Argentines were not stupid, although quite clearly some in the United Kingdom thought they were.

Captain L's conscience should at last be clear, for, as has been discussed, Operation Mikado would never have been sanctioned, regardless of what positive comments he might have offered in his reconnaissance report.

Commodore 'Wiggy' Bennett has since stated that, had he been in Andy L's shoes, he would have made the same decision. Knowing this, Andy L has felt able to comment further:

Dick Hutchings was annoyed that I queried his navigation and hasn't been able to see the wider picture with the passing of the years, but Wiggy has. Dick is entitled to his opinions, even today [as his own subjective account shows] but at the time it certainly felt as though we had been compromised. It was my prerogative as the patrol commander to make the choice, 'Emergency drop off point please'. That was my decision, not that of the pilot.

History shows that, whatever the reasons employed at the time, it was the correct decision.

In 2013 Brigadier Jonathan Thomson, who had commanded the SBS in 1982, also felt moved to comment:[25]

I feel for Captain L as I have no doubt that he did the right thing. Like him, I returned wondering whether I, too, had done the right thing over Operation Kettledrum; concerned that, perhaps, I had been found wanting at a crucial time. Having read your account of events I now know that that was not the case.

History also shows, now, that Captain Andy L and his men from B Squadron, 22 SAS Regiment, did everything that was asked of them, willingly, professionally and without hesitation. Despite the appalling circumstances into which they were pitched, coupled with the dreadful weather, the inadequate equipment and food, the lack of any form of intelligence, two useless maps and the unavoidable realization that they were written off and 'not expected to survive', they acted in the 'very highest traditions of their regiment'. Indeed, it might come to be realized that, through their stoic and uncomplaining fortitude, they themselves helped to 'maintain the myth'.

*   *   *

If little else comes of the telling of this disturbing, convoluted (and certainly frightening) saga, it is the recurring truth that one should never underestimate an enemy. Had Operation Mikado been conducted and had it ended, as predicted by everyone outside Hereford and Chelsea, in humiliating failure, then the SAS would have billed it, perhaps understandably, as a 'glorious attempt at the impossible'. Of course, had it succeeded it would have been hailed, paradoxically, as a 'glorious success against impossible odds'; the same might have been said of the SBS and Operation Kettledrum.

Either way, 'myths would have been maintained'. But that is not a wise premise on which to risk so many other men's lives, in addition to those whose proud and apt motto is, *Who Dares Wins*.

Notes

Introduction
1. Later, Sir Jeremy, KCB, OBE, MC and Bar.
2. Report of Proceedings, 18 October 1982.
3. See Julian Thompson's *3 Commando Brigade in the Falklands. No Picnic.*
4. Interestingly, the Argentine Ambassador to Paris was on leave in the south of France and, allegedly unaware of the 'crisis', did not return until four days later, according to his cousin Mireille, Comtesse d'Hérouville, married to a Frenchman and an *estancia* owner near Buenos Aires (conversation with the author, 9 July 2011).
5. Many books offer in-depth, historical and contemporary accounts of the two protagonists' claims and counter claims: the most notable is Professor Sir Lawrence Freedman's *The Official History of the Falklands Campaign*, Routledge, 2005. Others include Max Hastings' and Simon Jenkins' *The Battle for the Falkland Islands*, Michael Joseph, 1983 and the *Sunday Times* Insight Team's *The Falklands War*, André Deutsch, 1982.
6. Ewen Southby-Tailyour, *Reasons in Writing*, Leo Cooper, 1993.
7. Later, Sir Rex. See his *My Falkland Days*, David & Charles, 1992.
8. Later, Admiral of the Fleet, GCB, DL. See his *Endure No Makeshifts*, Pen & Sword, 1993.
9. Later, Admiral of the Fleet, Lord, KG, GCB, LVO, DSC.
10. *Endure No Makeshifts.*
11. Later, Sir John, KCB.

Chapter 1 RAF Laarbruch, West Germany
1. Later, Squadron Leader, AFC.
2. Later, AFC.
3. The RAF left in 1999. In May 2003 it became known as Flughafen Niederrhein (Lower Rhine Airport), but was more recently renamed Weeze Airport.
4. Later, Squadron Leader, MBE.
5. Later, Squadron Leader, MBE, QCVSA.
6. For ease of identification all such nautical and aeronautical publications are referred to as 'charts' and all terrestrial maps as 'maps'.
7. For a video of just such an exercise see http://www.youtube.com/watch?v=d6S789W31u4.
8. Awarded the AFC following Operation Agila in Rhodesia/Zimbabwe.
9. Later, General Sir Peter, KCB, KBE, DSO, MC and Bar, Mentioned in Dispatches, Legion of Merit (US).
10. See http://www.youtube.com/watch?v=ar-poc38C84 for a video clip of a C-130 landing on a carrier.

Chapter 2 Opening Shots
1. For the background to Naval Party 8901's Concept of Operations see Ewen Southby-Tailyour, *Reasons in Writing*, Leo Cooper, 1993.
2. Later, Major General, CB, OBE.
3. Preston was to be appointed Land Force Adviser to the Battle Group Commander, Rear Admiral Woodward, until after the San Carlos landings, following which he would rejoin Major General Jeremy Moore in HMS *Fearless*. Among other appointments, Preston had commanded the Royal Marines SBS Headquarters and Landing Craft base at Poole in Dorset. He had also attended various courses at Fort Monkton during his career.
4. Later, General Sir Michael, KCB, CBE, DSO, QGM, Mentioned in Dispatches.
5. Later, Brigadier, CBE, QGM, twice Mentioned in Dispatches.

6. Later, Lieutenant General Sir Martin, KCB, CMG, OBE. Then Colonel, General Staff, to the Commandant General Royal Marines. Commandant General Royal Marines, 1987–90.
7. In an e-mail to the author from the then Commanding Officer, SBS.
8. Later, CB. See his book *Amphibious Assault Falklands*, Leo Cooper, 1996.
9. See his book *3 Commando Brigade in the Falklands: No Picnic*, Pen & Sword, 2007.
10. Later, Rear Admiral, DSO.
11. Later, Admiral Sir John, GBE, KCB. He died in August 2013. See his book *One Hundred Days*. HarperCollins, 1992.
12. The pilots pronounced this 'Su-é'.
13. Jorge Muñoz, *¡Ataquen Rio Grande! Operación Mikado*, Instituto de Publicaciones Navales, 2005.
14. Later, Admiral of the Fleet Lord Fieldhouse of Gosport, GCB, GBE.
15. Professor Sir Lawrence Freedman, *The Official History of the Falklands Campaign. Volume II: War and Diplomacy*, Routledge, 2005.
16. Various conversations with the author, 2011–2013.
17. Charles Maisonneuve & Pierre Razoux, *La Guerre des Malouines*, Éditions Larivière, 2002.
18. Later, Commander, AFC.
19. E-mails to the author, 29 October–20 November 2012.
20. Later, Commodore, CBE.
21. Flag officer Naval Air Command. Later, Vice Admiral Sir Edward, KCB.
22. Later Commander, DSC, AFC.
23. Leo Cooper, 1992.
24. Later, Commodore. Letter to the *Daily Telegraph*, December 2011.
25. *The Downing Street Years*, HarperCollins, 1993.
26. *Here Today, Gone Tomorrow*, Politico's Publishing Ltd, 2002.
27. Hugh Bicheno, *Razor's Edge*, Weidenfeld and Nicolson, 2006.
28. Transcript of telephone conversation contained in the Thatcher Papers, National Archives.
29. *La Guerre des Malouines*.
30. Detailed in the Introduction.
31. From the Latin for flying fish, 'Exocoetus'.
32. 'Étendard' is French for 'battle ensign'.
33. Interview with McBain on 20 June 2005. Retrieved from the internet.
34. The information here is from conversations and e-mails between the author and a former Buzo Tactico officer, Diego Quiroga, in January and February 2012.
35. See also *La Guerre des Malouines* and *¡Ataquen Rio Grande! Operación Mikado!*
36. Later, Major, MBE. Then, a Royal Marines captain was equivalent to a Royal Navy Lieutenant Commander and a Royal Air Force Squadron Leader.
37. Later, Rear Admiral, CB.
38. Letter to the author, 22 February 2011.
39. Chief of Staff to the Commander-in-Chief and overall Task Force Commander, Admiral Sir John Fieldhouse, later Admiral Sir David, KCB, KBE, KCVO.
40. Later, Rear Admiral Sir Robert, KCVO, DL and Flag Officer Royal Yachts.
41. 18 Maritime Group RAF, commanded from Northwood by Air Marshal Sir John Curtiss.
42. Paddy Ashdown, *A Brilliant Little Operation*, Aurum Press, 2012.
43. Later, Lieutenant Colonel, DSO, OBE, Croix de Guerre, Mentioned in Dispatches.
44. Lately of the Royal Corps of Transport. Later, Brigadier, OBE.
45. A helicopter pilot. Later, Brigadier, MBE.
46. Conversation between the author and Woodard.
47. Author's interview with Woodard, 29 March 2011.
48. E-mails and conversations with the author.
49. Report of Proceedings, 18 October 1982.
50. Author's interview with Woodard, 29 March 2011.
51. Navy and Army slang for the RAF.

Chapter 3 Super Étendard fighter-bombers and Exocet missiles
1. *¡Ataquen Rio Grande!*
2. *La Guerre des Malouines*.

3. Capitán de Navío is the equivalent in the Royal Navy of a captain with over six years seniority. Lavezzo was later promoted to Vicealmirante.
4. Later, *Vice-amiral*.
5. E-mail from Super Étendard pilot Roberto Curilovic to the author, August 2011.
6. Not CANA, as has been reported.
7. *¡Ataquen Rio Grande!*
8. Ibid.
9. Ibid.
10. *Razor's Edge. The Unofficial History of the Falklands War*, Weidenfeld & Nicolson, 2006.
11. However, see Chapter 15.
12. Santiago Rivas, *Wings of the Malvinas. The Argentine Air War over the Falklands*, Buenos Aires, 2010. Published in the UK in 2012 by Hikoki Publications.
13. Confirmed in an e-mail from Capitán de Navío Miguel Pita, relayed by his son to the author, 25 October 2012.
14. *La Guerre des Malouines.*
15. *¡Ataquen Rio Grande!*
16. *La Guerre des Malouines.*
17. *¡Ataquen Rio Grande!*
18. The author in conversation with Woodard.
19. See *Daily Telegraph*, 28 December 2012. Later, Divall's accounts of these events was embellished, a mistake that did him no favours.
20. *¡Ataquen Rio Grande!*
21. *La Guerre des Malouines* and *¡Ataquen Rio Grande!*

Chapter 4   Base Aeronaval Almirante Quijada, Rio Grande, Tierra del Fuego
1. A prominent sheer, cliff 262 feet high producing an excellent radar 'picture'. Cabo Peñas, to the south of Rio Grande, is 98 feet high.
2. *South America Pilot. Volume II.*
3. E-mail exchanges with Capitán de Navío Miguel Pita via his son Alejandro Pita.
4. One of many e-mails to the author, 2011–12.
5. Letter to the author from DI4, May 1978.
6. Operation Sovereignty.
7. E-mails to the author, 2011–12.
8. Series of e-mails between Capitán Pita, his son Alejandro and the author.
9. Died on 29 September 2012.
10. Later, Sir Rex, KCMG. He died on 10 November 2012.
11. E-mail to the author 28 October 2012 relayed by his son Alejandro Pita, who also played a small part in the saga, as he explains: 'I was in Rio Grande with my father during the Malvinas conflict. As a student in Buenos Aires I was frustrated that I could not help. So I hitched a ride on an Argentine Navy Electra that was carrying ammo from Buenos Aires to Rio Grande, and surprised my father at the Rio Grande airfield. He gave me a war commission as a midshipman, and assigned me to the electronic warfare section in his command (because I spoke English well). The second day I was there I listened in on the frantic English open communications that were going on when the Port Pleasant/Bluff Cove disaster happened, and *Sir Tristram* and *Sir Galahad* were bombed by Argentine A-4s.'
12. Also known on some maps and charts as the Rio Carmen Sylva.
13. E-mail from Capitán de Navío Miguel Pita.
14. Jimmy Harvey and Alan Withington: see *Wings of the Malvinas*.
15. According to a member of the Special Operations Group, and discussed in detail later.
16. Later, Contraalmirante and author of *Historia de la Aviación Naval Argentina*, published by the Departamento de Estudios Historicos Navales (Conflicto Del Atlantico Sur), Buenos Aires, 1992 – a most detailed account of Argentine naval aviation in 1982.
17. *¡Ataquen Rio Grande!*
18. E-mail to the author from Miguel Pita.
19. There are number of different spellings for this *estancia*; this is from Captain Andy L's 1930s 'escape map'.

20. In an e-mail to the author from Mariano Sciaroni.
21. Courtesy of Santiago Rivas and his book *Wings of the Malvinas*.
22. Brigadier Mario Menéndez sent his own photograph of the crater to the author. He had climbed down into it.

Chapter 5   ARA *General Belgrano* and HMS *Sheffield*
1. Later, he commanded 45 Commando in Northern Ireland and Iraq (Kurdistan).
2. Later, DSO.
3. HMS *Conqueror*'s Report of Proceedings, Annex Bravo, 1 July 1982.
4. E-mail, 21 March 2013.
5. Later, Rear Admiral, CB. Now deceased.
6. Available via the internet.
7. Later, Captain.
8. Yorkshire Television, *The Falklands War – The Untold Story*. First broadcast 1 April 1987.
9. Board of Inquiry findings, 22 July 1982.
10. *Éditions Larivière*.
11. (With Patrick Robinson), *One Hundred Days*, HarperCollins ,1992.
12. Later, Admiral of the Fleet Lord Lewin of Greenwich, KG, GCB, LVO, DSC and three times Mentioned in Dispatches.
13. Later, Commander, MBE.

Chapter 6   RAF Lyneham
1. Later, Air Vice-Marshal, CBE.
2. Later, Air Vice-Marshal CB, CBE.
3. *Royal Air Force Historical Society Journal No 30*, 'The Royal Air Force in the Falklands Campaign', 8 April 2008.

Chapter 7   Deliberations: South Atlantic, Northwood and Hereford
1. *Endure No Makeshifts*, Leo Cooper, 1993.
2. Later, Rear Admiral CB, DSO, LVO.
3. Later, Rear Admiral CB, OBE.
4. 'The great defence against the air menace is to attack the enemy's aircraft as near as possible to their point of departure' (Winston Churchill).
5. E-mail to the author, 9 February 2011.
6. E-mail to the author, 1 May 2012.
7. The problem of 'hiding' in the 12-mile limit was to exercise the Prime Minister. On 28 May at a meeting of the Cabinet's Sub-Committee on the South Atlantic and the Falkland Islands , at which she was present, the Chief of the Defence Staff briefed (as reported in the minutes to the meeting): 'In discussion of the Ministry of Defence's note it was pointed out that Britain had lost four ships in the past week, two of them in British territorial waters. The Exocet missiles with which a number of Argentine Navy ships were armed constituted a serious threat to current operations, and the possibility of a sudden sally by such ships could not be ruled out. In these circumstances it was unreasonable and dangerous that the Argentine Navy should be allowed sanctuary if within the 12 miles of the coast of Argentina. There were two possible areas where operations within the 12-mile zone might be practicable. Public opinion would not understand if opportunities there were missed and later a major British ship such as the SS *Canberra* were in consequence sunk. Against this it was argued that there would be no legal justification for operations within what Britain herself regarded as Argentine territorial waters unless war had first been declared. The threat posed by the (Exocet-armed) Argentine Navy, while within these waters, was not direct enough to justify action under the right of self-defence. Force could not be used if it was disproportionate. There were also wider arguments against what would be seen as the equivalent of an attack on the Argentine mainland when no directly threatening target was involved. This might increase the danger of other Latin American countries joining the conflict on Argentina's side.' In summing up this discussion the Prime Minister acknowledged that decisions involving the 12-mile limit and operations on the mainland were indeed difficult ones that would need further consideration by the Sub-Committee early in the following week. (Thatcher Files, National Archives)
8. The author held this post between 1978 and 1979 and was briefed by Richard Preston in 1977.

9. Later, Admiral of the Fleet Lord Fieldhouse of Gosport, GCB, GBE.
10. Later, Lord Havers of St Edmundsbury.
11. A correspondent to the *The Times* noted, with apologies to Belloc, 'Whatever happens, they have got, the Exocet, and we have Nott.' From A.B. Sainsbury, *The Royal Navy Day by Day*, Ian Allan Publishing, 1992.
12. An unwritten, in-house SAS desire, and an expression first used publicly later during the First Gulf War, with almost tragic consequences.
13. Author's conversation with Captain C of the Special Operations Group.
14. Further considerations are raised in the Epilogue.
15. Telephone conversation with the author, 27 February 2011.
16. At that time, Cartwright was also the Vice Chairman of the RAF Mountaineering Association (RAFMA) and Deputy Leader of the RAFMA's 40th Anniversary Himalayan Expedition to Lahul.
17. In September 2012 the National Imagery Exploitation Centre moved to new, purpose-built accommodation at RAF Wyton, also in Cambridgeshire.
18. Later, Air Marshal Sir Donald, KCB, CBE, AFC.
19. United States Air Force reconnaissance (spy) satellites that sent their images back to earth in capsules for processing and interpretation. They had had their orbits altered in support of the UK.
20. This is discussed in Chapter 15.
21. E-mail to the author, 4 August 2012.
22. Professor Freedman, *The Official History of the Falklands Campaign. Volume II.*
23. The SAS were strongly advised by an officer with 'local' knowledge – the author – to land by helicopter, canoe or Gemini rubber raiding craft at Pebble Cove on the very north-west extremity of the island, 9 miles from the Pebble Island airstrip with no habitation (or enemy) 'guarding' the approach to the airfield from that direction. The three 'mountains' in between Pebble Cove and the objective would also have masked any movement from enemy eyes. However, the SAS chose to land by helicopter on West Falkland to the north of Port Purvis and overlooking Pebble Sound. This required them to cross the notorious Tamar Pass in canoes (probably the most inappropriate form of travel by sea throughout the archipelago) against currents that have been recorded at up to ten knots. Lieutenant Alan Bennett, one of the Sea King pilots, has confirmed their landing site. Using their own chosen route, once on Pebble Island the reconnaissance patrol had then to pass through not only the civilian settlement but the Argentine base before reaching its objective; thus it is not surprising that the reconnaissance was avoidably delayed.

Chapter 8 Ascension Island
1. From *The Dead Marines* ('Dead Marine' = an empty bottle) by Major W.P. Drury, Royal Marines Light Infantry.
2. Then Assistant Director Operations (Rest of the World) on the staff of the Assistant Defence Staff (Operations).
3. From the Rest of the World planning team on the United Kingdom's Commander-in-Chief's Committee.
4. Later, Air Vice-Marshal, CB.
5. As has been explained by Richard Preston, any such request would not have surprised the Americans, who had always offered to help over British use of Ascension Island.
6. *Royal Air Force Historical Society Journal*, No. 30.
7. Free letter forms issued to service personnel when on operations. Only known later as 'blueys', but the name is used here as all current servicemen know what is meant.
8. Later, Squadron Leader.

Chapter 9 Operation Plum Duff – Phase One: Hereford and the Mid-Atlantic
1. Later, Lieutenant General Sir Cedric, KCB, DSO.
2. Later, Colonel, OBE.
3. Later, Sir David, DSO, OBE.
4. Later, Brigadier, OBE, MC.
5. Later, Lieutenant Colonel OBE, MC. As a major he was to become a member of Brigadier Thompson's staff well before, and during, Operation Corporate. An 'exchange' Army officer was always attached to Headquarters, 3 Commando Brigade.
6. Detail from the SBS officer with the Special Operations Group.

7. Telephone conversation between the author and Sir John Nott on 27 February 2011, during which Nott also confirmed that he later sanctioned Operation Mikado to proceed once the recce had failed. This does not accord with a wider view aired in the Epilogue.

8. Position and Intended Movement, sent at noon each day by Royal Navy ships at sea.

9. Nautical readers should translate this RAF phrase as 'off the port bow'!

10. A USAF squadron flying aircraft in Soviet (and other) colours. Wearing Soviet flying suits, using Soviet doctrine and practices (and with some speaking Russian) this squadron's pilots introduced realism into 'Top Gun' training.

11. The senior RFA officer afloat. Later, CBE, DSO.

12. As a result of this incident, widely separated arrival and departure routes were devised and used thereafter.

Chapter 10   Operation Plum Duff – Phase Two: South Atlantic

1. Narrative and conversation paraphrased from an interview with Captain Andy L on 27 July 2011, plus his written account passed to the author.

2. Later, Rear Admiral, CB, DSO. Middleton died in December 2012.

3. Captain Middleton (and, as will be seen, Captain Black in *Invincible*) were not the only ones concerned at the loss of yet another troop-lift 'junglie' helicopter. Brigadier, later Major General, Julian Thompson, then commanding 3 Commando Brigade, along with Commodore Michael Clapp, the Commodore Amphibious Warfare, argued strongly for a troop-lift helicopter not to be used. The reply from Rear Admiral Sandy Woodward to Thompson was, 'Mind your own (effing) business!' The loss of such a helicopter was, of course, very much the business of Thompson and Clapp; indeed, such a loss, regardless of the purpose in hand, was their business almost more than anyone else's. Clapp retained operational command of all support helicopters and had only passed tactical control to Woodward for specific operations around the Falkland Islands as required by the Brigade Commander.

4. These army ranks were known to the sailors as 'the men from the Enchanted Forest', the expression coming from their permanently-worn camouflage uniform.

5. E-mail to the author, 21 November 2012.

6. See Chapter 11.

7. Later, Commodore, DSC, FRAeS. Most timings and events from now until 6 Troop becomes airborne in Sea King Victor Charlie are taken from Bennett's contemporary diary and from numerous meetings, conversations and e-mails between him and the author since.

8. Later, retired as a Major, DSC.

9. The nickname by which Bennetts are known in the Royal Navy.

10. Corporal Love was killed in a Sea King crash three days later. He was to be awarded a posthumous DSM in the campaign honours list.

11. Later, Lieutenant Commander, DSM.

12. Alan Bennett's diary.

13. Entitled *Puerto Santa Cruz to Cabo Pilar including the Falkland Islands*.

14. Entitled *Estracho de Magallanes*.

15. Entitled *Rio de la Plata to Cabo Hornos*.

16. 1:3,500,000.

17. Number ONC T-18 dated 10 June 1976.

18. To avoid confusion, note that this is not the map shown in West's *The Secret War for the Falklands*.

19. Interview with the author, 27 July 2011.

20. E-mail to the author, 3 June 2012.

21. Michael O'Mara Books Ltd, 2000.

22. Later, Admiral Sir Jeremy, GBE, KCB, DSO.

23. E-mail to the author, 20 September 2011.

24. E-mail to the author from Admiral Black, 24 September 2012.

25. Capitán de Navío Eugenio L. Facchin and José L. Speroni , *El Bouchard y El Fracaso de la Operación Británica Mikado*, and various e-mails between Capitán de Navio Barcena and the author. Also paraphrased from 'Informe del comandante del destructor ARA Bouchard, Procedimientos tacticos proprios y del enemigo' – the ship's Report of Proceedings; the 'Libro historicao del buque destructor ARA *Hipolito Bouchard*' – the 'historic' record of the ARA *Hipolito Bouchard*; the

Diario de Guerre (the ship's war diary) and the *Libro de Navigacion* (the ship's log). In 1982 Capitán de Navío Facchin had been ARA *Hipolito Bouchard*'s 'Chief of Operations'. See issue no XXX of the Argentine *Naval Center Bulletin* (Naval Centre Magazine).

26. On 19 May an interesting event took place that alerted the British Special Forces to the fact that the Argentines needed to be taken seriously. Via a link through Century House (then Headquarters, Secret Intelligence Service) Captain C of the SBS received a press clip filed during the 'advance force' stage, prior to the British landings at San Carlos. The Argentines had dressed a dead body in British camouflaged combat kit, photographed it and put the photo into the Reuters system. Before it reached the London press it passed across Captain C's desk. The dead man 'resembled' an SBS colleague that Captain C knew. 'Terribly clever bit of disinformation. "Here you are, we've killed a member of your advance special forces. Did you know that, you British". Very clever.'

27. *Reports of Proceedings* for the four British nuclear submarines sent to the author by Mariano Sciaroni, an Argentine lawyer based in Buenos Aires.

28. *¡Ataquen Rio Grande!*

29. Quoted by Brigadier-General Aubel in his 'alleged memorandum' to Mrs Thatcher, 25 March 1999.

30. 17 May was a busy day for those intimately concerned over the number and whereabouts of the Exocets. Even at the very highest levels in the conduct of the campaign there remained confusion over the number of Exocets that 6 Troop might be looking for, as the minutes of an MOD/FCO meeting suggest: 'The following points of interest in the Foreign and Commonwealth Office arose at this morning's meeting of the Chiefs of Staff. The Deputy Chief of Defence Staff (Intelligence) reported the latest assessment that the Argentines have two or three Exocet still operational, but thought that deliveries might raise this to total to five or ten within three or four weeks' time, including the four Exocets for Peru [other sources state that there were six Exocets destined for Peru], on which representations are being made to the French. The Chief of the Defence Staff asked whether there was any evidence that the *Belgrano* had had Exocets on board, pointing out that although the incident was fading from public interest [*sic*] this could be an important public relations point. [General Glover] undertook to look into it. [The Secretary] drew attention to a recent intelligence report, received from a community liaison service, which appeared to state categorically that the Argentines now have ten [air-launched] Exocets.'

Chapter 11   Operation Plum Duff – Phase Three: Tierra del Fuego

1. Positions and timings from here onwards are taken from Bennett's contemporary notes, seen by the author.

2. Flying Command: control room in the carrier's island, adjacent to the ship's bridge and overlooking the full length of the flight deck.

3. A very few large hand-held sets were in the Task Force, mostly used by ships and the Task Force Landing Craft Squadron. With few satellites then in orbit, the sets were not accurate and were extremely slow.

4. Confirmed by Admiral Black, e-mail to the author, 24 September 2012.

5. Ibid. See Chapter 14.

6. The same make that Burgoyne's crew had obtained from Royal Naval Air Station, Yeovilton.

7. Interview with the author, 27 July 2011.

8. This temporary deviation from the planned course is not mentioned in *Special Forces Pilot*.

9. Miguel Pita was referring to 'large para-illuminating flares', for it is known that some of the infantry set off small flares.

10. In conversation with the author.

11. Neither has spoken publicly before.

12. At Estancia la Sara the Ruta Nacional 3 is about 4 miles from the coast and runs towards it in a south-easterly direction.

13. Conversation with the author, 27 July 2011.

14. E-mail to the author, 15 August 2013.

15. *¡Ataquen Rio Grande!*

16. A Buenos Aires newspaper, 21 May 2007.

17. E-mail, 9 August 2011, from (now) Capitán de Navío Luis Bonanni.

18. E-mail to the author, 22 November 2011.
19. This fable was first aired by West in *The Secret War for the Falklands* in 1997, then (rather surprisingly, bearing in mind Hutchings' comments on the accuracy of some of West's book) repeated by Hutchings in *Special Forces Pilot* in 1998.
20. Only the tense has been changed from present to past in order to make sense.
21. The range and bearing would have been helpful, but as Captain L had (at that stage) no charts or maps with latitude and longitude marked, this extra information would have been superfluous.
22. Unlike his pilot, Bennett did not recognize this as an AN/TPS-43 and regards any such description as a 'gross leap of imagination'. 'The observers in the "pinging" squadrons got pretty good at assessing what they were listening to', he says, 'but we had no training whatsoever. Even if we had, it takes a very good ear and tons of practice with the rudimentary kit we had to state with any degree of certainty what we were listening to.' Either way, it was never the continuous 'growl' of a fire control radar; nor were there any anti-aircraft missiles either on board the destroyers or at Rio Grande.
23. With the radar warning receiver's bearing estimation no better than +/−20°, this was more likely to have been ARA *Hipolito Bouchard*'s SPS 10 surface-search radar.
24. It was just as well that the navigator was allowing a 2-nautical-mile error, for on the Admiralty chart his indicated position was exactly 1 mile offshore and 1 mile from the substantial Estancia Cameron.
25. Tab – Tactical Advance to Battle – is the Parachute Regiment's equivalent of the Royal Marines' expression 'yomp'.
26. 'Diddle-dee' is *Empetrum rubrum*, a low, heather-like shrub with, in season, edible red berries from which jam and 'wine' can be made.
27. *¡Ataquen Rio Grande!*
28. According to Muñoz. See also Chapter 10 and the Epilogue.
29. Which makes subsequent events in Porvenir difficult to understand.
30. From post-war interpretation this has been identified as the bridge close to Estancia California that carries the road, now numbered Y-85, across a small stream, about 3 nautical miles further north-east from the beach where they had been landed.
31. Stokes and Lane had, earlier and in a roundabout manner, been involved with the retaking of South Georgia. Following their experiences on Mount Everest in 1976, they had stated that the Fortuna Glacier was passable during the reconnaissance phase. This opinion contradicted advice offered by those with personal experience of the area. See also Major Neri G. Terri Jnr, USMC, *Selected Intelligence Issues from the Falkland Islands Conflict of 1982*, Faculty of the Defense Intelligence College, December 1989.
32. In conversation with the author, 27 July 2011.
33. Letter to the author dated 22 February 2011.
34. In one of many post-operation discussions circa October 1982 Moore commented that, 'There were more Special Forces than could be allocated tasks ... which were given more through a sense of obligation than because of a valid requirement.' Additionally, the Land Force Commander had never been consulted on Special Force force levels. Moore also believed that the Special Boat Squadron was adequate for the number and range of tasks that had to be met by Special Forces and that, being amphibious, they were already integrated into the order of battle with compatible communications. Furthermore, both Moore and Thompson accepted that the Royal Marines' Mountain and Arctic Warfare Cadre, recently returned from winter training in arctic Norway, were better prepared for operations in South Georgia than any other unit.
35. On 24 May 1982, the *Daily Telegraph* announced: 'Wrecked [Sea King] keeps its secret ... It could have landed troops on Chilean soil ... 12 miles from ... Ushuaia ... British and Chilean authorities ... anxious to let the matter rest.' Two days later the paper revised its view: 'Crash helicopter on SAS raid ... An obvious target would be Rio Gallegos.' On 24 May the *Daily Mail* speculated, 'The SAS might have knocked out the Super Étendards with their Exocet missiles', but offered no details. The next day, the *Daily Express*'s reporter in Buenos Aires went further: 'British commandos [*sic*] ... have destroyed Argentina's deadliest planes ...at Rio Gallegos ... Having been dropped by Sea King helicopter near the airfield ... then, under cover of darkness, they slipped in ... and planted explosives [on] Argentina's five [*sic*] Super Étendards ... The commandos' amazing triumph has taken so long to come to light because it was in everyone's

interest to keep it secret. They are now believed to be back in Britain or even back with the Task Force.'

Chapter 12   Operation Mikado – Outline Plan: Rio Grande

1. General Sir Peter de la Billière, *Looking for Trouble*, Harper Collins, 1994.
2. Tragically, he has since been badly injured in a parachuting accident in South Africa. Having commanded 23 SAS Crooke became the managing director of Kilo Alpha Services.
3. First of many interviews with the author. This one held on 10 May 2011.
4. Sleeping pills cleared for aircrew use by the RAF's doctors.

Chapter 13   MV *Atlantic Conveyor*

1. E-mails to the author, and from Santiago Rivas' *Wings of the Malvinas*.
2. Dated 21 July 1982.
3. Both of whom were awarded Argentina's Medalla La Nación Argentina al Valor en Combate.
4. Later, Admiral Sir Michael, KCB, CBE.
5. John Johnson-Allen, *They Couldn't Have Done it without Us*, Seafarer Books, 2011.
6. Later, Captain, Mentioned in Dispatches. In 2012 he was Master of the MV *Discovery*.
7. Specialist in seamanship.
8. E-mail to the author.
9. Naval slang for food or a meal.
10. Ironically, perhaps, these were for a prisoner-of-war camp.

Chapter 14   Operation Mikado – Detailed Plan: Rio Grande

1. Not to be confused with the Omega radar warning receiver.
2. Cartwright gathered his data through a GCHQ Cheltenham communications network that was totally separate from the SAS. This was information that could only be passed on to those senior officers and commanders who had themselves been cleared to receive such a high level of intelligence. Thus, strictly speaking, Roberts and Burgoyne should not have been privy to the whereabouts of the destroyers. The position of the radar pickets was passed – in the same signal – to the Commander-in-Chief Fleet for forward transmission to HMS *Hermes*; at this remove in time it remains unclear whether this actually happened. This vital information certainly never reached Captain Black in HMS *Invincible* – as it should have done – in order for him to brief the aircrew of Operation Plum Duff. See Chapter 11.
3. Discussion between the author and Rear Admiral Sir Robert Woodard. The submarine has never been identified.
4. The shortest route between two points on a globe.
5. Operational Navigation Chart.
6. Major Neri G. Terry Jnr, 'Selected Intelligence Issues from the Falkland Islands Conflict of 1982', USMC, December 1989.
7. Now known as the Defence Evaluation and Research Agency, Malvern.
8. Although the incorrect spelling of the Spanish word 'Aerea' on the RAF Hercules (on an unrelated mission) and the aircrew masquerading as Chileans but wearing RAF flying suits tended to give the game away.
9. Nowadays, three-dimensional elevation modelling software speeds up the process. It is now infinitely more accurate and, especially within special forces operations, widely used for 'dead ground' studies and sniper operations.
10. It is now interesting to 'fly' the route using Google Earth.
11. A large and heavy aircraft; engine power alone might not have overcome the down-draughts. The C-130 is stressed from plus 3G (gravity) to minus 1G, but these safety limits can be exceeded in severe, low-level turbulence.
12. Later, Air Marshal Sir Kenneth, KCB, KBE, AFC and Bar.
13. Phoenix, 2002.
14. See West's *The Secret War for the Falklands*.
15. E-mail to the author, 19 August 2011.
16. Various e-mails to the author via the Capitán's son, Alejandro Pita.
17. Flight Lieutenant Jeff Glover, an RAF Harrier pilot who became a prisoner of war after he was shot down over the Falkland Islands. He was well and properly treated.

18. Article Number 823 written for the Argentine Naval Bureau in 2009 entitled 'El *Bouchard* y El *Fracaso* de la Operación Británica Mikado' by Capitan de Navío Eugenio Luis Facchin and Army Engineer Colonel José Luis Speroni.

19. The position or location has been deleted by Ministry of Defence censors.

Chapter 15   Operation Plum Duff – Mark Two: Tierra del Fuego

1. Not an expression used at the time by either the RAF or B Squadron but useful here for the lack of anything more descriptive.

2. Likewise, various members of the SAS have claimed that they trained with HMS *Onyx* for a raid on to the Argentine mainland. They did not.

3. Bloomsbury Publishing, 1996.

4. *Fighting Scared. Para, Mercenary, SAS, Sniper, Bodyguard*. W&N, 10 October 2002. Kindle.

5. 3 September 2011.

6. E-mails to the author, 7–9 February 2013.

7. The author's name for the alternative operation, used here simply to describe an updated version of the same overall plan.

8. Despite reports in a number of publications, the SAS never embarked in HMS *Onyx* for operations on the Argentine mainland nor did they practise for such an operation in San Carlos; sadly, a number of authors have been taken in by these 'first-hand' stories (for example, see the *Daily Telegraph*, 8 March 2002). Indeed, there were never plans for the SAS to do so (other than in the minds of their own members), for the same reasons that the SBS considered such an operation unfeasible ... and if the SBS considered such an operation unworkable then it certainly would not have been possible using those inexperienced in the art of submarine operations.

9. Subsequent research has shown that this dirt track is barely 18 feet wide in places and either flanked by drainage ditches or raised a few feet above the surrounding countryside.

10. E-mail 'conversations' between the pilots and the author.

Chapter 16   Operation Kettledrum – Puerto Deseado

1. Recharging the batteries at periscope depth through the use of a snorkel to provide fresh air for the diesel engines.

2. Later, Rear Admiral, DSO.

3. Various e-mails to the author, 2011–2012.

4. E-mails to the author, 8 and 19 November 2012.

5. Later, Major and Squadron Commander in the New Zealand SAS. Appointed a Member of the New Zealand Order of Merit (MNZM) in 2005. Now the owner of the Lynfer Estates vineyard, Wellington.

6. Later, Captain, Royal Marines.

7. Later, 'local' Lieutenant Colonel while serving with the United Arab Emirates; retired as Major, MBE.

8. E-mail to the author, 26 August 2013.

9. E-mail to the author, 12 September 2013.

10. E-mail to the author, 20 November 2012.

11. One of many e-mails to the author.

12. E-mail to the author, 27 August 2013.

Chapter 17   HMS *Avenger*, HMS *Fearless*, HMS *Intrepid* and HMS *Glamorgan*

1. Knowing that returning Sea Harriers were always low on fuel and thus unwilling to take a circuitous route back to their ships, it was not difficult for the Argentines to deduce that any aircraft flying away from the islands in a specific direction had to be heading for either HMS *Invincible* or HMS *Hermes*.

2. *Wings of the Malvinas*.

3. Later, Admiral Sir Hugo, GCB, CBE, Commander-in-Chief Fleet and Governor of Gibraltar.

4. The puzzle surrounding the last Argentine air-launched Exocet is compounded by the following entry in HMS *Invincible*'s log for 30 May 1982 (all times GMT): 'Daily Summary: ... Patrolling eastern part of Total Exclusion Zone ... Attack by Super Étendard – no damage. 1731 Air Raid Warning Red. 1735 Two missiles sighted by helicopter. Explosions sighted at 230[°]. 1745 Air Raid Warning Yellow. 2229 Action Stations. Detection of Super Étendard radar. 2255 Air Raid

Warning Yellow.' At 2000 HMS *Invincible*'s position was given as 51°3.4′ S, 54°34.6′W. By deduction from the ship's log this gives her position at the time of the radar detection as 50°47′ S, 54°43′ W.

5. Both surviving Skyhawk pilots were awarded the Medalla al Heroico Valor en Combate.
6. Later, Commander.
7. Teniente de Navío Omar Castillo.
8. E-mail to the author, October 2012.
9. On 13 June the Super Étendards were ordered back to Rio Grande fitted with 'iron' bombs.
10. Pebble Island was on the ship's starboard side; thus the order to turn to port.
11. Later, Rear Admiral CB, DSO.
12. 12,000-ton Landing Platform Dock and amphibious command ships. *Fearless* and *Intrepid* were sisters.
13. Contained in Ewen Southby-Tailyour's *Reasons in Writing*, Leo Cooper, 1993. See also Michael Clapp and Ewen Southby-Tailyour, *Amphibious Assault, Falklands*, Leo Cooper, 1996.
14. For a full account of this incident, see Southby-Tailyour's *Reasons in Writing* and his and Clapp's *Amphibious Assault Falklands*.
15. To whom the author is grateful for permission to quote and paraphrase. Dr Amendolara has a Master's degree in History of Warfare from Argentina's Army War College, is a member of the Argentine Commission of Military History, a member of the Argentine Army's Institute of Military History and Associate Professor at the Joint War College of the Argentine Armed Forces.
16. Presented to the 38th International Commission of Military History Congress, *Technology and Warfare*, at Sofia, Bulgaria, between 25 August and 1 September 2012.
17. Apart from the almost nightly resupply run using the ubiquitous C-130 into Stanley and the occasional night bombing run of ageing Canberra bombers.
18. Quoted here with permission.
19. *Ordeal by Exocet*, Frontline Books, 2012.
20. Whose team, each night, performed the Mexican Rain Dance to encourage a target to appear on their radar screen. E-mail to the author.
21. Letter to the author, 22 July 2011. He died 28 April 2013.
22. A descriptive word coined by Martin van Creveld in *The Age of Airpower*, PublicAffairs, 2011.
23. Capitán de Corbeta Bedacarratz, quoted in *Wings of the Malvinas*.

Epilogue
1. E-mail to the author, 11 December 2012. The same restraints would have applied to the SAS had they planned to use a submarine.
2. Author's emphasis.
3. The Chilean Brigadier-General Aubel claims that the Chilean Air Force had a radar overlooking Comodoro Rivadavia that tracked Argentine aircraft up to 50 miles offshore. Aubel further claims (allegedly in a 'memorandum' to Mrs Thatcher dated 25 March 1999) that this information plus that from an RAF Nimrod was relayed direct to the Task Force by Group Captain Sid Edwards, the British Air Attaché in Santiago. Neither of these two alleged 'facts' have ever been substantiated and so could have been part of a ruse, after the event, to show how much Chile had been supporting the United Kingdom in 1982, in order to help obtain ex-President Pinochet's release from house arrest in England in 1999. As this radar did not cover Rio Grande (Comodoro Rivadavia is 480 nautical miles to the north of Rio Grande and over 500 nautical miles from Stanley), it would not have been of use against any of the Super Étendards, Sky Hawks and Daggers, while just four (out of a total of eight) of the Mirages were based at Comodoro Rivadavia, together with an assortment of tanker and transport C-130s. The Nimrod flew just three sorties over Chilean airspace until withdrawn following the discovery of Victor Charlie. The Sea King's incursion into Chilean airspace had not been agreed with Chile.
4. Infantry description of an unsubtle, full-frontal, bayonets-fixed assault: two 'units' (usually platoons) leading, with one following up 'in reserve' through a heavy screen of smoke.
5. Which could only come from the highest possible level.
6. Letter to the author, 22 February 2011.
7. Although Sir John Nott told the author that he, personally, gave approval for the 'planning' of Operation Mikado he never mentioned giving approval for the 'execution' of the operation.

8. E-mail to the author, 14 December 2012.
9. Later, Major General, CB, OBE, MC.
10. Moore was obliged to state in the covering letter to his Report of Proceedings dated 18 October 1982: 'I deprecate the fact that the Director Special Air Service feels unable to forward to me the report on the operations by 22 Special Air Service, particularly since, after 21 May, the Special Air Service's ability to integrate with the land force operations as a whole and to provide the accurate and timely reports that I required were not always impressive. I believe that, despite their undoubted quality, there are improvements that should be made ... Director SAS was asked to forward a report on 22 SAS's operations (in support of my ground forces) but felt unable to comply as he had been instructed by the Director of Military Operations to report direct to the Ministry of Defence (Army).' In making these statements Moore recognized that four major SAS reconnaissance tasks had been conducted in a 'less than impressive' manner and he needed to read why – in the SAS's own words – in order to apply the 'lessons learned' to any future such conventional operation. The reconnaissance patrols at South Georgia, Goose Green (where it is alleged that no reconnaissance worthy of the title took place and yet a report was sent to the 2nd Battalion the Parachute Regiment prior to the battle) and Pebble Island were uppermost in his mind. For this latter operation, General Moore commented further, 'The pre-attack reconnaissance took longer than anticipated ... and [so the attack] was eventually mounted on the last night when it was possible to do so without delaying the main landing.'Although not under Moore's command or his control – but of paramount interest to him – Operation Plum Duff was the fourth 'unimpressive' major reconnaissance; yet on this occasion the operation, as has been explained, failed for less culpable reasons.
11. A helicopter pilot. Later, Lieutenant Colonel.
12. Chief of the General Staff during the Falklands campaign. Later, Chief of the Defence Staff and finally Field Marshal the Lord Bramall, KG, GCB, OBE, MC, JP, DL.
13. Taken from numerous discussions with, and e-mails from, Blundell and Donkin to the author.
14. As noted by Major General Moore. See Chapter 2.
15. The SAS, unlike the SBS and the Parachute Regiment, had never participated in 3 Commando Brigade's annual amphibious Arctic training in Norway and so had no concept of how such operations are conducted.
16. E-mail to the author, 11 December 2012.
17. Various telephone conversations between de la Billière and the author, from early 2011 to late 2012.
18. E-mail to the author 23 January 2013.
19. The Kettledrum team lead by Boyd was described thus: 'They were the most competent and tough Marines in the business and might well have succeeded, but for all the reasons explained the odds were still stacked against them'.
20. E-mail to the author, 17 August 2013.
21. E-mail to the author, 4 January 2013.
22. As noted by HMS *Fearless*.
23. Later, Air Chief Marshall Sir Peter, GCB, DFC, AFC, DL.
24. Including – but regrettably with no space for elaboration here – the remarkable air-bridge between, to begin with, Ascension Island and the Task Force and then direct to Stanley once hostilities had ended.
25. Series of e-mails to the author, 7–14 August 2013.

Bibliography

Published books and papers

Amendolara, Dr Alejandro, 'Inventiveness under Pressure: The Exocet Coastal Launcher in the Malvinas/Falklands War'.

Ashdown, Paddy, *A Brilliant Little Operation*, Aurum Press, 2012.

Barker, Nick, *Beyond Endurance. An Epic of Whitehall and the South Atlantic Conflict*, Leo Cooper, 1997.

Bicheno, Hugh , *Razor's Edge*, Weidenfeld and Nicolson, 2006.

Borge, Jacques and Viasnoff, Nicolas, *The Dakota: the DC3 Story*, Frederick Warne, 1982.

Brown, David, *The Royal Navy and the Falklands War*, Leo Cooper, 1987.

Brown, Jeremy, *A South American War*, Book Guild Publishing, 2013.

Clapp, Michael and Southby-Tailyour, Ewen, *Amphibious Assault Falklands*, Leo Cooper, 1996.

Connor, Ken, *Ghost Force*, Phoenix, 2002.

de la Billière, General Sir Peter, *Looking for Trouble*, HarperCollins, 1994.

Falconer, Duncan, *First Into Action. Dramatic Personal Account of Life Inside the SBS*, Sphere, 2001.

Freedman, Professor Sir Lawrence, *The Official History of the Falklands Campaign, Volume II: War and Diplomacy*, Routledge, 2005.

Hastings, Max and Jenkins, Simon, *The Battle for the Falkland Islands*, Michael Joseph, 1983.

Horsfall, Robin, *Fighting Scared*, W&N, 2002.

Hunt, Sir Rex, *My Falkland Days*, David & Charles, 1992.

Hutchings, Richard, *Special Forces Pilot*, Pen & Sword, 2008.

Inskip, Ian, *Ordeal by Exocet*, Frontline Books, 2012.

Jane's All the World's Aircraft, 1982.

Jane's Fighting Ships, 1982.

Johnson-Allen, John, *They Couldn't Have Done it Without Us*, Seafarer Books, 2011.

Leach, Admiral of the Fleet Sir Henry, *Endure No Makeshift*, Pen & Sword, 1993.

London Gazette (supplement), 8 October 1982: Honours and Awards.

McCallion, Harry, *The Killing Zone*, Bloomsbury, 1996.

MacKenzie, Alastair, *Special Force.The Untold Story of 22 Special Air Service Regiment*, I.B. Taurus, 2011.

Maisonneuve, Charles and Razoux, Pierre, *La Guerre des Malouines*, Éditions Larivière, 2002.

Middlebrook, Martin, *Operation Corporate. The Story of the Falklands War*, Viking, 1985.

Martini, Contraalmirante Hector, 'Historia de la Aviación Naval Argentina. Conflicto Del Atlantico Sur', Departamento de Estudios Historicos Navales, Buenos Aires, 1992.

Muñoz, Jorge, *¡Ataquen Rio Grande! Operación Mikado*, Instituto de Publicaciones Navales, 2005.

Terry, Major Neri G. Jnr, USMC, 'Selected Intelligence Issues from the Falkland Islands Conflict of 1982', Faculty of the Defense Intelligence College, December 1989.

Nott, Sir John, *Here Today, Gone Tomorrow*, Politico's Publishing, 2002.

Oakley, Derek, *The Falklands Military Machine*, Spellmount, 1989.

Ratcliffe, Peter, *The Eye of the Storm*, Michael O'Mara Books, 2000.

Reynolds, David, *Task Force. The Illustrated History of the Falklands War*, Sutton, 2002.

Rivas, Santiago, *Wings of the Malvinas. The Argentine Air War over the Falklands*, Hikoki Publications (UK), 2012.

Southby-Tailyour, Ewen, *Reasons in Writing*, Leo Cooper, 1993.

Southby-Tailyour, Ewen, *HMS Fearless. The Mighty Lion*, Pen & Sword, 2006.

The Sunday Times Insight Team, *The Falklands War*, André Deutsch, 1982.

Thatcher, Margaret, *The Downing Street Years*, HarperCollins, 1993.

Thompson, Julian, *3 Commando Brigade in the Falklands. No Picnic*, Pen & Sword, 2007.

United Kingdom Hydrographic Office, *South America Pilot. Volume II*, fifteenth edition, 1971.

van Creveld, Martin, *The Age of Airpower*, PublicAffairs, 2011.

Vaux, Nick, *March to the South Atlantic*, Buchan & Enright, 1986.
Ward, Commander 'Sharkey', *Sea Harrier over the Falklands*, Leo Cooper, 1992.
West, Nigel, *The Secret War for the Falklands*, Little Brown, 1997.
Woodward, Admiral Sandy, *One Hundred* Days, Harper Collins, 1992.

The National Archives
The Thatcher Papers.
Headquarters Commando Forces: Operation Corporate Report of Proceedings.
HMS *Conqueror* Report of Proceedings.
HMS *Splendid* Report of Proceedings.
HMS *Valiant* Report of Proceedings.
HMS *Spartan* Report of Proceedings.
HMS *Onyx* log.
HMS *Invincible* log.

Royal Air Force Archives
'The Royal Air Force in the Falklands Campaign', *Royal Air Force Historical Society Journal*, No. 30,
  8 April, 2008.

Argentine Reports of Proceedings and Logs
Facchin, Capitán de Navío Eugenio L. and Speroni, José L., 'El Bouchard y El Fracaso de la
  Operación Británica Mikado', Article No. 823, Argentine Naval Bureau, 2009.
'Informe del comandante del destructor ARA *Bouchard*', Procedimientos tacticos proprios y del
  enemigo.
Libro historicao del buque destructor ARA *Hipolito Bouchard*.
Diario de Guerre Libro de Navigacion, ARA *Hipolito Bouchard*.
Argentine Naval Center Bulletin, Issue No. XXX.

British Boards of Inquiry
Loss of HMS *Sheffield*.
Loss of MV *Atlantic Conveyor*.

Interview
Sir Richard Parsons, Churchill College, 20 June 2005.

American magazine
Time Magazine 17 May 1982 (Rio Grande).

Argentine newspapers
Buenos Aires Herald 25 April 1982 (Rio Grande).
Clarín 21 May 2007 (Estancia la Sara).

British Newspapers
Daily Telegraph 24 May 1982 (Crashed Sea King).
Daily Mail 24 May 1982 (Crashed Sea King).
Daily Express 25 May 1982 (Crashed Sea King).
Sunday Times 31 October 1982 (SIS operations).
Daily Telegraph 8 March 2002 (SAS in submarines).
Guardian 24 July 2004 (Operation Algeciras).
Independent 4 April 2007 (Operation Algeciras).
Daily Mail 3 September 2011 (SAS at Ascension Island).
Daily Telegraph December 2011 (French assistance).
Daily Telegraph 22 March 2012 (Operation Plum Duff).
Daily Telegraph 28 December 2012 (SIS operations).

Television
Yorkshire Television: *The Falklands War – the Untold Story*. First broadcast 1 April 1987.

Video on the internet
TALO operation: http://www.youtube.com/watch?v=d6S789W31u4.
US Hercules landing on an aircraft carrier: http://www.youtube.com/watch?v=ar-poc38C84

Index

Ranks and titles shown are those held at the time. Subsequent ranks and decorations will be found in the notes.